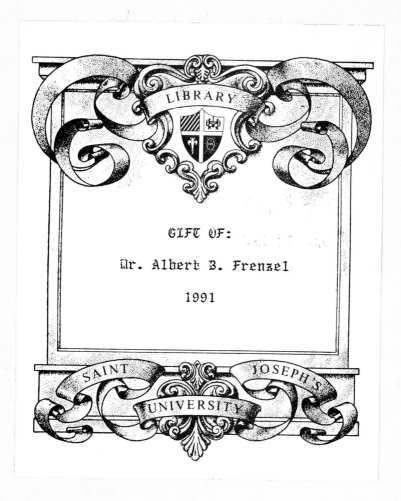

THE DEATH OF CLASSICAL PAGANISM

For Vonla

The Death of Classical Paganism

John Holland Smith

Charles Scribner's Sons New York

Printed in Great Britain
Library of Congress Catalog Card Number 76–28906
ISBN 0–684–14449–2

Contents

Chapter Six
Julian's character and the history of his religious opinions – Libanius and his circle – Julian's chosen associates: Maximus and the theurges – his accession as autocrator – his accession and enactments – his attitude to Christians – Julian at Antioch: the *Misopogon* – his revival of the pagan "church"—the Persian Expedition – Julian's untimely death and unfitting funeral – pagan assessments of his achievement

Chapter Seven
The Emperor Jovian – the Persian peace – divisions among the Christians – Valentinian I and Valens – agitation against the theurges – Praetextatus and the threat to the mysteries – corruption in Africa – Procopius' revolt and its suppression – the barbarians on the Rhine – corruption at Rome – Praetextatus and Pope Damasus – Maximinus and the oppression of Roman pagans – the Emperor Valens and the pagans of the east – the "Theodorus Conspiracy" – war on the Danube – death of Valentinian I and accession of Gratian – death of Valens – the appointment of Theodosius I

Chapter Eight
Policy of Theodosius I – anti-pagan legislation – character of the Emperor Gratian – suppression of the Mithras-cult on the Vatican Hill – Ambrose of Milan – his theory of history – Symmachus and his circle – suppression of the imperial title *Pontifex Maximus* – the controversy over the Altar of Victory, priestly privileges and the Vestals – the revolt of Magnus Maximus – Symmachus' *Relatio III* and Ambrose's replies – the significance of the Priscillian affair – Prudentius' poems *contra Symmachum*

Chapter Nine
Theodosius' hardening attitude towards paganism after Gratian's murder – new laws against divination and sacrifice – Cynegius' campaign against the temples – the destruction of Jupiter of Apamea – Libanius' defence of the temples – the five accounts of the destructions at Alexandria – alleged pagan atrocities – John Chrysostom and the temples of Syria – Martin of Tours and the temples of the Loire

Chapter Ten
A new *Gigantomachia* foretold – political developments to the fall of Maximus – Arbogast and the death of Valentinian II – proclamation of Eugenius and the pagan revival – counter-legislation and reactions to it – Stilicho, Alaric and the wars of Eugenius – consequences of the victory of Theodosius – his death – Alaric's sack of Greece – the end of the mysteries of Eleusis

Chapter Eleven
The Emperors Arcadius and Honorius I – the prefects Rufinus, Eutropius

and Stilicho – destruction of the temples of Africa – the re-Romanisation policy in east and west – Stilicho's ambiguities – first Vandal incursions – Radagais' horde – second Vandal incursions – rebellion of Constantine III – the burning of the Sibylline Books – execution of Stilicho – Alaric's invasion of Italy – the pagan Emperor Attalus – events leading to Alaric's sack of Rome

Many of the dates mentioned in this book are uncertain. Rather than interrupt the flow of the text to argue the case for each one of them, I have in most instances adopted that date which on the basis of the evidence seems most likely to me. The three most important dates about which there is controversy are those of Constantine's conquest of the East, the composition of Libanius' *In defence of the temples* and the accession of Alaric's puppet-emperor Attalus at Rome. The complications of the first are discussed in my *Constantine the Great* (Hamish Hamilton and Scribners, 1971); the problems surrounding the other two are considered in some detail in chapters nine and eleven of this book.

Philosophies of Life in the Roman Empire

One tradition, the Christian, has it that when the Emperor Julian lay dying he mourned in his own death the ending of the old world with the words, "Thou has conquered, O Galilean".

Another tradition, the pagan, has it that the Emperor Julian was assassinated by a Christian.

In all probability, neither tradition is true (although there is more likelihood in the second than in the first).

"And Pilate asked, What is truth?"

There are many, perhaps too many, histories of Christianity in the years of the church's triumph over the gods and traditions of the classical pagan world. This book is not another of them. Nor is it a plain history of the decline of Rome. It is rather a review of the years of Rome's decline, and the death-agony of Jupiter and his children, as seen through the admittedly biased eyes of an educated pagan living far enough away from the events to see them with some objectivity despite his biases and with sufficient freedom to be able to express himself honestly.

There can be no doubt that Christianity played a major part in Rome's decline. But Christianity did not exist in a void, or fight its battle with paganism on a plane separate from that of daily life. In this struggle, the characters and experiences of those principally involved from decade to decade were always at least as significant as the ideas about which they were allegedly fighting. As we shall be driven often to repeat, in later imperial history, religion, politics and social life were one and indivisible: the name of the imperial god, the foibles of the imperial temper, and the size of the imperial gold reserves were all of day-to-day significance in the lives of citizens from Hadrian's Wall to the River Euphrates. That is why it is impossible to write a true history of Rome without discussing Roman religion, or a valid history of western religion which takes little account of political and social life under the emperors. This book tells the story of the end of classical paganism, but a great many of its pages are filled with details about whom emperors married and whom they fought or executed, the bribes that officials accepted and the enemies that they made. At times, such details may seem irrelevant, but finally they will all be seen to have had their significance in this story's sad, inevitable, chaotic end.

Everyone—whether pagan or Christian—alive at the time, providing he thought about the question at all, convinced himself that the old Rome and its empire died on 24 August 410, the day that Alaric the Visigoth gave his men the city to loot.

If in any sense they all were right, the teasing question must be, why did the City die that day, after having survived so much?

It was important—but precisely how important it is difficult to assess—that the first recorded pandemic of plague had just about burned itself out by that time, leaving large areas underpopulated and, worse, widespread uncertainty and depression among those who had survived.

It was also important that imperial finances had long been in a chaotic state, gold was for ever in short supply, and much of what good coin could be collected was being paid out in bribes to keep enemies away.

Again, the geophysical structure and climate of the Mediterranean basin were changing. The consequent droughts, floods, famines and earthquakes were perils which men could fear but not control.

And again, after centuries of assault, the frontiers had collapsed, partly from internal weakness, partly from intolerable external pressure, with the result that there were barbarians everywhere, not merely the untamed, recent invaders rampaging through the countryside in recognisable hordes, but also thousands superficially civilised in dress and language but alien nonetheless, although among them were the holders of some of the highest offices in the state.

And yet again, the sons and daughters—especially the daughters—of solid citizen families were turning in confusion and distress of mind to one or other of the eastern religions offering salvation, often to Christianity, with the result that the service of the gods was being neglected and the foundation-stone of the state undermined.

To many at the time, it seemed that these last two menaces were the greatest of all. The Christians and barbarians between them were killing the gods and the state. We can ask today: how far was this true? And how could such circumstances have been allowed to arise?

That last question can be answered in a single sentence (which then, of course, instantly needs qualification): the state and its gods were succumbing to Christians and barbarians because Roman morale had failed.

We cannot talk about the dying gods apart from politics, or the Roman emperors without their gods. The traditional gods of the empire were lordly companions, sometimes capricious or intolerant, but friendly when it pleased them—as it had pleased them to uphold the superiority of the Roman state. But they were not saviours; they did not promise all who worshipped them fittingly ease in a life-to-come. They were gods who, when their own chief was angry, could sit talking over what to do for the best until the sun went down. And, as they were gods under whom the empire had prospered, men had for centuries accepted the Immortals as they had found them. But by late in the third century, although the mass of the citizens still paid lip-service to the superiority of life in the empire, they had stopped believing in it. The empire and its gods no longer offered sufficient security. For every human being life has always been uncertain, but to many in the third century its shortcomings were not a challenge nor even a background to daily events fatalistically accepted; they were a mountainous burden, so that even free men felt themselves to be the oppressed slaves of fate. Allowing themselves to be crushed by the pressures of the times at just that stage in the development of civilisation when they also felt within themselves the stirrings of individual self-awareness and responsibility, people of all classes began to demand more of the Immortals than they had ever undertaken to provide. So the "saving religions" began to make large numbers of converts, while other aberrations, such as theurgy (the magic of the élite) and astrology, brought fortunes to those who learned their jargon well.

From the beginning the Christians set out to destroy the gods of the classical world. They all but succeeded. And there can be no doubt that of all the crimes committed in Christ's name this has been the most devastating in its consequences. During their attempt to murder the gods, the Christians destroyed the world of those who loved them and could laugh at them while serving them. The result was that, after their victory, chaos ruled again.

To the Christians that killing was, of course, no murder. Most of them did not deny that the gods existed, but believed them to be devils, the spawn of the evil one. Tertullian, a second-century north African Christian, described Satan's champions down in hell sharing out the names of the gods between them the better to deceive mankind (although naturally to him this was no joke).[1] In sound Christian opinion, to kill off such depraved monsters was praiseworthy. It loosened the arch-devil Satan's grip on the world and brought nearer the kingdom of heaven.

Delighting in their success as deicides, Christians have understandably been chary of admitting the high cost to the world of their victory. Jesus' divine father swallowed up Jupiter the Best and Greatest together with all his family so completely that next to nothing visible of them remained, apart from their ruined shrines. After an initial period of apparently total disappearance, all in the gods that seemed good to the bishops was absorbed into the mediaeval Jesus and his attendant army of heroes and martyrs, while all that orthodoxy could accept of the goddesses appeared in the Virgin Mary and her retinue of female saints. The story of that transformation has often been told. Its narrators, when Christian, have usually claimed that in the process little of value was lost. That claim is untrue. Western civilisation was immeasurably impoverished by the totality of the gods' eclipse. Art, philosophy, literature, the very psychology of Western man, all suffered by the victory of the bishops. The Christianity forced upon the Graeco-Roman world by imperial and episcopal policy in the fourth century and confirmed in the post-Roman world by barbarian and Byzantine ignorance in the fifth was too narrow a religion to satisfy all the needs of human beings; the god it offered was too tenuous and the goals it set too restricted. In the pagan view—the view of the author of this book, and many of the writers whose works are quoted in it—the havoc could scarcely have been greater if in the crucial battle of the beginning, the *Gigantomachia* celebrated in so many classical sculptures, the giants had overcome the gods and forced upon the world their own uncultured tyranny.

Legend says that when rival chiefs among the ancient Celts confronted one another in battle, being wise leaders and proud men, they did their best to ensure the safety of their bards, so that whatever the outcome of the conflict a trained observer from each side would live to tell the tale of great deeds done by the princes and their champions. When Christians and pagans fought for the soul of the empire, no such care was taken to preserve both stories. Only the Christians survived and inevitably the story their bards told afterwards was partial and myopic. The balance has remained unredressed through the centuries since. But some record of what individual pagans thought and did during the long-drawn conflict has survived, chiefly in letters and orations preserved by Christian copyists, and the deeds of pagans in defence of their world are often reflected in the chronicles of their opponents. It is these survivals which form the main materials of this book.

They are relatively rare, for two reasons. In the first place, despite the apparently contradictory evidence of the persecutions, most pagans appear not to have been worried by the success of Christianity until it was too late, while those who were troubled tended to be too law-abiding to offer any other than verbal resistance, except when encouraged to do so by the law. And secondly, so great was the hatred of the Christian historians for their defeated enemies that they almost never wrote of them with even respect, let alone affection.

It would be fascinating to know what picture the average pagan had of the Christians at about the year 300, when the great battle was joined. The contempt of the official class is reflected in some of the *Acta* of the third-century martyrs recording the exchanges in African and Palestinian courtrooms between Christians and their judges. But little else has been allowed to survive. The most famous reasoned attack on Christianity, that made by Celsus at the end of the second century, is known only through Origen's *Contra Celsum*[2] and represented the intellectual's approach to the problem. What was said on the street-corners is largely lost, although it is known that in third-century comedy the Christian slave—slandered continually as whining, hypocritical, and dishonest—had become a stock villain (which accounts in part for the Christians' hatred of the theatre). The common attitude is perhaps best reflected in the wicked Christian miller's wife vividly drawn in Apuleius' *Metamorphoses* and in the satirical "pagan" account of Christianity given in the Christian Minucius Felix' *Octavius*, composed about the year 200, the less intellectual and reasoned parts of which may fairly be taken to represent the sort of gossip against themselves that Christians were then likely to overhear: they were "the ultimate filth", a gang "of ignorant men and credulous women", who "with meetings at night, solemn fasts and inhuman food" made up "a hole-in-the-corner, shadow-loving crew", "silent in public but clacking away in corners", "spitting on the gods and laughing at holy things".

> "They know one another by secret signs and signals and they make love together before they know one another—for there is a certain amount of lust mixed up with their religion, and they promiscuously call themselves brothers and sisters. . . . It is said that among them the head of the lowest of beasts, the ass, is most improperly consecrated to I cannot imagine what kind of worship. They are said to reverence the genitals of their presidents and priests, worshipping the nature of their begetters as it were—I do not know whether by wicked rites of the sort you would expect, but I do know for a certainty that it is by secret ones in the dark. And when the master of their ceremonies has told the tale of a man punished for his crimes by the supreme penalty, the deadly wood of the cross, a sacrifice is offered in a suitably corrupt and vicious way. A baby is smothered in flour and . . . offered to one to be initiated, who kills it . . . with blows on the floury outer surface—blows, of course, apparently innocuous. . . . They lap the blood up thirstily and eagerly share out the limbs. . . . They assemble for their feasts with all licentiousness . . . people of every age and sex. And after sumptuous feastings, during which amoral living is extolled and lustful, drunken excitement exhibited . . . they couple in abominable lust in the shameless darkness. . . ."[3]

Despite their setting these are not, essentially, anti-Christian stories: they are of the common stock of human insult as directed towards a hated minority, given verisimilitude in a particular context by a sprinkling of known facts about the peculiar customs of the despised people.

At the other end of the propaganda scale, about eighty years after Minucius put together this scandal in order to refute it, Porphyry, the disciple and biographer of the greatest of the third century's philosophers, Plotinus, compiled an attack on the Christians in a very different vein. Unfortunately, it was accounted so deadly that no part of it has been allowed to survive; it was destroyed by imperial decree in 448. But sufficient references to it may be culled from other works to reveal the main grounds for Porphyry's rejection of Christian teaching. They are especially interesting because several of them are not arguments which would be likely to spring to mind today.

Porphyry's main complaint was against the weakness of the testimony offered with regard to the life of the historical Jesus. His own training was as a literary critic. It was he who first proved on literary and historical grounds that the Book of Daniel was not an ancient prophecy but belonged to the time of Alexander the Great's successors, a critical judgement generally accepted today. He found many inconsistencies among the gospel stories, and between the gospels and the *Acts of the Apostles* on the one hand, and the New Testament as a whole and later Christian teaching on the other. He found Christianity unjust, because it offered salvation only to the generation of the New Testament and those who came after. He claimed that the Apostle Peter murdered Ananias and Sapphira. He found that the apostles were liars, that they practised magic to make money, and they promised blessings—especially resurrection—which they could not provide. Above all, he found the whole story of Jesus as incarnate son of God, dying by the will of God, impossible to accept, because it made the supreme and holy God responsible for evil actions and for death.[4]

The average pagan's reactions to Christianity must have lain somewhere between these two extremes of abuse and intellectual rejection. Paradoxically, part of the reason that they are difficult to deduce is that "paganism" to the pagan never existed. It was a figment of the Christian imagination. "Paganism" was a loose mixture of cults, blended in different proportions at different times and places. It is not far from the truth to say that before Christianity invented it, there was no Roman religion,[5] but only worship, expressed in a hundred-and-one different ways, all the different cults establishing a relationship between the citizen and the divine powers above and below, the universe in which he lived and the state which he served.

To Libanius, the defender of the cults against the Christian destroyer, Theodosius, each of the cults had its own practical usefulness: "In the forces, not every soldier performs the same services, but all have their role in the victory. And it is the same with companies of rowers: not every arm is as strong as every other, but even the weakest are useful. [So it is with the gods.] Some protect Roman rule, others defend their client cities, others watch over the fields. . ."[6]

It was once commonplace among Christians to claim that the gods were already moribund before the Christians stepped in to end their misery. Like most misrepresentations, this one has a grain of truth in it. Some forms of cult were weakening, some views of divinity had begun to seem outmoded or even laughable. But apathy was not universal, despite the failure of Roman morale, and some forms of cult were flourishing as never before. The gods did not die of old age. The Christians assassinated them.

Every way of life has a special quality of its own, easier to sense than to define. The religion of the empire was part of the imperial way of life—a very important part, an essential one in the opinion of many of the empire's thinking men. The principal elements of Roman religion have often been tabulated, but to tabulate is inevitably to falsify. No sensible and sensitive Christian would claim that the whole of what Christianity means to him is summed up in the Nicene Creed or even that it could be compressed into any form of words. So it was with paganism. The cults can be described. The psychological realities behind them can be discussed. But only a pagan knew what being a pagan meant. Paganism was a life-style, a cogitation upon "all those things pertaining to the worship of the gods",[7] never a definition in a text-book and certainly not a collection of statues in a museum.

Because the empire repeatedly condemned Christians and members of other exclusivist sects, at times seeking to extirpate them all, Roman rule is often depicted as narrowminded, hard, and cruelly oppressive. A number of influential pagans, notably among the emperors, exhibited all these faults, sometimes to a grotesque degree. Generally speaking, however, the world ruled from Rome was extremely tolerant. In republican days, vigorous attempts were made to keep foreign cults out of the city of Rome itself, especially those which seemed to threaten public order (the cult of the great mother of Syria and her son-lover Attis was considered especially dangerous), but in the empire as a whole throughout most of its existence local expressions of religious sentiment were tolerated and even encouraged. It was more common for Roman thinkers to look for parallels between local cults and their own than to emphasize and so exaggerate the differences. Christians (and the members of certain other religious groups, notably the Jews, the dualist gnostics and the Manichees) were branded as atheists because they preached and practised intolerance and exclusivism. They were thought godless not because they put their trust in a different god from most men but because they refused to recognise certain aspects of divinity obvious in the gods worshipped by their fellow citizens, and so were led to deny that they were gods at all.

It is generally recognised that Christians and other atheists were not alone in attacking the traditional polytheism of the Graeco-Roman world. Centuries before Christ, poets and philosophers had begun to look into and beyond the multiplicity of the gods and godlings in a quest for the One, the Mind, the Reason behind the universe. Unlike the Christians, they did not often deny the validity of the religious experience of those who could not follow them in their refinements of current ideas. Few pagan thinkers would have questioned that all religions lead human minds and hearts in the direction of *divinitas*, "whatever is enthroned in heaven", while most Christian teachers of the time thought that all other religions but their own led straight to the devil.

The official gods of the third century empire were still, as they had always been, the divine family of Jupiter the Best and Greatest, a family long since universally identified with the Hellenic Olympians who had sat talking until the sun set. It was the popular and often debased concept of the official gods as expressed in folklore and fairy tale, stage play and novel, which made them such easy targets for Christian propagandists. But it would be wrong to conclude, for instance, from the portrayal—I all but wrote "betrayal"—of Venus-Aphrodite as a sharp-tongued bitch of a goddess in Apuleius' second century version of the story of Cupid and Psyche, that respect for the goddess's power was already dead and true devotion to her forgotten. Far from it. She was still the goddess of whom it was first said "her service is perfect freedom" and she was to remain so, one of those whom no amount of ridicule, or even later Christian hatred, could kill.The lyrics of mediaeval poets alone are enough to show her continuing power. As for the Best and Greatest himself, despite the crudeness of some of the jokes made, and the sermons preached, at his expense, his stock continued to rise throughout imperial times, so that he was untouchable by any satire, however barbed. Beyond the reach of blasphemy, to the Christians he became the most potent of the black devils, while to the popular pagan mind he was the image of what philosophers meant when they spoke of "the divine".

As deeply engraved on the subconscious mind of the Romans as the worship of the great Sky-Lord Jupiter and his family was reverence for the law and the state, embodied in pre-Republican times in awe for the king, as common father of the tribe, responsible for its religious as well as its material well-being, and in Imperial Rome in the divine presence of the Emperor. Although, during republican times, the title *Rex* was publicly spurned by every good Roman, the tradition of a *rex sacrorum*, a King of the Cult, lived on at Rome. The sacred priest-king himself still haunted the woods around the lake of Nemi in the mysterious person of the escaped slave who was king of the forest until a challenger slew him and the actual title *rex sacrorum* was among those of the high priest of Rome until it was assumed by the emperors. No early emperor dared to allow himself to be called King (or even Lord) of Rome, but there had undoubtedly survived among the people a profound subconscious longing for a quasi-divine leader, a yearning which expressed itself in an extreme reverence for the emperors spilling over into actual worship as soon as the emperors themselves would permit it.[8]

The tradition of the ancient sacred king of Latium was not the only element—although it may have been the most profound—in the cult of the divine emperors. From the beginning of imperial times, there were two ways in which it was always accounted legitimate for awe felt for the ruler to be expressed. The first was in adoration offered to the *genius*, the guiding spirit, of the reigning emperor. The other was by the worship of a dead emperor as a *divus*, a divine being dwelling with the gods, a hero in the tradition of Hercules, translated after this life to the courts of heaven.

The genius of an emperor was, essentially, the spark of divinity in him setting him above other men and making him fit to rule. To some degree, every human being was believed to possess—or be possessed by—a genius, and every Roman reverenced his own genius, especially on his birthday.

The genius of the head of a family was held in special honour by his whole household, including its slaves, and it was as the *paterfamilias* of the whole empire that the emperor was first honoured with offerings of incense, made publicly to his genius or to the *numen* of his power.

An imperial cult of this kind was intelligible and even defensible. But partly under the influence of subconscious folk memories, and partly in sycophantic response to the paranoia of certain emperors, extravagance crept in, finding it especially easy to do so because it became frequent (though not inevitable) practice to honour a dead emperor as divine. Augustus was ranked among the gods by a decree of the senate made less than a month after his death. From there it was a short but monumental step to acknowledgement of the divinity of the living ruler. Official Rome took it only with the greatest hesitancy. It was not until the self-made Aurelian had been proclaimed Augustus by the army in 270 that any emperor allowed himself to be advertised as divine: his coins offered him to his people as Recreator of the World and Our Lord and God. During the chaotic years after his death, his divine titles were briefly claimed by the short-lived Probus and Carus, but most significantly the first man proud enough consistently to equate himself with the Best and Greatest was the last of the pagans to enjoy a long reign, the Emperor Diocletian, who seized the throne in an officers' coup in 284. Calling himself Jovius, "son" or "servant" of Jove, and assuming the diadem, he let it be known in every possible way that he was to be regarded as more than a mere man. His arrogant claims may have been made partly to impress his less sophisticated barbarian-born subjects, but their main inspiration was probably in the last resort his fear of lesser men. His own birth was not brilliant and he was constantly alive to the danger of assassination. Although, through his decrees and propaganda, one of paganism's great champions, he was not praiseworthy as a pagan.

He was guilty of *hubris*, the arrogant assumption of superiority which the gods are bound to punish, and in the end the Furies hunted him down, driving him first to institute the great persecution of the Christians for which he is infamous and then to suffer a mental breakdown which forced his abdication.[9]

Official religion has never satisfied everyone. There have always been those in every culture who have asked more from the gods than they have seemed to the tribal ancestors willing to offer. This being so, there have understandably also always been those who have believed that they themselves knew more about the gods than the tribal priests have revealed. Throughout history, such people have tried to win extra favours from the gods, either by coercion or by cogitation, and sometimes by a combination of the two. Roman religious life was not different from any other. The empire had both its magicians and its philosophers, as well as its sophistical-magicians, bringing disrepute to both.

Divination had always been a part of the worship of Jupiter and his family. Omens and auguries were given official status in the national life. (There is no evidence that they gave any less trustworthy results than the ritual consultation of statistical projections and prognostications in modern times.) It was believed that the will of the gods both in public and private affairs could be deduced from a variety of observations of natural phenomena, especially the flight of birds, the occurrence of abnormal births among both men and animals, the behaviour of lightning, and the condition of the entrails of sacrificial beasts. Such official omens, interpreted according to age-old traditions, did not, however, satisfy everyone. Astrologers had a big following, especially after Augustus gave them his favour. Though the state never appointed astrologers as such to the priestly hierarchy, horoscopes were widely consulted in great causes as well as small. Cities—Constantinople among them—were founded at moments declared propitious by astrologers, and leading experts in the art of reading the heavens could command great influence as well as, often, great wealth.

Less respectable, but hardly less widely respected, were witches and necromancers who undertook not merely to read the will of the gods from signs which the gods themselves had provided but also to bend the divine will to human desires. Official policy was to condemn practitioners of these dark skills—while walking very warily of offending them, not only because witches and their like were believed to be knowledgeable in the matter of poisons but also because their goddess Hekate, a rural Greek by origin, could not be proved even by the most sceptical not to exist and not to take vengeance on those who scorned her.

Moreover the witches formed a secret society and such societies, especially those meeting by night, were always suspect. But as successful witchcraft offered definite advantages over other forms of religious practice, it continued to thrive. As time went on, through a perversion of Platonist philosophical and metaphysical studies, a new and apparently loftier style of magic found its way into all but the most respectable circles of paganism, the corruption—as both imperial lawmakers and true philosophers saw it—known as theurgy, "god-power".

Like cruder magic, god-power sought to bring pressure to bear on the divine, to bend its will to human ends. But philosophy gave it a respectable ancestry and an evocative vocabulary. It claimed that its ultimate goal was that of philosophy itself, knowledge of the divine, but what it sought above all to know was the ultimate secret name of the divine being, so as to be able to control the *afreet* in the wineskin, the genie in the lamp, the dwarf Rumpelstiltskin, the terrible reality beyond the veil. All the art of the magician, all his *techne magike*, was essentially directed towards this lower goal.[10]

The unscrupulous made fortunes from theurgy and, even more important, gained power and influence through it. Not all practitioners of the art were unscrupulous or self-seeking, of course, but it was simply not true that as Proclus claimed, "the art is quite humble and, so to speak, creeps about the world, the slave-girl of thaumaturges, making a home for itself among the dead, clinging to weeds, giving obedience to magic utterances. . . ."

Theurges sought power in this world and over the other. As will become evident as our story unfolds, too many of them were greedy men.

Many of the anti-pagan laws of the fourth century were directed against theurgy and forms of divination so like it as to be indistinguishable from it, but some cults offering near-magical advantages were tolerated until all paganism was banned. These were the Greater Mysteries attaching to the names of more-or-less respectable gods accepted (although at first often only grudgingly) by the Roman state.

The Immortals did not usually offer eternal bliss in the style so characteristic of mediaeval Christianity. The unenviable task of the genius of the average dead man was to watch over him in the dismal gloom of *dis*, with nothing to look forward to except the painful chance that some necromancer might pull him back temporarily from the grave to answer questions boringly insignificant to the dead. There were, naturally, those who were not satisfied with this cheerless doctrine, so cults offering more than mere existence to the dead found adherents among the romantic at all levels in society—just as philosophers teaching a doctrine of meaningful survival also found ready listeners. What the Mysteries promised by imperial times to those willing to undergo their initiation rites was on the one hand the enjoyable experience of belonging to a closed society and on the other a satisfying place in the divine scheme of things. Through the Mysteries, the individual found significance: every initiate became an immortal, a divine being through communication with the divine in the secret worship peculiar to his sect.

The origins of the Mysteries are lost in the hills and forests, the dark nights and lonely shepherds' days of antiquity. By the second and third Christian centuries, there were six great mysteries offering their own brands of companionship, enlightenment and salvation in the empire. They were not generally competing, although anyone who had found what he sought in one of them was unlikely to seek more from the others. The six were those of Cybele-Attis, Demeter, Dionysos, Isis, Mithras and Orpheus. The first four of these were still intimately linked with the corn-myths and harvest-myths which gave rise to them. Mithras was also a sun and vegetation hero. And even Orpheus was Master of the Animals before he became the chief guide to the spirit world.

It is as impossible to estimate how many adherents each of the mysteries could muster at any particular time as it is to reconstruct the detail of their ceremonies, let alone experience the atmosphere in which they were performed or share the special joy the devout found in any of them. Everyone who was ever enthralled by a theatrical performance or has even got drunk at a party has stood on the fringes of the mystery of Dionysos (the

Latin Liber and Bacchus) but no one will ever know how many used to experience the true Dionysiac frenzy or were carried into a world beyond speech by the revelations of Orpheus. Now and again the veil between us and the mystagogues is momentarily drawn aside in some fragment of literature, but it falls again almost at once. Perhaps the best-known of these survivals is Apuleius' *Metamorphoses* (often known as "The Golden Ass") which, as well as containing some glorious knock-about farce and awful warnings against dabbling in witchcraft also preserves one of the most moving prayers ever written and an emotionally charged description of the Egyptian Isis, identifying her with the Great Mother by whatever name she was known. Mystery and genuine devotion also pervade the surviving Orphic Hymns, which reflect the divine fear of those brought into the presence of the numinous by fasting and prayer. The deep fulfilment the followers of Dionysos found in his companionship is mirrored in the faces of his priestesses. There is peace-beyond-torment on the face of every Mithras Bull-slayer. . . . But how many found this peace, this hope, this fulfilment, this felicity, there is no means of discovering.[11]

The name of the philosopher who first propounded the idea that all cults have ultimately a common aim and concluded from that that they all have a common object, the One-at-the-heart-of-things, is another secret which time has not revealed. Some faint glimmering of this idea seems to have been instinctive to the Roman mind and permitted acceptance by the Roman people of the great variety of tolerated cults. From the earliest days of Roman expansion, when the army came into contact with a new race or tribe every effort was made to discover the nature of its gods and identify them with their nearest Roman counterparts, so that the process of assimilation—the first stage in syncretism—was immediately begun. Of course, at the outset interest in the name and character of an alien god was purely practical and military. Knowing the name and tastes of a god—and actually taking him into one's own camp, if he could be captured—gave one power over him and so over his devotees. Very soon, however, interest in the gods for their own sake emerged and formal identication of a foreign god with one native to Rome—technically, establishing his *interpretatio Romana*—led the way if not immediately to the introduction of foreign modes of worship into Rome itself then at least to acceptance of the philosophical concept that all worship had much in common and so at last to the idea that there is a common divine something, a *divinitas*, shared by all gods.

The first identification of Zeus with Jupiter is lost in the mists of time. Apollo—the most "Greek" of all the Hellenic gods, a deity without a native Roman counterpart—was already worshipped in Italy five centuries before Christ's birth and formally became one of the official gods at Rome itself when Augustus vowed him a temple on the Capitoline Hill. A very important stage in the Romanisation of Gaul was reached when the Romans admitted that such local gods as the horned Cerunnos were but foreign manifestations of Roman deities and equally worthy with them of human respect. All the Mysteries were foreign imports (sometimes vigorously resisted before being welcomed at Rome itself). No god was alien to the empire excepting always those gods like Christ demanding the suppression of insights already won, or those, like druidism's deities, which seemed to pose a political threat to stability. Not all the cults reached Rome itself. Perhaps the majority did not. But all were respected by Romans on their home ground, as it were, and inscriptions are common from the provinces uniting the names of Roman and local gods.

The philosophers of the empire carried this process of recognition and assimilation much further along the road towards syncretism. But they were also responsible for much more besides. If their influence on everyday life is hard to pinpoint, it is because it was all-pervasive. There existed, even in the most difficult times, a large leisured and educated class for whom ideas—any ideas—held a deep fascination. They were the philosophers' special patrons and targets. Many rich young citizens studied—even if only desultorily—at the Athenian schools; others heard and disputed over the doctrines taught at Alexandria, or Apamea or Rome itself. Nor did ideas attract the leisured class alone, though it especially had the time to pursue them. A philosopher with a powerful personality could attract a following from all classes, and where professional philosophers were lacking there was no shortage of local teachers and logicians, schoolmasters and lawyers, argumentative pedants and out-and-out charlatans, who had heard the masters' names and some earcatching sentences from their teachings, and were ready to use both to advance their own theories about man and his world. Paradoxical though it may appear at first sight, these totally unknown men are of more importance to our story than their masters, for it was they who kept philosophy alive from day to day, it was they who inculcated into the mass of the citizens the reverence for law which kept the empire alive for so long, and it was they who by their incompetence finally allowed Christian teachers to overwhelm both philosophy and the law.

By the third and fourth centuries, philosophy had moved far from the relatively pure forms of Hellenistic and Early Roman times. Its fundamental aim was theoretically still to account for life, but in practice its goal was often identical with that of non-official religion, the giving of meaning and hope to the individual. So the most influential pagan philosophers of these years were also the most influential religious teachers, and their language was imitated (though often garbled) by those ignorant· know-alls, the gnostics, the "Men of Knowledge" whose doctrines were often so esoteric as to seem meaningless today. Moreover, throughout much of the fourth century, philosophers also concerned themselves with the practices of the theurges, and as platonist-magicians were often known as the "sophists", "the wise ones".

The most mystical, least formally educated, least philosophical—and, I believe, most influential (in the very long run)—of all third-century thinkers was a Persian named Mani. Professional philosophers might argue that Mani was not a philosopher at all, but a sophistic charlatan who took elements from several religious systems and blended them together to give the people what they seemed to want. He was a supreme plagiarist and a supreme showman; his ideas touched a chord in thousands in his own century and deeply influenced millions in later times, down to the reign of Pope Innocent III and beyond.(Francis of Assisi's enemies accused him of teaching the current form of Mani's doctrines.) In the Persian empire, he was first lauded, then executed (in the year 276): in the Roman world, his dualist, gnostic ideas caught the attention of philosophers as well as of the naturally and naively religious, and deeply influenced the development of ideas.

To Mani—as to most gnostics before him and many ascetics since—this world is evil. The whole of life is a struggle between good and evil, light and darkness, truth and the lie. The aim of life is to redeem from the darkness of the world and the flesh the divine spark trapped in it, and reunite that divine spark with the glory of light and truth. This aim can be achieved, Mani taught, only by self-denial and withdrawal from the world, giving up everything in pursuit of ascetic perfection. Those who thus dedicated themselves to becoming "Perfect (Men)" were forbidden to indulge themselves in any way, except by excesses of fasting and prayerful contemplation, so that at the end their spirits might be freed from the weary wheel of fortune, fate and rebirth, and be reunited to the light. The less than perfect followers of the way of Mani, the Hearers, were permitted to support the Perfect with gifts and prayers, hoping that in their next incarnations they might be born as Perfect themselves; but while still imperfect they were free to indulge themselves as they chose, because nothing can further dirty utter pollution.

Unlike many of the religions which found themselves with followers in the empire, Mani's religion demanded the exclusive attention of those adopting it. It became powerful because its dualist approach appealed on different levels to both the intellectual—like Augustine of Hippo—and to the ascetic, like Priscillianus of Avila. Its particular strength lay in the emphasis it gave to ideas about the nature of good and evil, and to ethical and non-ethical behaviour by the individual, a field left to so large a degree unexplored by traditional Roman religion.

In contrast to Mani, Ammonius of Alexandria and his disciples were philosophers first and mighty champions of pagan freedom only in consequence of their philosophical ideas. Ammonius, a contemporary of the influential Christian Clement of Alexandria, was born into a Christian family but abandoned Christianity when he grew up and by about the year 235 had begun to teach a revitalised philosophy based on Platonic ideas and ideals. What precisely he added to the common teaching is not known because nothing he may have written has survived. But his famous pupils unanimously acknowledged their immeasurable debt to him.

The aim of the new Platonists inspired by Ammonius was not merely to revive the teachings of Plato but to produce a synthesis of all knowledge within the framework of their centuries-dead master's ideas about the universe. It was an impossible task, but Ammonius and his followers made advances in history, literary criticism, medical theory and logic, as well as in philosophy and metaphysics, progress so valuable as to suggest that the methods and approaches Ammonius taught were original, stimulating and effective.[12] It was no accident that it was a pupil of his, the great Plotinus, who raised neo-Platonism to its greatest heights.

Plotinus studied under Ammonius for eleven years before travelling to the east in search of wisdom with the Roman expedition against the Persians under Gordian III. The expedition failed and by 245 Plotinus had reached Rome, where he lived for the next thirty years teaching and later writing in the furtherance of the new Platonism both as a system of thought and as a way of life. He rejected the dualist approach to philosophy because he saw no proof that the material world is ruled by evil. To him, everything in physical, spiritual or mental reality emanates ultimately from a single source, the One, the Good, the ultimate origin and focus of all values. The closer any lesser goods or values stand to the One, the higher they are, so that it is theoretically possible to establish a hierarchy of values, with mere matter at the periphery, the least of goods, and at the centre, beyond the natural world, beyond the world-soul and even the world-mind, Good itself, Thought-thinking-itself, the One. The ultimate aim of all philosophy, all religion, all living, is union of man the microcosm with the One at the heart of all things.

This union can—although rarely—be foreshadowed in this life by the achievement of a state of ecstasy through contemplation and introspection lifting the seeker to the level of the intensity of being of the world-mind. Plotinus himself had achieved this ecstasy and described it in language showing him to have been a mystic worthy of comparison with the greatest doctors of the soul. His biographer Porphyry says that he often went without food, not so much in defiance of the body's needs but because physical satiation clouds contemplation. He never called the body evil as the gnostics habitually did. In fact, he denied the existence of total evil. Nevertheless, Porphyry says, "he seemed ashamed of being in the body—and therefore . . . would not tolerate talk of his race, or parentage, or native city".[13] He reached ecstasy without the support of any organised religious cult, and could teach others to reach it:

"this god-like being many times raised himself to the first and transcendent god . . . that god without shape or intelligible form, enthroned above all mind and thinking. And I, Porphyry, declare that once I also, in my sixty-eighth year, drew close and was made one with him . . . but four times while I was with him, he achieved this ultimate good in actuality and not in potentiality only."[14]

For Plotinus, there were no short cuts to this beatitude. Like scholarship, it needed application and training:

> "Once for three days I myself, Porphyry, went on questioning him about how the mind is linked with the body, he going on explaining, until a certain Thammasius chanced by, a man concerned with definitive statements, who wanted him to talk like a book. . . . And he said to him: but if when Porphyry asks questions we do not resolve his difficulties, we shall never be able to express anything in cut-and-dried form to you."[15]

The cut-and-dried formulae of salvation offered by the gnostics and Christians had no appeal to Plotinus. Of the gnostics, he once said "the fact that they say they can see does not actually make them any more perceptive". The Christians certainly feared his influence long after his death, although he seems never to have attacked them directly. But there is one paragraph in Porphyry's edition of his work which deserves quotation here because it epitomises the antithesis between the best pagan and the common Christian teaching at the end of the third century on the key doctrine of providence; rejecting in it all concepts of salvation from outside, and thus making impossible any doctrine of redemption, Plotinus ends all possibility of any dialogue between himself and orthodox Christians:

> "Providence cannot be of such a kind that we ourselves are nothing. . . . And Providence says that one growing in goodness shall have a good life now and in store for him in the future, and the wicked the reverse. It is not right for those who have gone to the bad to solicit others to be their saviours or to sacrifice themselves at their behest, nor yet is it right for them to demand of the gods that they should order their affairs for them, laying aside their own existence [to do so], or that good people, leading another kind of life superior to the common human rule should do as much for them. . . ."[16]

So for Plotinus there could be no incarnation, no redemption, no salvation through the prayers of the saints. There could be only growth into goodness, by following the laws of the providence of one's kind. To ask for salvation was weak as well as wrong.

When this was his view, it is not surprising that his dedicated disciple Porphyry should, in the time of trial, prove to be one of the most dedicated (if not most successful) enemies that Christianity was ever to encounter.[17]

Notes

1 See Tertullian *Apologeticus, xxiii* in Migne, P. L. 1. Cf. also his *Liber de Idolatria* for a Christian view of the cult offered to statues and the "devils" the statues represent.

2 *Contra Celsum*, ed. H. Chadwick (C.U.P., 1965 ed.); see also H. Chadwick, *Early Christian Thought and Classical Tradition* (1966).

3 Minucius Felix, *Octavius*, J. Beaujeu (Paris, 1964); see also J. Becker in Paully-Wissowa, *Supp. XI*, 952ff.; 1365ff. See also Tertullian, *Apologeticus*, cap 9 in Migne, P. L., vol. 1.

4 See A. von Harnack, "Porphyrius 'Gegen die Christen' 15 Becher", etc., (Berlin, 1916) in *Abhandlungen der Koeniglichen Preussichen Akademie der Wissenschaft* (1916, 1).

Porphyry wrote, Harnack believed, from Sicily in about the year 270 with the intention of playing his part in Claudius II's announced Restoration of the World. Peter's murder of Ananias and Sapphira is described at Acts 5:1ff.

The kind of contradiction Porphyry found in the gospel is well illustrated by the pair of quotations Mark 10:18 ("There is none good but God") and Luke 6:45 ("A good man out of the good treasure of his heart bringeth forth that which is good").

The apostles lie, Porphyry claims, at Matt. 1:22ff. and many times in the Infancy Narratives.

But Porphyry's chief argument, many times repeated, was that Jesus was not a good man: if he had been, the government would not have executed him, and his followers, pursuing his example, would not have committed the endless crimes against the state which had necessitated their persecution.

5 The word *religio* existed, of course, but thinking men were hard put to it to define it, not because it had no meaning but because the religion of Rome and her dependent allies was so closely bound up with everyday life that it seemed to need definition to none but pedants. As the empire changed and developed, so did the scope of the word *religio*. Often said to have derived from the word *religere*, "to bind back" or "bind again", *religio* seems in the earliest times to have referred to the tabus binding the people, and so to have been largely negative in its connotation, religious actions being those required for safety at certain places or seasons of the year, or in connexion with certain family events or offices in the state. By the time of Cicero, however, the scope of the word had been very much enlarged and become more positive, so that his definition "all those things pertaining to the worship of the gods—*omnia que ad cultum deorum pertinerent . . . sunt dicti religiosi*—are called religious" is acceptable today. But not so his derivation of the word from *relegendo*: re-read, re-studied, cogitated upon. The falseness of the derivation was pointed out by the Christian Lactantius, who derives *religio* firmly from *religere* and notes "by this fetter (*vinculo*) we are bound (*obstricti*) and rebound (*religati*) to god: hence comes its name *religio*, and not as Cicero interpreted it from *relegendo*".

Lactantius, the tutor to the son of the Emperor Constantine, was anxious to see Christianity made a binding state religion.

The quotation from Cicero is at *De Nat. Deorum*, II, 72.

6 *In defence of the temples*, 34.

7 For details of the cults of Rome, see especially K. Latte, *Roemische Religionsgeschichte* (Munich, 1960).

8 Augustus' successor Tiberius complained that he was being mocked and insulted when he was called "master and lord" like an oriental god. Caligula was laughed at when he took to wearing the diadem, the visible symbol of the superhuman status of a Persian king. A hundred and fifty years later, Elegabalus may not actually have objected if some of his subjects identified him with the sun-

god whose priest he was. But such extravagances did not go down well while the empire remained "Roman". On sacred Kingship, see J. Frazer. *The Golden Bough*, 12 vols. (Macmillan, 1907–1915); M. Frankfurt, *Kingship and the Gods* (University of Chicago, 1948).

9 It is noteworthy that the Christian emperors of the fourth century used the title *divis* when speaking or writing of one of their number who had died: in this usage, *divus* can only mean "filled with divinity" or "united to the divine", and not "divine by his own right". The same title was later used by the Roman Church of its officially-canonised saints.

10 But the magician's skill is not limited to the manipulation of words alone. Although words do have divine power, in fact the divine is also diffused throughout the material world, so that if the right plants, animals, stones, bodily secretions, secret signs and power-filled words can all be brought together the magician can achieve any desired end by focussing upon the Ultimate, as it were, along a preselected line of related sympathetic entities. Proclus wrote in his *On sacrificing* "each individual object does in fact have within it a certain characteristic of the divine, but one that is in itself not enough to invoke the presence of the god. So by combining various [sympathetic] substances, the emanations of the divine from above are brought down and the One made from so many together brings into play the One ruling over the many." Hence, he goes on to say, statues are often made out of such mutually sympathetic substances, and compound statues of this kind are specially powerful (although single-substance images are not to be despised). For this reason also, particular animals are offered to particular gods, and so on. Theurges learn "first the powers of the demons linked with things in nature, so as to call them into bodily manifestation through those things with which they are sympathetically linked; then they move on from the demons to the powers and functions of the gods themselves—for they learn a great deal from the instruction the demons give, and much again from the symbols. . . . And so finally they come to knowledge of the god himself."

The progression is ultimately Platonist—from the visible to the invisible, from the lower to the higher, and thus on to the Highest of all. In theory, it could sound straightforward enough, but there were many tricky bypaths which the theurge had to learn to avoid. By general consent among the theurges, the lower demons in any series could be mischievous and might prove malicious. The fourth-century theurge Iamblichus warned that most manifestations of divine beings engineered by theurges (rather than achieved by meditation and prayer) were only revelations of lesser beings standing in the same line of sympathies as the divine being invoked, and could be dangerous (even if their manifestation was not faked, as modern pseudo-mediums fake spirit manifestations for the credulous, with lights and linen cloths). The warning was often ignored. In his *Lives of the Sophists* Eunapius related the story of one such seance at which Iamblichus was present:

> "When a certain Egyptian invoked Apollo and to the great amazement of those who saw what was manifested Apollo came, the great Iamblichus said, 'Do not be surprised, friends: it is only the ghost of a gladiator'."

The gladiator dedicated to Apollo, or with Appollonine qualities, was not malicious on that occasion, so no great harm was done—except to the Egyptian's reputation.

Stories like this circulated freely around the late Roman world, but most of them were not even cautionary, let alone deflating of the theurge's pretensions.

According to the theurges, the most powerful names are the secret titles of the Demiurge, the maker and ruler of the world, merely to speak which might be fatal to the uninitiated, although fully-fledged theurges are taught them by the Egyptian god Thoth in his Helleno-Roman manifestation as Hermes Trimegistos "Hermes of the three great things" (truth, faith and love), leading the faithful follower of his way to the Good and the Beautiful and so ultimately to the fulness of Knowledge. Platonist theurges seem to have envisaged the soul with two parts, a higher and a lower. The higher stems from the Demiurge. The lower, binding us to the world from which it emanates, binds us also to the weary wheel of destiny. Through theurgy, the higher soul can break free from the wheel of fortune and, becoming dominant, raise man above the physical world, above the realm of Fate, to the realm of the planets—the visible gods—and so on to the divine. . . . So theurgy was a synthesis of the old magic of the woods and fields, the astrological teaching of the east, the remnants of Egyptian classical religion, and the dominant philosophy of the Greeks. Not surprisingly, it was a synthesis which almost everyone who was not a theurge—either initiated or postulant—found deeply disturbing and darkly menacing to the wellbeing of individuals and the state. Purists made distinctions between religion and magic, between pagan worshippers and theurges—a distinction often reflected in the laws of, especially, Valentinian and Theodosius. Responsible pagans themselves made that distinction and many of them would have been content if the Christian emperors had set out to cleanse paganism of magic. But even while they were contemptuous of the theurges, they feared them (as the Christians did also) and made use of them (as the Christians claimed not to do).

11 It is often said that only the rich could afford to undergo full initiation into any of the mysteries; certainly Apuleius writes as though he had impoverished himself for his goddess's sake and it would seem unlikely that any but the richest and their chosen companions could afford the expenses of the ceremonies admitting a man to the higher ranks of the devotees of Mithras or of killing a bull (or even a ram) in his honour of Attis and his mother Cybele. There is, however, no evidence that the lowest-ranking of Mithrean initiates, the members of the Raven Order, had any less devotion (or found any less satisfaction) than did those who could afford the time and money—and accept the disciplines—allowing them to rise to the seventh grade and become Fathers. Although only a rich man could afford the costs involved in the ritual bath in bull's blood that was the ultimate sacrifice open to citizen-worshippers of Attis and Cybele, nothing suggests that only the rich were "saved". Indeed, the taurobolium seems not to have been performed for the sake of winning salvation until the reign of Julian: before the mid-fourth century the idea behind the rite would appear rather to have been to offer something—oneself, one's city, one's province—to the mother of all. Even in Phrygia, where the worship of Cybele is first recorded, only an individual with a peculiarly perverse psychology could enter into the state of ecstasy which led men to castrate themselves in Cybele's honour (a sacrifice which the empire made a criminal offence for a citizen), but lack neither of cash nor courage prevented anyone, Roman or not, from taking part in the public rites of her festival around the spring equinox and deriving hope, comfort and pleasure from the ceremonies of the cutting of the pine, the day of blood, and the *hilaria*. That many did find

benefit in them is surely indicated by the fact that the mystery was supported by public funds in Gaul and Africa as well as at Rome.

The importance given to the individual in the mysteries shows most clearly in our broken records of the worship of Isis and Sarapis, and of Mithras. There were daily services at temples of Isis with simple ceremonies—the awakening of the statues, the blessing with Nile water—and congregational singing from the hymn-book, the *Praises of Isis*. All her initiates had personal rôles in the dances and processions held in her honour, and the evidence is that the devotion of the *Isiaci* to their goddess was profound. Sarapis, her fellow-Egyptian, worked miracles, especially of healing, and protected the dead.

An even more intense personal relationship would appear to have bound the initiates of Mithras to their hero. (Mithras was so untypical a cult-leader that it is misleading to call him a god without further definition: Jerome thought he had been specially invented by the Devil to deceive potential Christian converts.) Mithras, the original "companion of the sun", was the protector of men, a man himself, yet more than a man, one of the principal actors in creation—his myth related how he created rain by striking a rock—and destined to be the restorer of the world at the end of time. In the original Persian myth, there stood behind him Ahura Mazda, the god of light and Ahriman, the god of death, with beyond them again Zervan akarana, boundless time, but in Roman Mithraism, the hero and his sun-comrade appear to have sufficed—though even now, after intensive research, the myth that justified and explained the ceremonies in the cave-chapels of the cult remains obscure.

12 Among Ammonius' pupils later achieving fame were Longinus, head of the school at Athens, Origen the Philosopher, and, as well as the great Plotinus, the Christian Origen whose *Hexapla* was the first attempt at literary criticism of the text of the bible by comparison of various versions and whose imitation of an ecstatic priest of Attis in castrating himself (allegedly in fulfilment of the gospel saying "there are eunuchs who have made themselves so . . . for the kingdom") earned him notoriety, while the extravagance of his speculations in platonist style won for him condemnation by the church.

13 *Life of Plotinus*, 1.

14 *Life of Plotinus*, 13.

15 *ibid*.

16 *Enneads*, 3, 2, 9.

17 It is a pity that, inevitably, so much emphasis has to be placed on Porphyry's antagonism towards Christianity. He was a very solid thinker and a tireless worker, who produced at least seventy books of value, many of which have been lost owing to Christian dislike of his name. He wrote the *Life of Plotinus* and edited his master's thoughts (unskilfully) in the *Enneads*: he also wrote valuable studies of Homer, Plato and Aristotle. His treatise on logic—*Categories*—became the standard mediaeval textbook and his essay *On the formation of the embryo* formed part of the Galenian corpus. He was in many ways the most typical of late pagans (and so the model of later renascence man), a polymath of real ability and application, a man worthy of his civilisation and fully at home in the world of the gods.

Religion in Politics

Throughout the centuries the hereditary principle has always been much resented by those who have little or nothing to gain from the deaths of their fathers. The histories of the Germanic peoples in the middle ages, and the Roman empire in late antiquity, however, show the great weakness into which a state is betrayed by uncertainty about the succession. In both societies if the soldiers had known precisely who was destined to inherit the throne and had been convinced that any rebellion on their part would be met by opposition from the overwhelming majority of the people, the whole bloody history would have been transformed. As things were in the empire, from the day that Tiberius established the Praetorian Guard in barracks under the shadow of Rome's very walls, no imperial family was safe in the palace. The list of those assassinated or driven to suicide makes sickening reading. By the middle of the third century, it had become obvious that only a really strong man with a ruthlessly thorough approach to the problems of power could hold the empire together. Many thought that they had the strength, but time—sometimes no more than a few days—proved them mistaken. This terrible period began when Alexander Severus was murdered in 235, and Maximinus in 238; the same year, Gordian I committed suicide after his son and co-ruler Gordian II had been murdered, and the emperors appointed by the senate to follow the Gordians, Balbius and Pupienus, were assassinated. Then the puppet child-emperor Gordian III was dressed in the trappings of power for almost six years till in 244 he was murdered by Philip the Arabian. Philip died in a mutiny in 249; his successor Decius was killed in battle in 251. Trebonius Gallus was murdered in 253, Valerian vanished in Persia in 260, Gallienus was murdered in 268, Claudius II died of plague in 270, Aurelian was murdered in 275, Tacitus in 276, Florian also in 276, Probus in 282, and Carus the same year. His sons Numerian and Carinus survived almost eighteen months, till Numerian was murdered, perhaps by Diocletian (who blamed General Aper for the killing), and Carinus was killed by Diocletian's supporters in battle. . . . Terrible times, indeed—yet these were only the most public of the empire's evils. Not every attempt at revolution was automatically successful. And while emperors put down plotters or succumbed to them, enemies from the north and east struck again and again at the frontiers, while famine, plague, chronic inflation, every imaginable evil, it seemed, sapped public confidence, weakening the foundations which the first two centuries of imperial government had so painfully laid.

It speaks very highly for the inherent strength of the Roman system of law and administration that under this unrelenting strain civil government did not totally collapse and men remained proud to call themselves Roman citizens. On the other hand, it is not surprising that, with stability so devastatingly shaken, all the institutions of the empire seemed to be rocking, ready to fall. Even the gods, upon whom the fabric of the state rested, were shaken, while peculiar sects, like the gnostics, and various forms of nastiness, like necromancy, found ready adherents.

It was against this background that edicts of persecution against the Christians were issued by Maximinus, Decius and Valerian.[1] All three were disciplinarians; Maximinus was a crude soldier of peasant origins, but both Decius and Valerian were renowned for their very real devotion to old standards and traditional ways. Both were convinced that Rome could be made secure only by a restoration of true government. To both of them, that meant government by the senate and the emperor working together under the true leaders of the state, the old gods worshipped since republican times. Their persecution of the adherents of alien cults was accompanied by powerful propaganda intended to stimulate loyalty to all that was truly Roman. Their aims found wide support. The Christians themselves admitted that Decius' persecution came close to achieving its object. Cyprian, bishop of Carthage during the persecution, and Eusebius of Caesarea, the fourth-century historian, both told how presbyters of the church flocked to swear their allegiance to the empire and its divine rulers and to receive the precious *libellus* certifying their loyalty. But as Pontius' *Acts of Cyprian* show,[2] the Christians were already making a distinction which pagans could not make between loyalty to the state and loyalty to its gods. When Cyprian was called upon to surrender himself to the magistrates during Valerian's persecution, loyalty to his citizenship drove him to present himself at court although he knew that inevitably he was going to his death for his loyalty to an alien god.

It is obvious from the records that Cyprian understood fully what he was doing, but it is doubtful if any non-Christian citizen could have understood his reasoning, let alone applauded it. To most people the two loyalties Cyprian honoured could not be two; they were conceivable only as one and indivisible. Nobody could be loyal to the state who was not also loyal to its gods.

Decius died fighting for the old ways on the north-eastern frontier near Beroea; Valerian died after losing a war for the old frontiers in the east, no one ever knew quite where or when. After Valerian's disappearance, his son Gallienus stopped the persecution of the Christians, but the fight to restore traditional values continued alongside that to reconstitute the old frontiers. Despite his granting Christians permission to exist and himself calling on another foreign god, Mithras, to help him as "the augustus' preserver", Gallienus was forced to retreat everywhere until his officers murdered him. His assassination seemed temporarily to mark a turning-point in the fortunes of the imperial office, a turning-point reached only just in time, for Gaul was in rebel hands and Gothic and Herulian raiders had swept deep enough into Greece to succeed in sacking Athens itself.

His successor, elected by the soldiers, was Claudius II, a skilful and courageous soldier born in Illyria. In a reign of less than two years before plague, then raging through the northern provinces, brought his life to an end, Claudius revitalised the senate and people by a stubborn demonstration of his own devotion to the imperial ideal. On paper, his achievements do not look very impressive; he was not strong enough to end the revolt in Gaul, or prevent the growth of the ambiguously-loyal semi-independent state centred on Palmyra, but he restored the Danube frontier, destroying invading hordes of Alamanni in the autumn of 268, and so weakened the Gothic tribes ravaging the Balkans in 269 that he felt it safe to enlist the remnants as auxiliaries in his army and settle them as farmers guarding the frontiers in Dacia and Thrace. His master of horse, Aurelian, elected by the army to succeed him, regained the whole of the Danube area, Asia Minor and the East for the empire, continuing Claudius' work of restoration with such vigour that it was recognised as quite fitting when he called himself on his coins "Recreator of the World".

It was not only in the military field that Aurelian fought to regain what was being lost. He took stern measures against corruption wherever he found it, especially in the civil administration, issued new and improved coins in an attempt to halt rising prices and restore confidence, and towards the end of his reign sought to crown his work by bringing sound military discipline to the worship of the gods by appointing a new supreme commander over them, simultaneously preparing edicts (apparently never promulgated) against all those, including the Christians, who could be expected to refuse recognition to the new overlord.

The new head of the Roman pantheon was *Sol invictus deus*,[3] the Invincible God Sun. Aurelian discovered—or was discovered by—the Invincible Sun at Emesa immediately after a victory there over the forces of Zenovia of Palmyra. Emesa's sun-god was the El Gabel worshipped at Rome under Elagabalus and banned from the city after that emperor's death. Now, at Emesa, he gave Aurelian victory: "when his horsemen were exhausted and on the point of showing their backs, suddenly, by a numinous power as it was afterwards demonstrated, a divine form spread encouragement among the infantry and even rallied the cavalry. . . . So Aurelian entered Emesa as Victor and went straight to the temple of Elagabalus to pay his vows in fulfilment of the common duty of all. And the fact is that he saw there that same numinous form which he had seen supporting him in battle. Therefore, he not only founded temples there,

giving them vast donations, but also dedicated a temple to the sun at
Rome, amid still greater pomp."[4]

The historian Eutropius recalled that this Roman temple contained "an
infinite amount of gold and jewels". It stood in the Campus Agrippa and
its dedication-day was 25 December, the feast-day of Mithras Bull-slayer,
the saviour beloved of soldiers. Aurelian's god was not purely Mithras, any
more than he was purely El Gabel, or Rome's *sol indiges*, whose festival fell
in the burning days of August and whose temple in the Circus Maximus
showed him driving a four-horse chariot across the sky, or the primitive
Pannonian sun-god whose priestess the emperor's mother had been,[5] or
the sun-god worshipped at Palmyra, whose native name was Malachbelus,
"King Bel", but who was known to Latin speakers as *Sol sanctissimus*, "Most
Holy Sun". He was all these gods, and none of them, an essay in synthesis.
His name related him to the eastern gods, but his cult at Rome connected
him with the primitive deity of the Circus Maximus by celebrating his feast
with horse-races and games. He was also apparently linked with the
originally Greek Apollo Phoibos by the institution of four-yearly
competitions in his honour, known as the *agon solis*.[6]

The only known representations of Aurelian's god are those on the coins
of his reign, on which he is shown as a young man wearing a short Greek
riding-cloak, either walking carrying a whip in one hand and the orb of the
world in the other, or driving the chariot of the sun.[7]

Since Christ displaced Sol as the chief object of Roman worship,
Christians have always found it easy to laugh at Aurelian's god as an
artificial confection, but the evidence suggests that his invention—in
whatever sense that word is taken—met a real need. The sun is a universal
symbol, life-giving and death-dealing, so that by whatever name he is
known, he is universally recognised. What Aurelian had succeeded in
doing was providing this universal symbol with an exterior form to which
everyone could respond, together with a form of response in worship
which seemed worthy of the symbol projected: he had tapped the universal
consciousness, the Self we all share.

Sol invictus deus did not demand that other gods should be forgotten
where he was worshipped: indeed, he was identifiable with a good many of
them. How important men felt this to be is shown by the fact that when
Aurelian died, the victim of a murder-plot among his officers, his god did
not die with him or go into exile as El Gabel had done at Elagabalus' fall
fifty years earlier. His successor Tacitus further enriched the temple at
Rome with a silver statue of himself, and both Probus and Carus
reverenced him.

But despite the unifying force provided by the wide recognition of the
Invincible God Sun, the weakness draining away the life of the empire was
not even temporarily halted until the success of the plot which gave
supreme power to Diocletian.

A great question mark hangs over Diocletian. In broad outline what he achieved is well known, as are also even the methods by which he achieved it. But the man himself remains remote and inexplicable.

Born in Dalmatia, probably about the year 230, and originally named Diocles, he became a professional soldier early in life, rising rapidly through the ranks to achieve command under Aurelian and further promotion under his short-lived successors. He made himself emperor under the name Diocletian in a military coup so skilful in its execution that it has never been possible to prove the case against him. Once securely in command, he appointed an old comrade in arms, the cunning but ignorant Maximian as his Caesar and sent him to subdue the rebels in Gaul. Diocletian and Maximian ruled together for twenty years.

Diocletian has been called an organising genius. The details of his political and military reforms have often been recounted and show him certainly to have had a firmer grasp of men and affairs than any imperial commander for a century, with the possible exceptions of Zenovia of Palmyra and the short-lived Claudius II. Like most successful leaders, he was a pragmatist, but if any over-riding principle can be said to have guided him, it was that the old ways are the best. Himself by origin Nobody of Nowhere, he looked back to the great days of the empire and (like Aurelian, "the Restorer of the World", before him) set himself the task of recreating the order and respect for authority of the legendary golden age of imperial power. Naturally, this task was impossible. The accidents and incidents of the centuries since Augustus could not simply be wiped out. Nor would Diocletian's organising genius permit him to try to expunge them. For the sake of power he allowed himself to be all but deified during his lifetime, becoming the Lord and Master that not even Tiberius could imagine himself to be. In many other ways he made innovations unthinkable to his less imaginative predecessors, reforming the army and the civil service, attempting to fix prices and so end inflation, inventing a new system of taxation, dividing his authority first with Maximian alone, then with three associates together, so that the empire was ruled from four capitals simultaneously and no frontier was more than a week or so from the nearest centre of all power. Nevertheless his dream was not of innovation but of reconstruction. And that dream lured him into excesses from which the pagan world never recovered.

Unlike Aurelian, Diocletian never called himself god or even recreator of the world. The name he took for himself was Jovius, "son of Jupiter's household" or "Jupiter's slave". Maximian he named Herculius, son of the hero Hercules who became an immortal. His inscriptions throw the spotlight onto the god and the hero—but leave Diocletian himself and Maximian standing clearly clearly lit in the shimmering halo reflected back from the divine beings: "To the begotten of the gods and created by the gods, our Lords Diocletian and Maximian, Augusti. . . ." "To Jovius Maximus, procreated by divine authority for the enrichment of the state. . . ." In the last resort, Diocletian's god was probably Diocletian, but there can be no doubt that he himself believed that he was worshipping not himself and his own ideals but the true gods, the old gods of the state.[8]

It was this conviction that what was old was best which drove him to persecute the divine saviours, Mani the Paraclete and Jesus the Messiah. They threatened the old values and the new world which Diocletian was unwittingly building upon those values. The weight of imperial displeasure fell first upon the Manichees. The edict issued against them has been preserved. Significantly it was promulgated about the year 287 from Alexandria, a city frequently in ferment, where new ideas found a welcome from wherever they had come, and so a city which Diocletian was bound to find uncongenial under whatever circumstances he had visited it. In 287 he had been fighting revolutionaries there. The edict commands the Proconsul in Africa to burn Manichees "together with their abominable writings"[9] because members of this "damnable sect" were setting their own beliefs "against the old cults" and so disturbing the peace of mind of persons hitherto tranquil and content: "it is a most hateful thing that people should be exhorted to go beyond our common human nature [*the Manichees urged extremes of asceticism on the would-be perfect*] and persuaded to adopt every sort of quite futile and evil superstitious teaching. For the immortal gods have seen fit by their providence to ordain and arrange things that are good and true by the counsel of a multitude of good, outstanding, wise persons . . . which things it is good neither to stray from nor to fight against. . . . For it is the greatest of crimes to gainsay what has once been established and defined by those of old. . . ."

As persecutors have found time and again, killing alone did not eliminate distasteful ideas. No doubt Diocletian's magistrates did their best to put a stop to the spread of Manichaeism, but it was too deeply rooted for the empire to eradicate it by mere pruning. A hundred years later there were still Manichees in every city of North Africa and Italy, and Christianity had absorbed so many of the sect's ideas that it has never wholly recovered from the infection of dualism which it then received. However, in 287, when Diocletian signed the edict "On Malefactors and Manichees", he could not see so far into the future. He had just put down a rebellion in the physical world, and now aimed to put down another in the spiritual, for precisely the same reasons, because "it is the greatest of crimes to gainsay what has once been established". Jupiter was the god of old Rome. The Manichees did not recognise Jupiter. Therefore, before they destroyed Rome, Jovius, the servant of old Rome's Jupiter, must destroy them. The policy was partly cynical, partly idealistic, wholly paradoxical, yet practical in both its stated object, the preservation of Rome, and its unstated, the preservation of Diocletian.

On the official level, the level of public life, Diocletian's restoration of Jupiter was, temporarily at least, wholly successful. Jupiter, Hercules and Victory were Diocletian's gods, and while Victory smiled on him the citizens were content to worship them. It seems strange to us, after one god has been established so long as sole arbiter of western affairs, to see the supreme deity changed by imperial decree from Jupiter to Sol and from Sol back to Jupiter again. But when we find it strange, we are thinking with minds conditioned by our Judaeo-Christian culture—and Porphyry, Diocletian's contemporary, accuses us of being "atheistical" on the grounds that we understand nothing about the divine nature. Certainly, we have much to forget, much to unlearn, if we are to begin to understand.

The decades of Diocletian's rule were those when the Christians made their greatest inroads yet into the empire of Jupiter. It would, therefore, seem that many of Diocletian's subjects were also atheistical in Porphyry's sense. But the majority of citizens was still pagan and still looked at things with a "religious" mind. Diocletian and his preferences did not worry and confuse these traditionalists in the way that the exclusive Manichees and Christians did. Although he might believe that in recent years too much had been made of other gods at Jupiter's expense, he did not forbid the worship of Sol, or close the theatres sacred to Dionysos, or deny the power of Aphrodite. With a little more co-operation from the Goddess Fortune—in whom, like any soldier, he was bound to believe—and a little less ruthlessness, he might have succeeded in the religious reforms he attempted. Fortune, however, smiled on him only fitfully.

Like a neglected cancer, the chaos of the previous fifty years had sown seeds of destruction in many of the organs of the body politic, so many that no one man could hope to cut them all out. Realising the desperateness of the situation, Diocletian tried to shape and train a team capable of the radical surgery which alone could save his patient, by first appointing Maximian as his fellow Augustus to rule the West, and shortly afterwards promoting the Governor of Dalmatia, Constantius, as his Caesar and successor there, while himself adopting another soldier, Galerius, as his own subordinate in the East. It was a bold action, but luck was against him, the providence which "ordains and arranges things which are good and true". His chosen assistants were good, but not good enough. None of them could wield the knife as skilfully and ruthlessly as he.

Although a successful soldier, Maximian was a schemer, devious and double-dealing, wholly loyal only to his supreme commander Diocletian, whom he both revered and feared. He was incapable of initiating strategy, although dedicated in fulfilling the demands of tactics. When in later life he was faced with personal decision-making, the results were disastrous.

Constantius, his son-in-law, nicknamed Chlorus "The Pale", was a general with administrative experience. His busts show a man with a pugnacious, heavy face, and suggest a solid, hard-working, determined character, capable of great obstinacy. Although as later events showed, he had the self-assurance to turn a deaf ear to superior orders when it seemed to him the local situation demanded it, he also was totally loyal to Diocletian. His own chosen god was Sol, "to whom all hearts are open". He was happier fighting rebels—as he did very successfully in ending the secession of Britain in 296—or smashing barbarian tribes invading the empire—as he did on the Rhine in 298 and at Hadrian's wall in 305—than in hatching plots against his superiors.

The fourth member of the Tetrarchy, Diocletian's Caesar and son-in-law Galerius, was yet another general used to fighting barbarians and obeying Diocletian, but so ignorant of everything apart from warfare that no one except the military historians ever had a good word for him. On being confronted with a problem, his first instinct was to squash it flat under his heavy military boots. On the frontiers, that was sound strategy. He beat the Sarmatians in 294, the Carpi in 295, and—after an initial setback—the Persians in 298. When confronted with the problem of the Christians his reaction was to declare, "They may not exist" and to set about eliminating them. His men nicknamed him "the Drover" and it was a name aptly chosen. He was a hard-working, hard-bargaining, hard-drinking man, no more subtle than a rhinoceros or even-tempered than a frustrated bull. But like Maximian and Constantius, he had absolute loyalty for Diocletian.

With only such men as these to rely upon, and no formal training in the art of government himself, it is surprising only that Diocletian did not make more mistakes, especially in the quaggy fields of religion and law. Because he was a man from nowhere, the old aristocrats of the empire not unnaturally ignored him—and he reciprocated their indifference. It was a grave error on his part, and probably on theirs also. They lived safe within their pale, the hundred-mile circle of the City Prefecture around Rome itself, where, under the nominal control of the Prefect, they ruled according to their own customs, protected from taxation and harassment by their own laws, and often contemptuous in their attitude to the problems of the rest of the empire. The fact that it was from Milan or Arles, and not from Rome, that Maximian's praetorian prefect ruled the south-west was a great weakness in Diocletian's system. Diocletian himself issued commands disguised as requests to the senators through the City Prefect, and spent vast sums on the temples and other public buildings of Rome. But he himself visited the city only once, to attend the celebrations of his own twentieth jubilee in 303, and Maximian is recorded as having visited it only once prior to that, in 298 when, after a victory over the Moors, he attended the ceremonies held for the foundation of the great Baths of Diocletian. Meanwhile, the administration undermined the very real powers hitherto enjoyed by the senate in a series of reforms ostensibly intended to improve the administration of the provinces, using the civil service rather than elected magistrates to enforce the laws, and destroying the old traditions of Roman public service by making separate careers of military and civil administration, so that magistrates and civil governors no longer commanded the instant respect of fighting men through reputations earned, albeit long ago, in the field. The aristocratic reaction to these and similar measures was not immediately to embrace rebellion, even on the level of non-violent opposition (perhaps by adopting Christianity or one of the other radical religions), but to withdraw into the very real comfort afforded by long-established wealth and privilege. Within the City Prefecture, men now bought such once-proud offices as the quaestorship for their adolescent sons. While the rest of the empire foundered slowly through lack of a stable monetary system, families like the Agorii, Symmachi and Rufini, cushioned by vast accumulated (and largely untaxable) wealth in land and slaves as well as gold and silver, continued to fulfil all the religious and civil functions the law still left to them and gravely to debate the clearly approaching crisis, though impotent to do anything to avert it. When the decisive battle with the Christians was joined, after Constantine's usurpation of power, it was some of these families who stood most firmly for the old ways and the old religion, although others naturally adapted themselves to the new world to preserve what they could of their wealth and influence.

The head-on clash between the forceful Diocletian and the Christians was not, perhaps, inevitable from the first, though with the benefit of hindsight it is difficult to see how all conflict could have been avoided in a situation where neither party would withdraw. Although in the Danube provinces and the West generally Christians were few as yet, they had established themselves firmly in all the cities on the shores of the Mediterranean and may actually have been in the majority in a few centres. As their numbers increased, and memories of the last great persecution faded, their propadanda grew ever more aggressive. The days when they hid themselves away, meeting only at night or at dawn, were long behind them. At Nicomedia, Diocletian's eastern capital, their church was actually visible from the palace, a fine, new building on a prime site, a daily insult to the followers of Jovius and his Caesar. When the Christians asked themselves why their god allowed the persecution, they found a variety of answers. Eusebius of Caesarea, who lived through the terror, claimed in his *History of the Church* that the Christians brought it on themselves, a divine punishment for their laxity. Lactantius, who was a pagan *rhetor*, teaching and practising the art of eloquent pleading and argument, when the persecution began and a committed Christian before it ended, drew a parallel in his *Deaths of the Persecutors* between the terror suffered by the Christians and the oppression of the Jews in Egypt which ended in the Exodus, and his reading of it was generally followed by later Christians, who were at pains to prove that there had been ten persecutions, as there had been ten plagues of Egypt.[10] To the historians, then, these things were because they had to be: they were part of the divine plan for the world. Their view of history was as mechanical as a modern dialectical materialist's.

There are no detailed accounts of the persecution from pagan sources, but from Lactantius' story and the *Acts* of the Christian martyrs it is clear that the terror grew out of small beginnings. At the outset, in fact, around the year 298, there was no clear intention to initiate a persecution at all, but merely a drive for a disciplinary purge of the army.

The regulations laid it down that on enlistment, re-engagement or promotion a man had to swear an oath of allegiance to the patron gods of his legion and the reigning emperor. This some Christian soldiers believed it wrong to do and a few—though it would seem, very few, mostly veterans on the reserve—refused their duty when called to active service. For these offences, some were executed in the Danube provinces and others in North Africa, in accordance with the law. Probably matters would have ended there if during the next five years financial and political problems had not multiplied as fast as the Christians seemed to be doing. Many reforms were achieved between 298 and 303 but the situation generally seemed nevertheless not to improve but actually to worsen in several important ways. Prices rose, natural disasters multiplied and the number of Christians increased. Diocletian developed symptoms of acute anxiety—and many throughout the empire shared his distress. Some people convinced themselves that the world was ending. Catchpenny astrologers and fashionable prophets encouraged this conviction. Pessimists quoted at one another such undated prophecies as a notorious line from the Sibylline Books foretelling that *Roma* would become *rhume*, a path beaten out in the wilderness by pack-animals. When Lactantius wrote in his *Divine Institutes* "the fall and ruin of the world will soon come . . . when the Head of the World is cut off",[11] he was echoing a common fear. From the time of Noah and Cassandra, there have always been prophets of doom. People listen to them only when anxiety is all but universal. Traditionally, clever but ruthless rulers have used them to rid their realms of some unwanted foreign element, of aliens in either the racial or cultural sense. So now Diocletian—or perhaps more properly Galerius with Diocletian's acquiescence—used the anxiety of the times to rid his world of Christians.

The case against the Christians was, of course, a strong one. They were potential traitors, as the trouble in the army had shown. And in their preaching, they called all traditional values into question and so undermined the foundations of the state. But even the Christians themselves make it clear that Diocletian hesitated to order them to abandon their foreign superstition, although some time before the year 300 Porphyry had published his fifteen books *Against the Christians*, so providing the regime with the intellectual material it needed to justify an attack. Some prominent men in the administration, notably Hierocles, the governor of Bithynia, who had been a contemporary of Porphyry at Plotinus' school in Rome, had the skill to use its arguments effectively. But to men like Galerius, who boasted of their ignorance, the intellectual approach to sworn enemies of the government was uncertain and much too slow. Urged on by his mother Romula, "a priestess of the mountain gods",[12] who hated Christians in part because they hated her and in part, one feels, because she was of the kind who can never really enjoy themselves unless they have someone to hate, Galerius prodded Diocletian reluctantly into action. In the winter of 302 the senior emperor called a conference at Antioch in Syria to discuss the Christian menace. Hierocles was among the provincial governors present. The chief religious representative was the Master of Haruscopy, whom Lactantius calls Tagis, though this may be a generic rather than a personal name for the Etruscan divinely-wise child. Tages had been the first haruspex seeking to discern the will of the gods in the entrails, especially the livers, of animals offered as sacrifices.[13] Other members included Galerius and military and civilian chiefs from most of the eastern half of the empire.

Surviving accounts of the Antioch conference are confused but it would seem that the delegates were told that what had finally decided Diocletian to hold it was a particularly glaring example of failure of the omens. Such failure was not unprecedented. In the course of Rome's long history it had not infrequently happened that the haruspex had been unable to find any sign, good or bad, in the entrails of the sacrifices. The established procedure in such a case was to repeat the offering until some message from the gods was found. It had been followed in this instance. The sacrifices were repeated "several times", but no omens could be read. As sacrifice had followed unrewarding sacrifice, the tension had grown until the question why? in everybody's mind was answered by someone accusing the Christians present in their rôles as members of the imperial household and bodyguard of having made their magic sign of the cross to drive away the gods or blind the priests to their message.

Lactantius, who tells the story in some detail, obviously believed that the sign had "driven the devils away".[14] The probable truth—that the alleged failure of the omens was part of a plot to drive Diocletian to persecution—seems not to have occurred to him as an explanation. Anyway, whether the Christian god organised it, so that the Christians might have to suffer the plagues of persecution, or Tagis did, as seems more likely, the plot worked, the conference was called, and a long wrangle about how to deal with the Christian menace ensued. Details of the deliberations have not been preserved, but it is clear that Diocletian still hung back from the use of force until someone suggested that he should take the advice of the oracle of Apollo at Didyma near Miletus, and act upon it.

As anyone must who has been there, Diocletian had a special devotion to the shrine at Didyma, where the vast temple, already in his time two hundred years and more in building and still unfinished, surrounded an ancient laurel grove where the oracular the Branchidae, the Grunters, had been proclaiming the will of the god since at least the time of Croesus of Lydia. In 286 and 293 Diocletian had dedicated statues of Zeus and Leto, father and mother of Apollo, to the temple in the names of himself and Maximian. Now that in his anxiety to do the right thing with regard to the

Christians he turned to the god for help, the oracle told him that he was being prevented from uttering by those who called themselves "the just upon earth".

"So," Lactantius says, "Diocletian was led to review his decision. Being unable to resist both his old friends, Caesar (Galerius) and Apollo, he nevertheless held firm to his opinion that everything ought to be accomplished without bloodshed, although the Caesar wanted to burn alive all those who would not offer sacrifice."[15] The result was that the first persecutory edict ordered only that everyone suspected of disloyalty should make an oath of loyalty in the prescribed form and that places of Christian worship—like the offensive church opposite the palace gate at Nicomedia—should be closed.[16] It was only later, when these mild measures were resisted and the fundamental disloyalty of Christians thus demonstrated, that Diocletian yielded to Galerius' demands with further edicts requiring a thorough-going purge of public life. Although the actual order of events is difficult to establish it would seem that what finally clinched the argument for him was an omen of the most terrible import: the palace at Nicomedia was struck by lightning and caught fire not once, but twice, and the second time Diocletian's own "sacred" bedchamber was destroyed. All emperors were what would now be called superstitious of lightning; to them, as to all Romans, it was a direct message from the gods (as late as 320, Constantine was to pass a law confirming the need for careful evaluation of the omen "if any part of our palace or some other public building has been struck by lightning").[17] In 303 the divine warning was reinforced with news of threatening rebellion in Syria and Cappadocia. No emperor, least of all the traditionalist Diocletian, could have ignored such a combination of events. The terror ordered by the persecuting edicts outlasted Diocletian's reign by several years. During it churches were wrecked, Christians executed, religious books destroyed and church life disrupted through all the provinces of the south and east where Christianity was strong. But in the north-west, where Constantius Chlorus ruled, there was no more than token action and after his death he was remembered with gratitude by the church historians.

Diocletian's reaction to the failure of the omens and the fall of the lightning reflects the unrational aspect of paganism. Superstition of this kind was one of its greatest weaknesses in many pagan as well as Christian eyes. But superstition was part of the general climate of the times. It was by no means limited to pagans. The inexplicable question in relation to the year 303 is why had the situation apparently become so desperate from the pagan viewpoint? Plotinus' generation had felt it safe on the whole to ignore Christians: that of his pupils Porphyry and Hierocles felt compelled to take up the cudgels against them. The last great persecution has a new quality about it. In comparison with it, the others—deadly though they may have been—were mere Christian-baiting. The texts of Diocletian's persecuting edicts have not survived, but the third of them, issued from

Rome just before the jubilee amnesty of 17 September 303 ordered that all Christians must offer sacrifice on pain of death and so amounted in practice to a formal expression of Galerius' opinion that Christians should not be allowed to exist. It was a declaration of war, a war that was to end only when the old world was no more.

Notes

1 On Maximus' persecution (235) see Eusebius *History*, 6, 28. The Decian Persecution (249–51) is the subject of Cyprian's *De Lapsis*; it was during this persecution that such persons famous in later history as St Babylos of Antioch and St Pios of Smyrna were murdered for refusing to participate in pagan worship. Valerius' persecution (257–60) is described in the *Acta Cyprian*, 1ff. and Eusebius' *History*, 7, 11.

2 Pontius. *Life of St. Cyprian*, ed. W. von Hartel, *Corpus Script. Eccles. Lat.*, 3.

3 The title *Sol Invictus Deus* can be variously translated. In their Latin order the words mean "(The) Sun Invincible (*or* Unconquered) God": whether they are translated "God the Unconquered Sun" or "The Invincible God, (the) Sun", or, as I have translated them, using the word Sun as a proper name; the concept is essentially unaltered, and only the emphasis changed.

4 *Historia augusta, Aurelian*, 25.

5 *ibid.*, 4.

6 A great deal of ingenuity has been exercised in attempts to identify Aurelian's Invincible God Sun precisely, but no totally compelling answer has emerged. In my own opinion, he was intended to be a synthesis, a practical soldier's expression of the One, the Truth, the Light, the Reality-beyond-reality sought by philosophers of the time. Aurelian's childhood god is likely to have been a primitive manifestation of the sun, but at this late date even in remote Dacia the god of his infancy would not have been an unadulterated expression of peasant piety. At Rome—and although a Dacian by birth, Aurelian was a true Roman, a soldier under the influence of the gods of the army from his late adolescence onwards—the old nature-god *Sol indiges* had been worshipped side-by-side with the Greek Apollo Phoibos since early times, and eastern influence had been detectable in the sun-cult since at least Augustus' triumphs in Egypt, when columns sacred to the sun were brought from Heliopolis, the Sun City, and set up in the Circus Maximus and the Campus Martius. By A.D. 158, as is known from inscriptions, the sun had already been awarded titles of honour which were translations of his Oriental names, *Sol invictus, Sol aeternus,* and *Sol divus,* "the unconquered, eternal, divine sun". At the beginning of the third century, Septimius Severus was shown on coins driving the sun's chariot and carrying the charioteer's whip. His son Caracalla was at least once called "the Emperor Unconquered Sun" (*Sol invictus imperator*, in an inscription found at Friedburg in Hesse, dated 187), and his successor Elagabalus made himself notorious by his excesses in the worship of the sun-stone El Gabel, of whom he was an hereditary priest. Rome rejected El Gabel together with Elagabalus in 222, but the way had

been prepared for a more respectable cult of the sun without those aspects of it offensive to Roman *gravitas*, the pretty boys, the dancing girls and dropping rose petals (see *Antoninus Heliogabalus*, in the *Scriptores Historiae Augustae* vol. 2 (Loeb Classical Library), pp. 104ff. Heinemann).

7 On one coin, Aurelian himself is identified with the god, himself wearing the nimbus. On another, he is called "Aurelian born Lord and God". He perhaps himself acted as his god's first high priest but the cult was overseen by a special college of priests bearing the ancient title *pontifices* hitherto used only for the hierarchy headed by the emperor as *pontifex maximus* and presiding over the state cults.

8 Even the Christian historians had no doubt about the genuineness of his conscious devotion to the gods. See Aurelius Victor 39, 45, where it is said that he put his trust in "the oldest religions most purely preserved".

9 John of Antioch, *Frag. 165* maintains that this decree was actually put into effect. The edict is preserved in the *Codex Gregorianus*, col. 15, 13, 1.

10 *Eusebius Ecclesiastical History*, ed. Lake and Oulton (Loeb Classical Library, 1932). Lactantius, "De Mortibus Persecutorum", ed. Brandt, *Vienna Corpus*, vol. 19 (1890); English version, *Library of the Ante-Nicene Fathers*, vol. 7 (Scribners, New York, 1867).

11 Lactantius, *Divine Institutes*, 7 (English Version, *Library of the Ante-Nicene Fathers*, vol. 7 (Scribners, New York, 1867).

12 Her gods were probably Silvanus, Diana and Liber Pater (or their locally-named equivalents), "country" gods with ecstatic elements in their cults.

13 Cicero, *de Divinatione*, 2, 23. The Order of Imperial Haruspices was founded by the Emperor Claudius I. At its head was the *haruspex maximus*, "the first of the sixty" and master of the public haruspices (see C.I.L. VI. 2066, 2161, 2163).

14 See Lactantius, *Divine Institutes*, 27, 3: "If anyone present when they sacrifice to the gods makes this sign on his forehead, the sacrifice can in no wise offer anything."

Also, *ibid.*, 4, 27: where Lactantius claims that the devils are terrified of the cross.

15 Lactantius, *De Mort. Pers.*, XI, 6.

16 *Lactantius, De Mort. Pers.*, XII, 1: the date was the feast of Terminus, 23 February 303.

17 The law is preserved in the *Codex Theodosianus* at XVI, X, 1

Christian and Pagan Catholics

A few months after the promulgation of the first edict of persecution, the eastern emperors' entourage moved to Italy, for the celebrations marking Diocletian's twentieth jubilee.

Grand preparations were made for the festivities, which were timed to begin on 20 November[1] and continue for six weeks, through the period of the Saturnalia and the feast of the Most Holy Sun to a culmination in the ceremonies of the 1 January, when the emperor was to be invested with his ninth consulship. After a pause, celebrations would then be renewed in the year 304 with the dedication of the baths founded in Diocletian's honour in 298 and—in the expectation of many—would be concluded with the celebration of the secular games, last held during the reign of Septimius Severus.[2]

The celebrations began as planned, but they quickly turned sour. By this time Rome, the nominal capital, was out of step with the rest of the empire, and the city proved to be the one place above all in his vast holdings where Diocletian was not at home. He was, he discovered, to the Romans a barbarian in all but name—and he was certainly, despite all his years of practice at playing the deity, still at heart rather a fighting general than a suave diplomat. Rome worried him. He did the right things: he rode in triumph into the city, made the offerings at Capitoline Jupiter, declared an amnesty for all in prison (but ordered Christians to take oaths of allegiance to himself and the gods, so putting them immediately back behind bars again), accepted some days of glory and feasting from the citizens, and declined everything else they offered.

He complained that the city was overcivilised for his taste: its people were corrupt and effete, its nightly banquets too rich and its daily games too long. Before the extravagances of December's Saturnalia, "the best of days", turned the city into a madhouse, as they did every year, he left for Ravenna, on Italy's Adriatic coast. It was there, on the way to his beloved Illyria, that he accepted the consulship, and there, during a bitterly cold and wet winter, that he developed the debilitating fever which depressed him so much during the ensuing months that he decided to resign.

The importance of the nominally Roman emperor's rejection of Rome cannot be overemphasised. It presaged not only the disintegration of Diocletian but also, at very long range, of the empire itself. It offered the senate and citizens an insult so enormous that no munificence towards the city could wipe it out. Zosimus, one of the few substantial pagan historians of the period, dates the decline of Roman hegemony from this year, linking it with the failure to celebrate the secular games:

> "Events themselves have demonstrated to us that as long as [the games] were still performed exactly as the [Sibylline] oracle directed and prevailing conditions decreed, the Romans kept their empire and continued to hold under their domination almost the whole civilised world. But no one seems to have noticed that the ceremonies having been neglected around the time of Diocletian's abdication the empire has gradually slipped away, becoming largely barbarianised. . . ."

No modern historian could accept that the decline of the empire began from the failure to hold the Secular Games, but the thought that the neglect of religious ceremonies (and so of the gods themselves) was linked with the fall of Rome was one wholly acceptable in the fourth century. Diocletian himself believed that restoration could begin only with a renewal of dedication to the gods, while the Christian historian Lactantius was convinced that all the persecuting emperors died horrible deaths because they had opposed Christ (which is a kind of reverse image of Diocletian's belief). Zosimus, writing at the time of Odoacer, the first barbarian king of Italy, certainly believed that the neglect of the rites had led to barbarianisation and decay—and in as much as the empire rested on Roman religion and Roman law, both embodied in and directed by a Roman emperor, he was right, as we shall see.

The battering-ram of Fate struck Rome's foundations three mighty blows between 303 and 305. The first fell when Diocletian refused to stay and worship any longer in Jupiter's own city; the second, when Diocletian himself fell so ill at Ravenna that for the next year he could take little direct part in the government; and the third when Diocletian abdicated at Nicomedia on 1 May 305, dragging Maximian into retirement with him, leaving Constantius (wholly occupied with troubles in far-off Britain) as Supreme Augustus but real executive power in the hands of the new Augustus Galerius.

When the names of the Caesars to the new Augusti were announced, it was obvious to everyone that Galerius had so played on the old emperor's fears that he had won complete ascendency over him.[3] The adult sons and natural heirs of both Constantius and Maximian were passed over in favour of Galerius' nephew, Maximin Daia, and Galerius' most amenable subordinate commander, a general named Severus.

Maximin Daia, a youth newly commissioned, became Caesar in the East and Egypt, heir-apparent to Galerius himself, while Severus was appointed Caesar to Constantius, with responsibility for Italy, Africa and Spain.

Many were offended by this redistribution of power, but those most obviously injured by it were Constantius' son Constantine and Maximian's son Maxentius. At the time, Constantine was a tribune of the guard at Nicomedia,[4] while Maxentius (a man until now apparently little active in affairs of state) lived quietly on an estate within the City Prefecture of Rome. Little more than a year later, both men rebelled, Constantine when his soldiers proclaimed him Augustus at York on his father's death in July 306, Maxentius three months later when the Praetorians declared Severus' rule in Italy at an end and acclaimed him as their emperor, welcoming his father out of retirement to help him run the world from Rome.

It would be difficult to imagine two men more different than these young rebel emperors, Constantine and Maxentius, who were soon to become such deadly enemies. Maxentius, married to Galerius' daughter Valeria Maximilla, had until now lived the most civilised of lives, as a Roman country gentleman with a villa on the Via Labicana and interests in the city. He was pious in the old Roman tradition, observing all the customs and conventions of Roman upper-class life. He had named his only son Romulus in a double act of homage, on the one hand to his city and on the other to his wife's grandmother, the priestess Romula. When in 309 his son was murdered, he had him proclaimed divine by the senate and built in his honour the delicate little temple in the forum which bears his name.[5]

Constantine was a man of an altogether different stamp, a man of the courts and camps, a man of war and intrigue, a man who had been forced to use both his wits and his physical strength to survive. His religion, if he had any, would seem to have been purely nominal. His nephew—the Emperor Julian, who hated his memory—said that he was a lifelong devotee of the sun-god, and he was praised by the panegyrist Eumenius for the size of his donation to the temple of Apollo at Flavia Aeduorum. But his devotion to the sun can be explained by his anxiety to prove himself (falsely) a descendant of the sun-worshipping family of Claudius II and a true son of his father Constantius, whose lifelong devotion to the sun appears to have been quite genuine. His coins—those bill-boards of the emperors, by which they proclaimed their policies to the people —associate him early in his reign with Mars. Although persecution continued and was even intensified under Galerius, Constantine neither persecuted Christians nor, apparently, favoured them until it became expedient for him to do so, when he needed them as allies in the war for Rome. (Later in life, he maintained that before the battle of Mulvian Bridge, in which Maxentius died, he had never heard of Christ, and when he saw him in a vision had to ask who he was: this was a lie, for he had been a witness of the beginning of the persecution at Nicomedia.)[6]

Galerius' reaction to the illegal assumption of power by these two young men reflected his estimate of them. Constantine he demoted to Caesar under the Augustus Severus; Maxentius he declared proscribed, urging Severus to put down his revolt. In 307, Severus marched on Rome, but he was driven back from the city by a combination of spirited defence from the

Praetorians and propaganda in support of Maxentius and Maximian, which induced many of his troops to desert. Under this reverse, his battle-sense evaporated and he allowed himself to driven back to Ravenna, his retreating troops so ravaging the countryside that it was many years before agriculture recovered. Soon he was forced to surrender, and committed suicide in prison.

Delighted by this proof that his old magic name was not forgotten, Maximian hastened to Gaul, to propose an alliance with Constantine against Galerius. At Trier, he offered Constantine the title Augustus (presumably on the authority he had abdicated in 305 and since illegally resumed) and hastily married him to Maxentius' half-sister, Fausta, daughter of himself and Diocletian's daughter Theodora. How seriously Constantine took his plots against Galerius is not known, but he accepted the title and the bride, divorcing his wife, Minervina, in order to be able to do so. The only indication of his personal feelings at this time is that he helped neither side when Galerius himself invaded Italy.

Faced with this new threat, Maxentius, "the Unconquered Prince of the Romans" as he now called himself, sat at Rome and waited for his enemy to come to him, secure in the knowledge that he alone of all the emperors was recognised as a true Roman by the old capital. Galerius made the mistake of letting it be known that he felt vindictive towards the city: when he had taken it, he would revenge himself upon it by abolishing the guard, cancelling the privileges of the senators, and suspending the law which relieved Rome of taxation. Naturally, the whole City Prefecture united against him, and would have done so even if "the Unconquered Prince" had not been genuinely popular.

Despite his bad reputation among Christian authors, Maxentius was at the outset a very mild-mannered usurper. Severus, during his brief period of authority in Italy, had beheaded the Christian menace by executing the bishop of Rome, Pope Marcellinus, and imprisoning so many of his followers that the rest dared not meet to elect a successor for over a year, but Maxentius harmed no one and endeared himself to many by his devotion to Rome and its laws. He was reverent towards the senate, liberal towards the people, and pious in his devotion to the gods. His father had just allied him to Constantine and his victory over Severus had brought him the allegiance of Africa, Mauretania and the Iberian peninsula. A victory for Galerius could only mean changes for the worse. Everybody at Rome united to deny him that victory and, by presenting a united front against him, they succeeded in doing so. After losing as many of his troops by desertion as in war, he was compelled to withdraw. He had not met with such humiliation since his defeat during his first campaign against the Persians fifteen years earlier, a defeat occasioned by a similar fundamental error, underestimation of the enemy amounting to contempt. Leaving all Italy to the Unconquered Prince and his unprincipled father, he withdrew to the Danube and plotted revenge.

The next development was an insane attempt by Maximian to unseat his victorious son; appealing to the soldiers as their old commander, he was rejected by them so decisively that he had to flee for his life. He found refuge with his son-in-law Constantine and went on plotting.

At about this time someone renewed an earlier proposal, that the retired Diocletian should resume control and restore order. Diocletian refused to give up his hard-won ease, but reluctantly consented to meet Galerius and Maximian at the military capital of Pannonia, Carnuntum on the Danube.

The conference had one unexpected result. The three rulers united in a kind of soldiers' freemasonry, joining together to re-endow a Mithraeum, the altar from which survives. It bears the inscription: "The most pious Augusti, Jovius and Herculius, his emperors and devotees, together with the caesars, have restored (this) shrine to the God, the Unconquered Sun, Mithras."[7] It was typical of Diocletian that he should lead puzzled officers to the soldiers' hero, the Creator and Recreator, at this crisis of affairs.

The solution proposed to the crisis was the appointment of a new Augustus, over Constantine's head as it were. The man chosen was Valerius Licinius, a general of Dacian peasant stock who contented himself for the time being with establishing his authority in the Danube area, securing his bases before any aggressive action.

While Licinius pursued his policy of masterly inactivity in the west Balkans, Maxentius' luck began to run out. Nothing went right for him for long. In 308 his father tried to replace him and he was refused recognition at Carnuntum. Either that same year or early in 309, encouraged by his outright condemnation at Carnuntum, his governor in Africa rebelled against him and succeeded in having himself recognised there as Augustus under Galerius. The most unhappy result of his defection was that the supplies of African corn upon which Rome depended for survival failed to reach the city. There were no large food stocks and famine soon appeared, to be greeted with rioting. Then, offering an omen which no one could ignore, the Temple of Fortune burned down. Zosimus tells the story:

> "At this time, a fire started, though whether from the air or from the earth is uncertain (*were the gods above or those below dissatisfied?*), and the temple of Fortune was burned down. As everyone rushed to put out the fire, a certain soldier who had sworn blasphemously against Providence was attacked and killed by the people in their zeal for religion. This started a mutiny among the troops. They would have come close to destroying the city if Maxentius himself had not quickly blunted their anger."[8]

Obviously, the Unconquered Prince was still the soldiers' hero. But in their days of rioting they had, other reports say, killed six thousand citizens, and people naturally asked themselves whether the ill-luck threatened by the omen was exhausted by this slaughter or was worse still to come?

As far as Maxentius was concerned, worse was still to come. During the disturbances his only son, the beloved Romulus, was murdered and early in 310 his father Maximian was executed by Constantine for attempting to raise a rebellion against him in Gaul and trying to assassinate him after it had failed. From that moment on, war between Gaul and Italy was inevitable, for although Maxentius had had no cause to trust his father during his life, he could not forgive his murderer.[9]

The food riots and Fortune riots were not the only disturbances at Rome. The Christians plucked up courage to elect a successor to the executed Pope Marcellinus and promptly quarrelled over his policies, some claiming that he was too harsh towards those who had obeyed the law and surrendered their sacred books at the beginning of the persecution: these dissenters held a counter-election which produced another pope, and supporters of the two men, Marcellus and Eusebius, fought out their quarrel in the streets. Maxentius had them both arrested and exiled them to islands off the Italian coast. It was scarcely his fault that they both died before the first edict of toleration would have allowed their return to the city; he did permit their successor, Militiades, to live there in peace. Nevertheless, he was labelled a persecutor, and Christian historians blacken his name with all manner of crimes, alleging that he sacrificed children to read the omens in their entrails and snatched decent Christian matrons from their homes to offer them to his friends at orgies. There is no proof that he committed these crimes: the only "evidence" for them was offered by Constantine's propaganda machine immediately after he had struck the tyrant down, and so can be safely ignored.[10]

Although the proscription of Constantine at Rome was to prove in the long run the most dangerous of Maxentius' policy decisions, the most immediate and obvious threat to his rule was the defection of Africa, followed shortly afterwards by the secession of Spain to Constantine. Maxentius met the African threat firmly and in the most practical way by despatching an army under one of the most able of his commanders, to bring the usurper down. In the opinion of contemporaries, the army was ridiculously small, but it met with only the most inept resistance in Africa and its commander was soon able to report that the revolt was over and the leader of the rebels dead. However, the damage had been done. The victorious troops, Zosimus relates, could not be stopped from ravaging "Carthage and the lovelier parts of Africa" and it proved impossible to restore full corn rations at Rome before the reign ended. From Zosimus' account, it would appear that Maxentius lost control either of his officers or of himself at this time, and a reign of terror fell upon Africa; the mean and envious were encouraged "to inform against practically everyone in Africa well-born or well-to-do, denouncing them as partisans of [the rebels]. No one was spared. Some lost all they had. Others lost their lives as well—and a triumph was held at Rome to celebrate the evil perpetrated at Carthage."[11]

Meanwhile in the eastern half of the empire, also, events were not proceeding smoothly. Galerius' Caesar, Maximin Daia, rejected the title "Son of the Emperors" granted to him at Carnuntum and arbitrarily declared himself Augustus, the equal at least of Licinius and Constantine if not of Galerius. Despite his youth and lack of experience there can be little doubt of his fitness to hold equal rank with them. Under his rule, the East and Egypt were more peaceful and prosperous than in living memory. The Christians have always hated Daia: he despised them and sought to stamp them out, not as worthy, human opponents, but as unclean, subhuman vermin. His portrait-busts show a hard, unyielding face set in an obstinate sneer—but one also that is quick and lively, not ponderous like Constantius' or brutal in the manner of Galerius' unthinking militarism. He had all the limitations of his generation, but great gifts to go with them. In 310 he was at the height of his powers and, recognising his strength, Galerius acquiesced in his assumption of the supreme title—perhaps because he realised that in any case it would soon be his by right, for it is probable that the senior emperor already felt in himself the stirrings of the multiple cancer which was to kill him, a few months later.

Galerius' was a horrible death. The end came unmercifully slowly at Sirmium in May 311. One of his last recorded acts was to suspend the legislation against the Christians "because we have observed that they neither give the gods the honour due to them nor worship the god of the Christians [fear of the authorities having ended all public manifestations of Christianity]. Wherefore . . . we feel we ought to extend our indulgence towards them, permitting Christians to exist henceforward and to re-establish their congregations. . . . In the light of this our indulgence, let them pray to their god for our health, and for the state, and for themselves."[12] There can be no doubt that superstition alone drove Galerius to issue this edict. But for whatever reason, it was undeniably promulgated in legal form and persecution ceased everywhere, at Rome, where Maxentius was scrupulous in fulfilling the letter of the law, no less than in the East and Egypt. Eusebius' *History* contains a copy of the grudging letter Maximin Daia sent to his Prefect Sabinus on the question: "Since many were involving themselves in danger [by continuing as Christians] . . . our divine masters [*Galerius and Licinius*] holding it alien to their own divine design that men should be embroiled in such danger for such a cause, have issued a command that Your Wisdom should be informed through my Devoted Person that if any of the Christians is apprehended in practising his people's religion, you are to protect him from molestation and peril, and are to hold no one guilty on this ground alone. . . ."[13]

According to Optatus, at Rome Maxentius wrote personally to his Prefect of Italy and Africa to order Christian property restored and called on the City Prefect to invite Pope Eusebius to return from exile: the pope died on the journey, and Militiades was elected, without police intervention, to succeed him. "The storm of persecution was finished and over: by the indulgence of god, liberty was restored to the Christians by Maxentius".[14]

Within a very short time of news of Galerius' death reaching the East, Maximin Daia's armies had crossed the Orontes and were marching north for the Bosphorus, while Licinius hurried south-east through the Danube area to claim for himself all that Galerius had held. Briefly, the empire seemed to be tottering on the brink of civil war, but when the two emperors met—some accounts suggest, in boats on the Bosphorus midway between Byzantium and Chalcedon—they agreed that Asia Minor should go to Daia, while Licinius took the Danube provinces and Thrace.

At about this time, or possibly before even Galerius died, Daia opened the secret negotiations with Maxentius which the Christians later claimed were intended to unite a thoroughly repaganised empire against them. Throughout the summer and autumn, however, they were everywhere left in peace. Daia was preoccupied with politics. He seized and married Galerius' widow, Valeria, despite protests from both Licinius, her legal guardian under her husband's will, and Diocletian, her father. In a law promulgated on 1 June, before he himself visited Asia Minor, he suspended Galerius' census there, so saving the citizens large increases in taxes—for which relief they fêted him when he made a progress to Nicomedia later in the year. But difficulties soon arose because so much new money had to be raised for increased arms production, and trade between Europe and Asia came almost to a standstill, as merchants learned that Daia's frontier guards were treating all travellers as spies.

It was not until six months after Galerius' death that Daia felt secure enough to resume his bitter struggle with the Christians. Our sources for this new campaign are fragmentary, and the precise course of events consequently difficult to follow, but it would appear that before the end of the year soldiers had killed Archbishop Peter at Alexandria, the famous teacher Lucian of Antioch had been murdered at Nicomedia, the emperor had forbidden Christians to hold assemblies in the cemeteries where they were making it their custom to commemorate the martyrs of the recent persecution (thus keeping old bitternesses alive), and the citizens of Nicomedia had petitioned their new ruler to allow them to expel Christians from their city.

Christian sources insinuate that Daia himself inspired this petition and others which followed it, from Antioch and other cities in Asia and the East, but there is no real reason for believing that he did more than indicate—perhaps by allowing the first of them—that he would receive them favourably. Where Christians had once been mocked, they were now hated and feared, both on religious and economic grounds (especially by those who had benefited by the sequestrations during the persecution). Given the climate of the times, it was inevitable that someone should point out that the edict permitting them to exist had been followed by one of the worst harvests in history, so that the whole east lay under the threat of famine: the gods were understandably angry, and must be propitiated.

The text of the original petition pleading for the Christians' expulsion from Nicomedia has not been preserved, but extensive fragments of that from Aricanda, a small town in Lycia, were discovered at Aruf in 1892: it is significant that the Aricandans thought their petition of sufficient importance to be recorded on stone for posterity. The restored text reads:

> "[To the Saviours] of all mankind, the [August] Caesars, Valerius Maximinus and Valerius Licinianus Licinius: the people of [the Lycians] and Pamphylians begs and beseeches:
>
> The gods, your cogenitors, O Divine Emperors, have [always repaid] with acts of philanthropy those who have their worship close to their hearts [and pray for] your [?eternal] wellbeing. We have therefore, O Invincible Masters, thought it right to appeal to [? your undying] authority and beseech you some day to suppress the Christians, who have been impious so long and still [?persist in] the same sickness, and to forbid them to violate with their sinister and novel [?worship] what is owed to the gods. If your divine and eternal [?will] decides to suppress and forbid the odious freedom of worship of these atheists [? imposing on all the obligation] to practise the worship of the gods your cogenitors, we shall expect you to enjoy eternal and incorruptible peace: and, obviously, it would [? in the highest degree] contribute to the wellbeing of your subjects."

The imperial reply to the Aricandans is lost, but it must have closely resembled that addressed to the governor of Tyre in similar circumstances and preserved by Eusebius in his *History*:

> "When [your city] saw the adherents of that damnable foolishness spreading once more, it instantly . . . took refuge in our Piety . . . appealing for some remedy . . . It was the Most High, Mighty Jupiter . . . who inspired your breasts with this well-conceived resolve [. . . *as a result of which crops will improve and an age of plenty dawn*].
>
> As far as those are concerned who have been led safely back from the blind error into which they had strayed . . . let them rejoice. But as for those who persist in their most damnable foolishness, let them be ejected as you request, and driven far away from your city and vicinity, so that . . . your city may be purged and . . . give itself with fitting reverence to the normal worship of the immortals."[15]

As the winter progressed, the threatened famine became a reality and, their resistance lowered by poor feeding, the citizens found themselves at the mercy of an epidemic of smallpox (or perhaps measles; Lactantius describes it as "a malignant pustule . . . spreading over the whole body . . . mainly affecting the eyes: hundreds of men, women and children were blinded"). The pagans blamed the Christians; the Christians the Christhater. To add to the universal misery, Christians driven from the cities on their neighbours' petitions, dying of exposure and hunger, littered the country roads, where they were harried by pagan fanatics, seeking not to kill but to convert them. The more fortunate crossed the frontier into Christian Armenia, but the pagans followed them there, giving great offence to the country's Christian king, who threatened to declare war on Maximin Daia if his missionaries were not withdrawn.

Imperial policy was, however, not entirely negative. Inspired, obviously, by Christian teachings about divine fatherhood, and developing old, but often underrated, pagan concepts of Zeus as the Father of All, Theotecnos, the treasurer (*logistes*) of Antioch, set up an altar to Zeus "the Friend of Man" in his city and (according to Eusebius) "invented diabolical rites, unholy initiations, horrible purifications and in the emperor's very presence gave a demonstration of his magic arts in false oracular pronouncements". In the long run it might have been better to have ignored the Christians rather than flatter them by introducing a cult which could be represented as an imitation of their own, but Daia and his advisers did not see Theotecnos' initiative in that light—and the evidence is that neither did the pagan citizens of Antioch, whatever the Christians among them thought. The fame of the shrine spread as rapidly as later did that of any mediaeval saint. Theotecnos was rewarded with the governorship of his province, and pagan intellectuals and administrators set themselves to give direction to all the pagan zeal this revival liberated by constructing a pagan hierarchy as efficient as the civil administration.

Unfortunately, the main records of this "church" (as it must inevitably be called) are those preserved by its Christian enemies, to whom it seemed naturally no more than an imitation of their own administrative and spiritual organisation. But Eusebius himself makes the point—though perhaps not intentionally—that this revival was a canalisation of genuine zeal: "Priests—priests, if you please!—were appointed in every town by Maximin [Daia] personally—priests of the idols and high priests also— men of the greatest fame in political life, well-known to the public and filled with enthusiasm for the gods they served. . . ."

The old priesthoods, many of them hereditary, were not swept away, but the new religious administrators were accorded ranks and honours comparable to those to be earned in the civil and military services. High priests acted as magistrates and were given military escorts. No effort was spared to do honour to the gods through them. The pride men felt in representing their towns before the gods is reflected in this epitaph from Oturak in Phrygia:

"I, Athanatos Epitynchanos, son of Pios, honoured by Hecate, first, and afterwards by Manes Daos, Sunrunner of Zeus, and third by Phoibos, *archegetos* and oracular god,
I have genuinely received the gift of prophesying truth in my land and

of establishing what is law within [city] boundaries. This gift I hold from
the immortal Athanatos Pios, first high priest, father of a fine line, and
from [my] mother Tatiá III, who has brought fine children into the world,
first among them bring—

Athanatos Epitychanos, High Priest, Saviour of his Country, Nomothetes.

In the year 398 [A.D. 313–4], obedient to the commandments of the
immortals, I can say this of myself: I, Athanatos Epitychanos, was initiated by
the demotic high priestess of high repute, Ispatales, whom the immortal gods
have honoured within city limits and beyond. And in truth, she saved many
from bitter torments.

The two brothers, Athanatos Diogenes and Athanatos Epitychanos, First
High Priests, Saviours of their Country, Nomothetes [have erected this
inscription]."

Athanatos Epitychanos, "the undying" Epitychanos, High Priest
and Saviour, had what he would probably have considered the good
fortune to die a matter of months at the most before the pagan "church" he
so devotedly served was smashed together with the empire of Maximin
Daia its founder. It is clear from his titles, and those of the gods who
honoured him that in his part of Phrygia (always an unorthodox area)
syncretism was far advanced[16] but it is also obvious that he and his family
were not floundering in confusion because of that. They knew what they
were doing and believed in it.

It is in the light of their understanding and belief that we should read
Lactantius' brief and vituperative account of Daia's pagan institutions, and
the excesses towards Christians in which they resulted:

"he created a new style of high priests, appointing one from the men of first
rank in each city. They both made daily sacrifices to all his gods and gave an
eye to the ministry maintained by the old priesthood. Christians might
neither build [meeting-houses] nor assemble either publicly or privately, but
coming within reach of his law were either constrained to the sacrifices or
brought before the magistrates. Not content with that, he put others as some
kind of pontiffs over provinces with a higher degree of status, and ordered
both them and the others to parade decked out in white robes. And to present
a contrast to what had recently been going on in the eastern areas, so that he
would show a merciful face to the world, he forbade the killing of the servants
of God, ordering that they should be maimed [*or* unnerved]. So the eyes of
confessors were gouged out; their hands were cut off; their feet amputated,
their nostrils and ears slit. . . ."

These excesses were counterbalanced by offers of rewards to those who
would return to the old gods. (Theotecnos offered one Theodotos, town
governor at Ancyra, a position as priest of Apollo, with its legal and
financial advantages, if he would abjure Christ; he refused it and was
deposed from his governorship.)[17]

The rescript in which Daia showed his "merciful face" to the world has survived: it makes no mention of the physical constraints which were certainly used in persuading Christians to worship with the new priesthood. Eusebius claims that this letter was not sent until after Constantine, newly appointed Augustus Maximus and Pontifex Maximus by the Roman senate after a successful invasion of Italy in 312, wrote to Maximin Daia reminding him of Galerius' edict of toleration. The letter reads in part:

> "When last year [311] I paid an auspicious visit to Nicomedia . . . some of the citizens presented themselves before me . . . requesting that [no Christians] should be permitted to live in their city. . . . I thanked them warmly for their petition, but realised that it was by no means unanimous. If any are still persisting in that superstition, let them keep to their resolve. . . . It is rather by acts of grace and exhortations that you should increase the care for the gods in our provinces . . . if some wish to follow their own religion, let them do what it is legal for them to do . . . But let no one trouble our provinces with violence. . . ."[18]

Further to encourage support for the established religion and discourage the young from probing the nature of Christian teaching, new schoolbooks were introduced, presenting the pagan view of Christ as a criminal justly condemned to a slave's death and unworthy of a citizen's respect—books which seem to have been based principally on the arguments popularised in Porphyry's *Against the Christians* and (in the most notorious instance at least, *The Acts of Pilate*) so convincingly modelled on Christian popular works as to give the bishops real cause for concern.[19]

The low level at which the debate was conducted on both sides can perhaps best be illustrated by an example. Some time about the year 200 Flavius Philostratus, a philosopher friend of the Emperor Septimius Severus, wrote a life of a philosopher and mystic named Apollonius of Tyana who had lived about a century earlier. During Maximin's reign, Hierocles, the governor of Bithynia, offered Apollonius to the world as a rival to Christ, showing him as a good man, full of wisdom, so close to the divine that he could work miracles. Wonders being relatively few in Philostratus' original study, Hierocles filled out the record in his book, which he entitled *The Friend of Man*, with inventive additions of his own. The book was so well received that Eusebius, whose *History* we have so often quoted, felt constrained to write a denigration of Apollonius in reply. Neither the *Friend of Man* (it would appear from the fragments Eusebius quotes: the original has not survived) nor Eusebius' treatise is worth a moment's consideration as a serious treatment of the subject: a single incident, that of the Plague at Ephesus will illustrate this quite clearly:

In chapter seven of Book 8 of Philostratus' *Life*, in which Apollonius is shown defending himself before the Emperor Domitian on charges including witchcraft and illegal wonder-working, the philosopher describes how he saved the city of Ephesus from an outbreak of plague. It is well known, he says, that exhalations from the earth cause disease. Being himself an ascetic and abstemious man, he can sense such exhalations before other people. So at Ephesus he "sensed" or "saw" a plague threatening the city before anyone else realised its presence. "The spirit of the pestilence took the form of an aged, poverty-stricken man. I both detected its presence and made it captive. So I did not so much retard the disease as actually drive it away."

This is the language of mysticism, and is not intended to be taken literally. Apollonius himself says that he cannot explain what he feels and sees in the surroundings of a courtroom, but he would be glad to try to help the emperor to understand in a private interview elsewhere.

So far, so good: in the world of the New Testament no less than that of the pagan mystics, the "demons" can be sensed by those gifted to detect them, and once sensed can be driven away. But what did Hierocles make of this story? As quoted by Eusebius, his account in the *Friend of Man* claimed that "the plague was seen [by people generally] in the form of an old man, a beggar, dressed in rags, who, when Apollonius called on the crowd to stone him, first shot darts of fire out of his eyes, then, when crushed under the weight of the stones, metamorphosed himself into a dog, crushed-looking and foaming at the mouth, like a rabid animal. . . ." Eusebius, of course, had no difficulty in laughing away this story. Plague, he pointed out, is not a little old man but, as Apollonius had first said, "nothing other than a corruption and vitiation of the atmosphere, the air around us going rotten". Neither Hierocles nor Eusebius comes well out of such exchanges as this. Would that so crucial a debate had been conducted on a level above that of fiction and abuse.

Daia's experiments in popular religious education were doomed to be suspended after little more than three years. Before negotiations between Daia and Maxentius could lead to any working agreement, Constantine had decided that the time had come for the "liberation" of Italy, and soon both "tyrants" were dead.

All kinds of historical problems surround the story of the invasion of the peninsula in 312, and especially the nature of Constantine's vision before the battle of Mulvian Bridge which won Rome for him and ended Maxentius' life.[20] Reduced to its brutal outlines, the story is one of a war of aggressive self-aggrandisement undertaken in the name of liberty and legality. It has been made famous by Christian historians because it led ultimately, by way of subsidies to the Christian clergy and the re-enactment of laws calling for toleration in the so-called "Edict of Milan", to the emperor's founding of Constantinople as the capital of a Christian-dominated empire. But the earliest account of the campaign, the summary given before Constantine himself by a panegyrist only months after Rome fell, mentions no vision, concentrating wholly on the evil of Maxentius' regime and the personal psycho-spiritual power, the charismatic and inspired leadership, of the story's hero: "For what god was it that made you feel that the time had come for the liberation of the city against the advice of men and even against the warning of the auspices? Assuredly, O Constantine, there is in you some secret communication from the divine mind which delegating the care of us to lesser gods, deigns to reveal itself to you alone. If that is not so, most mighty emperor, as you have conquered, so tell us how...."[21]

The same mysterious, compelling inspiration is hinted at in the inscription on the Arch of Constantine, erected by the senate in the Victor's honour: "To the Emperor Caesar Flavius Constantine who being instinct with divinity (*instinctu divinitatis*) and by the greatness of his spirit with his forces avenged the commonwealth in a just cause on both the tyrant and all his party."

What mattered to Constantine in 312 was that the world should believe that "divinity" had chosen him to be the Victor. What little evidence there is suggests that this ultra-superstitious man had been deeply disturbed by the religious turmoil of recent years. He was certainly not yet a Christian himself but on the one hand had vague yearnings towards a supreme god—the *summus sanctus deus* of the philosophers—and on the other stood in urgent, superstitious need of a divine name under which to fight and with which to inspire his soldiers. As the Christian historian Socrates put it in the fifth century, when the story of Constantine's vision had already gone through several mythographical metamorphoses,

"The Emperor Constantine . . . set himself to free the Romans . . . and . . . while his mind was full of this great objective, he debated within himself what god's help he should invoke in the conduct of the war. He had reached the conclusion that Diocletian's party had not profited at all from the pagan deities whom they had sought to propitiate, but that his own father Constantius, who had renounced the various religions of the Greeks, had passed through life far more prosperously than they. In this state of uncertainty, a preternatural vision . . . appeared to him."[22]

The earliest account of the vision, Lactantius', written perhaps a year after the event, describes an inspiration very like the vision which came to Aurelian at a crisis during the battle of Emesa, except, of course, that the divine hero was changed. "Constantine was directed in a dream to cause a heavenly sign to be marked on the shields of his soldiers and so proceed to battle. He did as he had been commanded, and marked on their shields the letter X with a perpendicular line through it, turned over at the top, this being the monogram of Christ."[23]

Later, the vision was transferred from night-time to daylight, and from the camp on the night before the battle to mid-afternoon in the Alps, before the campaign had begun. Christ's monogram ☧, appeared in the sky with the inscription around it: "In this sign you shall be the victor"—and it was as the Victor that Constantine preferred to be lauded throughout the rest of his long career.

Maxentius' men, especially the Praetorians, fought well for him throughout the summer-long campaign. They were defeated in a series of hard-fought battles which reduced the north-Italian fortresses one by one. The stubbornness of the resistance, even after the defenders' commanding general, the Prefect, had been killed, suggests not that Italy felt itself to be groaning under the tyrant's heel, but that it saw itself slipping into slavery if Constantine won. Once established as Victor he in fact showed himself a very mild conqueror, soon restoring to their offices several of the chief administrators who had been most strongly opposed to him. But in the long run, their early assessment of his character and policies proved right: his defeat of Maxentius at Mulvian Bridge spelled the end of the old Rome, the world their forefathers had built and they had loved and served.

No more than Diocletian had did Constantine linger in Rome, and that for fundamentally the same reason: it was his city, but he was a foreigner there, a barbarian, though a frighteningly competent one. In the three months he spent there, he won the support of Pope Melitiades and of the "Catholic" Church of Africa (then involved in a conflict of personalities and doctrine with the rigorist Donatists)[24] with bribes of money, influence and judicial favour, dissolved the Praetorian Guard, reorganised the city's food supplies, restored the regular grain-shipments from Africa, accepted what honours the cities offered him and in short confirmed himself in every possible way as master of the western half of the world. Then, in mid-winter, armed with the precious title Augustus Maximus awarded to him by the senate, he left for the old imperial palace at Milan, to confront the next problem presenting itself to his divine genius, his future relations with his elder colleague in the imperial college, the divine—but surely puzzled and perhaps apprehensive—Licinius.

The difficulties inherent in the situation were resolved amiably and in Constantine's favour. He offered Licinius his half-sister Constantia in exchange for legal title to Italy, Africa, Mauretania and Spain, and had his offer accepted. He must also have promised his benevolent neutrality while Licinius measured swords with Maximin Daia—an expedition he undertook immediately after the wedding celebration—but naturally no word of this was allowed to creep out. One of the documents prepared for universal promulgation after Licinius' expected victory was the "Edict of Milan", a document giving "to Christians and everyone else the right freely to follow whatever rule of faith they choose, so that, whatever divinity [is] enthroned in heaven may be well-disposed and propitious towards us and all those under our authority"[25]—the charter of Christian (and Manichaean) liberty.

Although no longer young, Licinius had been a good general in his time, and still retained enough of his old skills and enthusiasm to defeat one unpractised in war. Daia made it easy for him by invading Thrace while he was at Milan, taking first Byzantium, then Heraclea-ad-Europa, but shortsightedly leaving the bulk of his army in Asia. There was no time for Licinius to collect and equip his field army. He marched east at a very sharp pace with a mere thirty-thousand men and smashed Daia's army in a single battle. What is interesting about this battle, apart from Maximin Daia's overwhelming defeat, is that according to Lactantius the notoriously godless Licinius thought it worthwhile to encourage his troops on the eve of the conflict with the news that, like Aurelian and Constantine before him, he had been promised victory in a dream sent by the supreme god. In these years, religion and politics were inseparable. Licinius' newly-discovered god had no name, only a title, and he taught the emperor a prayer which the troops were to recite three times as they marched to their battle lines—a prayer which Eusebius says Constantine also used among his multi-sectarian armies—and ending with the battle-cry *Summe sancte Deus!*, "Supreme and Holy God!"[26]

Daia saved himself but very little besides from his defeat. He was still master of all Asia Minor, Egypt and the East, but he hid in the Taurus Mountains, frantically trying to rally men to himself without actually showing himself in places where his enemy might find him. Panic was destroying him. By mid-June, 313, Licinius was in control at Nicomedia, and shortly afterwards, no one knows quite when, but while still issuing orders from his mountain retreat, Daia contracted a terrible, dehydrating disease (probably cholera) and died, after, it is said, executing the diviners who had promised him victory and humbly begging pardon of the Christians' god in an edict granting the persecuted all that he had hitherto refused them. After his death, no mercy was shown to those who had been closest to him. Licinius executed even his wife and her mother, Diocletian's daughter and widow. The high priests of the new pagan church also fell victims of the purge, "first Theotecnos himself," Eusebius says, "and then his partners in the fraud were subjected to complicated tortures and afterwards delivered to the executioner."[27] The supreme and holy god had not taught his servant Licinius mercy.

So the Roman world was divided between Constantine in the West and Licinius in the East, with the Christians at first treated in both halves of the empire as the equals of the rest, their property restored to them, their congregations free to worship where they would, their priests free to come and go as they chose and their bishops, especially in the western half of the empire, gradually growing in influence as Constantine, the new man, found that he could trust these new men to serve his ends as long as he did not obstruct them in the pursuit of theirs. The key to the years to come was the fact that Constantine and the Christians needed one another.

Notes

1 His accession day, the nineteenth anniversary of his usurpation, and thus the first day of his twentieth year, was 17 September. It is not known why the celebrations were delayed until November.

2 The whole concept of "secular" games, to celebrate the centuries of Roman domination as they passed, was in fact an artificial one. The games had been omitted as often as they had been celebrated, and no one knew whether they should be celebrated after ninety, one hundred, or even one hundred and ten years. By one system of reckoning they were due in 304: by another, not until 314. But Zosimus thought that they were important—for reasons which emerge in the main text—and it is certain that his was not an isolated view. He continually reflects "reactionary" pagan opinion.

3 *De Mort. Pers.*, 19 describes the events at Diocletian's abdication as seen by an eye-witness with a taste for scandalous speculation about what he could not see.

4 The story of Constantine's flight from Nicomedia and subsequent rebellion is told in *De Mort. Pers.*, 24; Zosimus 2, 8; Anon. Vales. 2, 4.

5 The temple which has traditionally been called Romulus' for many centuries, and now forms part of the Church of Saints Cosmas and Damian. Some modern commentators deny the validity of this identification, and look for the original temple of Romulus at the Circus of Maxentius where inscriptions relating to the murdered youth have been discovered.

6 *De Vit. Const.*, 1, 28; cf. Socrates, *History*, 1, 2; Sozomen, *History*, 1, 3–4.

7 D.S.I.M. (Deo Soli Invicto Mithrae) fautorii imperii sui Iovi et Herculii religiosissimi Augusti et Caesari sacrarium resistuerunt.

8 Zosimus, 2, 13.

9 C.I.L. VI. i. 1138. He was, it seems, a man of very warm family feelings. He persuaded the senate to proclaim both Romulus and Maximian divine: the inscriptions cut in Romulus' honour reflect a deep affection for the dead youth:

"To divine Romulus, for love, from the esteem of his most loving father . . . for love, from the affection of his dearest mother" and

"To divine Romulus of most noble memory, duly elected consul for the second time, the son of the Lord Maxentius the unconquered and abiding emperor, the grandson of the divine Maximian the Elder".

10 *Paneg. Lat.*, XII, 14, 3; 16, 3; 18, 1; *Paneg. Lat.*, IV, 8, 3. At XII, 14, 4, *superstitiosa maleficia* is the explicit charge: it was seized upon by Eusebius when later he came to write up the history of the times: *History*, 8, 14 and *De Vit. Const.*, 1, 36.

11 Zosimus, II, 14; cf. *Paneg. Lat.*, IV, 32; XII, 16.

12 Eusebius, *History*, 8, 17.

13 Eusebius, *History*, 9, 9.

14 Optatus, *Contra Donat.*, 1, 18.

15 Eusebius, *History*, 9, 9.

16 Hecate was the Greek goddess of magic and divination, one of the many manifestations of the great Earth Mother of the East Mediterranean area. Manes-

Daos would appear to have been a synthesis of Manes, the father of Atys, a Phrygian deity, and Daos, the spirit of Dacia on the Danube, so that (it has been suggested) he is the divine expression of the political union between Asia and SE Europe. Phoibos was the oracular Apollo.

17 *De Mort. Pers.*, 35.

18 Eusebius, *History*, 9, 9.

19 The original *Acts of Pilate* has not survived. The extant book so named is a Christian forgery, probably composed to combat the influence of the original work. See M. R. James, *The Apocryphal New Testament* (Oxford, 1953) pp. 94ff.

20 See John Holland Smith, *Constantine the Great* (Hamish Hamilton, Scribners, 1971) ch. 5 and 7, and refs.

21 *Paneg. Lat.*, XI, 3, 4–5.

22 Socrates Scholasticus, *Ecclesiastical History*, 1, 2.

23 *De Mort. Pers.*, 48.

24 On the Donatists, see G. G. Willis, *St Augustine and the Donatist Controversy* (S.P.C.K. 1950). W. H. C. Frend, *The Donatist Church*, (Clarendon Press, 1952).

25 For the text of the Edict, see Eusebius, *History*, 10, 5. Lactantius, *De Mort. Pers.*, 48; M. Anastos, art. *The Edict of Milan* in *Revue des Etudes Byzantines*, 1967, pp. 13ff.

26 Lactantius, *De Mort. Pers.*, 46; Eusebius, *De Vit. Const.*, 4, 20.

27 Eusebius, *History*, 9, 11.

The Revolution under Constantine

There is no record of any oracle ever having been bold enough to order Constantine to leave his temple: the Voice of the Sun at Emesa once told Aurelian to get out because he was "A single hawk: herald of cold woe to many doves. They shiver at the murderer." But Constantine, the murderer of the oracles, at first wore a gentle mask, and perhaps for a time even deceiving Apollo was deceived.

Some Christians believed, of course, that it needed only a Christian hand to wave for the gods to creep back, cringing, to the Satan who had begotten them. Lactantius, who became tutor to Constantine's eldest son Crispus shortly after the rape of Rome, was one of them. He wrote in his *Divine Institutes* "if anyone present when they sacrifice to their gods makes the sign [of the cross] on his forehead, the sacrifice offers nothing whatsoever".[1] But Constantine's superstition would not allow him to accept so simplistic a view (even if, indeed, he would have been happy as early as 313–14 to sweep away all that had gone before and surround himself solely with Christians). In the ten years during which he and Licinius shared the empire, no temple was closed by imperial action, and no priest, except Theotecnos and his allies, lost his living. The mintmasters of the empire continued to use the old gods in their inscriptions. Constantine specially favoured the unconquered sun; Licinius promoted Jupiter, "the Preserver of the Augustus". There are coins of Constantine from this decade lauding the Divine Claudius (II, Gothicus), the Divine Constantius, and surprisingly, as late as 325, the Divine "Jovius" and "Herculius", Diocletian and Maximian. Outwardly, the empire continued much as it had for the past thirty years, with Constantine proving himself year by year an administrator even more able than the great Diocletian had been, beginning reforms of the army, the currency and the civil service which when complete were to give them structures they were to preserve in the Byzantine Empire (although not, of course, without changes in detail) for more than a thousand years.

Naturally, the two emperors quarrelled—and that only four months after Licinius' eastern victory. The story was a tangled one, but it seems that Licinius overreached himself. At his suggestion Constantine appointed a certain Bassianus, his half-sister Anastasia's husband and a distant relation of Licinius himself, as his Caesar in Italy, only to learn shortly afterwards that the family was plotting against him, or so his propaganda department announced when war was declared in October 315. The fighting was brief and bloody: a battle on the Save River, and another eastwards in Thrace gave Constantine Byzantium, from where he was able to dictate his terms. Neither he nor Licinius was yet ready for a fight to the end. They agreed a peace which gave Constantine all Europe apart from Thrace. He withdrew his garrison from Byzantium and for the next decade the frontiers of the Roman world remained unchanged.

By specifically naming the Christians as of special concern to the emperors the Edict of Milan had in fact given them a special status as protected persons. In the east, this did not mean a great deal. Licinius remained the conventionally blasphemous god-fearer he had been all his life (though his empress Constantia became a devotee of the martyred teacher Lucian of Antioch whose shrine at Nicomedia was a rallying-point among the eastern Christians). Constantine, on the other hand, subsidised the western Christians and employed their leaders, especially Bishops Hosius of Cordoba, and Melitiades of Rome, as his advisers, so naturally winning Christian support for his own rule. The great persecution had proved it impossible to destroy the Christians: Constantine intended to rule them, making a legally-sanctioned place for them in his empire and so bringing them under control. It was a dangerous game. In pagan opinion, if the emperor was not very careful, the Christians would soon rule him. They showed their disapproval of his policy at the earliest opportunity.

When in the summer of 315 he visited Rome for the celebrations marking the tenth anniversary of his usurpation, he showed his graciousness towards the still largely pagan city by such acts as the appointment of the aged augur and high priest of the sun Vettius Rufinus as his governor there, but spoiled the effect by refusing to play his part, as emperor and pontifex maximus, in the sacrifices of thanksgiving for his rule. "He ordered general celebrations" Eusebius recorded in his *History*, "and offered prayers of thanksgiving to God the King of All as sacrifices without flame and smoke."[2]

There was a school of thought among the pagans which rejected animal sacrifices. Some of its adherents, including the influential Porphyry at one stage in his career, even advocated vegetarianism, on the grounds that men had no right to end lives which the gods had created. But no one believed that the emperor was a follower of that school. His refusal to take part in Rome's traditional ceremonies was an insult to tradition, the act of a crypto-Christian, an atheist. The Roman pagans never forgave him for it.

It is a pity that he was so misguided by his advisers and his own temperament. because if there was ever a moment when compromise was possible between pagans and Christians it was after the fall of Maximin Daia, while both Licinius and Constantine were attracted by the worship of "whatever divinity is enthroned in heaven", the unnamed "Supreme and Holy God".

Although the received history of Christianity makes no reference to any such compromise, its achievement was in fact possible, if never probable. Unfortunately, in the fourth century especially, both sides tended to listen to their extremists. The Great Persecution—itself a symptom of extremism—provoked violent reactions within the Christian church which tended to boil over in street fighting not infrequently ending in murder. Mauretania, Africa, Egypt, Syria, even Rome itself—wherever persecution had been severe, for however short a period, there was strife among Christians afterwards as those who had watched members of their families suffer, or even suffered themselves, protested against the leniency of many bishops in allowing those who had apostatised in times of trouble easily return to the church once peace was restored. So the schism of Donatus arose in Africa and that led by Meletius[3] in Egypt: so arose the riots at Rome which Maxentius had rightly but ruthlessly put down.

Extremism in discipline was often paralleled by extremism in doctrine. In parts of the Christian world where persecution had not been extreme, moderation towards those who had lapsed prevailed and in Spain—where there was virtually no persecution—a council of Christian bishops held at Elvira about the year 306 went so far as to rule that a Christian offered a magistracy could make the customary sacrifices and swear the traditional oaths without forswearing his citizenship of heaven. Although Constantine's chief adviser in religious affairs was Hosius of Cordoba, the mild and understanding attitude of the Spanish bishops unfortunately did not prevail, any more than in the long run did the moderate and sensible teaching about Christ proposed early in the 320s by Arius of Lycopolis in much-persecuted Egypt, whose view that Christ was not in the last resort "of the same substance eternally" as the one, holy and supreme God "the Father" opened the way to comparison between him and the deified heroes of pagan tradition, and might ultimately have made an understanding possible between Christians and pagans—for Christianity was constantly absorbing elements of pagan thinking, and there were many unorthodox pagans who included Jesus in their lists of heroes.[4] One wonders what would have been the result if paganism had produced more men like Plotinus and in the church Arianism had prevailed. Unfortunately, neither of these desirable developments occurred. Arianism was crushed,[5] and paganism produced Iamblichus, a writer whose influence was far greater than his intellect, a man whose importance endured only because there was no one greater to overshadow him.

Iamblichus, a Semite by race, was born at Chalcis in Coele-Syria about the year 250 and had the good fortune to study at Rome under Porphyry at the time when Porphyry was editing the ideas of the great master Plotinus. But later in life he returned to Syria and there opened a school where, during the reigns of Maximin Daia and Licinius, he taught extremist pagan doctrines, rejecting the logic of his masters as leading to conclusions too remote for ordinary people to grasp.

Plotinus had found temples and sacrifices unnecessary, and Porphyry had argued cogently against animal sacrifices. Both had sought to create a rational picture of the universe, where the mind of man reflected, however dimly, the mind of "the One" so that Man the Microcosm was a true if limited echo of the Macrocosm, and intellect and emotion, physics and metaphysics, head and heart all had their places in the scheme of things. Iamblichus turned his back on this balanced approach, unconsciously allowing his mystery-loving, sentimental, Oriental heart to rule his platonist-trained mind, and by his influence setting pagan speculation on a course bound to lead to disaster.

Among Porphyry's works was a treatise against the magic even then threatening to overwhelm paganism in the form of a letter to a (mythical) Egyptian priest named Anebo. It was a powerful and valuable contribution to rational thinking, rejecting magic as unworthy of either gods or men. Iamblichus signalised his retreat into extremism by writing a "Reply of Abammon ['the son of Ra'] to Porphyry's Letter to Anebo". In it, he strung together all the magical practices current in his times, applauding them all, as though the weight of the evidence that magic was popular could demonstrate the logic and rationality of magic itself. In this and other works, he retreated entirely from reason into a world full of magical numbers, as beloved by the Pythagoreans: he found evidence for 360 divine beings—one for every day of the sacred Egyptian year—with twenty-one (three times seven) Lords of the World and forty-two (two times three times seven) Lords of Nature. The presiding deities of the great mysteries (Serapis, Isis, Hecate, Demeter, Dionysos, and Cybele) were his divine guides to the truth beloved of "King Helios", the ruling sun, Lord of the Intelligible World, the Sun's companion Aphrodite and his doubles Zeus and Serapis. Arguing that the people needed symbols, Iamblichus forced every religion except Christianity to provide them. The supreme syncretist, he was the inventor of the "religion of the Greeks", the Hellenism condemned so bitterly by later Byzantine Christians (and unfortunately he was also the most direct influence upon the Emperor Julian and his pagan friends).[6] According to Eunapius, huge crowds made pilgrimages to Iamblichus' school at Apamea on the Orontes, in order to hear him talk. He would offer sacrifices in their presence and—whether by deception or suggestion—would appear to undergo a metamorphosis as he was speaking, seeming to emit a golden glow and to float at knee-height or more above the ground, as the Christian preacher Joseph of Cupertino is said to have levitated a millennium or so later.

The man and his act were no doubt worth a day's journey to see, but the instruction he gave seemed to many not to provide a stable foundation upon which to build a life.

While pagans thus drifted towards one kind of extremism, the unbalanced dream of theurgy, Christians were fighting their way towards another in the controversy over Arius' teaching. The attempts of Arius and his associates minutely to define the relationship between Jesus and his divine Father seemed to some Christians to reduce or restrict Jesus' eternal divinity. Their most forceful summary of their teaching, the catch-phrase "there was a time when he [Jesus] was not" drove their opponents constantly to seek new definitions of their own ideas about Christ which would exclude any thought that his being the Son of God made him in any way inferior to, or less eternally divine than, his Father. Partly because all the leaders on both sides of this controversy were strong characters and partly because the question was of real significance to them, and was not merely a debating point, the argument became continually more acrimonious and indeed ultimately threatened the peace of the state (although not until after Licinius' death). Long before Arianism was finally defeated, the non-Arians, "the catholics", had been forced into attitudes which made impossible any real discussion, let alone compromise, between them and the pagans.

Another extremist development within Licinius' empire which was to have an important place in the story of the death of paganism was the gradual Christian acceptance, first in the districts around Alexandria, then later elsewhere, of self-wounding asceticism as a normal if heroic expression of devotion to Christ. The name is lost of the first Egyptian to go out into the desert to make himself a celibate hermit for the love of God but the first to organise hermits into groups supported by local communities is said to have been Saint Pachomius, a contemporary of Constantine. In the years following the great persecution there was an eremetical explosion, erupting into the life of the church with frightening force. Soon such pathological figures as the tortured Anthony of the Desert, hag-ridden by frustrated sexuality, and the suncrazed, worm-eaten Simon Stylites, who sat for years on top of a stone column, became the heroes of contemporary Christians. There had always been a puritanical streak in Christianity, but the logical foundation for the way of life of these heroes must be sought in dualist and gnostic thinking, not in the New Testament. Whatever the origins of their behaviour, it was another blow to the established Roman world when admiration for the horrific voluntary sufferings of these figures made them arbiters of holiness. Within a few decades so many were calling themselves monks, and justifying such odd and often criminous behaviour by appeals to their alleged vocation, that, as we shall see in later chapters, the peace was threatened and steps had to be taken to control them.

While Licinius' realm was nurturing figures as various as Iamblichus, Arius and Pachomius, in Constantine's half of the empire developments were less colourful, but not less baleful for the pagan world. After 315, Constantine did not visit Rome again for ten years, and Roman life went on very much as before, except that Christian worship was no longer proscribed. But very slowly the world outside the City Prefecture began to change. New laws were introduced, making Christian leaders the equal of their pagan counterparts, and Constantine's attitude to non-Christian institutions gradually became more overtly contemptuous. The first small steps in establishing the new precedences were the provision of subsidies for "the catholic church" of Caecilian, bishop of Carthage in Africa, immediately after the province became Constantine's in 312–13, and the granting of immunities from taxation and conscription to the clergy, immunities hitherto restricted to pagan priests. Next came imperial recognition of the right of bishops to judge the actions of Christians, signalised by the convocation first of a synod at Rome under Pope Melitiades in 313, and then of the Council of Arles in 314 as an imperial consistory (not merely a church synod) to try the case of Donatus. Only three years later, having told his *Vicarius* in Africa that he intended personally to "make plain . . . what kind of worship is to be offered to the divinity" and "cause those I judge hostile to the divine law to pay the penalty", the emperor ordered the army to occupy three basilicas in Carthage used by the Donatists. The date of this action, 12 March 317, deserves to be remembered, for it marked the beginning of the sad mediaeval story of the use of troops to enforce Christian uniformity. Just four years after that, and a decade after the dying Galerius had issued his ruling that "Christians may exist", imperial catholicism became a truly persecuting religion with the issue of a general order to the army of Africa decreeing the annihilation of the Donatist sect.[7]

The year 318 saw another development which must have caused the pagans to look at one another, wondering where they stood. The higher clergy were made equal with pagan high priests, being granted the honours and authority of magistrates, entitled to a guard and lights when engaged upon their functions. Further laws, dated 321 and 323 extended these privileges down the ranks, till there was hardly a minister who was not entitled to honours by imperial decree, and for the first time in history it became fashionable to seek office in the church as a career—so fashionable, indeed, that in the end more edicts had to be promulgated forbidding anyone to become a Christian minister whose birth made him eligible for appointment to any of the time-consuming and costly offices of the state.

However, no positive steps were yet taken against paganism as such. There are in fact laws of Constantine from this decade which show his attitude to have been either wholly ambiguous or wholly self-glorificatory, depending upon one's reading of them. On the one hand he favoured Christians, building them up as a body of privileged citizens, headed by his son Crispus, and soon joined by his mother, later "the Augusta" and after her death "Saint" Helena. But on the other hand, he did not lose his fear of omens which had traditionally been held threatening, and expressly forbade anyone to attack pagans for believing in the gods. The armies prayed to the gods (and sacrificed to their legionary standards) in his name. As late as 330, he gave pagan admirers at Hispellum in Umbria permission to endow a priesthood and build a temple in honour of his genius and family, though he forbade any offerings there except prayer. Talking to Christian bishops in 325 he sneered at Diocletian for his lifelong fear of lightning, but only five years earlier he had signed an edict, never repealed, reaffirming the importance of *fulguratores*, the diviners whose duty it was to expound the omen if "any part of the palace or some other public building has been struck by lightning",[8] expressly permitting private persons also to consult them if the supreme god gave them similar cause to think on him. The only legislation from the years 314–24 directed against any pagans was aimed at those who had traditionally been reckoned enemies of the state. So in 318 an edict forbade making magic to charm away the life of any citizen and laws of 319 and 320 prohibited private and secret divination, exhorting pagans to "go to the public altars" adding that "we do not forbid the performance in daylight of ceremonies hitherto permitted".[9] What has often been called "white" magic, performed to secure the return to good health of the sick, was actually encouraged in a law of 318. Even the well-known "Sunday Observance" laws of 321, closing the courts for any work except the consideration of urgent petitions, especially those relating to the emancipation of slaves, and permitting no labour except field-work which could not be delayed are not anti-pagan but are so worded as to offend no one. Although they can be claimed to have been inspired by Christianity, they actually refer not to Christ as their inspiration, but to "the Venerable Day of the Sun", the weekly festival of King Sol only then becoming fashionable among devout pagans. Constantine's mind at this time is unreadable from the evidence. Probably he was deliberately ambiguous, so as to win credit from as many directions as possible, and lose it in none.

Outside the field of religion, the first half of the decade passed largely in the "Blessed Tranquillity" which Constantine's coins claimed were the chief gift brought by his reign. His eldest son Crispus (Minerva's, not Fausta's child) was proclaimed Caesar in 317 simultaneously with his younger half-brother Constantine II, Maximian's grandson, and Licinianus, the son of Licinius. Three years later, at the age of about twenty, Crispus undertook a winter campaign against the Franks and acquitted himself well enough to be fêted by his father; the next year he returned to Gaul in command of an expedition against the Alamanni. All this must have been most gratifying, but Constantine was not satisfied. He had moved his capital eastwards to Serdica, and he dreamed of pushing it still further east, forcing Licinius' retirement and making himself sole master of the Roman world. Soon, two excuses for war had been found: the alleged persecution of the Christians by Licinius despite the toleration shown to them in laws written by the Supreme Augustus Constantine and approved by the Pontifex Maximus (Constantine again) and the alleged provocation of Licinius in moving the bulk of his army into European Thrace after Constantine had violated his frontiers in pursuit of the marauding king of the Sarmatians, who had invaded Dacia. The closer the evidence for either of Licinius' alleged crimes is examined, the more tenuous it appears. While Constantine was pursuing a policy of Blessed Tranquillity, he was also building a great new naval harbour at Thessalonika and a warfleet big enough to fill it, too big to be used against any imaginable enemy except his fellow-emperor.

Licinius' alleged decline into persecution is described only in Christian sources. In an appendix to Eusebius' *History of the Church*, written specially to show why God had to inspire Constantine to end all authority but his own, the course of events is graphically but unconvincingly described as follows: at first, after the defeat of Maximin Daia, the church was free: synods were held, bishops elected, and meeting-houses built; then, Licinius forbade the election of bishops to replace those lost to death or heresy; a little later, he purged bishops and priests from his civil service; next he ordered that Christian males and females were to worship separately and be separately instructed, the women by female teachers; finally, Christians were forbidden to congregate within city limits anywhere, though worship was allowed "outside the gates, in the open country". Just before the war broke out, some bishops were arrested on charges (unconsciously betrayed by Eusebius) of treasonable magic-making in Constantine's cause "because he would not believe that prayers were offered for him . . . but convinced himself that we did everything and made our petitions to god only for the emperor whom god loved".[10] If there was any "persecution", it was of traitors—who proved on examination to be Christians, devoted to Constantine.

The date when Constantine's troops crossed into Thrace to begin the final struggle is not known. There were battles in Thrace, with Constantine directing the western armies, and at sea, with Crispus commanding the fleet. Soon, probably by late summer 323, Constantine held Byzantium and Licinius had fallen back on Nicomedia. According to Eusebius, both sides took their gods to war with them. Constantine's armies fought under the banner of the *labarum*, the battle-standard elaborated out of the *Chi-Rho* symbol, "the monogram of Christ", revealed to the emperor before the battle of Mulvian Bridge, and their battle-cry was *Deus Summus Salvator*: God Supreme, Saviour! Battles commenced, we are told, when Constantine himself was inspired to rush, drawn sword in hand, out of the shrine-tent, "the tabernacle of the cross", he had set up to pray in wherever the army camped. Licinius recruited a special corps of élite soothsayers, augurers and prophets to guide his men and before the decisive battle of Chrysopolis, the city guarding the road to Nicomedia, gathered his troops together in a sacred grove full of votive offerings and images to the gods, to exhort them to fight for "the gods of the fatherland" and the forms of worship "handed down to us from our remotest ancestors". The issues are unlikely to have been as clearcut on the day of the battle—18 September 323—as Eusebius thus presents them, but reviewed in retrospect, the campaign can be seen to have been decisive, in that it brought Constantine finally to appreciate that his future—and that of his empire—lay with the Christians. In 324, as soon as was practicable after his victory, he issued summonses to the bishops of the world to attend him at the crucial consistory now remembered as the Council of Nicaea: in 325 and 326, he deliberately offered unforgivable insults to the pagans of Rome, and began to rebuild Byzantium as Constantinople, Christian from the first; yet he himself was still not baptised.

Licinius' life was saved immediately after his defeat by the negotiation of a truce and surrender by his wife Constantia. For perhaps six months or a little more he was allowed to live in peace at Thessalonika, then all his acts were annulled and he was murdered "secretly," Jerome's Chronicle says, "in defiance of civilised custom when oaths have been sworn". Nor was his the only death ordered by the Victor. His Master of Offices, Martianus, whom he had named Augustus during the war, was also put to death in 324 and not much more than a year later his young son Licinianus, together with the Empress Fausta, the Caesar Crispus and "numbers of his friends" were "judicially executed for an undisclosed reason".[11] Henceforward the chief persons in Constantine's entourage were to be his mother, Helena Augusta, and his legitimate sons Constantine II, Constantius (named Caesar on 8 November 324 at the age of seven) and Constans, the baby of the family.

The Council of Nicaea met in May of 325. It was an occasion never to be forgotten by the Christians, for it set them on a course from which no deviation was afterwards possible, a course dictated by extremists from Alexandria on the one hand and the temper of the Augustus on the other. Throughout the proceedings, Constantine was at his most engaging; he flattered (and impressed) the bishops at the opening ceremony with a show of imperial splendour which would have done honour to the court of Persia, chatting to those without Latin in his execrable Greek, seeing personally that they were provided with their little comforts, wooing and winning them with his pious charm.[12] He was determined to end their squabbling and although in that he was only temporarily successful (largely because Arius and his closest followers chose exile rather than submission) by the day of the great banquet ending the council the principle was firmly established that the emperor could—and, as the Christian Pontifex Maximus, probably should—exercise ultimate authority over the disciplinary affairs of the "catholic" church. In exchange, the bishops were assured of imperial favour and a privileged place among the counsellors of the empire. The Christian bishops had, in short, been constituted a branch of the imperial civil service, in practice though not in law occupying the position hitherto filled by the chief priests of Roman paganism, the ancient College of Pontiffs and College of Fifteen. Seen from this angle, the Council of Nicaea clearly appears to have marked an important stage in Constantine's divorcing of the empire from the city,

in the "byzantinisation"—or as Zosimus would have it, "the decline"—of
Rome.

The importance of this development was underlined by the significant
place and date of the council. It was held at Nicaea so that Constantine
could divide his time between its debates and conferences with the
architects of his new headquarters at Byzantium. And it was held in May
325 not merely because that was the earliest convenient date after the
unification of the empire but as a deliberate snub to Rome. The year was
that of Constantine's twentieth jubilee. He had celebrated his *decennalia* at
Rome in 315 with the senate. Now in 325, the principal celebrations of his
vincennalia were held away from Rome among the leaders of the new world.
As though to emphasise the point still more strongly, in this same year,
325, he appointed to Rome her first Christian governor, Acilius Severus.

At some time during the year somebody must have urged upon the
emperor that Victor and Sole Augustus although he might be, he was not
yet himself god, to do entirely as it pleased him. He could not simply
ignore Rome, turn his back on the past, trample on the susceptibilities of
half—or more than half—the world. He agreed to travel to Italy in 326 for
a joint celebration of his twentieth year of power and his Caesars' tenth. It
was during that journey that Crispus, Fausta, Licinianus and their friends
were murdered. At Rome, Constantine was more uneasy than he had been
ten years earlier; Hosius of Cordoba was still constantly with him and it
was to Hosius that pagan tradition later attributed the counsel which
triggered off the ultimate explosion.

The fullest account of what happened is Zosimus'. Historically, it is
inaccurate (in particular, in that Constantine was not baptised in 326) but it
must be quoted at length here because it gives the clearest view we have of
an intelligent pagan's picture of what was happening to the world:

"The universal sovereignty having devolved upon Constantine alone, he no
longer hid his congenital viciousness, but indulged in every licentiousness.
However, he continued nonetheless to make use of the ancestral ceremonies,
though this was for necessity rather than out of respect. This was the reason
that he used soothsayers." [*He murdered Crispus and Fausta and*] "having
feelings of guilt both about these crimes and the oaths he had broken, he went
to the priests, asking for lustration. They told him that there was no means of
purification known to the tradition that was capable of washing away such
abominations. But a certain Spaniard, known as the Egyptian [i.e. the
Magician, Hosius], who had slid into Rome and made himself the intimate
of the women of the palace, confidently claimed in conversation with
Constantine that what the Christians taught could cleanse any crime,
promising that it would immediately liberate any wrongdoer who accepted it,
leaving him free from all sin. Constantine swallowed this and set aside the
rites of our forefathers for the sake of those revealed by the Egyptian. The first
stage in his impiety was marked by his coming to hold divination suspect,
because a lot of good luck having been predicted for him by it, he was afraid

that if others consulted it against him what was predicted for them might also actually happen. It was on this grounds that he strove to do away with such things. And when the festival of the ancestors came round, when the custom was to go up from the camp to the Capitol and there fulfil the traditional ceremonies, Constantine was to have taken part in the festival with the soldiers. But the Egyptian told him of an oracle to the effect that to go up to the Capitol Hill would be a shameful thing, so he stayed away from the holy rites of the temples, thus demonstrating hatred of the Senate and people".[13]

The Pontifex Maximus was refusing in Rome to attend to his ancestral duties. There is no wonder that later pagans believed that it was in 326 that Constantine was baptised. During this vicennial visit, he gave Apollo's shrine at Nero's circus to the Christians as a church to be dedicated to St Peter and (according to mediaeval tradition) carried away the first baskets of topsoil himself. He may also have made over to the reigning pope the site of St-Paul's-without-the walls. Certainly both churches were later endowed with properties in Asia which had belonged to Licinius. When he left Rome, shortly after finally refusing his duty to the gods, he robbed the city of her most sacred treasure, to bury it at the foot of a colossal statue of himself set up in the heart of Constantinople—or so the legends said. In Roman tradition, this treasure, the mysterious (and unidentified) *palladium*, had been brought from Troy (whose luck it had once embodied) to Rome by Aeneas and given into the care of the Vestals. On its safety Rome's security depended: to take it away was to announce and promote the ruin of the city. To put it into the city which a Christian poet was the first to call "another Rome" was to transfer the luck of the Romans from one city to the other. . . . The story of the legalised theft of an actual physical object from the Vestals' keeping cannot be confirmed from contemporary sources, but if it is a late invention, its symbolism is nonetheless perfect. From now on, Constantine's attitude to the old Rome was consistently one of rejection, and preference for his own new city—to which the mystery-mongers gave the secret, mystical name Anthusa, "flourishing", the Greek equivalent of their Latin name "Flora" for Rome.[14]

Despite all the indications clear to later ages that, at the time of the foundation of Constantinople, its founder was committed to the Christians, he himself seems not to have been consciously aware of it. Although "the Unconquered Sun Comrade of Our Augustus" did not appear on his coins after 325, when the site of New Rome was consecrated and the line of the walls marked out by the emperor himself (probably on 4 November 328, "in the first year of the 276th Olympiad, when the sun was in the constellation of the bowman and at an hour dominated by the crab") his chief advisers in the art of successful city-founding were the chief priest and a neoplatonist teacher named Sopater. (As Zosimus said, he continued to use the ancestral rites from necessity, and city founding was an ancient pagan skill, ruled by the oracles and the stars; naturally, no superstitious emperor could trust Christians yet to have had sufficient experience in it.)

Someone also persuaded Constantine that no city could be safe without its protecting deities, so he set up shrines there: one to himself, the colossal statue with the *palladium* at its foot, one to Holy Peace (the "Blessed Tranquillity" of the Augustus), a Christian church on the acropolis, and two temples dedicated to traditional pagan deities in the hippodrome, one of them to the Heavenly Twins, the other to the *Tyche*, the tutelary spirit, the *genius* and luck of the city. Both these pagan temples had priesthoods but probably neither had a sacrificial cult. The only offerings publicly permitted in the city were prayers in the church and flowers and candles around the imperial statue.

It was now, with the founding of Constantinople, that the emperor at last made an open attack upon the old aristocracy of the empire and the pagans. Having tried and failed to persuade a significant number of the old leading families in Rome to migrate to Constantinople, he created a new order of aristocrats for the new city, naming them the *clari* (at Rome, he had created an order of *clarissimi* to outvote the old aristocracy, the *honestiores*, but they proved no more ready to move to the new city than the oldest of Rome's leading families). The attack on paganism was more direct, but still restrained. In part, it consisted in the appointment of Christians to posts of honour; in part, in attacks on the reverence shown to the gods.

In his eulogy of the emperor, the *Life of Constantine*, Eusebius of Caesarea naturally describes the desecration of shrines and images as victories. The reader is left to imagine for himself the pain and distress such triumphs caused to those who did not share the emperor's views. At first, Constantine's aim seems to have been to obtain for his city on the one hand the most powerful trophies (as good-luck pieces and tokens of his glory) and on the other the most beautiful works of art that the old world could be induced to surrender without rebelling. He robbed Apollo at Delphi of the pythoness' tripod; he brought statues of the muses from Mount Helicon and collected likenesses of gods, heroes and philosophers from all over the world to decorate the streets, markets, baths and other public buildings of the city. But it was not only pagan luck that he coveted. His mother Helena claimed to have found the true cross of Christ in Jerusalem: Constantine enclosed a fragment of it in the orb held by his colossal statue in the new forum. Agents travelling through the empire collected all kinds of Christian relics for forwarding to Constantinople. Whereas in Christian centres, however, they were empowered to spend imperial funds on improvements, at pagan shrines they left desolation behind them:

"In various cities, the entrances to their temples were left open to the weather, being stripped of their doors at his command; the tiling of others was removed and their roofs thus destroyed. From others again the aged bronze statues . . . were exposed to public view in public places in Constantinople . . . bronzes . . . which the victims of superstition had long honoured as gods —though now at last they learned to renounce their error when their own emperor held up the very objects of their worship to the ridicule and scorn of all who saw them.

He acted differently with regard to gold images. Realising that the ignorant masses were filled with a vain and childish dread of these teachers of error . . . he sent . . . a few of his personal friends into each province . . . to abolish this old error. They ordered the priests themselves to bring their gods from their dark inner chambers into the light of day, stripped them of their ornaments and . . . chipped off whatever seemed valuable and melted it down for assay . . . leaving what was of no value to the worshippers, as a token of their shame. . . ."[15]

According to critics, Constantine was "a man mocking rather than honey-tongued": "a banker with the outlook of a pastrycook":[16] to combine self-enrichment with the delights of ridiculing opponents might well appeal to such a man. But superstition made him hesitate actually to destroy the temples. Only in a few isolated instances did his other scruples overcome his fears. His legislation shows a strong puritan streak in him. Two Syrian temples of Aphrodite fell victim to it, one at Aphaca, the other at Heliopolis; the medical centre dedicated to Aesculapius at Aegea was also destroyed, presumably because it was too successful, and one school of pagan priests, the *galli* of Cybele at Alexandria, was dissolved:

"Like a keen-sighted eagle, while residing at his own city, he espied as from a watchtower a hidden and secret deadly snare in the province of Phoenicia. It was a grove and temple not situated in the middle of a city or in any public place . . . but away from the beaten, busy track at Aphaca, on part of the summit of Mount Libanus, and dedicated to the foul demon going by the name of Venus. It was a school for vice for all the abandoned votaries of sensuality and impurity where men undeserving of the name forgot the honour of their sex and propitiated the demon by their effeminate conduct; here too in this temple, as at a place beyond the range and restrictions of law, were perpetrated prostitution of women and adulterous intercourse, with other terrible and infamous practices. . . . Our august Emperor . . . having himself inspected these proceedings, gave orders that this building with its votives should be utterly destroyed . . . and military force was made the instrument of the place's purging. . . .

Many of the pretenders to wisdom were deluded votaries of the demon worshipped in Cilicia [the wholly beneficent Asclepios of Aegea] whom thousands reverenced as the possessor of saving and healing power, who sometimes appeared to those spending nights in his temple and sometimes restored the sick to health. The emperor . . . gave instructions that this temple was to be razed. In prompt obedience to his command, a band of soldiers laid this building, the object of admiration even to noble philosophers, flat in the dust, together with its unseen inmate, neither demon nor god, but rather deceiver of souls.

Among the emperor's most noble achievements . . . we may reckon the Phoenician city of Heliopolis [Baalbek] where those who dignify licentious pleasure with the distinguished name of reverence had permitted their women and children to commit shameless fornication. But now a new law, breathing the very spirit of chastity, was promulgated by the emperor, peremptorily forbidding these practices to continue. . . . And besides this, he also sent written exhortations, not disdaining to communicate by letter even with such as these. . . . At the same time, he followed up his words with matching deeds, erecting even in this city a church of great size and magnificence . . . and further, he made great provision for the poor.

And inasmuch as the Egyptians, especially of Alexandria, had been accustomed to honour their river by a priesthood made up of effeminate men, a further law was passed commanding the extirpation of this corrupt and vicious class, in order that in future no one might be found tainted by the like impurity."[17]

"Every gloomy cavern" Eusebius says elsewhere, "every hidden recess, offered access easily to the emperor's emissaries: the inaccessible and secret chambers, the inmost shrines of temples were trampled under the soldiers' feet": there was very little resistance, partly because the army was used to ensure that there was none, partly because many pagans shared Christian views of the immorality of such shrines as that at Aphaca, but partly also—and this factor was of growing importance as time passed—because obedience to the law, to the expressed will of an emperor as well as the laws of the ancestors, was an essential part of Roman paganism. There must have been protests. Perhaps there was fighting. No one recorded any details. But two recorded deaths leave a question mark hanging over these days. Sopater the Neoplatonist who had so prominent a role in Constantinople's consecration in 328 had been executed before the walls were completed and the city dedicated in 330, and a philosopher named Canonaris was killed for making an oration on the theme: "Do not think yourself above our ancestors simply because you have brought our ancestors down to nothing." Did Constantine actually order the closing of all temples at this time? Eusebius' *Life* claims that he did, but the pagan orator Libanius, who lived through these difficult years, declared in his *Defence of the Temples* (written about 386) that he left them impoverished but changed nothing in the laws regarding them. Certainly, no edict ordering their closure survives.

Constantine lived seven years after the dedication of his New Rome. His most important work during this time was the resettlement of a third of a million Sarmatians in the Danube provinces, Macedonia and Northern Italy. Later pagan historians attacked him strongly for this act of humane expediency, especially those who believed that barbarisation was the main cause of imperial decline. The tribesmen were, however, a valuable and loyal addition to the population. The Danube area was the poorest and least-developed in the Empire; the new settlers proved good frontiersmen, only too anxious once farming south of the river to protect their new prosperity from their less fortunate brethren to the north.

By the year 336, Constantine had been personally directing the affairs of his empire with great energy for thirty of his sixty-three years. Since the battle of Mulvian Bridge, he had effected a revolution in Roman affairs. But the problems looked as serious as ever. Rampant inflation exacerbated the effects of bad harvests, poverty and endemic disease. His favourites, the Christians, were deeply divided in everything except their opposition to paganism. The forty years' peace signed between Diocletian and the Persians was coming to an end and Persia, under King Sapor II, had made it clear that she did not intend to renew the treaty except for brief periods at a time. The pro-pagan aristocracy had risen in Armenia, driving out Constantine's ally, the Christian king. No emperor except Augustus had ever lived to celebrate a thirty-year jubilee. Constantine decided that the main festivities should be neither at Rome nor at Constantinople, but at Jerusalem, and should consist not of the traditional sacrifices, banquets and games, but of the solemn dedication of a new church, the glorious, gilded shrine built to house the cross discovered by his mother. First, he decreed, there should be a church council to settle all disagreements; then everyone who counted would go up to Jerusalem. . . .

Naturally, the year's events did not unroll smoothly. The council was held—and the Christians quarrelled over it. However, the Holy Sepulchre was dedicated, and the world saw that Constantine meant all that he had said and done in the religious sphere.

It was time to look to the future. Constantine had three sons: Constantine II, Constantius, and Constans. The elder two—probably born of different mothers, though both usually described as legitimate—were still under twenty, the youngest was about fourteen. The emperor must have had misgivings about their abilities, for when he divided the empire, it was to give power to others besides them. Constantine II he left as his Caesar in Gaul, Spain and the Britains, where he was already well known. Constans, the child, he made his Caesar in Italy and Africa, which were at peace. The most important command went to Constantius, as Caesar in the diocese of Oriens, the East, with its long Persian frontier, Dalmatius, the son of his eldest half-brother, who had served him as his prefect on the Danube since 332, received supreme power in that region, and Hannibalianus, Dalmatius' younger brother, went to Pontus with the oriental title King of Kings and Constantine's daughter Constantia [Constantina] as his wife.

The year 336 saw protracted negotiations between the aging emperor and ambassadors from Persia. By the end of the year it was obvious that the forty years' truce then ending would not be replaced by permanent peace on the eastern frontier. Constantine prepared for war, sending his Caesar Constantius to Mesopotamia in command of the frontier legions while he himself remained in Asia Minor to oversee the equipment and training of reinforcements. While preparing for the coming conflict, he died on Whitsunday, 22 May 337, one week after being baptised by the Arian Bishop Eusebius of Nicomedia.[18]

Notes

1 Lactantius, *Divine Institutes*, IV, 27, 3; there is an English Version in the *Library of the Ante-Nicene Fathers*, vol. 7 (Scribners, 1867).

2 Eusebius, *History*, 10, 8.

3 On the Meletian Schism, see John Holland Smith, *Constantine the Great*, chaps. 10 and 13.

4 The third-century apocryphal *Acts of Thomas* (cap. 27) contains an interesting prayer combining traditional Christian with Manichee teaching. (The female person mentioned is the Holy Spirit—divine wisdom to many gnostics—for the Syriac word for "spirit" was feminine and this was originally a Syriac text):

"Come thou holy name of Christ that is above every name.
Come, thou power of the Most High.
Come, charism of the Most High.
Come, compassionate Mother.
Come, communion of the male.
Come, lady revealing hidden secrets.
Come, mother of the seven houses, to rest in the ninth.
Come, elder of the five attributes: mind, thought, reflection, consideration, reason. . . ."

Such syncretism was, of course, banned to orthodox Christians, but combinations of Christian and pagan ideas are frequent in mediaeval magical texts.

5 There were, it seems, always two schools of thought among Christians regarding the nature of Christ. The "extremist" view, a modification of which ultimately prevailed and is that officially taught by the Christian churches today, saw Christ as God absolutely, the Son of God completely equal with the Father (and in the developed trinitarian doctrine, also with the Spirit). The other view, expressed in many different ways by different teachers, saw him as more clearly differentiated from the Father: sometimes as a man superabundantly endowed with divinity; sometimes as a god manifesting himself on earth in a more-or-less real mortal guise, so that he might be either less than fully and perfectly divine, or less than fully and perfectly human. The only view of Christ totally incompatible with pagan thinking was the orthodox trinitarian one, that Christ was perfect God and perfect man, co-equal, co-eternal and "consubstantial" with the Father. Advocates of any other could find parallels for their Christ among the pagan gods and heroes: if any one of them had been accepted by the Christians, the full tragedy of the fourth and fifth centuries might have been avoided. If traditional Christianity had allowed gradation between Father, Son and Spirit, no Platonist, at least, would have shrugged off its doctrine as Critius did Triephon's oath "by God, the great, the holy, the heavenly, the son of the father, the spirit proceeding from the father: one from three and from one three" with the contemptuous,

"You are teaching me a sort of arithmetic I don't know: you're saying one is equal to three and three to one!"

Arius' doctrine, which he first taught at Alexandria around the year 312, was subtle and appealing. The touchstone by which he tested all other doctrinal statements was the deliberately obscure (because tenuous and ill-defined) phrase "there was when he was not", meaning that there was a moment in time or eternity when the Father was alone, a "when" before the Son was begotten. The Father was thus "the supreme and holy god" (as Licinius would have called him) superior in time, or existence, or nature—call it what you will (and whatever you call it, some fourth-century theologian would have disagreed with you)—to the divine Christ, equal to the Father in every respect except this.

Arius and his followers were pupils and admirers of Lucian of Antioch, the martyr honoured at Nicomedia by, among others, Constantine's sister Constantia, Licinius' empress. So, after Licinius' defeat, Arius' views entered the court through the bishops and priests who had admired and sat as disciples at the feet of the martyr. These influential men, "those who were with Lucian" (the *Collucianists*, as Arius himself called them, playing on their emotions as well as their intellects) were bound by loyalty and outlook in united opposition to the party which became known as the *consubstantialists* (because they thought that Christ as the Word of God is "of one substance with" the Father) or the *catholics* (because they claimed the support of the universal church, the faction universally recognised throughout Constantine's western empire as teachers of official doctrine and recipients of official privileges).

Lucian's own views about Christ may be traced back ultimately to the Christian Origen, the pupil of Ammonius Saccas, whose other famous disciples included Longinus of Athens and Plotinus of Rome. Thus although the bond between Arian and pagan thinking might be called tenuous, it was undeniably there: both sides used the same, fundamentally neo-platonist, vocabulary, even when they disagreed as to its true interpretation.

In its finest and most subtle expression, the world Arius presented to his followers was one combining the best of contemporary Platonist philosophy with Christian ethics and a universally-acceptable religion. Moreover, Arius and some of his immediate followers were brilliant propagandists, expressing themselves with lucidity and popular appeal as well as with logical and philosophical genius. To millions within the empire and beyond its borders (for the Arians were successful missionaries) their teaching seemed to express what the ordinary human being felt about the divine nature and the Christ of the gospels and epistles of the New Testament. Although represented to the world by orthodox theologians of a later date as perhaps the greatest of all heretics, Arius was in fact a religious genius whose Christ personified the half-hidden, all but ineffable, yearnings of the masses for a *summus, sanctus deus* whose inner, mystical life was nevertheless interpreted upon earth in intelligible, human form by the life, death and resurrection of the divine Jesus.

Arianism was ultimately destroyed by the extremist consubstantialists, whose "Nicene" creed was so incomprehensible that its exponents were finally compelled to exalt the divine virtue of faith above—and so to put it beyond the reach of—the human virtues of logic, reason and understanding. But the struggle to suppress Arian doctrines and the Arian church occupied the minds of consubstantialists for a period of at least three hundred years. (It is in fact debatable whether all traces of Arianism have been eliminated from the minds of all Christians today; there would appear to be an echo of Arian thought in every grant of especial status by Christians to such non-Christian "heroes" and interpreters of the Divine as Mahommet, Confucius or the Buddha). Most histories of early Christianity devote many pages to the intricacies of the Arian conflict and the later, but closely related, "monophysite" controversy, which arose in the fifth century and was again concerned with the essential nature of Christ. (The monophysites, under the leadership of Patriarch Nestorius of Constantinople, taught that the eternal Christ, reigning in heaven, is wholly divine by nature, his humanity having been absorbed by his divinity as a drop of water is lost in the immensity of the ocean.) The following notes on the developments of the Arian dispute are intended to be no more than pointers indicating important stages in it in so far as they have bearing on the major subject of our present interest, the death of the classical world.

It cannot be indicated in these notes, but should never be forgotten that Arius' was a popular Christianity, not only because he studied to make it so by writing slogans and popular songs for use by his youth sections, workers' councils and ladies' guilds (as we should perhaps call them today) but also because it permitted speculative thinking and pious practices of kinds long suspect to more extreme "catholics". Although in theory teaching among both Arians and Anti-Arians on such matters as the right use of relics and pilgrimage shrines, miracles and martyrs was the same, in practice the Arians were more liberal with regard to them. This made passage from paganism to Arianism easier than from paganism to orthodox Christianity.

(For more orthodox views of Arianism, see J. H. Newman, *Arians of the Fourth Century*; H. A. Gwatkin, *Studies in Arianism*; *Reallexikon fuer Antike und Christentum*, art. *Arius*, and especially the writings of St Athanasius and his orthodox contemporaries).

Ca. 312: Arius, a confessor who had suffered during the persecution, having been ordained deacon by orthodox bishop Peter of Alexandria (died 310) begins to preach popular sermons at Baucalis, a suburb of Alexandria, and so collects a following of devotees of the doctrines and cult of the martyr Lucian of Antioch, killed at Nicomedia at the beginning of that year.

Ca. 318: Arius, condemned by Archbishop Alexander of Alexandria, finds supporters among "those who were with Lucian" now in prominent positions throughout the eastern church.

321: Athanasius, later Arius' most dedicated opponent, made deacon by Archbishop Alexander.

325: Constantine, seeking peace and unity, "the Blessed Tranquillity of the Augustus" in his newly-united empire, himself attends the Council of Nicaea and gives his support to the consubstantialists, being guided to this ruling by the advice of such western theologians as Hosius of Cordoba to the effect that the doctrine of Alexander and Athanasius of Alexandria is that of the western church which had co-operated so loyally with the imperial authorities since 312. Arius and other collucianists threatened with exile and worse.

326: On the death of Alexander, Athanasius is elected Archbishop of Alexandria.

325–37: The Arian Bishops, led by Eusebius of Caesarea (the Historian of the Church) and Eusebius of Nicomedia, both "collucianists", gradually seduce

Constantine from his championship of the consubstantialists, until he is finally baptised an Arian (337) after exiling Athanasius and other consubstantialist bishops, following their condemnation by the Council of Tyre (335) and Arius' own death.

338–9: Constantius, himself under Arian influence, nevertheless permits the return of exiled consubstantialists to their sees. Riots in Alexandria following Athanasius' return in 339: consubstantialist Paul of Constantinople succeeded by Arian Eusebius of Nicomedia immediately upon Constantius' receiving the city as a gift from his consubstantialist brother Constans.

340: Death of Eusebius of Caesarea: exile of Athanasius on charges of having used imperial institutions to further his own ends by, for example, distributing aid for widows and orphans partially. The Arian Pistos (or Pistis) chosen to replace him at Alexandria.

340–1: After at first accepting Pistos' account of events at Alexandria as veracious Pope Julian calls for a council at Antioch to elect a new bishop for Alexandria: Eusebius of Edessa elected, but refuses to serve; Gregory of Cappadocia, another Arian, accepts the position, but after Athanasius has pleaded his own cause at Rome Julius feels obliged to call a synod which reverses the earlier decision of the Roman church. Henceforward, Rome—and the Emperor Constans—remain not only advocates of "Nicene" Christianity but also staunch supporters of the rights of deposed consubstantialist bishops. A second synod at Antioch, however, confirms the appointment of Gregory to Alexandria and Athanasius is prevented from returning there before 341.

341: On the death of Eusebius of Constantinople, the consubstantialist Paul attempts to return to that city, but rioting leads to the appointment as patriarch of another Arian, Macedonius; after fierce and bloody encounters between supporters of the rival factions, Constantius himself confirms the appointment of Macedonius and exiles Paul, who thereafter conducts a vigorous campaign by pamphlet and letter for his reinstatement until his death.

341–361: Arian missionaries enjoy wide success both within the empire and beyond its frontiers, with the result that large areas of the west, notably the Milan archdiocese, become Arian, and such later barbarian leaders as Alaric the Visigoth are brought up in the Arian faith and educated at Arian schools—the first Christian schools established in Europe.

346: The Council of Serdica, one of the many attempts by Constantius to bring unity under the banner of Arianism, or "semi-Arianism" (which attempted, by a careful avoidance of controversial terms, to bring all Christians together under one, somewhat floppy, umbrella): Athanasius among the many obdurately "Nicene" bishops exiled for refusing to accept the creeds of the council.

349: Gregory of Cappadocia murdered at Alexandria; Athanasius returns to the city and is allowed to remain there unmolested until deposed and exiled by Constantius' decree in 356, Constantius having by then been convinced that his successes against Magnentius were due to the aid given to him by Arian martyrs and councils at Arles and Milan having confirmed Arianism as the faith of the church.

357: The Council of Sirmium, Constantius' most determined attempt to unite the church, collapses in deadlock, but mild (semi-) Arianism finds many supporters in the west.

360: The Council of Rimini, a purely western council, accepts the semi-Arian creed of Bishops Valens and Ursacius of Illyricum so that, in Jerome's words, "the world wakes up and wonders at finding itself Arian"; once back home from the council, many of the bishops rethink their position and return to strict orthodoxy.

361: Julian, educated as an Arian Christian, but converted to paganism and indifferent to Christian quarrels, allows the return of all exiled bishops in both east and west. Rioting at Alexandria follows Athanasius' attempt to return there. Again exiled, he withdraws to the desert, to live and teach among the monks and hermits; thereafter they are the chief standard-bearers and assault troops of consubstantialist doctrines in the east.

363 onwards: constant conflict between Arians, semi-Arians and Catholics throughout the reigns of Jovian (who declared for the catholic faith, so permitting the return of Athanasius to his see, in occupation of which he died in 373), Valentinian and Valens. Persecution of eastern "catholics" under Valens from 367 to 378 (under the influence of the Empress Domnica) by exile and the confiscation of their goods. Then, under Gratian and Theodosius, the gradual elimination of Arian influence first in the west (where Auxentius, the last Arian bishop of Milan was succeeded by Ambrose, a Catholic, in 376) and later in the east, where Theodosius imposed on everyone by decree "the Catholic Faith" of the Bishops of Rome and Alexandria before the opening of the Council of Constantinople (381), which made its "Nicene Creed" (as it is now called) the rule of faith for the whole Romano-Christian world. Naturally, individual Arians continued to make trouble. More importantly, the barbarians tribes maintained their Arianism so that Greece was sacked (395–6) in the name of Visigothic Arianism and Vandal Spain, and afterwards, Africa, were spiritually guided by Arian bishops. Moreover, from the 420s onwards, the east was split by the adherents of Nestorius, despite his condemnation by the Council of Antioch of 431 and at later synods. Arianism was eliminated from Vandal Africa only after its reconquest for the Byzantine Empire by the generals of Justinian early in the sixth century and from Spain by the labours of Martin of Braga and his contemporaries early in the seventh.

Nestorian Christianity was carried by eminently heroic missionaries to India and the Far East, where the remnants of this ancient heretical church were still to be found until this present century.

6 "Seek out for me all Iamblichus' writings" the Emperor Julian once wrote to Priscus (*Letters, II*), "and all those by my namesake: for you know I honour Iamblichus for his philosophy and my namesake for his theurgy. And—like Apollodorus—I think the rest are nothing beside these two. . . ."

7 See the relevant chapters in N. H. Baynes, *Constantine the Great and the Christian Church* (Proc. British Academy, 1929). A. H. M. Jones, *Constantine and the Conversion of Europe* (Hodder and Stoughton, 1948).

8 *Cod. Theod.* XVI, x, 1—the first of the laws in that section of the Codex Theodosianus, made under Theodosius II in 438, entitled "On Pagans, Sacrifices and Temples."

9 Constantly, it was private and nocturnal divination which was forbidden —and had been since the days of Augustus. One of the reasons that Pliny the Younger, when governor of Bithynia, was troubled by the early Christians was that they met at night, when conspiracies were generally thought to be hatched. The passage from Minucius Felix in chapter one seems fairly to reflect opinion about those who could not do their business in the daytime.

10 Eusebius, *History*, 10, 8.

11 Victor, *Caesars*, 41, 11. The wave of murders is inexplicable except as the expression of the fears of an aging tyrant. Fabulous tales were later told about Fausta's murder: it may be true that she had been behaving promiscuously with either Crispus (as one suggests) or a stable-boy. But it seems unlikely. The baby of the legitimate family, Constans, was only a few months old.

12 Eusebius, *On the Life of Constantine*, 3, 10.

13 Zosimus, 2, 29.

14 Zosimus saw the dedication of Constantinople as one of the most significant steps in the decline of Rome. Searching the oracles he found only one which seemed to refer to this baleful event. Beginning happily enough, "Soon rule will pass to men dwelling at the seat of Byzas [that is, Byzantium] on Thrice-Blessed Hellespont", it ended, "Soon a great bane will come to birth: a child sowing evil. . . . A huge blane rising on the old man's flanks will swell until bursting it oozes blood" (Zosimus, 3, 27).

15 *De Vit. Const.*, LIV, *passim*.

16 Julian, *Caesars*, Greek text and an English translation in Cave-Wright, *Julian*, vol. 2 (Heinemann, 1913).

17 *De Vit. Const.*, LV.

18 Eusebius of Nicomedia was himself a distant relation of the imperial house, in as much as his niece Basilena was the wife of Constantine's half-brother, Julius Constantius, and mother of the future Emperor Julian.

Paganism under Constantine's sons

When Constantine died, he had been sole ruler of the Roman world for thirteen years and had worn the purple for over thirty, an average lifetime in the crowded towns of his empire. He left a revolution half completed and a tangle of heirs not all of whom were convinced that to have started it had been wise. Worst of all, he left no clear instructions for the future.

Constantius was not at the imperial villa near Nicomedia where his father lost consciouness for the last time, but arrived their either shortly before his death or immediately after it and began to plan for the future with the bishops and eunuchs of the palace. They decided to remove the corpse to Constantinople, where the fact that it was lifeless could be concealed for a time in the pseudo-mystical rituals of the palace.[1] The historians suggest that the deception was maintained for three months, but the truth is rather that for three months the future hung in the balance, while opinions were taken and reactions tested to the proposition that only Constantine's sons should rule. The army apparently welcomed the proposal: "The soldiers . . . all . . . swore . . .", Eusebius afterwards claimed, "to recognise no one but his sons as rulers of the Roman world."[2] We may doubt the force of that "all": it covers some very bitter arguments and a great deal of Christian lobbying, if nothing worse. Constantius and the bishops have never shaken off the suspicion that settled on them during these weeks. Constantine had dictated a will, but the document later produced by the bishops as that testament is certainly a forgery. In it, Constantine is made to warn his sons that his half-brothers, Dalmatius and Julius Constantius, had slowly poisoned him. In fact, no emperor had more loyal relatives.[3]

The funeral, at Constantinople late in the summer, was a triumph for Constantius and diplomacy. Its public element, a display of military power and imperial glory through the streets of the newly-built city, filled every unthinking man with nostalgia for the glorious past—and fixed every thinking man's eye on Constantius, the Master of Ceremonies. The actual interment, at the Church of the Apostles, which the dead emperor had planned as his tomb, reflected Constantine's final religious opinions and the deal that Constantius had made with the bishops. The soldiers and the pagan public were excluded. Only Christians were allowed to see the imperial coffin enclosed in the great catafalque constructed at the top of tall pillars where Constantine was expected to lie, surrounded by alleged relics of all the apostles, until the General Resurrection of the Dead.

The funeral as a whole—military and ecclesiastical—was symbolic of what was to come.

Meanwhile, Rome was claiming the right to bury her erstwhile liberator. His mother, the Empress Helena, and his favourite sister, Licinius' widow Constantia, were already buried there. Some enthusiastic pagans, displaying their loyalty but ignoring all the signs of the times, went so far as to declare Constantine a god, dressing in mourning and displaying the customary banners on their houses depicting the dead ruler in the glory of heaven.[4]

Very soon after the funeral, the killing began. In implementation of the decision that only Constantine's sons should rule, every possible rival to them was eliminated. Hannibalianus the King of Kings, and Dalmatius, the Ceasar on the Danube, were murdered at their frontier stations by their own troops. Then Ablavius, Constantine's Christian Praetorian Prefect to whose infant daughter Constans was betrothed, Dalmatius and Julius Constantius, Constantine's half-brothers, Julius' wife Basilena the niece of Bishop Eusebius of Nicomedia, and Flavius Optatus, a former consul married to Constantine's half-sister Anastasia, were all murdered by judicial process, to be joined in death shortly afterwards by no one could estimate how many more, the majority of them the victims of anonymous denunciations.[5] The terror went on until it seemed to decent people impossible that it should ever stop. What finally ended it was the pressure of public opinion, coupled with the urgent need to establish stable government if the empire was not to fragment. On 9 September 337[6] the three brothers were declared Augusti, but that in itself was not enough. Their spheres of influence had to be fixed and public confidence restored, especially as the Persians were pressing their claims and it was certain that war could not be delayed much beyond the next harvest. So, early in the summer of 338, the three met at Viminacium in Moesia, a Danube fortress lying in the overlap of their chosen areas, to fix the boundaries of the world between them.

The personal qualities of the three were crucial to the outcome of this, their first and also last attempt at fraternal cooperation. Constantius, aged nearly twenty-one, was a strange, twisted character, who was to be haunted for years by the murders he had authorised, a man closely under the influence of the bishops he made his friends, the eunuchs and the women of his court, none of whom could bring him peace of mind.

Constantine II, although usually reckoned the legitimate son of Constantine and Fausta, was Constantius' senior by only seven months. He had worn the purple for thirteen years already, and was a seasoned soldier, but he was no match for Constantius in deviousness; he showed his independence bluntly, by such acts as sheltering at his headquarters in

Gaul exiles from the East, among them Bishop Athanasius of Alexandria, the Arians' sworn enemy, whom his father, Constantine, had exiled for refusing to live in amity with his friends, the Arian bishops. The catholics later remembered Constantine II with gratitude, but whether he ever formally became a Christian himself by baptism is not recorded. The events of his brief life suggest that he was arrogant and lacking in judgement, and that these two shortcomings made his early death inevitable.

Constans, the third brother, had probably not yet passed his fifteenth birthday when he arrived at Viminacium, but he was already showing determination and independence of mind. A baptised Christian, opposed to the Arians supported by Constantius, he quarrelled with his dangerous brother, defying him by offering the shelter of his court to Ablavius' daughter, his affianced bride Olympia, although she was far too young for him to marry yet. He wanted the killing stopped, and it may be assumed that at the conference he said so very clearly.

The course of the discussions between the brothers has not been recorded, but the outcome of the conference was well-publicised. Constantius had to bow to the demand that the murders should end. It was announced that no more anonymous denunciations would be accepted and the Peace of the Emperors was symbolised in a public bonfire of all the unsigned accusations already held by the Quaestor's office, the fact being announced in an edict published throughout the empire.[7]

Then boundaries were drawn, defining the territory each of the brothers was to hold. Constantius naturally absorbed Hannibalianus' Kingdom of Pontus, but Dalmatius Caesar's former holding presented a problem. Eastern Augusti had traditionally maintained a foothold in the West, but Constantius did not want it said that he had profited by Dalmatius' execution (although he had shown no such scruples about confiscating his other victims' property), so he urged that Constans' holding should be extended to include the whole Balkan area, including Constantinople, while he himself held the East and Egypt, and Constantine II, Gaul and the Britains.

With the same aim of promoting stability, it was also agreed—in the face of opposition from Constantius—that all exiled bishops of whatever Christian sect banished during Constantine's reign for refusing to accept his decisions on matters of faith and practice should be permitted to return to their former sees. But this was a bad provision, as no action could be taken to ensure them a peaceful welcome there. The essential prerequisite for peace in the church (and so in the empire) was that factionalism should be ended. Everyone recognised that a doctrinal settlement was the primary need and constant attempts were made to bring the parties together under imperial authority at a council—attempts which the warring Christians continually thwarted by refusing to attend assemblies at which their own parties would not have guaranteed majorities. No compromise was possible, although a formula acceptable to everyone was urgently sought. When such a one was apparently found, it merely provoked the evolution of a new party, that known to church historians as the semi-Arian. The problem was not merely that the leaders of all parties were obstinate men, but also that defeat at a council often also led to exile and loss of property. Furthermore, the imperial brothers were suspicious of one another and divided on the subject of Christianity as upon everything else. Constans, brought up as a Christian from his earliest days, and to a lesser extent Constantine II, were both under the influence of anti-Arian westerners, who thought in Latin. And they both distrusted the thrusting Constantius, whose advisers remained Arian and Greek. . . . Despite the religious and political upheavals of the past forty years, religion and politics were still as inextricably entangled as when Diocletian had published *On Malefactors and Manichees*.

In this conflict, the pagans were largely forgotten—and it would seem that the best of them were content to be so, withdrawing into their own communities and closing their minds to outside influences. Their attitude generally towards Christianity would appear to have been "ignore it and it will go away". But in the end, as we shall see, they were forced reluctantly into revolt.

It is to Constans that there belongs the doubtful honour of having been the first emperor to declare the official religion of the state illegal, although the wording of his edict on the subject makes it appear that he believed that he was following in his father's footsteps:

"Let superstition end [and this] unsoundness of thinking be abolished: whosoever dares to have sacrifices celebrated contrary to the laws of the Divine Prince our Father and to this command of our Clemency shall be justly punished on that ground alone."[8]

The pagans tried to ignore this law, but the Christianisation of the urban masses continued apace both at Rome and elsewhere. The temples were impoverished, and partly (it would appear) from confused thinking and partly from a desire to perpetuate everything apparently in danger of being lost, a few individuals took upon themselves the burden of one priesthood after another, so that from their epitaphs it seems that they must have spent a large part of their lives and their fortunes fulfilling religious obligations. Simpler people merely had themselves baptised as a safeguard and went on as before, often to be buried at last with Charon's penny on their tongues and a cross in their hands.

Constantius celebrated his fifth jubilee in 338 with a month of festivities at Antioch, consecrating a new church on the day his fifth year actually began, 25 December, the feast of Mithras already recognised in Egypt and Italy, but not yet in Syria, as Christmas. At the time, his general standing was very low, but events moved for him, as Constans discovered the disadvantages of having an elder brother in Gaul; Constantine had assumed uninvited the rôle of his mentor and protector, writing laws in both their names and foisting advisers on his junior. Feeling threatened by Constantine's overbearing attitude, Constans decided to take action. He did not want open warfare, probably believing that he would be bound to lose, so to win a breathing-space he asked for Constantius' protection, offering him in payment the turbulent province of Thrace, including, of course, the city of Constantinople. Naturally, Constantius accepted this bribe, although there is no evidence that he actually did anything to pay off the debt it created. Sharing his father's vision of the Constantinople of the future, as soon as he had authority there, he set himself the task of making the city the equal of old Rome in every way, promoting the welfare of the second senate there, granting new tax concessions to residents, appointing a Prefect of the City, and striking new coins showing Constantinople, sometimes with old Rome and sometimes alone, enthroned above the empire.

The wars for which Constantine I had been preparing at the time of his death in 337 did not actually break out until 339. Then Constantius found himself unable to put off any longer action against the rebels of Rome's ally Armenia and their supporters, the Persians. In Armenia he succeeded in restoring the Christian king, but the Mesopotamian campaign was a frustrating affair, setting a pattern followed for years to come: The emperor could always build and man forts on the Tigris. He could never stop the open country between them being devastated by raiders who melted away on the approach of a large force. So the Persian frontier became an open, running sore, constantly draining away the resources of the Empire.

Constantius' was not the only war that year; towards autumn, Constans was called to the Danube frontier, where the tribes were on the move again. While he was in the region, Constantine—untroubled by foreign enemies—persuaded himself that the division of the empire agreed at Viminacium had been unfair to him and demanded that the rich province of Africa should be handed over, to be added with Spain to his own holdings. Constans not unnaturally refused to consider making such a gift, which would have given Constantine control of Rome's corn supply, so Constantine led an army into Italy. By forced marches, recalling his father's in speed and endurance, Constans brought his troops to a confrontation with Constantine's at Aquileia. In a battle about 9 April 340, Constantine was killed and his brother left master of all Western Europe. The imperial corpse was thrown into the River Alsa and an edict promulgated declaring the dead man a public enemy, his acts annulled and his property sequestered. The triumphant Constans was aged seventeen.

The prospects for adolescent emperors were notoriously poor. In the opinion of contemporaries, the next few years ruined Constans' character.

His huge empire was too unwieldy for his inexperience to control (though he spent himself tirelessly, rushing from one place to another personally to oversee action undertaken in his name) and the flattery of place-seekers overwhelmed his innate good sense. To add to his difficulties, the days of quiescent acceptance of Roman rule in the north and west were running out. The tribes of what is now western Russia were under pressure from peoples further east and in their turn were weighing heavily on those of Germany. The Germanic tribes could escape only west and south. When Constantine II died, a major thrust westward by the Franks of the middle Rhine lay only a year in the future: when it came, in the middle of 341, the army of Gaul proved incapable of stemming the flood. Constans tried to bring the invaders to a decisive battle, but failed, probably because their thoughts were not on conquest as such but on settlement. After a year of mopping-up operations which achieved nothing of significance, the emperor made a bargain with the barbarian chiefs under which he granted them what they really wanted, peaceful homes in fertile Gaul; in exchange they accepted him as their overlord. Traditionalists naturally saw this as another step in the decline of Rome—and, from their point of view, worse followed because Constans, himself the child of barbarian parents in their Romano-Greek eyes, found that he enjoyed the company of young men from the tribes better than that of staider Latin counsellors: "his chosen companions were handsome barbarian hostages," Zosimus records, echoing older jaundiced views of events. The emperor frightened Roman opinion and shocked puritanical minds by "allowing them to perpetrate any such misdeeds against his subjects as served him with occasion for sexual depravity".[9] Rich as he was in property, he was always short of cash and took to selling offices in the civil administration in order to raise money for his extravagances.

The troubles of the Christian church dragged on, using time and energy which could have been far more usefully employed. Thoroughly to review all that happened would require a volume in itself. Fundamentally, the struggle was still between the Arians and the consubstantialist "Catholics", but Constantius and, to a lesser degree, Constans were constantly dragged in on one side or the other. The return of exiled bishops to their sees under the terms of the agreement at Viminacium was an expensive mistake. Violence often accompanied it, violence reaching extremes in two of the eastern empire's most important centres, Alexandria and Constantinople.[10]

Month after month, the troubles of the church multiplied. In 343, the western bishops tried to browbeat Constantius into accepting their view of things at a council held at Serdica, attended by both emperors, but nothing significant came of the meeting, perhaps because neither of the brothers was a figure powerful enough to force his opinions on the world. What Libanius later said of Constantius was true of them both: his authority "was a power in name rather than in fact, because the *imperium* was in the hands of others, [the bishops] who had been given charge of his childhood almost from the outset".[11]

Meanwhile, as Christian differences threatened the stability of the empire, the continuing pagans daily lost confidence in their rulers. There was a brief honeymoon between Constans and the leaders of Roman society when he invited to his court the learned Proaeresius, who had won his way to the head of the school of rhetoric at Athens despite the disability of being a Christian. The senate voted Proaeresius a statue and invited him to teach at Rome (an offer which he declined) but Constans frittered away the prestige the friendship of such a man had earned for him by frivolously naming him Master of the Soldiers and showering gifts upon him. Professional military men could see in such behaviour only contempt for their service. Apparently, Proaeresius did nothing to save the situaation but allowed himself to be flattered and spoiled until public admiration turned to disgust at the sight of the 55-year-old professor making a fool of himself with a boy of twenty and a gang of beautiful barbarians. Pagan opinion turned against Proaeresius and, inevitably, hardened against Constans. When at last, in 350, the army rebelled, there were many among the westerners ready to back its choice of a pagan to rule.

The year 346, when the brothers shared the consulship, saw two edicts against pagan worship addressed to the City Prefecture: "To Catulinus, Prefect of the City: Although all superstition is in the course of being utterly rooted out, it is nonetheless our will that temple buildings situated outside city limits should remain intact and undamaged. Moreover, regarding those from which games, circuses or competitions derive their origin, it is not appropriate that those places should be destroyed from which the celebration of privately-endowed spectacles is offered to the Roman people"[12] and "To Taurus, Prefect of the City: It is resolved that temples should instantly be closed in every locality and at every city, the right to enter any forbidden place or perform any forbidden act being denied. For it is our will that all should abstain from sacrifices. If anyone should involve himself in anything at all of this kind, let him fall by the avenging sword. And we decree that the property of those so slain be arrogated to the public fisc. Governors of provinces shall be similarly punished if they fail to punish contraventions."[13]

If these two laws had been instantly and wholeheartedly obeyed, the result would have been an explosion. Not even the "bread-and-circuses" concession in the first of them could have disguised the fact that pagans were from now on to be public enemies. However, later events make it clear that in many places they were ineffectual because they were premature. Priesthoods were officially declared dissolved and the temples were deserted in towns, where local bishops in their capacity as magistrates and local monks in their self-appointed rôles as watch-dogs could raise sufficient forces to compel fulfilment of the law. But country celebrations could not so easily be prevented, and the more "philosophical" pagan religions—Manichaeism, Neoplatonism, and the private mysteries—could not be stopped. Thoughts cannot be vetoed nor silent opinions censored. The great schools of the empire continued to teach from the traditional texts. And a few—like the future emperor Julian—were so sickened by the excesses of some of the men calling themselves Christian that they turned away from Christianity even though it meant surrendering all chance of advancement and even, as time went by, all public respect. Although Latin-speaking Christians since the time of Tertullian had been calling non-Christians *pagani*, applying the soldiers' word for cowards and stay-at-homes to those who would not fight in the army of Christ, the word now doubled its vituperative force; the pagan was henceforward not only a contemptible non-combatant but also—in the other traditional meaning of the word—a rustic, unsophisticated, boorish peasant, to be laughed at for his obstinacy in clinging to old ways his grandfather would have done well to have abandoned. Nowadays the pressure is on everyone to be "liberal": fourth-century propaganda relentlessly proclaimed the view that not to be a Christian was to be ridiculous.

Nevertheless, despite the laws and the ridicule, pagans continued loyally to obey and to serve the empire while they were permitted to do so. The early career of Vettius Agorius Praetextatus illustrates how well Constans was served.

Praetextatus was the son (or perhaps grandson) of that Vettius Rufinus whom Constantine made his first governor of Rome in 315 and rewarded with a consulship in 323. He was a few years senior to Constans, having been born about the year 320. In 340 he married Anconia Fabia Paulina, whose family had been prominent in Roman history since the beginning of recorded time. Praetextatus was rich. In middle life he owned two houses in Rome, one on the Aventine Hill, the other on the Esquiline, and a villa at Baia, the imperially-favoured resort on the bay of Naples. His epitaph records that during his lifetime he was "an augur, high priest of Vesta, high priest of the sun, a member of the venerable Council of Fifteen [originally charged with controlling foreign cults at Rome and guarding the Sibylline books], a priest of Hercules, an initiate of the mysteries of Dionysos and Eleusis, priest and temple guardian in the mystery of Cybele initiated by the taurobolium, and Father in the mystery of Mithras."[14] Some of these honours and duties may have accrued to him in later life, but in his late twenties, his career in public life had already been a meteoric rise through the civilian civil service: first quaestor, then praetor in the City, next Corrector of Tuscany and Umbria and afterwards Consular in Lusitania, an area covering the whole of western Spain and Portugal. At this point, his devotion to the old religion put a stop to his progress and, still only about thirty, he retired to Rome, for the soldiers and pagan senators had endured as much as they could from Constans and there had been a revolt; its outcome had been unhappy, and the new master of the world,

Constantius, had purged the higher offices of the empire of all traditionalists.

The standard of rebellion against Constans was raised first in 349 by soldiers cheering for an officer named Magnentius, a pagan dedicated to the pagan cause. Magnentius was a military Count, commander of the Jovian and Herculian legions first raised by Diocletian. He owed his prominence not to birth, but to favour from Constans and his father. Zosimus emphasises that although greatly praised by later Romans, he was not an estimable man. Little is known of his first attempt to seize power. Apparently Constans was unwilling to take it seriously; he is said to have announced pardons for all those involved in it and to have charmed the soldiers into revoking their call for a change. After this incident, he—not unnaturally, one feels—convinced himself that the feelings of soldiers were not worth taking into consideration: the authorities agree that when trouble recurred, Constans was hated by the soldiers for the "contempt" he had shown for them.[15]

The new plot—hatched while the legions of the bodyguard were in winter quarters in 349–50—was probably much better laid than surviving accounts of it suggest. Its leaders were Count Magnentius, Count Marcellinus, who as *Comes sacrarum largitionum* had control of the all-important treasury, and a certain general Chrestus. There is no direct evidence for saying so, but they may have had the promise of support from Rome before they made a move, and possibly even had contacts among Constantius' officers in the East. Certainly when their revolt was successful they did not lack backing in the West and there was some hesitancy in the East before steps were taken to control them.

The fullest account of the beginning of the rising, Zosimus's story, mentions nothing of this but presents a scene almost farcical in its suggestion of bored officers at a midwinter mess dinner letting themselves be talked into military enormities.

> "The disgruntled officers . . . noted that [Constans] was devoted to the pleasures of hunting. The leadership they relied on was that of Marcellinus the treasury prefect and Magnentius, who had been appointed to command of the Jovians and Herculians . . . Marcellinus talked about celebrating his son's birthday and invited many of the leading men in camp, including Magnentius, to a feast. The party went on till midnight when Magnentius, getting up from the table as though to answer a call of nature and absenting himself briefly from the assembled guests, made a theatrical re-entrance, dressed in imperial costume."

Banging on the tables and stamping their feet, his fellow-generals hailed him as emperor. Nobody thought the idea impossible and the rebellion spread. When Constans and his wild boys rode in from the woods, it was to the news that his camp was being held against him. This time, there was no talking his way out of trouble. No one still looked up to him except the leader of the Franks he had allowed to settle in south-western France. But Franks also helped in hunting him down, and it was in their area that he was trapped, at Castle Helena on the Spanish frontier, and killed by a former Frankish friend.

The rebellion began on 18 January. Within six weeks at the latest, Magnentius was in control at Rome, where he named a new city prefect on Constantine's birthday—the date may have been deliberately chosen—27 February. By early in March, he felt secure enough to travel on to Africa, where he quickly won control of Cyrenaica.

At this point in the story, the family of Constantine roused themselves to avenge Constans—or perhaps merely to take advantage of his death to advance themselves. The first to act was Constans' sister, Constantia, who had once been married to Hannibalianus, the King of Kings. At this time, she was living in Dacia and when news of her brother's death reached her she persuaded Count Vetranio, the Master of Infantry on the Danube frontier, to declare himself Caesar there. In a letter to her surviving brother Constantius she explained that this apparently treasonable action had been necessary to create a buffer state between east and west—although, of course there was no immediate danger that Magnentius, then heading south and west, might strike at Constantinople and Asia. Her motives may have been genuine, but it looks very much as though she was trying to win advantage for herself by using Vetranio's ambition rather than defend the empire of Constantius.

Constantia's success awakened the ambitions of another woman of the family, Eutropia, the great Constantine's half-sister who had represented the family at Rome through marriage to a senator named Popilius Nepotianus. Her husband had died but her son, Flavius Popilius Nepotianus, must have felt unsafe in the city from February onwards and was easily aroused by his mother to act before he was made to suffer. On 3 June he had himself proclaimed Caesar at a town on the edge of the City Prefecture by a motley crew of rebel gladiators, discharged soldiers and malcontents, and marched on Rome. Magnentius' City Prefect hastily organised a home guard against him. Zosimus tells the story: "[The Prefect] . . . armed some plebeians and led them out of the city to do battle with Nepotianus. A sharp encounter followed in which the Romans were routed without much difficulty on account of their lack of experience and military discipline. Seeing them flee, and afraid for the City, the Praetorian Prefect closed the gates. As they were now without an escape route, Nepotianus' soldiers ran them down and slaughtered them all," afterwards, naturally, laying siege to the city itself. A few days later, the garrison surrendered, the Prefect was murdered, and with him hundreds of citizens who would not shout for the Emperor Nepotianus and his mother Eutropia.

Although temporarily successful, the rebellion was ill-conceived and ill-executed. When Marcellinus, now promoted to Master of the Offices, brought a regular army to the relief of the city, Nepotianus was easily captured, a traditionalist senator betraying his whereabouts to the soldiers. He was executed on 30 June, and his death was followed by those of his chief supporters, including that of his mother, the instigator of the whole affair. So Magnentius' rule was restored at Rome and sacrifices of thanksgiving were offered everywhere.

It was not until the late autumn of that same year that Constantius felt free to come and investigate for himself the situation on his western frontier. By then, Magnentius had made himself master of the whole of the West, the temples were re-opened, and it looked to pagan optimists as though the evil dream of the last few years might be over. During the summer both Magnentius and Constantius had sent envoys to the self-styled Caesar Vetrantio. No one knew quite what he intended to do—perhaps not even himself. But from Edessa at the end of the summer's campaigning against the Persians, Constantius sent him a diadem, so apparently recognising his right to call himself an emperor, and on the basis of this gift, Vetranio dismissed the envoys from the West.

Constantius travelled with deliberate slowness to Constantinople. He had a great deal to think about. Could he trust Constantia? Years earlier, he had murdered her husband of a few months, and ever since he had been hounded on the battlefield by the fear of his ghost's revenge—or so Julian said: "he was always careful not to involve himself in skirmishes, for fear of avenging spirits".[16] He had left a deputy on the eastern front and the news was that the deputy was in difficulties, besieged at Nisibis. While he sat thinking at Constantinople, a messenger arrived from Magnentius, warning him not to trust Vetranio and proposing a union of the east and the west against the centre. When he turned this suggestion down, another followed it: Marcellinus, Magnentius' Master of the Offices, travelled by way of Libya and Egypt to offer Constantius leadership of a college of emperors with the title Augustus Maximus and both Magnentius and Vetranio as his juniors. To seal the bargain it was suggested that Magnentius' sister should marry Constantius and Magnentius himself the troublesome Constantia.

The Christian historians claim that a dream from heaven warned Constantius not to accept these proposals, but he may also have been influenced in his decision to some degree by the fact that he had just taken (or perhaps was about to take) a new wife of his own choice. She was the daughter of a man of low rank from Thessalonika. Her name was Eusebia. The new empress was a woman typical of many in her generation. Although she was not a Christian when she first came to prominence, she grew very angry when anyone—even her husband—disagreed with the bishops, whom she viewed with superstitious awe. And the bishops could never have agreed with Constantius' making peace with Magnentius. So the peace-proposals were doomed from the start, and Constantius went on from Constantinople to a confrontation with Vetranio.

Although the Danube provinces had never been a part of Constantius' dominions, Vetranio had given orders that he should be welcomed to Dacia, and himself received him with full honours at Serdica. The two then travelled together in great state to Naissus, where Constantine I had been born. By that time Constantius obviously felt that he had the measure of his sister's Caesar for (again to quote Zosimus) on his own accession day, the feast of the Sun, Mithras and Christ, 25 December, "Vetranio having been deceived by what Constantius had been saying to him, they both appeared on a platform built for the occasion" to address the assembled troops. "Because of his illustrious ancestry, Constantius was accorded the privilege of speaking first. All through his speech he constantly reminded the soldiers of his father's generosity and of the oaths they had sworn always to maintain goodwill towards his son." (Most of those present had never served under Constantine I, dead thirteen years earlier, but the speech was obviously addressed to the senior officers, and the occasion was an emotional one, so such a small point did not matter.) "Simultaneously he insinuated a demand that they ought not to allow Magnentius to go unpunished; Magnentius, the murderer of one of the sons of Constantine, with whom they had laboured through many campaigns and by whom they had been favoured with great rewards. When the soldiers—already primed with liberal donations—heard this, they shouted that Rome must be kept free from bastards, and forthwith stripped Vetranio of his robes and led him off the platform as a private citizen."

For once in his life, Constantius was generous in his judgement of another man's actions. He did not order Vetranio executed, but calling him "father", granted him a pension and sent him to live at Prusa in Bithynia, where he remained for six years until his death. He would probably have done even better to have trusted him as his Caesar, for Constantia had been right in her assessment of the situation: her brother needed a deputy he could trust either to hold the empire together while he fought Magnentius or to undertake that war wholeheartedly for him.

Other problems had not vanished simply because there was a revolt in the empire. Although the Persians were kept busy with the Massagetes on their own eastern frontier, there was no reason to believe that the danger from their brilliant King Sapor was permanently passed. And in the north, the Germanic tribes were restless. Magnentius had already been forced to appoint a kinsman named Magnus Decentius as his Caesar to keep the Rhine safe. Constantius tried to stir up trouble for his rival there, by writing to the tribal chiefs telling them that they could keep whatever they could conquer in Gaul. It was, perhaps, the most dangerous proposal ever made by an emperor. But the tribes were Arian Christians and the Gauls under Magnentius were reverting to paganism. The bishops' advice was that Christian barbarians were to be preferred to pagan citizens. So, while Constantius waited in the east until that frontier was safe, the dangerous letters went out.

He dared not believe that the east was safe until he had found a member of the family to guard it for him. But in fact only two of his kinsmen had survived his murder-squads in 338, the two sons of Julius Constantius, Gallus and Julian. Both had been brought up as virtual prisoners and educated largely with pro-Christian and pro-Constantinian propaganda. Gallus was now twenty-five. All through a very hard winter, which kept everyone inactive, Constantius hesitated. Then in spring he gave Gallus the high-sounding title "brother of the Augustus" and the right to call himself Flavius Claudius Constantius, announcing that he had betrothed him to Constantia, swearing an oath with him that neither would hold the past against the other. Before all this could be arranged, the Persians had turned west and smashed through the Mesopotamiam provinces to lay siege to Syrian Antioch. Gallus' first task was to drive them off. He fulfilled it brilliantly.

In the west, the issue was now clear-cut. Magnentius realised that he was soon to be fighting for his life. Learning that Constantius had bribed the Germans to attack his Caesar Decentius, he offered them even larger payments to stay where they were and withdrew every man possible from Gaul. A special levy of half a year's income from every citizen of the West raised sufficient funds to support the troops. In a surprise move at the end of winter, he brought his army into Pannonia where it forced an unwelcome battle on Constantius' vanguard during the first days of its spring offensive. The eastern forces managed to disengage, but obviously not before they had been severely mauled, for Constantius sent his Prefect to Magnentius with the offer of an honourable settlement: Magnentius could have Gaul and the Britains if he would surrender Italy and Africa. Magnentius' reply was to declare all-out war by seizing the Prefect as a hostage and pushing on eastwards towards Siscia. Constantius claimed a victory at a ford on the Rive Save, but had to pull back nonetheless towards the marshes around Cibalae, where his father had fought Licinius nearly forty years earlier. For the whole summer of 351 the issue was in doubt. Magnentius took Siscia by storm and sacked it, but could not take either Sirmium or Cibalae. In the September, he decided that he must by-pass Cibalae and occupy the Danube valley, and the decisive battle was fought at Mursa on 28 September for control of the valley of the River Drau. Both emperors were present, but neither had anything like his full forces with him. It would appear that neither side expected a major battle that day, and both hesitated to begin, Magnentius because his force was outnumbered two to one and Constantius because he had the Drau on his right and the Danube behind him, leaving him little room for movement. Whether from conviction or bravado, Magnentius had public sacrifices made before the fighting started in the afternoon. The gods, however, did not fight for him. Overwhelmed by weight of numbers, his centre broke almost at the outset and he was able to do no more than save himself as best he could. But his men fought on, especially strongly on the right where his

Master of Cavalry led repeated charges and did terrible damage, continuing the struggle till long after dark. Two-thirds of the western army—twenty-four thousand men—are said to have died that day, while Constantius lost thirty thousand but was left with fifty thousand.

Magnentius never recovered from that defeat. Once he had started retreating, he could not stop. To encourage western cities to close their gates against him, Constantius offered a general amnesty to everyone not directly involved in the death of Constans. Perhaps he even meant the offer when he made it, but when he had power to do as he liked, he did not spare anyone. Fear of his vengeance prolonged the war, but slowly he pushed Magnentius back, till he held only Gaul and the Britains. The pagans felt his vengeance worst of all groups. Valuable men like Praetextatus, realising that there was no future for them while he lived, retired into obscurity if they survived at all. The temples were closed and abandoned, and the laws already in existence reinforced with new edicts such as this sent to Constantius' newly-appointed Prefect at Rome in 353, the year that Magnentius and his Caesar Decentius committed suicide rather than surrender in Gaul: "Let nocturnal sacrifices permitted by the authority of Magnentius be abolished and the impious licence consequent thereupon be done away with."[17] Naturally, as Zosimus puts it, "the whole empire being invested in Constantius alone, his arrogance increased, because he could not cope with good fortune. And there increased also the rôle of the informers. . . ."

A brilliant man in many ways, Constantius was none the less afflicted by a fatal flaw of character, a flaw which showed itself time and again in the cruel killing of any whom he could imagine to represent the slightest threat to his authority. His next notable victim was the Caesar Gallus, his last surviving male relative apart from Julian. Gallus had in fact served him well; not a likeable man, harsh and distant, not at all at ease with human beings, he had nevertheless held the loyalty of the army entrusted to him and kept the eastern frontier safe. While the outcome of Constantius' fight for the West was still in doubt, there were two attempts at rebellion in the East, insignificant in normal circumstances but dangerous in these difficult times. The first occurred among the Isaurians of the Taurus Mountains, a wild inhospitable area where the inhabitants' traditional main source of income was banditry and living standards always sagged below those of the coastlands. The other was in Palestine, where the Jews and other dispossessed peoples found a leader in a man who called himself King Patricius, took Jerusalem and other hill centres, and for months defied an army sent to put them down. Hardly had these affairs been settled in the East, and Constantius himself tightened his hold upon the West, before the whispering campaign against Gallus began. He was a horrible and cruel character, but there is no evidence that he had planned a rebellion. Nevertheless, "informers . . . took as their confederates in wickedness some of the court eunuchs and . . . persuaded [Constantius] that Gallus was discontented and was attempting to clothe himself with the *imperium*. . . . They drove him to plan Gallus' murder, a murder devised by . . . vile men, willing to better themselves through evils of this kind. Lampadius, the Praetorian Prefect, joined them in their plot: he was a man always anxious to be more powerful than anyone else close to the emperor. And in due time Constantius . . . summoned Gallus . . . stripped him of his imperial rank . . . and delivered him to the executioners."[18] The year was 354. And as was usual with Constantius' murders, the Caesar Gallus did not die alone. His friends were dragged into the plot and executed, as also apparently was his wife Constantia.

It was all very well for the emperor to rid himself of rivals in this way but a man in his exposed position needed friends. Constantius had admirers: both the Empress's brothers, Flavius Eusebius and Flavius Hypatius, would do anything for him—except pay taxes, from which they and all the members of her family were excused by a special decree. But she and the emperor had no children, despite all the best efforts of both pagan priests and Christian bishops to interest the supreme god in her problem. Of all the descendants of Constantius Chlorus by both his marriages the only survivors were now Constantius himself, his sister Helena and his cousin Julian.

Eusebia had saved Julian's life when his mother was executed; now she pleaded for his marriage to his cousin and his appointment as Constantius' Caesar and putative heir. As far as anyone knew at that time, Julian was a good Arian Christian, thoroughly cowed by his pious upbringing, a worthy holder of the office of reader in the church to which both he and the dead Gallus had been ordained. So tame did he seem in fact that, when Gallus had been made Brother of the Augustus, he had been allowed to leave his palace-prison and complete his education in Nicomedia and Ephesus. Immediately after Gallus' death, he was called to Milan, from where Constantius was directing operations in the West. The obvious intention was to make him Caesar, but he remained at court for seven months without receiving promotion and was actually on his way back to Nicomedia when his appointment was announced. He assumed the purple on 6 November 355 and was married to Helena a few days later.

As all the world was soon to know, Julian had ideas of his own about both how the empire should be managed and the gods worshipped. But while Constantius lived, it was more than life was worth to express them. In eighteen years as emperor, Constantius had solved none of the problems he had inherited from his father. The Persians still menaced the eastern frontier. The Germanic peoples had recently mounted a massive invasion of the west. During Magnentius' rebellion, the pagans had shown that they were ready to follow any leadership which would halt the despoliation of old Rome. And among their enemies, the Christians, divisions ran deeper than ever: Athanasius was still intriguing to force his way back into Alexandria, Hosius of Cordoba still conspiring with the western bishops to keep Constantius' Arians from gaining influence beyond Macedonia. Riots continued to mar the peace at Constantinople—a terrible one occurred when Constantine's body had to be moved because his Church of the Apostles threatened to collapse—and throughout the empire famine was never more than a harvest-time thunderstorm away.

In 355 the Franks had poured across the Rhine in an unprecedented flood, to be followed a few months later by their cousins the Alamanni. Constantius fought the Franks inconclusively; Julian took on the Alamanni and beat them soundly at Argentorate late in 356. The danger was not thereby averted, but already Constantius had withdrawn from the western command. He had other business, notably at Rome where he was determined to make his supreme authority felt. To prepare the ground, his Empress Eusebia had preceded him there and to their surprise the Romans had found her a very pleasant and openhanded lady, anxious only to please. They fêted her, but did not come to love her husband any better, especially when attempts were made to enforce his most recent law to stamp out paganism: "We envisage that capital punishment will be suffered by those causing sacrifices to be performed or making provision for devotion to idols".[19] It is on record that Constantius greatly admired the treasures of the Forum and the Palatine, but he showed no desire to remain in Rome or to mitigate his decrees against the religion which had inspired so many of them. Instead, he was busy with a new scheme, to reunite all the Christians under a creed of his own—or rather, his bishops'—devising. The great council at which this formula was to be imposed was held at Sirmium that same year. One of those who, after imprisonment and torture it is said, set his name to this essentially Arian creed was the now very aged Hosius of Cordoba, who had guided the great Constantine through the intricacies of African Christianity in 312, stage-managed the Council of Nicaea in 325, and attended synods throughout Constantius' reign in defence of western views, but now in obedience to the emperor signed the formula which became known as "the Blasphemy of Sirmium". The consubstantialist bishops were not, of course, satisfied with this defeat as an end to the struggle, and the last three years of Constantius' life were overshadowed by continuing arguments in the church. During these years, Eusebia's star shone ever brighter, until suddenly it was eclipsed by death. In 358, her husband created a new civil diocese around Nicomedia, naming it Pietas in her honour; in 359, he named her brothers Eusebius and Hypatius consuls; in 360, he freed Thessalonika from taxes because she had been born there. But that year she died, poisoned, it was rumoured, by a medicine she took to make her fertile; with almost indecent haste, as though he knew that his own time was almost run, Constantius married again. His new bride, named Faustina, conceived within months of their marriage, but her daughter, Constantia "Posthuma", was not born until after Constantius' death. He died of a fever at Mopsucrene in Cilicia on 3 November 361, after a futile last hunt for the elusive Persians and while pondering the necessity of a war to destroy Julian. Surprisingly, among the last acts of this great champion of Christianity was to become a Christian himself, having himself baptised by his friend Bishop Euzoius;[20] his last significant act of government was to acknowledge himself defeated in his dream of founding a dynasty by signing the instrument appointing Julian his legal heir.

Julian claimed to have foreseen his death in a vision in which he heard the voice of the Unconquered Sun speaking to him. Zosimus records the verse—for naturally the sun-god spoke in the poetic form used by the most ancient and credible oracles of Phoibos Apollo:

"When Jupiter approaches the wide shores of the Waterman
And Saturn walks in the Virgin's twenty-fifth degree
A horrible, painfilled end will close the sweet life
Of the Lord of all Asia's lands."[21]

There were those who believed that such an oracle was just too convenient and claimed that Julian had plotted his cousin's death by poison. But tradition called for an oracle when an emperor died and Julian, when tradition called, had a wonderful imagination.

Notes

1 Although its approach was apparently blazoned on the heavens: "His death was presaged by a star with a tail of unusual size, which shone for a long time; it was one of the kind the Greeks call comets" (*Eutropius VIII*).

2 *De Vit. Const.*, 4, 68.

3 Philostorgius, *Ecclesiastical History*, 2, 16.

4 *De Vit. Const.*, 4, 69.

5 Zosimus, II, 40.

6 Idatius' Chronicle fixes the date.

7 *Cod. Theod.* IX, 34, 5.

8 *Cod. Theod.* XVI, 10, 2; cf. Sozomen, *Ecclesiastical History*, 3, 17.

9 Zosimus, II, 42.

10 Athanasius, deposed and exiled by Constantine I in 335 returned to Alexandria on 23 November 338. Although as bishop he had no official position in the civil service of the empire (except certain magisterial functions), he immediately set himself to use imperial institutions for his own ends, demanding that government doles of free corn to the needy should be withheld from the widows and orphans of known Arians. Constantius wrote asking him to soften his attitude and at a Synod held at Antioch in the emperor's presence he was condemned and declared deposed, one Pistis or Pistos, a notorious Arian, being elected to replace him. Pistos and others then wrote to Pope Julius at Rome describing Athanasius' crimes so graphically that Julius accepted that he had been rightfully replaced.

Hearing this judgement, Athanasius called a synod of his own supporters at Alexandria which concoted its own account of events, justifying Athanasius and condemning Pistos (Athanasius, *Apologia contra Arianos*, 2ff.). This new account was accepted at Rome as true and found favour with the western emperors so Julius sent two Roman priests to the bishop of Constantinople urging him to summon both Athanasius and Pistos to the imperial court at Antioch to argue the case out before imperial assessors. Julius can scarcely have believed that such a court would find in favour of Athanasius, for not only was the emperor himself an Arian but now that Constantinople was in Constantius' hands, the bishop there was also an Arian. Paul of Constantinople, a consubstantialist, had returned in 338, but riots had greeted his arrival and on taking over the city Constantius had deposed him in favour of Eusebius of Nicomedia, the Arian bishop who had played so large a part in his own advancement and had baptised his father on his deathbed.

A synod was in fact held at Antioch as Julius had requested. Accusations and counter-accusations made a proper assessment of the Alexandrian scene impossible, and after some delay it was announced that the slate would be wiped clean; everyone could start over again, with nothing remembered to his disadvantage. Both Athanasius and Pistos were now declared deposed and the see of Alexandria was offered to another Arian, Eusebius, the bishop of Edessa. He refused the doubtful honour, so Constantius made an appointment by imperial decree, naming as bishop Gregory of Cappadocia.

The riots following the announcement of his promotion at Alexandria were terrifying in their violence. On 19 March 339 Athanasius fled the city. Four days later, Gregory was duly installed as bishop under the protection of the army. Athanasius' followers showed their dissent by burning down the church in which the ceremonies were held, while he himself made his way to Rome to prevail upon Pope Julius to convoke a synod to overturn the previous Roman judgement and condemn Gregory. Constans and Constantine II both accepted the rulings of this western synod, but Constantius unsurprisingly refused to recognise it. The dispute went on for years. In 341, another synod at Antioch confirmed the appointment of Gregory to Alexandria where, his enemies said, he was behaving in an abominable way, even going so far as to dig up one of Athanasius' dead relations to prove from his grave ornaments that he had not been a good Christian.

Later that same year, Eusebius of Constantinople died, while earthquake after earthquake shook the cities of Asia Minor and Syria. Naturally in so superstitious a society the two events were said not to be unconnected: either god or the devil was welcoming his loyal subject home. Hardly had he been buried before the deposed bishop Paul reappeared in the city to a riotous welcome from his backers. The political bishops of the Antiochene synod could not, however, agree to his reinstatement. They reconvened their assembly at Constantinople and elected one Macedonius as successor to Eusebius. Bloody riots were the inevitable consequence. By this time, Constantius was in the middle of that year's campaign against the Persians. When news of the troubles reached him, he despatched Herogenes, his Master of Horse, to the city with orders to restore normal life there and take firm control of all Thrace. Hermogenes was met with stones and curses: his troops dispersed the rioters and drove Bishop Paul out of the city. The only result was a worsening of the trouble. Hermogenes' palaces was burned down and he himself killed, his corpse being dragged ignominiously around the streets. Disturbances continued for many months until at last Constantius himself was forced to give up his other concerns and travel to Constantinople. By the time he arrived, the people had recovered their reason. He was rapturously received and lauded by Bishop Macedonius, now in firm control, while the unfortunate Paul was exiled to Mesopotamia, from where he conducted a bitter campaign for his own reinstatement.

So the troubles of the church dragged on.

11 *In defence of the Temples.*

12 *Cod. Theod.* XVI, 10, 3.

13 *Cod. Theod.* XVI, 10, 4.

14 C.I.L. 6, i, 1799: D. M. Vettius Agorius Praetextatus, auger, pontifex Vestae, pontifex solis, quindecimvir, curialis Herculis, sacratus libero et eleusinis, hierophanta neocorus tauroboliatus, pater patrum.

His wife, Anconia Fabia Paulina, held the religious titles: Sacrata cerveri et eleusinis sacrata apud Eginam Hecatae, tauroboliata, hierophanta.

15 Eutropius X. 9. 3; Zosimus II, 47, 3.

16 Julian, *ad Athen.*, 271.

17 *Cod. Theod.* XVI, 10, 5.

18 The story of Magnentius' revolt, Vetranio's "rebellion" and Gallus' murder is told in Zosimus III.

19 *Cod. Theod.*, XVI, 10, 6.

20 Socrates, *Ecclesiastical History*, II, 47: "While the Emperor Constantius continued to reside at Antioch, Julian the Caesar engaged in battle a vast army of barbarians in Gaul and was victorious over them, so that he became very popular with the soldiers and was proclaimed their emperor. When this became known, the Emperor Constantius was most painfully afflicted by it; he therefore had himself baptised by Euzoius, and immediately prepared to undertake an expedition against Julian. . . ."

21 Zosimus, III, 9.

Julian

To understand the glory and the tragedy of the life of the Emperor Julian it is necessary to go back far beyond the day when the sun-god announced Constantius' death to him, back to the year 337 when, his uncle Constantine having died, his father and mother were both murdered on the orders of his cousin Constantius and he himself was spared because at six he was considered too young to be dangerous. Throughout his life, he hated the memory of his uncle, whom he believed to have been a hypocrite, and feared his cousin, whom he knew to be a murderer.

Historians have generally agreed that Julian was a liar. It is doubtful that he intended to lie, but he had an unwillingness which many will readily understand to curb his vivid imagination with bitter facts. He was a very literate man and although educated in the Christian religion from his earliest days, in later life became a Hellene, the first of all the emperors, apart from his hero Marcus Aurelius, dedicated to making himself a Greek philosopher. And, as every Roman knew, "all Greeks are liars". He wrote a great deal and, despite the claims the critics make against his style, wrote very well about what immediately concerned him. Hence there are two accounts of almost everything that happened to him, his own and his enemies'. Historians have usually preferred that of his enemies.

At the age of six or seven he was given into the care of the eunuch Mardonius, a Goth by race, who had once been his mother's tutor. Although as an adult he had no time for the "male-women" with whom Constantius surrounded himself, he gladly admitted that he owed much to Mardonius and to the masters to whose schools Mardonius sent him for his formal education, Nicocles the grammarian and Hecebolios, a Christian like Proaeresius skilled in rhetoric. Hecebolios tried loyally to fulfil an instruction from Constantius that the boy was not to be taught the myths of the Hellenes, but in fact it was impossible at that time for anyone to be educated without hearing stories of the old gods and heroes. Even the simplest elementary grammars used the ancient names in examples and exercises, and all more advanced studies had their roots in Homer and the later poets, whose references would have been meaningless if the gods they mentioned had remained unexplained.

The instruction in comportment which Mardonius gave to his prince would have satisfied one of the old fathers of Rome concerned for his son's *gravitas*. In later life Julian was laughed at for failing to find pleasure in the common entertainments: in his *Misopogon* ("Beard-Hater") he explained sarcastically to the people of Antioch that it was his tutor who should be blamed: "My tutor taught me to look at the ground going to school. I never saw a theatre until there was more hair on my chin than on my head . . . and then my kinsman ordered my attendance there. . . . It was Mardonius who created in my soul [the gravity] I should otherwise in no way have desired. . . . [What you call] churlishness he called 'decent behaviour', want of good taste 'sobermindedness' and not surrendering to one's desires and so getting one's pleasures 'manliness'.[1]

"He was a barbarian, by the gods and goddesses! A Scythian by race . . . and a eunuch . . . brought in by my grandfather to teach my mother the poems of Homer and Hesiod."[2]

Mardonius' teaching struck a chord in Julian's soul, but left him with none of the fine manners then regarded as essential to a gentleman. By the time he came to assume responsibilities at court, he was a shambling figure of fun to Constantius' courtiers: "None of the beautifyings of these wretches suited me. I did not even walk like them, staring around me and strutting about, but I gazed at the ground as the pedagogue who had brought me up had taught me."[3]

Five years after his education began, Julian was moved from Constantinople to Nicomedia. Now aged about twelve, he must already have been aware of the struggle for the soul of the empire being fought out there. His attention was caught by the circle of those most strongly opposed to Constantius' bishops, the friends of the Antiochene rhetor Libanius, although he was not actually invited to join Libanius' students; he was too young—and perhaps as a princeling too dangerous. "He did not come to my lectures," Libanius himself recalled in his funeral oration for Julian, "although I had for some time been holding classes there, having exchanged one city [Constantinople] for another [Nicomedia], choosing the one offering tranquillity in the place of one swarming with dangers. But by buying copies of my lectures he maintained a constant intercourse with me."[4]

Libanius was eighteen years older than Julian, came from a good family and had been expensively educated first at home, then at Athens. He remembered the first impact of Constantine's Christian nobodies on the East, and he did not like what he remembered. But he was one of those whose delight it was to sit talking with the gods, a pagan gentleman too aware of his duties towards legitimate authority and too immersed in his own learned studies to do more than feebly protest while his world was dismantled about him. During the year that Julian studied at Nicomedia, most of Libanius' greatest works still lay before him; already, however, he was a man of wide influence, so well known that a few years later Constantius would invite him to return to Constantinople and teach at the new university there.

After only a year at Nicomedia, Julian was ordered (together with his brother Gallus, who had been studying at Ephesus) to the Fundus Macellum, an imperial estate in Cappadocia in central Asia Minor. Julian saw this as an exile, imposed by his cousin to check his further development. Whether it was intended to be so or not, Macellum certainly closed around both boys like a prison. Although the estate was on the main road from Constantinople to Antioch, Constantius could—and did—regulate who stayed there. Julian said, "We lived as though on the estate of a stranger, and were watched as though by the Persians." The boys' main complaint was that they had no companions of their own age, but could share their time only with slaves. Constantius' choice of instructors for them favoured bishops and monks; one of their tutors who afterwards became infamous was George of Cappadocia, who was in 356 promoted bishop of Alexandria in succession to Athenasius.

At Macellum, the young princes were baptised—though Constantius himself had not yet been—and were ultimately ordained as church Readers. In his *Against the Galileans*[5] and other later writings Julian gives ample proof of the soundness of his biblical and theological training.

Julian claimed that his early life was miserable, and it was, after all, its impression on him that shaped his future. But it is interesting to compare his reading of it with that made twenty years after his death by a man who had known him well, and come to hate him, Gregory of Nazianzus, who preached two sermons damning his memory without ever once mentioning his name. The emperor Constantius, Gregory claimed, made one big mistake in life: he let Julian survive the massacre of the Flavians. "He committed one mistake unworthy of his ancestral piety, he did not realise that he was training up for Christians an enemy of Christ. In this one thing he did not do well, in showing kindness, saving the life and giving rule to him who was saved and crowned for evil."

"In the first place this man, having been saved by the great Constantius immediately after he had succeeded to his father . . . together with his brother . . . never felt gratitude to God for his escape, nor yet to the emperor through whose agency he had been preserved, but showed himself antagonistic towards both, by conceiving apostasy against the one and rebellion against the other. . . .
[The brothers] were honoured with princely accommodation and education at one of the royal castles, being safeguarded for imperial power by this most humane emperor, as the sole survivors of his family. . . . While they were there, enjoying complete leisure—imperial power still lying in the future for them—they had masters in all branches of learning, their uncle and sovereign causing them to be instructed in complete and regular courses of instruction. They also studied—and even more fully—our own [Christian] philosophy. . . . One of them was sincerely pious—for although he was quick-tempered, his piety was genuine—while the other, waiting his time, concealed his evil character under a mask of goodness. . . . How could [so

great a man as Constantius] show himself so ignorant and thoughtless in this
one respect? . . . But who would not have expected at least to have tamed
[Julian] by the honours lavished on him? . . . In truth, wickedness is a thing
defying all calculation: there is no way to make bad better".[6]

Julian was squeezed by the narrow régime at Macellum from thirteen to
eighteen. It ended only in 351 when Gallus was suddenly summoned to
power. That summer, when the new Brother of the Augustus reached
Constantinople on the road back from Sirmium to his eastern provinces,
Julian left Macellum, apparently without permission, to meet him at the
Bosphorus and accompany him into Asia, riding with him as far as
Nicomedia on the road to Antioch. From then on, the younger prince
seems to have done as he liked. Perhaps Gallus had demanded freedom for
him. He made only a brief stay at Nicomedia, then moved on to beautiful
Pergamum, where he must have revelled in the vast collection of books
in the great library, certainly came to love the hero-god Asclepios, and
made perhaps the most baleful acquaintance of his life, the theurge
Maximus.

There were two sorts of medical practitioners at a centre like Pergamum,
the genuine sons of Asclepios, students of medicine and morbid
psychology, men like Julian's friend Oribasius, worthy of being spoken of
in the same breath as Galen and Hippocrates, and people like Maximus,
whose claimed miracle-cures rival only those of more recent fairground
quacks and charlatans. But Maximus was not entirely a fake; his
scholarship was genuine enough. A pupil of Aedesius, who himself had
studied under Iamblichus, he was one of those brilliant men of whom we
can only say "If only . . .". His influence on Julian was profound and
almost wholly to be deprecated. He fed Julian's imagination with talk of
wonders and omens, magic spells and numbers, helping him to deceive
himself into believing that what he wished really was so—self-deception to
which Julian was, in any case, by nature all too prone.

While Constantius ended Magnentius' revolt and tightened his hold on
the western world, and Gallus loyally if cruelly represented the régime in
the East, Julian enjoyed the happiest days of his life, first at Pergamum,
later in Nicomedia once more, reading, talking, beginning to write,
making himself what he most wanted to be, a philosopher. His idyll ended
suddenly, when Gallus was summoned to Constantius' presence, accused of
treason and executed. At first, Constantius seems to have tried to convince
himself that Julian must have been involved in the alleged plot, but was
finally persuaded that nothing could have been less likely. A new rising in
the West, led by one Silvanus, and an invasion by the Germanic peoples
lent weight to the argument of the Empress Eusebia and others that Julian
would have to be taught to take his place in the power-structure of the
empire. By this time, Maximus had talked Julian into believing that he
ought to want to rule, so when the summons from Constantius arrived in

the late summer of 354, he answered it willingly, though he was by no means sure whether it would lead to his promotion or his death.

It was while on his journey from Nicomedia to Milan that Julian experienced his conversion to paganism. He claimed in a letter to an unknown priest that it happened at New Ilium, the Helleno-Roman city which had grown up on the site of ancient Troy, an evocative place for any romantic spirit. Whether the events he describes actually occurred or were only imaginary is not so important as the effect they exerted on Julian's mind:

"When I was summoned to headquarters by the blessed Constantius . . . getting up [one morning] at first light I reached Ilium from Troas about midmorning. And [Bishop Pegasios] came to meet me and (as I wanted to explore the city—this being my excuse for visiting the temples) to act as my guide, showing me all that there was to be seen. But now—listen to what he said and did! There is a heroön of Hector with a bronze statue set up in a tiny shrine. Standing opposite it, they have a great Achilles in an open court. . . . And I found fires—I might almost say great beacons—burning on the altars and the statue of Hector had been anointed until it glistened. I looked at Pegasios. 'What's this' I said, cautiously testing him to see how he himself thought, 'Do the Ilians sacrifice?'

'Is it at all out of place that they should worship a good man, their fellow citizens, as we [Christians] do the martyrs?' he said.

Now, the analogy was not quite sound, but for the times his attitude was commendable. But, look what came next! 'Let us go over to the shrine of Athena of Ilium,' he said, and led me there with great enthusiasm, to open the temple—and as though proving something—show me all the statues quite undamaged. And he did not behave at all as these ungodly people usually do, sketching the sign on their godless foreheads, or hissing to himself as they do. For the high point of their theology consists in these two things, hissing at the spirits (*daimones*) and sketching the cross on their foreheads."[7]

Pegasios, Julian went on to explain, had deliberately deceived the local Christians by disfiguring the façade of Achilles' tomb in order to preserve from desecration the pagan treasure within.

This incident was important because it awakened in Julian the belief that paganism was far from dead in the world at large. Offered the right leadership—his leadership—it could yet be revived and reinvigorated. His later initiation into the mystery of Mithras at Ephesus, during which he experienced intimate communion with the Undying Sun, was perhaps even more important for his personal development, but for Julian as Leader what happened at New Ilium, so soon after Magnentius' rising, was decisive.

So the prince arrived at Milan filled with secret zeal. Already he affected the philosopher's beard and plain clothing. The Empress alone seems to have understood him. No one else tried to do so. Constantius granted him only one brief interview in six months. The courtiers mocked him: "they set up a mock barbers' shop, cut off my beard, threw a military cloak around me and turned me—as they obviously thought—into a rather comical soldier." Then in the summer of 355 he was suddenly dismissed to Nicomedia, to await orders. He left gladly, but with no sense of need to obey quickly. While he loitered at Sirmium, seeing the sights, fresh orders reached him, redirecting him to Athens, the mother-city of Hellenism, the one place above all he longed to see.

It was from Athens that he travelled to Ephesus and was initiated into the Mithras-cult. Although by his own evidence his personal experience there transformed his inner life, he was depressed by the neglect and decay of the shrines both there and in Greece itself. Nevertheless, Athens was exciting and he made deeper friendships there than he had ever known before. Gregory of Nazianzus, the friend who betrayed him, tried to dissociate himself afterwards from any possible charge of having enjoyed that late summer in Greece, but it is obvious that the whole circle spent a delightful three months as students, talking, arguing, speculating wildly on the whys and wherefores of the world. It is amusing to compare Gregory's description of Julian at this time with Libanius' account of him:

"His character was revealed to some by personal experience and to all by his coming to the throne [Gregory told his congregation] . . . [I have known it] ever since I lived with him at Athens. . . . There was a double reason for this journey, the hypocritical public one of acquainting himself with Greece and that country's schools, and the more secret one, communicated only to a few, of consulting the sacrifices and oracles there upon matters relating to himself. So far back in time did his paganism extend! At that time, I remember, I became not at all a bad judge of his character, though I am far from being very clever in that way. What gave me true insight was the inconsistency of his behaviour and his extreme excitability . . . his neck unsteady . . . his shoulders going up and down like scales . . . his eye rolling . . . his feet restless . . . his nostrils . . . his laughter bursting out unrestrainedly . . . his head nodding . . . his speech stuttering, broken up by his irregular breathing. . . . As soon as I saw these signs, I exclaimed, 'What an evil the Roman world is breeding!' "[8]

The excited student, feverish with intellectual discovery, was not as repulsive—even to Gregory—as Gregory pretended. Libanius wrote, "His reputation spreading in every direction, all those devoted to serving the Muses (and the other gods besides) flocked to him. . . . And when they arrived, they did not find it easy to go away again, for this Siren detained them not only by what he said but also by his natural powers of enchantment. . . ."

At this time, of course, speculation was rife about Julian's future. Gaul had been invaded and soon news came of Silvanus' rising. "The prayer in every sensible mouth," Libanius continued, "was that this youth might be made the director of affairs, to put an end to the pain being suffered by the state. . . . He himself also desired it . . . not out of love of luxury or wealth, or the purple itself, but for the sake of then being able to restore . . . the blessed estate from which man had fallen, both generally and especially with respect to worship of the gods."

Julian knew that he could expect a further communication from his cousin soon, but did not know whether his fate would be to be crowned or killed. There is no wonder that he was tense. When the letter came, in October, it summoned him to present himself immediately at Milan, prepared to assume the highest office in the state, apart from Constantius' own. He was named Caesar on 6 November 355 at Milan and a few days later was given the Augustus' sister Helena as his wife.

His command was to be Gaul. He rode out from Milan to assume it on 1 December accompanied by an immediate bodyguard of three hundred and sixty soldiers whom he personally judged "fit for nothing but to pray". At Turin, he learned that the Franks had broken out from the enclave granted to them on the west bank of the Rhine as a reward for their part in the operations against Magnentius and were ravaging the countryside. When he reached his command headquarters at Vienne, it soon became clear that the Franks were not to be his only enemies. Several members of the high command also showed themselves hostile, and had to be outmanœuvred before the real operations of the year could begin on the date Constantius had ordered, 1 June.

Between mid-356 and late 359, Julian earned himself an undying reputation both as a commander of troops,[9] and an administrator. He secured the Rhine frontier, settling uprooted Franks in Toxandria (N. Belgium), rebuilt the ravaged cities of the north, re-established the corn supply from the granary of southern Britain by building a fleet of armed merchantmen under military control to foil the northern pirates, and through measures curtailing corruption in the civil service and reducing expenses succeeded in cutting taxes by almost three-quarters, from twenty-five to seven *solidi* for each unit of production (*caput, iugum*). But more important than any of this, he won the total allegiance of his soldiers.

By 359 Constantius, on the other hand, felt himself menaced on every side. He had spent a great deal of time and energy in trying to unite the Christians, but had failed. He had devoted many of the summers of his life to trying to end the Persian threat to the East, but recent developments showed that he had failed in that also. It had been necessary to fortify Constantinople itself lest King Sapor's troops should overrun all Syria and Asia Minor to the Bosphorus. Then again, Eusebia was still childless. Whether it was jealousy—as Julian seems to have believed—or the real demands of grand strategy which made him try to milk the western armies of reinforcements at this juncture cannot now be decided. What is certain is that receipt at Paris of the order transferring eastwards no more than two *auxilia* of Celts in the first instance had devastating results.

Julian did not refuse to fulfil his cousin's command. The Celtic horsemen were started on their way. But then another order arrived, demanding several legions, two of which were already fully engaged in Britain, and four others acting as Julian's guard. According to Zosimus,[10] Julian did not refuse his orders. He called a staff conference and explained them to the assembled commanders, leaving the next developments to them. The junior staff officers, the tribunes—colonels—of the legions decided on subversion of the troops as the best safeguard of their own future, circulating pamphlets among their men alleging that "Caesar . . . would soon be exposed to extreme danger because the Emperor was secretly stealing his troops". While the officers worked on their men, Julian wrote to Constantius, telling him the truth, that soldiers recruited from barbarians born east of the Rhine were on local engagements only. Their conditions of service expressly excluded their being deployed *ad partes transalpinas*, in areas beyond the Alps. Then, following up the colonels' action, the chief legal officer suggested that the whole garrison army ought to be reviewed at Paris, so that the Caesar himself could explain why their contracts would have to be broken. At the review, Julian was hailed as Augustus, lifted up on a shield in the barbarian ceremony of coronation and—despite his protests, whether real or for-the-record—forcibly crowned with a standard-bearer's ornate helmet. The next day, he sent each soldier a donation of five gold pieces and a pound of silver, and wrote to Constantius to explain what had happened:

> "He sent legates to explain that the coronation had taken place against his will and better judgement, begging forgiveness for what had happened and going on to say that he was ready to lay aside the diadem and maintain only the rank of Caesar; but Constantius was carried away by anger and arrogance [as Galerius had been in similar circumstances, when auxiliary troops had crowned Constantine at York in 306] and ordered that Julian should revert to private life."

So the die was cast, for the next order to be expected would obviously be one for Julian's arrest. Delaying the moment when he would be forced into open rebellion in order to survive, he wrote to Constantius telling him that he intended himself immediately to bring all possible reinforcements to the East—a message guaranteed to throw Constantius into a panic.

Constantius received news of western developments at Caesarea in Cappadocia on 1 March. His reaction was to despatch his Praetorian Prefect to the west with orders to relieve Julian of his command, impound all his possessions, and replace all his senior officers. Julian received his cousin's legate respectfully, and had the letter he carried containing his orders read to the assembled troops. This tendentious action had the desired effect. Realising that everyone associated in any way with Julian was bound to be considered in some measure a traitor if he was condemned, the troops chose open rebellion and declared him their Augustus once more. But even now Julian seems to have been genuinely hesitant to attack his cousin. He spent the winter of 360–1 at Vienne, celebrating his *quinquennalia* there. It was during these months that his wife Helena died. He sent her body to Rome, where it was buried beside those of Constantine's sister, Licinius' empress Constantia, and his daughter Constantia (Constantina), widow of Hannibalianus and Gallus, in a mausoleum built for the family on the Via Nomentana.[11] Julian did not marry again, nor, it is said, did he ever again mention his dead wife's name.

Just as Julian made no overt move against Constantius in 360, so Constantius made none against him. He waited in Cappadocia, fearing that whichever way he moved he would precipitate an attack on the other front. But he wrote to the chief of the Alamanni suggesting that he should invade Gaul as soon as spring weather permitted, promising him—as he had promised the Franks when bribing them to attack Magnentius—that whatever he could take he could keep. His treachery against the west (for it could only be seen as treachery) was exposed when Julian smashed an Alamannic invasion and captured the leader to whom the offer had been addressed. Even now, however, he refused a decisive march against Constantius. The Alamanni were defeated in May; by July, the western command headquarters had only just reached the Danube when a certain Bishop Epictetus reached Julian from Constantius' court with new proposals, but no promises except that Julian's life would not be forfeit if he retired from the principate. During that summer, Julian's troops quietly took over Italy, while he himself led the occupation of Illyricum. He reached Sirmium on 10 October; the city surrendered and its garrison was ordered to Gaul while Julian pushed on to Constantine's birthplace, Naissus. During his stay there news reached him that Aquileia had rebelled against his newly-appointed commander. He could not afford to leave a rebellion behind him in the West, so he decided to stay at Naissus and await further news, spending the impatient weeks writing propaganda messages to the Greeks in the form of autobiographical letters addressed to the Athenians, Corinthians and Spartans, only the first of which survives. From Naissus, he sent Oribasius the Physician to Delphi, seeking an oracle. The outcome of the embassy is notorious. The glory was long gone from the most famous shrine in the world. The half-crazed priestess living there nevertheless rose to the occasion, with the bitter last utterance of the god:

Tell the king—
Dirt lies heavy on Daidalos' hall:
Phoebus has no cell, nor mantic laurel, nor place to speak.
Even the speaking spring is choked and dead.

Julian would not, could not allow himself to believe it. And he was able to put it out of his mind when a report reached him from the East that Constantius had died on 3 November, naming him as his heir. The rebellion at Aquileia collapsed. The whole West stood firmly behind the new *autocrator*. Julian marched in triumph to Serdica and from there to Constantinople, entering the city on 11 December 361.

The Christians waited in appalled silence for the terror they believed must begin. But almost nothing happened. Some Christians, Gregory of Nazianzus among them, wanted to convince themselves that Julian had plotted Constantius' death: "O, the mad soul!. . . He marches out against the emperor, coming out of the West, under the pretence of excusing his behaviour in assuming the diadem . . . and forcing a passage rather by stealth than force of arms, he draws near to the capital of the empire—impelled into this expedition, his supporters say, by prophecies, the devils promising him revolution at a time soon to come and foreseeing a change of government—or rather, as those who know the truth tell it, acting in accordance with a pre-arranged plot, a secret and deeply laid one, reckoning on a death, a death he himself has contrived, plotting the execution of the crime through someone on the inside."[12]

But the bloodbath the Christians expected did not follow. As Gregory put it, seeking desperately to find something to allege against "the Apostate", "he begrudged to our soldiers the honour of martyrdom—and so contrived to use compulsion without appearing to do so. In order that we might suffer, and yet not win honour as we should, suffering for Christ's sake . . . he attacked our religion in a very villainous and ungenerous way, introducing into his persecution the traps and snares of argument."[13]

As Julian said in his *Misopogon*, excusing his eccentricities, "Perhaps some god made me the way I am!"[14]

There were very few trials and even fewer executions at Constantinople, and none of those who suffered could be made by anyone to look like a martyr. They included the state prosecutor, and Apodemios, head of the infamous *Agentes in rebus*, the secret police, men who had been deeply involved in the plot to secure the execution of Gallus. A third to die was Eusebius, another plotter against Gallus, Constantius' Sacred Chamberlain and evil genius, a man so influential that a Christian once said that Constantius was believed to have some influence with him. Ursulus, the *Comes largitionem*, who had cursed the gods when Julian restored their worship, was also executed, but Florentius, once Praetorian Prefect in Gaul and the bitterest opponent of Julian's success both in war and administration, was condemned in his absence and never pursued. The only other official to die was the *Dux* of Egypt, Artemius, who had persecuted both pagans and non-Arian Christians there.

A few others, like Taurus, Constantius' consul with Florentius in 361, were banished. But most officers were left in their former positions, as long as Julian and his investigators could be convinced that they were worth their salaries. Corruption and waste appalled Julian all his life, and at the palace the two evils had always gone hand in hand. Men (and "male-women") had bought and sold places there, expecting to make profits from such transactions. Now barbers, cooks, beauticians, domestics and hangers-on of all ranks suddenly found themselves out of work. So too did many of Apodemius' secret policemen. The corps of Men of Affairs, *agentes in rebus*, had been founded by Constantine to replace the discredited *frumentarii* of earlier times. They had proved no less corruptible than their predecessors. In fact, corruption had been rife among them. As overseers of the imperial posting service, upon which communications within the empire depended, some of their chief officers had made illicit fortunes out of selling to unauthorised persons warrants offering unlimited free travel. Lesser officers had been running equally lucrative rackets. A specially nauseous one much in favour at this period, according to Libanius, was the blackmailing of Christian leaders famous for their protestations of celibacy. In an ingenious variant of the age-old "badger-game" notorious prostitutes were hired by agents to visit the clergy and seek advice. While the girl and her victim were closeted together, the agent would break in and threaten to denounce the wretched man to his congregation (and their pagan neighbours) unless he paid regularly for silence. To these and similar abuses Julian's reforms put a very sudden end.

It was not all as easy as this reform, of course. In fact, Julian found himself constantly misunderstood. How complicated the results of even the simplest judicial action might be is clear from what happened at Alexandria. The situation there was chaotic. Serapis, the wonder-worker, still had a multitude of followers. Christ, too, had acquired many, though his were divided between catholics and Arians. Bishop Gregory of Cappadocia, an Arian appointed by Constantius, had been murdered in 349 and the troublesome Athanasius, first exiled by Constantine, reinstated in 338, but exiled again within a few months, had returned to rule the Christians undisturbed until 356, when rioting had driven him into hiding and Constantius had appointed another Arian, Julian's tutor, George, once an army contractor and called by his enemies "the Porkbutcher", as bishop in his place.

Very quickly, George had made himself one of the most hated men in Egypt, but supported by the *Dux* Artemius he had felt free to behave as he chose. Determined to leave his mark in the country, he decided to lead an army of Christians to sack the temple of Serapis. There was no shortage of volunteers. Genuine Christians hated the place. Superstitious Christians feared it. And light-fingered citizens, of whatever persuasion, could hope to pick up valuable and rare prizes from its ruins. When the mob arrived at the shrine, it was met by an equal mob ready to defend its inheritance. The attempt made under Constantine to eradicate the worship of Serapis had failed (although Eusebius the historian claimed otherwise) and the Alexandrians were determined that this new attack should fail also. But Bishop George was equally determined: he called on the military for help and Artemius supplied it. The temple was sacked, but not destroyed. The Arians triumphed while Constantius lived.

News of the wholly justified execution at Constantinople of the corrupt and partial Artemius reached Alexandria almost simultaneously with the first copies of edicts by Julian setting all exiled bishops free to return to their native towns (although not, be it noticed, to their former positions), and ordering the restoration of all pagan property stolen during previous reigns. The consequences may easily be imagined. The mobs filled the streets; the pagans demanding the return of temple treasures, the Consubstantialist Christians clamouring for Athanasius' restoration not merely to his city, as the law allowed, but also to the cathedral from which he had been several times expelled, and the Arians protesting both Artemius' execution and the threat of Athanasius' return. If he had reached the city while George the Arian still lived, a general massacre might have resulted. But as it happened the pagans had already killed George by that time, tearing him limb from limb for having dared to bring Artemius and the army into the city to sack their shrine, and at the time of his arrival the shock of their violence had left the city momentarily numb, seemingly unable to react to further provocation.

Julian wrote two letters on the subject of this crime, one to the faithful pagans of Alexandria, the other to Ecdecius, his newly-appointed Prefect in Egypt. Whether Christians lived or died was a matter of indifference to Julian. He would not persecute, but neither would he specially protect them. The murders by pagans were few, and the Christians often provoked them: it is difficult to have sympathy for either George of Alexandria or Marcus of Arethusa, another bishop murdered for trying to incite a riot when pagans built a temple in his city. In neither of Julian's letters to Alexandria did he express any real regret for George's death or propose any punishment for it. Indeed, in his letter to the citizens, he spelled out for them the defence they should use if the case were brought to court:

> "The gods, and the great god Serapis above all, judged it right to make me the ruler of the world. The proper thing for you therefore would be to reserve decisions regarding offenders to me. But perhaps anger and rage have led you astray. . . . Tell me, in Serapis' name! What crimes do you allege against George? Your reply will doubtless be: he aroused the anger of Constantius of Blessed Memory against yourselves, brought an army into your holy city, and its general with it . . . seized the god's most sacred shrine, and stripped it of its statues and offerings and of all the fittings customary in temples. Then when being justly provoked you tried to come to the god's aid, Artemius dared to turn the soldiers on to you . . . so you, in your turn . . . dared to rend a human being in pieces, as a dog tears a wolf. And after all that you are not ashamed to lift to the gods hands still dripping with blood."[15]

He wrote to Ecdesius in an entirely different vein; one revealing of his essential indifference to Christians and their difficulties:

> "Some men have a passion for horses, others for birds, others again for savage animals—but I for books. So grant me this personal favour: let all the

books which once belonged to George be sought out. . . . Let George's slave-secretary be put in charge of this search and give him to understand that if he carries it out faithfully, freedom shall be his reward, but that if he is in any way dishonest in connexion with it, he shall be tortured. I know George's books—most of them, if not precisely all. He lent them to me to copy in Cappadocia, and I returned them to him afterwards.''[16]

It was while the city was still in recoil from the horror of George's death that Athanasius returned. As we have seen, he was a man to whom no one was able to remain indifferent. His partisans would—and did—die for him. The pagans feared him because he made converts from among them. The Arians naturally hated him. Inevitably, as news of his return spread, new rioting ensued. At the beginning of March, Julian felt that for the sake of peace, he would have to exile him yet again.

However, although Julian would not tolerate troublemakers and was indifferent to Christians in the mass, he could accept, and even revere, such Christian advisers as Aetios, his brother Gallus' friend, or the great Basil of Caesarea whose knowledge of classical culture was as wide as anyone's then living. Nevertheless, it seemed to most Christians that he was not unbiased in his dealings with them. The truth is that he himself took his own religion very much to heart and—whether seriously or cynically—expected Christians to live up to their own alleged beliefs and moral code, being always ready to quote at them the texts used by his own childhood teachers to bring him to heel. When he decided to promote only pagans in the army, he reminded Christians that they were forbidden to "take the sword". When Christians protested about his rulings, he reminded them that it was blessed for them to suffer injustice patiently: he was therefore helping them by his injustice to save their souls. It was good for Christianity, he claimed, that he forbade legacies to the church and deprived the bishops of the tax concessions formerly granted them: the gospels preached the value of poverty. If challenged, he could find scriptural grounds for freeing the bishops of the burden so many of them had gladly assumed of operating as magistrates. The Christians called all this persecution; Julian thought he was being tolerant. How it worked in practice is illustrated by events at Bostra in Arabia, where pagans and Christians were about equal in numbers. The two groups did not live peaceably side by side but constantly provoked one another into acts of violence. Bishop Titus of Bostra, fearing that Julian would hold the clergy responsible for any breaches of the peace, wrote to Julian explaining that although Christians had not always been guiltless in the past they were now doing their best to be good citizens because he, their leader, had told them that they must behave themselves. Julian replied with a general letter to the city, dated 1 August 362, outlining his legislation regarding Christians and written in a half-mocking style acceptable, perhaps, among intellectual equals but guaranteed to arouse anger wherever it was misunderstood:

"I should have expected the leaders of the Galileans," the letter began, with an insult which was not an insult (for Jesus' original disciples were Galileans, and it was not insulting to be compared to them—unless you knew your bible well enough to realise that the Galileans were the "pagans" of Palestine, the country bumpkins, as the Acharnians were the boors of Greece),

"I should have expected the leaders of the Galileans to have more gratitude towards me than to my predecessor. For under him most of them were sent into exile, prosecuted and imprisoned. Many of them were actually butchered—as at Samosata and Cyzicus, and in Pamphylia, Bithynia and Galatia. Whereas under me, the opposite has occurred . . . under my laws, the exiled have been restored and the dispossessed repossessed of everything. I do not permit a single one of them to be dragged to the altars against his will—indeed, I have expressly said that if anyone chooses of his own free will to take part in our lustrations and libations, he must first offer sacrifices of purification and prayers of supplication to the gods who avert evil. . . .

Anyway, it is obvious that those led into error by the people called 'clerics' are now in rebellion because their [the clerics'] right to act lawlessly has been taken away. These people, who behave like tyrants, are not satisfied with not being punished for their crimes; they are yearning for the power they had before. No longer able to sit as magistrates and draw up wills, misappropriating other men's inheritances, assigning everything to themselves, they now twitch all the cords of disorder . . . [Christians are dolls in their bishops' hands, therefore] I have determined to publish this edict in all the cities . . . that they must not join in the clerics' feuds, or let themselves be persuaded by them as they like, offering prayers on their own They may meet together as long as they like, offering prayers on their own account just as they are accustomed to do, but from now on they must not consent to join in clerical quarrels. . . ."

It has been pointed out that so far this letter may have originally been a rescript to the empire as a whole, drawing attention to the legislation both already in force and projected regarding Christians. It does not relate directly to the situation at Bostra. References to that situation are restricted to the closing paragraphs, where the general rule that the clergy are to be held responsible for the behaviour of Christian congregations is offered as an invitation to the Bostrans in general to expel Bishop Titus, because he has such power over the Christians that he is above the law; the Christians are behaving decently, in accordance with the law, only because their bishop has told them to do so, whereas decent people "the Hellenes . . . are restrained by *our* commandment that no one is to break the peace anywhere". The argument is valid but much too subtle. Christians could only read it as an injustice and pagans as an invitation to mayhem.

Julian stayed at Christian Constantinople till the summer of 362, then moved his court to once-pagan Antioch, where he hoped to be better understood. It was at Antioch only forty years earlier that Maximin Daia's pagan "church" had been founded by the initiative of Theotecnos in setting up the altar of Zeus the Friend of Man. That altar still existed—or at least, the shrine still stood—for Julian visited it. But the inspiration behind it had all but died. Antioch was a deep disappointment to the little circle of seven who were trying to reverse the rotation of the eternal wheel. It seemed to Julian that the Antiochenes had lost the spirit of religion, and especially of community and communal religious duties. They would not support the temples—but they still enjoyed the orgiastic dances forming part of the ritual of their version of the East Mediterranean cult of the Great Mother and her son-lover; they still celebrated their own birthdays with feastings which had once been part of the religious ceremonies of the day, but would not feast the gods on their anniversaries. Antioch disgusted Julian. And Julian, in his puritanical and pietistic devotion, puzzled, amused and ultimately disgusted the Antiochenes. They lampooned him unmercifully and in reply to their insults he wrote that apology for himself which must forever remain one of the most remarkable self-revelations ever published by a reigning sovereign, the *Beard-hater*, part satire, part plea for understanding, part attack on declared enemies. The few extracts for which space can be spared here must be allowed largely to speak for themselves and for the most unusual man who wrote them:

"The *chi*, you say, never harmed the city, nor yet the *kappa*. What does your riddle mean? . . . I have been told that these letters are the initials of names, pointing to Christ and Constantius. . . . But in one thing Constantius did do you an injustice: he made me Caesar and he let me live. . . . I have angered most—perhaps I should say 'all'—of you: the senate, the middle classes and the people. Indeed, it is perhaps the people who hate me most universally: all of them hate me because they see me cling to the sacred rites of our fathers. The powerful hate me because they cannot now make a lot of money with inflated prices [*Julian had fixed the price of corn during a shortage*]. And you all hate me because of the dances and the theatre. . . . As though the length of my beard were not enough, my head is unkempt also: I am rarely barbered or manicured and my fingers are usually black from the pen. And if you would like to hear a secret: my chest is hairy! . . . I hate the racecourse as debtors hate the marketplace. So I rarely go, except on the feasts of the gods—and then I do not stay all day, as my cousin used to do, and my uncle. . . .

I rarely allow my belly to fill itself with great mounds of food. . . .

[You complain]: 'You always sleep alone at night' . . . and . . . 'the emperor offered sacrifice in the temple of Zeus, and at the temple of Tyche, and went three times to the temple of Demeter' . . . and 'then came the Syrian New Year, and the emperor went to Zeus the Friend. . . . [Why?] There is plenty else to be enjoyed here: men and lovely boys, and lots of dancing girls. . . .'

We came here only seven persons, one of us being a fellow-citizen of your own, a man beloved of Hermes and me, a wonderful wordsmith (*Libanius*)."[17]

The seven were misunderstood, laughed at, despised. But there was, in Julian's opinion, very little for the Antiochenes to be proud about in the way their lives were shaping:

"In what was by your reckoning the tenth month—Loös, I think you call it—there was a traditional festival of the god [Apollo] and you all ought to have been anxious to go to Daphne [his shrine]. I hurried there from Zeus on Mount Kosios, expecting to be able to enjoy there above all places a glimpse of your riches and public-spiritedness. Like a man dreaming, seeing things in his sleep, I pictured the procession to myself: sacrificial animals, libations, dancers for the god in their stations, and the young people of the place pressing around the shrine, their souls adorned in holiness and their bodies dressed in white and splendid clothing. But when I went into the sacred enclosure, I found there not a single grain of incense, not a single beast. For a moment, I was taken aback. Then I thought: I am still outside the sacred area, and that you were all doing me honour, as high priest, waiting for the signal to start from me. But when I enquired what the city planned as an offering to celebrate the annual festival of the god, a priest told me: I have brought a goose from home as the god's offering; the city has made no preparations."[18]

Julian suffered for the shame of Apollo at Daphne and it is difficult not to suffer with him. He believed that he belonged to Apollo, in a very special way. Accepting the legend originated by Constantine's propagandists, that the family was descended from Claudius II, the great Gothicus, he had convinced himself that Constantine had a life-long devotion to Claudius' god, Apollo, and that he himself should match it. Daphne, where Apollo had been worshipped at Antioch, was some five miles from the city centre, and since the reign of Gallus had been famous for the Christian shrine built there to house relics of St Babylas, a bishop of the place who had been martyred during persecutions a century earlier. Arriving at Antioch in June 362, in time to keep the midsummer festival of Adonis there, Julian had sent to Apollo at Daphne asking for an oracle on the future of his reign. No reply had been forthcoming from the god, but the priest had sent to tell the emperor that the nearness of Babylas' corpse had silenced the oracle. Julian sent men to remove the relics to Antioch, destroy the Christian shrine, and rebuild the temple. Julian himself discusses in *Misopogon* what happened next:

"Many of you condemned the newly erected altars of the gods. And when the Corpse of Daphne was expelled . . . some of you handed over the shrine of the god of Daphne to those who were upset about the corpse-pieces, and the rest, whether accidentally or by design, set torches to it. . . ."[19]

Julian did not explicitly claim that the Christians had set the fire. He was well aware that pagans not willing to meet the expense of an imperial foundation might well have been responsible. But Christian writers saw in the burning the hand of God, directed by Saint Babylas.[20]

In the opinion of many Christians, Julian's most overtly anti-Christian act was to forbid Christians to use classical texts in teaching, which meant, in effect, that they were prevented from teaching at all in the public schools of the empire. His argument against allowing Christians to teach was perfectly logical, and ironically was essentially that used against the public schools two generations later by Christian followers of Saint Jerome. But to Christians in 362, it looked most oppressive. He wrote in *Against the Galileans*:

> "If the reading of your scriptures is sufficient for you, why do you make such a fuss about the learning of the Hellenes? . . . It seems to me that you yourselves must be aware of the very different effect of your writings on the intellect compared to ours, and that from studying yours no man could achieve excellence or even ordinary human goodness, whereas from studying ours every man can become better than before. . . . Now—this would give you clear proof: select children from among you and train them up and educate them in your scriptures, and if when they come to manhood they prove to have nobler qualities than slaves, you may believe that I am talking nonsense."[21]

Hellene excellence is not Christian goodness: only Julian's phraseology is exceptionable. In one of his letters, he explained what he meant by education. The definition is still worth pondering.

> "I hold that a proper education results not in a laboriously acquired balance of phrases and language but in a healthy state of mind. . . . And those who profess to teach anything whatsoever ought to be people of upright character and ought not to harbour in their minds opinions irreconcilable with what they publicly proclaim."

Christians ought not therefore to teach the classics in the public schools, because for them to do so is hypocritical:

> "Was it not the gods who revealed all their learning to Homer [and the rest]? . . . I think it is absurd that men who expound the works of these writers should not hold in honour the gods whom the poets themselves used to hold in reverence. . . ."

The teachers should, therefore, either return to the temples or

> "take themselves off to the churches of the Galileans to expound Matthew and Luke, since you Galileans are obeying them when you hold back from the worship of the temples. . . .
> No youngster who wants to go to school should be shut out; naturally, it would be unreasonable to close the best way to boys who still do not know enough to know which way they ought to turn. . . ."[22]

Two Christians, father and son, the younger of them being bishop of Laodicea, took up the challenge offered by their emperor and set themselves to produce school books suitable for use by Christian teachers and children. The father completed an introduction to Greek grammar, and the son was well ahead with versions of the Books of Moses in Greek hexameters and of the gospels and teaching of the apostles in Platonic dialogue, before Julian died and the controversy concerning education was temporarily suspended.

Julian succeeded in embarrassing Christian attempts to subvert the empire, but his own endeavours to rebuild paganism led only to disappointment. The seven at Antioch and such friends of their movement as Praetextatus, who came out of retirement to accept appointment as Proconsul of Achaia, chief civil officer in Julian's beloved Greece, seem to have expected too much too soon.

Moreover, dazzled by Christian successes, Julian made a crippling mistake. He tried to revive Maximin Daia's united pagan "church", albeit in a modified form.

The Christian hierarchical structure, although itself loosely based on that of the pagan empire, was simply not applicable to paganism. The emperor as Pontifex Maximus did not and could not stand in the same relationship to the diverse cults of the empire as the Christian patriarchs did to the various churches of their provinces. Constantine had succeeded (or very nearly so) in making himself the Pontifex Maximus of the Christians in Council at Nicaea and later centuries would create a full pyramid of power within the Christian church, headed by the Emperor Justinian and his successors (under God) in the east, and by the pope in the west. But when the pope became Pontifex Maximus of the western Christians, he did not fulfil functions among them analogous to those performed by the old Pontifex Maximus among pagans. He was expected to "guard the deposit" of doctrine and preserve the unity of Christians. The pagan pontifex never imposed a saving uniformity of doctrine; there was none of the Christian type for him to preserve, guard and impose. Julian's mistake, like Daia's before him, was to try to foster an alien Christian-type unity and uniformity in paganism, primarily by foisting an unnatural power-structure upon it: he tried to construct a uniform paganism, "Hellenism", to present a united front against the army of the soldiers of the saving Christ.

Just how alien to the Roman world this united "paganism" was is indicated by the fact that the Christians had been forced to invent the word designating their opponents as a group. There was no word describing a worshipper of the gods strictly comparable with *Christianus* "a soldier in Christ's legion". No one in the following of the Best and Greatest was accustomed to give orders in the way that the commanders of Christ's troops had from the beginning. The definition of religion given by Porphyry when the battle between pagans and Christians was fiercest contains not a single word suggesting the idea of "binding" or "fulfilling a divine commandment revealed to man" or even of "driving on to a preordained goal" (in Christianity, the establishment of the kingdom or the salvation of souls). It reads:

> "We offer sacrifices to the gods for three reasons: that we may venerate, that we may give thanks, and that we may implore from them things necessary and avert from ourselves things evil."

By attempting to turn the somewhat quietist and generally tolerant company of pagans into a unified fighting force, Julian did great disservice to his cause. Moreover, the pattern chosen for the army of Zeus the Friend was, perhaps, the right pattern for missionary Christianity, but it was wrong for paganism. Following the mistakes made by Maximin Daia before him (as he followed Maximin Daia in worshipping at Zeus the Friend), he took upon himself in his rôle of Pontifex Maximus, as he misinterpreted that rôle, the sole direction of pagan affairs, planning to divide the whole empire into metropolitan areas, each led in its worship by a high priest subject to himself and responsible for all the priests of whatever cult within the bounds of his metropolitan diocese. If this scheme had gone through—and no doubt it would have been forced through, if Julian had lived—the temples would have been supported from general taxation and the high priests would have been made responsible for the administration of what we should now call social welfare services within their areas, distributing benefits under the aegis of the gods. According to Gregory of Nazianzus, Julian's dreams carried him even further than this in imitation of the Christians, to a world where regular communities of pagan monks fought for the true religion of the Helleno-Roman world.[23] The distribution of alms from temples was not unknown. Mortgages at special rates of interest had been arranged by Artemis of Sardis centuries earlier and the temples of Asclepios, Serapis and Isis performed their own variety of good works. But monks were a special expression of the Christian ideal. Although certain groups among the pagans offered superficial parallels, they were only superficial. To have introduced pagan monks meaningful to universal paganism, it would have been necessary first to create that universal paganism—and so distort the essence of Helleno-Roman religion beyond recognition. (It would be possible to argue the case that this is in fact what Christianity did, in creating itself out of a handful of moral precepts cohering around belief in the resurrection of Jesus; but the result was certainly not universal paganism.) Whatever Julian's dreams, practical or not, they were cut short by his death.

There was a sense in which Julian invented the syncretism of which the later pagan world is so often accused. He did not, of course, invent the conception of the supreme god, and his whole-hearted devotion to the temples ran contrary to philosophical trends in generations immediately prior to his own. But he and his friend Maximus were trying to find a popular expression of the philosophical ideal, and had been more deeply influenced by Christian monotheism than they would have believed. Their syncretism seems different in quality from that of a man like Praetextatus; as I have already suggested, Roman pagans like Praetextatus were preserving the religion of their forefathers, accepting offices and duties which but for their acceptance of them would have died, while Julian and Daia before him were experimental syncretists, pressing non-Christian religions together to produce a non-Christian amalgam which could be fed to the masses in the place of Christianity. The religion of the High Priest Athanatos Epitynchanos invented under Maximin Daia and in essence revived by Julian was not the true religion of Greece and Rome.

Julian's personal religion was, however, very genuine, colouring all his thoughts and activities. He may have invented it for himself, out of fragments drawn from the patchwork of the past, but it suited his temperament that he should drive himself to live up to his ideals. He was trying to be a complete man, in the style presented for admiration to Alexander by his tutor Aristotle and later made their ideal by men of the renascence: the philosopher-king, all-wise, all-knowing and if need be all-suffering. It is surprising how close he came to achieving what he aimed at. Whenever determination alone was enough, his success was all but complete. He made himself a good general and a hero to his men. He made himself a skilful polemicist and competent philosopher. What he could not do was either to give himself the judgement he lacked (perhaps in part by nature and certainly by lack of experience) in selecting advisers and fitting his language to his audience, or single-handed, in the brief time available to him, to reverse the current of imperial history. He could enthuse himself, and arouse enthusiasm in his circle, over the Great Mother of Pessinus or Apollo at Daphne; he could not rekindle the ashes in the hearts of the Pessinians or the Antiochenes. Like Marcus Aurelius, for whom he had great admiration and of whom he in some sense imagined himself the reincarnation, he could treat his own desires and appetites harshly in his pursuit of excellence, but it was unrealistic of him to expect the bedmakers and pastrycooks, or even the lawyers and clerks, of the palace immediately to make his goals and satisfactions their own.

Julian stayed at Antioch for about nine months. While he was there, the Persians sent an embassy to him, suing for peace. He sent it away, because peace on the basis of the existing frontiers would have meant leaving in Persian hands territories in Mesopotamia which had once been Roman. The army marched out of Antioch on 5 March. Julian, not yet thirty-one, had three months and a few days to live.[24]

From the memorials of him left by his admirers, it is possible to know where he was almost every day of those three months. There were two possible approaches to the Persian capital at Ctesiphon, from the south and from the north. An attack from west to east direct was judged bound to be slowed down excessively by the distance and difficulty of the terrain. By the southern route, Julian could expect help from the river-system, and a fleet of transports built on the orders of Constantius' commander in the area, but never yet effectively deployed against the enemy. In the north, he could hope to find allies among the Armenians, to whom the Persians were a continual threat. For ten days, until the army had crossed the Euphrates, Julian pondered the problem. From 14 to 16 March, the army rested at Carrhae, while pagans in the force joined their emperor in celebrating the spring festival of the moon. There, before the altar, Julian is said to have given the purple to a cousin on his mother's side named Procopius, appointing him to command a northern wing of the army while he himself marched south to the confluence of the Euphrates with the Tigris. In normal practice, this ceremony would have made Procopius Julian's heir and Caesar, but no witnesses were permitted to be present, and when the northern army marched, Procopius went with it merely as its commander-in-chief.

Julian's southern army reached Callinicum on 21 March, and remained there for a week. It was at Callinicum that the fleet was anchored, and the town had been appointed as the mustering-point for Saracen mercenaries. Julian kept the feast of the Mother there with great solemnity on 27 March. Early in April, marching overland, while the fleet made the two sides of the triangle of the confluence, the army crossed the old frontier of Persia near Zaitha, and Julian caused a search to be made for the grave of his predecessor, the Emperor Gordian III, who had been murdered and hastily buried there by partisans of his own Praetorian Prefect Philip "the Arab" a hundred and nineteen years earlier, a murder which had led to a shameful, hurried peace. A week's hard march from Zaitha brought the army back to the river again at Phathusa, and the first real battle of the war, a battle won by skilful deployment of land and water-borne forces. From Phathusa onwards every place was heavily fortified and bitterly defended by men familiar with the bewildering mixture of canals and mudflats that made up the terrain. Many of the defensive lines along the waterways so effectively used by the Persians had originally been the work of Roman engineers, employed in this frontier area (as it had then been) during the reigns of Hadrian and Septimius Severus. The army's first major objective was Seleucia; its second, the Tigris and Ctesiphon. Seleucia, built six hundred years earlier by Seleucus I as the capital of his empire, had been the most eastern outpost of Hellenism until the Romans themselves had been forced to destroy it, as a focus of revolt, in A.D. 164: when Julian reached it, the city was still a ruin, but the fortresses ringing it had been repaired, and the area was bitterly contested. To Julian, it was a great triumph to watch it day by day become Hellene once again.

Despite the stubbornness of the resistance, the Tigris was reached at Coche before the end of May. Coche and Ctesiphon faced one another across the waterway: so near did total victory seem when Julian celebrated birthday games in honour of his *genius* after the army had rested there for a week. The next day, legionaries were ferried across the waterway under continual fire from the enemy defences, and as parties of men landed they found themselves immediately sucked into a bloody and exhausting fight. The battle lasted from noon till well into the following day. The walls were not breached, but early in the afternoon an embassy arrived at Julian's headquarters with an offer to negotiate peace-terms. Julian refused to discuss surrender with it: he wanted total victory. But it was obvious that his men had done all they could that day. The engagement was broken off, and from that time on difficulties began to multiply. In a sense, Julian's military ambition killed him.

There was no news of Procopius' force, daily expected from the north. Provisions were running short and the boats had to be burned to forestall attempts at desertion. For a week, Julian hesitated; then he ordered that the army should march north to meet Procopius. It was no retreat into comparative safety, for the country was strongly defended, but it was a deliberate turning away from the decisive battle. The Persian king mounted a pursuit and brought Julian's army to bay at Tumarra on the Tigris during the third week in June. For five days (17–21 June) there was heavy fighting every day, with neither side gaining a decisive advantage, so that when on the evening of 21 June Julian's envoys called for a truce, the Persians did not hesitate to grant it. There was no more fighting until 25 June, when there was a bitter encounter at Maranga, which once more brought the Persians to the point of suing for terms. That night, the last of Julian's life, he was a happy man. He believed that he was in close communion with his god, who promised him undying renown, although at terrible personal cost. What happened next morning was never properly explained. A fight began early, with skirmishing near Julian's tent. He joined the battle, to share his soldiers' hardships, as he always had been anxious to do since the earliest days in Gaul. Perhaps because the day was so hot, or perhaps because the fighting was so close, he did not wear full body armour, although he did carry a shield. While riding in the skirmish, he was wounded by a javelin in the right arm and side. He managed to remain in the saddle for some time, but ultimately collapsed and had to be carried to his tent on a shield. The point of the weapon had smashed through his liver and everyone, including Julian himself, realised that he could not survive the wound. He spent most of the afternoon and evening talking with his philosopher friends Maximus and Priscus, and died shortly before midnight without having nominated his successor.

Ever since, the world has asked, who threw the fatal javelin? The only thing that seems fairly certain was that it was not a Persian, although to have been able to believe that would have been the most comfortable conclusion for everyone. The Christian historian Socrates, writing about eighty years later, summed up the prevailing uncertainty:

"A dart thrown by some unknown person pierced his arm through and entered his side, wounding him there. It was as a result of this wound that he died. Some say that a Persian hurled this javelin and then made good his escape; others assert that the deed was done by one of his own men, and this is in fact the corroborated and most generally accepted story. But Callistus, one of his bodyguards, who commemorated this emperor's acts in heroic verse, says in his account of the details of this war that his mortal wound was inflicted by a *daimon*, a being from the spirit world. This may be merely a poetic fiction, but perhaps it was the genuine fact, for many have undoubtedly been brought down by avenging Furies."[25]

At the time, Libanius believed that the avenging fury was a Christian. In the fifth century, the Christian Sozomen accepted that view: "Libanius clearly states that the emperor fell by the hand of a Christian, and this probably was the truth."[26] Libanius' account of his death, in the funeral oration he composed for his hero, is very long and full; when he wrote it, the Christians were already again in the ascendency, and it was daring of him to go so far as to say:

"Those persons to whom his existence was of no advantage—the people that is who did not live according to the laws—had previously plotted against him: now, seizing their moment, they effected their purpose, their natural wickedness impelling them to it, wickedness which under his rule had had no opportunity of exercising itself."

Libanius was no soldier, and his description of the skirmish in which Julian was mortally wounded is about as far removed from a battle-report as any such account could be: his interest, however, is not in military precision but in proving that Julian died like a hero and a philosopher.

"I must speak out and put an end to the false reports circulating with regard to his end. When the Persians were already reduced to despair, having clearly been defeated . . . a part of the army was cut off from the rest . . . The emperor hurried up with a single bodyguard to redress the broken line. And a horseman's spear thrown at him—he being without armour—pierced his arm and penetrated his side. The hero fell. . . . And so he is carried back to his tent, to the black bed, the lion-skin, the palliasse which is all his bed consists of. The surgeon says that there is no hope. The army . . . groans . . . and when all around him have fallen to weeping, not even the sophists present being able to control their feelings, he rebukes them all, but the sophists more than the rest, because 'the life he has led till now is about to bring him to the Islands of the Blessed, but they are weeping as though he had so lived as to deserve Tartarus'. The scene was like that in Socrates' prison cell: those there were like those with the philosopher; the wound was equivalent to the cup of poison; the words, to his words . . . but when his friends urged him to name a successor . . . he referred the election to the army."[27]

Not unnaturally, the sophists told many edifying tales about Julian's death-bed conversation. One that proved specially persistent and may have some basis in fact was that Julian had an intuition that his own death and a Roman victory were somehow bound up together; he would have to die for the people, like a saviour-god. In Libanius' *In Defence of the Temples*, written about 386, there is an echo of this prophecy: "Having learned from [the gods] that once he had humbled the pride of the Persians he would soon die, he bought glory at the price of his life . . . he delighted, therefore, in his wound, gazing joyfully upon it, asking those who were weeping if his lot was not preferable to growing old. . . ."[28]

The oracle itself is allegedly preserved in one fanciful life of Julian:

> "But when you have subjected the race of the Persians to your sceptre, pushing them back with your sword beyond Seleucia, a chariot of fire will carry you up to Olympus."[29]

So died Julian: a sacrifice to the gods, the victim of an avenging fury, the casualty of a brilliant Persian skirmisher's opportunism or a Christian assassin's courage—who killed him, and for what end, did not really matter. What mattered to both pagans and Christians was that at only thirty-one he was dead.

When Julian died, Procopius' northern army was no more than a few days' march away from the main southern group. The council of officers which had the task of appointing a new emperor was agreed that he must not be allowed to assume the purple. The argument as to who should be chosen to do so was fierce. During 26 June the staff split along predictable lines, on the one side Julian's friends, led by the Franks Nevitta (who had been consul the previous year) and Dagalaiphus, and on the other the left-overs from the reign of Constantius, determined as soon as possible to reverse the course events had taken since Julian's accession.[30] If the military situation had not been so precarious the quarrel might have become murderous, but the needs of the moment overruled long-term considerations. On the morning of 27 June, the imperium was offered to Sallustius, the most senior officer among the front-line troops, who had enjoyed a distinguished career before Julian had made him successively his Praetorian Prefect in Gaul and then Prefect of the East. "All unanimously agreed upon Sallustius", Ammianus recalled. If he had accepted the power so offered to him, the fate of the army he commanded under the emperor might have been different, but "he pleaded ill health and old age" and when his excuses were accepted (probably with relief among the old followers of Constantius), the fate of the army and the eastern provinces was sealed by the sudden switch of opinion to the "safe" compromise candidate, the keeper of the great seal, the *Primicerius* Jovian.

The sad task of burying Julian's body was entrusted to his cousin Procopius. Julian's wishes regarding his funeral—that he should be buried at Tarsus, in the midst of his mother's family—were acceded to.[31] No doubt there were those in Jovian's confidence who advised that Procopius should be killed, so that he could pose no threat for the future. But he disarmed his enemies by welcoming Jovian's election and proposing, once the funeral rites had been properly performed, to retire into private life.

"The army as a whole," Zosimus claims, with an understandable exaggeration, "followed in attendance upon Julian's corpse, which was transported to Cilicia and consigned to a royal sepulchre in a suburb of Tarsus. The following inscription was carved upon the tomb:

> "Here lies Julian, coming from swift-flowing Tigris: Just ruler and mighty warrior alike."[32]

It is to Jovian's credit that on a brief visit to Tarsus shortly afterwards he gave instructions that the tomb should be decorated as befitted the memorial to an emperor, but there were those who felt that even so not enough honour had been done to the philosopher-king. Ammianus the soldier-historian was among them: the tomb, he wrote, "was placed in the suburb on the road leading to the passes through Mount Taurus. But a sounder decision would have been that the remains of so great a prince ought not to lie within sight of the Cydnus, beautiful and clear though that river may be. To perpetuate the glory of what he achieved they ought rather to be placed where the Tiber would wash by them as it passes through the eternal city, winding around the monuments of the ancestral gods."[33]

The historian Eutropius, Julian's younger contemporary, and himself a pagan, says that "he was enrolled among the gods". Certainly, the Christians thought that he was a fitting companion to the devil Zeus in hell. Partisan though Eutropius was, however, his analysis of Julian's character is among the most perspicacious ever made in so few words:

> "He was a remarkable man and would have ruled the empire with honour if the Fates had but permitted it. He was eminent in the liberal arts, but much the better read in the literature of the Hellenes, so much so indeed that his Latin learning was by no means comparable to his Greek. He spoke very freely and skilfully and had the most tenacious memory. He was in some respects more a philosopher than a prince. He was open-handed with his friends, but not as discriminating in choosing subjects for his generosity as would have been fitting in so great a ruler: He was very just in his dealings with the people of the provinces, remitting their taxes as far as that was practicable. He was indulgent towards others, but not himself greatly interested in the contents of the public treasury. However, he was a great lover of glory and demonstrated a longing for it verging on intemperance. He was a persecutor of the Christian religion, but one who held back from shedding blood. He was not unlike Marcus Aurelius, whom in fact he did study to emulate."[34]

> "Such was the prince who rebuilt the temples, the author of deeds stronger than oblivion, himself more powerful than oblivion."[35]

Notes

1 Julian, *Misopogon*, f. 351; there is an English version of *Misopogon* with the Greek text in Cave-Wright's edition of Julian's works (Heinemann, 1913). The numbering here is from that edition.

2 *Misopogon*, f. 352.

3 Julian, *To the Athenians*, 174f.; Cave-Wright, *Julian: Works* (Heinemann, 1913).

4 There is a translation of Libanius' *Oration* at Julian's funeral in C. W. King, *Julian the Emperor* (Bell, London, 1888).

5 No complete text of *Against the Galileans* survives. Reconstructions of parts of it are possible from the works of later historians.

6 Gregory of Nazianzus, *Invective against Julian*, I, 3, 21, 22, 24, 35, 42. Gregory's two sermons against Julian are translated in C. W. King, *op. cit.*

7 Julian, *Letters*, 19; Greek text and translation in Cave-Wright, *op. cit.* If Julian is not merely being insulting here about whispered prayers, the phrase "hissing at the spirits" defines a recognised method of dispelling them not otherwise attested.

8 Gregory of Nazianzus, *Invective against Julian*, II, 23f.

9 Even his enemies admitted his enviable reputation as a commander. So Socrates, *Ecclesiastical History*, 2, 47: "Julian Caesar engaged with an immense army of barbarians in Gaul and gained a victory over them, so that he became very popular with the soldiers. . . ."

10 Zosimus, III, 9.

11 In A.D. 1275, this mausoleum was converted into the church of Santa Costanza. Some of the sarcophagi from it are preserved in the Vatican Galleries.

12 Gregory of Nazianzus, *Invective against Julian*, I, 42, 46.

13 Gregory of Nazianzus, *Invective against Julian*, I, 58, 61.

14 *Misopogon*, f. 346.

15 *Letters*, 21.

16 *Letters*, 23.

17 *Misopogon*, 357, 337, 340, 346, 354. The seven at Antioch were Julian himself, Libanius, Maximus, Priscus, Himerius, Oribasius and either Eusebius of Myndos or Chrysanthius of Sardis, both of whom he had met at Pergamum.

18 *Misopogon*, 362.

19 *Misopogon*, 361. cf. John Chrysostom, *De S. Babylas et Castra Julianum* and Libanius, *Oration on Apollo's Shrine at Daphne*.

20 A similar superstitious reaction to a sudden fire put an end to Julian's plan for rebuilding the temple of Jerusalem—an undertaking planned less to placate the Jews than anger the Christians.

21 *Against the Galileans*, f. 229f.

22 *Letters*, 36.

23 The Manichees—if their enemies are to be believed—ultimately succeeded in building a "church" paralleling in many particulars the western catholic church of the high middle ages: it was against this body that the Albigensian Crusade was preached.

24 The story of Julian's Persian Expedition is told in Ammianus Marcellinus' *Roman History*, Libanius, *Funeral Oration* and Zosimus' *Historia Nova*.

25 Socrates Scholasticus, *Ecclesiastical History*, III, 21.

26 Sozomen, *Ecclesiastical History*, VI, 2.

27 There is a translation of Libanius' *Funeral Oration for the Emperor Julian*, Oration 17 (together with Gregory of Nazianzus' two Invectives and Julian's own studies of the Sun and the Mother of the Gods) in C. W. King, *op. cit.*

28 The whole passage reads: ". . . the prince who once reigned and would have overcome the Persian Empire if treachery had not put an end to his plans. He is still great after his death. If, like Achilles, he died by treachery, his exploits before his death are remembered with honour—again like those of Achilles. This destiny was a gift to him from the gods whose temples he rebuilt, whose honours he restored, with their sacred enclosures, their altars, their blood. Having learned from them that once he had humbled the pride of the Persians he would soon die, he bought glory at the price of his life, taking many town, reducing large areas of country, taking the fight to those who had been hunting him, and finally dying—as everyone knows—on the eve of receiving a deputation bringing him the submission of his foes. He delighted therefore in his wound, gazing joyfully upon it, asking those who were weeping if his lot was not preferable to growing old"—*In Defence of the Temples*, 40–41.

29 Quoted in Suidas, *Julian*.

30 Ammianus, 25, 5, text and translation in Yonge: *The Roman History of Ammianus Marcellinus*, in Bohn's Classical Library, 1848.

31 After Nisibis had been surrendered "when the citizens had been withdrawn and the city surrendered, and the tribune Constantius had been sent to deliver up to the Persian nobles the fortresses and areas agreed upon, Procopius was sent on ahead with Julian's remains, to bury them in the suburbs of Tarsus, according to the directions he had given when alive"—Ammianus 25,9.

32 Zosimus, III, 34. The second line was a favourite quotation of Julian's.

33 Ammianus, 25, 10.

34 Eutropius, X, 6.

35 Libanius, *Defence of the Temples*, 41; the whole physical world, Libanius claimed, mourned Julian's passing:

"Earth has fittingly mourned her hero by shearing off her curls: many cities in Palestine, every single one in Libya, the biggest towns of Sicily lie flat, and all those of Greece but one; beautiful Nicaea lies in ruins. . . ."

The Soul of Rome

Roman historians found it difficult to praise Jovian for anything, though they found his blue eyes, great height and prodigious gluttony worthy of remark. Christians admired him for the steadfastness of his faith, but their admiration was probably misplaced: as he ruled less than eight months, his true character was hardly tested.

Details are lost of the intrigues he undertook to persuade the fighting men to elect him as Julian's successor. The throne he inherited was an unenviable one. Ammianus, who fought in that Persian campaign, alleges that King Sapor was apprised of his election by a traitor almost as soon as it had occurred. The divisions in the Roman army were such that the frightened informer dared not even wait to see what a Roman future held for him. The Persian king immediately understood that Julian's death meant more to him than any victory could have done, and from being the suppliant for terms he became the dictator of them, despite the fact that an ill-prepared attack with elephants on the Roman camp was beaten off. But although Sapor realised that Julian's death had changed everything, it is doubtful whether he guessed just how desperate Jovian felt his position to be. When Jovian sued for peace, the terms offered were not so immoderate as to cause him any perceptible hesitation over accepting them.

The peace Jovian made was a shameful one. In exchange for the right of unmolested retreat beyond the Euphrates and the promise of thirty years' truce, he guaranteed to surrender the five Mesopotamian provinces to the Persians, withdrawing the population from the cities and handing them over empty, ready for occupation. He also promised to refuse further support to Rome's ally, Armenia. Libanius claims that there were those ready to support him in his acceptance of the treaty: "There was many a one then at hand to persuade the prince of the Romans that what would remain [his] would be plenty for him to rule over, plenty for luxury, drunkenness and gluttony." It would be difficult to be more scathingly sarcastic about a man and his motives. These were in fact Jovian's failings, but it was not simply weakness of character which led him to surrender so much. He was a politician as well as a soldier, and must have been acutely aware of the dangers threatening his survival. Julian's Gauls and Franks were still with the army. Procopius' reaction to the election was still not known. None of the great cities of the empire had yet acquiesced in the army's choice of ruler. There was no absolute guarantee that even after a long siege the army could take Ctesiphon now that Sapor had found new courage. Supplies were short. Revolt was so easy. With Julian's corpse still in the camp, no one could not be excused for remembering where the paths of glory so often lead.

Jovian—Flavius Jovianus—was the son of a Pannonian who had risen to be Count of the Household (*Comes domesticorum*) under Constantius and was held in high regard by those who revered Constantius' memory. The father did not long survive his son's promotion. Jovian himself was married to the daughter of Lucillianus, Constantius' Master of Cavalry, and in 361, as Protector of the Household, chief of the bodyguard, had been in charge of the preparations for Constantius' funeral. Julian had appointed him Keeper of the Seal (*Primicerius*). It is said of him that one of his first actions after his election was to send to the soldiers, along with the promise of the customary donation, an order that they should be good Christians. It is also said that he had sacrifices made and the entrails read for auguries of his reign. Both stories may well be true. Like Constantine before him—and unlike Julian—he may well have wanted to cover himself in all directions. Despite the Christian authors' praise of him, it is doubtful if he had any deep convictions at all.

The retreat from the Tigris was a disaster. The Persians had promised only a cessation of warfare, and they did nothing to relieve Roman shortages. Nor, once the cities on the route realised that they were to be surrendered to the Persians, were their citizens willing to extend themselves to succour the army. That summer and autumn must have been a time of horrible bitterness and despair. Men abandoned not only their equipment but also their comrades in the flight. Zosimus says that a man who ended the journey having saved as much as a pair of boots was a hero. Nisibis, so stubbornly defended by Lucillianus and his cavalrymen, and Carrhae, were among the cities to be abandoned to the enemy. It is not surprising that the Carrhean mob threw the man unfortunate enough to carry the news to them down a well and heaped stones upon his body.[1] When in October the retreating emperor reached Antioch, to announce in the circus that he had won a victory, the ensuing riot spilled over into the streets of the city, and the court was compelled to withdraw to Edessa.

It was at Edessa that the Christian bishops caught up with Jovian. "The bishops now renewed their agitation," Sozomen recorded. "During the reign of Julian, they had been quiet . . . but now a council was called at Antioch in Syria and . . . when it was over, they wrote to the emperor."[2] Athanasius of Alexandria, knowing that a synod at Antioch could not speak favourably of him, called on Jovian in person and so won restoration to his see. But Jovian—although the consubstantialists claimed him as their champion—sensibly refused to decide between the various sorts of Christian and issued a law (no copy of which has survived) promising toleration to all religions, forbidding only the practice of magic and fortune telling; on the basis of this law the neoplatonist theurges were afterwards persecuted, Julian's friend Maximus being the first of them to die, but in 363 not even the gifts that Julian had made to the temples were rescinded, and certainly no action was taken to revive Constantius' threat of execution to anyone offering sacrifice.

The autumn and early winter put great strain on Jovian. No one wanted to have to believe in his depressing "victory" and the rumour spread that Julian was still alive, but being kept prisoner somewhere by Jovian the usurper. The heralds sent to the various cities of east and west to proclaim the new reign were not always well received. The Gauls whom Julian had left in Pannonia proved especially difficult to convince of its good auguries. "Jovian sent Lucillianus, his father-in-law, together with Procopius and Valentinian, who in after time became emperor, to announce that Julian had died and that he had received the *imperium*," Zosimus relates. "But at Sirmium the Betravi, who had been left to guard the city, when they heard the news killed Lucillianus, as though he had been the herald of great evils, and without regard to his relationship to the emperor. Procopius, however, they allowed to go free, because he was kin to Julian. And Valentinian escaped being killed only by running away."[3] Not even the news that Jovian had himself visited Julian's tomb at Tarsus could scotch the rumour that one day the dead prince would return, and it is likely that Jovian would soon have found himself involved in a civil war if he had not suddenly fallen sick and died at Dadastana on the road to Constantinople; the date was 17 February, and he had reigned 235 days.

Dangerous days of interregnum followed Jovian's death, days during which the court moved on to Nicaea and the generals quarrelled over the succession. As a compromise, Jovian had been a failure, if only because he had not lived long enough. Once again, if Zosimus is right, the choice fell on Sallustius, but once again, he pleaded old age. "They then asked that his son, as second best, should accept the *imperium*. Sallustius replied that he was too young and was, in any case, not the man to bear the burden of an empire so great. So, having failed to elect the best man then living, they voted instead for Valentinianus, who had been born at Cibalis, a town in Pannonia. He had been active in many wars but was without education. Although he was not there, they summoned him nonetheless. So passed an interval of several days while the state was without a ruler, till meeting the army at Nicaea, a city in Bithynia, he began his principate."

"Although he was not there, they summoned him nonetheless." The atmosphere must have been very explosive, Zosimus is suggesting, if none of the power-hungry generals dared to snatch at glory during these endless days of waiting.

The man on whom all their hopes and fears centred had won his way to the top through the army. He was short of temper and formal education. According to his critics, he could be cruel, but he was not a fool. He knew that he had been elected to keep the peace between the Christians and the pagans on the one hand and the barbarian-born and the Helleno-Romans on the other. Julian's reign had sharpened all differences: his death had brought affairs to a fine point and on that fine point, as it were, the empire teetered. Whichever way it might fall, chaos would be lying in wait. It was Valentinian's task, from the moment of his election, to see that it did not fall. Throughout his eleven-year reign, he fulfilled that primary obligation well.

His reign began on 28 February 364 amid scenes far removed from any suggestion of the *gravitas* honoured above all virtues in the long-dead republic. His appointment was confirmed by the soldiers in full Germanic style, with the new emperor of Rome carried by his champions on a shield around the camp. The only traditional element in the ceremony seems to have been the bribe, the donation, he promised to the soldiers. As soon as it was certain that no one intended immediately to challenge his election, he marched for Constantinople. His first major appointment, of his brother Valens as his Caesar, was not only of importance in itself but also indicative of the type of appointment to come, with the near-barbarian emperor promoting neighbours and guest-friends whenever that was possible. Valentinian was not a descendant of Constantius Chlorus, but the process begun under his family, of "Germanisation" of the empire through favours shown to men of the middle Danube area, was not to be halted by the new dynasty, though time and again Valentinian demonstrated that he was not willing to allow favouritism to upset the balance of the empire. If a man was useful, Valentinian used him.

That delicate balance upon which everything rested was all but upset during the first days of the brothers' joint reign when they both fell violently sick with a fever at about the time of their joint entry into Constantinople (28 March). Jovian had died so suddenly and so recently that suspicions were inevitably aroused. The magicians, the Christians said, must be responsible. And many were ready, in that superstitious age, to agree with that judgement. Orders were issued for the arrest of Julian's friend Maximus, but Sallustius, the one man in the empire whom Valentinian could be certain had no ambitions to the purple, persuaded him that this was not the moment for violent action of any kind. The emperors recovered their health, Maximus retired into obscurity, new events intervened, and for the time being the fervour for witch-hunting died down.

Valentinian spent as little time as possible in Constantinople. He was a man not of the cities but of the camps. Probably neither he nor his brother enjoyed themselves in the atmosphere of intrigue hanging like fog over the city—though later Valens grew accustomed to it: "While they were both at Constantinople, certain people there who were plotting against Julian's friends kept spreading the rumour wherever the emperor was that these men were laying traps for him."[4] Certainly by May, and perhaps even earlier, Valentinian had decided that the principal threat to his government was likely to be an external one, coming from north of the Danube and east of the Rhine. Perhaps also he felt that he would be more comfortable where men spoke with his native accent. Early in spring, he set out for Pannonia; part of July, the brothers ruled from Naissus, all August, from Sirmium. From Naissus, Valentinian—who was still issuing all orders in his own name alone—gave instructions for a general reconstruction of the frontier defences of Dacia. A few weeks later, he appointed Valens Augustus equal with himself, and the decision to divide the empire was reached by common agreement. Their frontiers were those fixed between Constantius and his brothers twenty-six years earlier. Valens took the east, with Thrace as a toe-hold in Europe; Valentinian held the west, with the addition of Libya to his north African provinces. Valens' capital was to be Antioch in Syria; Valentinian's, Maximian's old palace and headquarters at Milan. Both choices were made largely for strategic reasons.

Obviously, all that summer of 364 the problems of internal security nagged at Valentinian. The rumours about Julian's friends multiplied, following him wherever he went. Early in September he was driven to promulgate a new law[5] reinforcing Jovian's edict against magic-making with a re-enactment of the old prohibition against sacrifices at night, sacrifices which everyone agreed were dangerous, because they could be only offerings to the dark powers: any good and honest man, approaching the gods with petitions for his own and the emperor's welfare, prayed in the light.

The law was addressed to Praetextatus in his capacity as Proconsul in Achaia. Daringly displaying his pagan colours, Praetextatus protested. Zosimus tells the story: "He prohibited the performance of sacrifices at night. . . . By this law, he intended to put obstacles in the way of the mysteries. But when Praetextatus . . . maintained that such a law would make life not worth living for the Hellenes, since it would put an end to the most sacred mysteries ever to unite mankind [those of Eleusis and Dionysos] the emperor rescinded the law and permitted the mysteries to be performed in the customary way."[6] So boldness saved the mysteries, but the law against abnormal (and magic-making) sacrifices continued in force. It was soon to have violent and frightening effects both in Rome and the east.

From Sirmium, Valentinian slowly progressed to Milan through Aquileia and Verona, reaching his capital city early in November. The last news from the north before winter closed the alpine passes was disastrous. Having learned that Julian was dead, the Alamanni had crossed the Rhine and thrust deep into Gaul and Rhaetia. Throughout the next spring and summer, the situation worsened. The Quadi and Sarmatians swept by the half-refurbished forts of Dacia and ravaged Pannonia. The Picts, Scots and Attacots broke through Hadrian's Wall and rampaged through the northern British Provinces, while the Saxons plundered the southern ones, and robbed and burned settlements all along the coast of the Low Countries. Almost simultaneously, a confederation of Moorish tribes from the Atlas Mountains invaded Numidia and Africa, whilst in the farthest east the Persians denounced their treaty with the dead Jovian and set upon free Armenia. And finally, while Valens' attentions were fixed on the Persians, Julian's cousin Procopius came out of hiding, appearing in Constantinople clothed in purple and calling himself Augustus.

Valentinian met these threats as decisively as befitted his reputation as a man of action. He ordered three commissioners to Africa, with instructions that they must safeguard the Italian corn supply. His generals in the Danube area were coping with the Carpi and Sarmatians, but the news from Britain and Gaul continued grave. Early in 365, an entire Roman army had been wiped out west of the Rhine and by summer the position had still not been stabilised. Valentinian moved his headquarters from Milan to Paris, and from there named Julian's friend Dagalaifus commander against the Alamanni, and Count Theodosius of Cauca in Spain commander in the Britains. While he was at Paris, news reached him of Procopius' revolt. Valentinian refused to let himself be disturbed by it, saying (according to Ammianus) that "Procopius was the enemy only of his brother and himself, but the Germans of the whole Roman world".[7] He ordered Equitius, his Praetorian Prefect in the Danube provinces, to block the mountain passes from Moesia into Dacia, and left his brother Valens to deal with his own troubles, while he himself moved on from Paris to Rheims to keep winter watch on the invaders in the north.

Procopius' rising failed to unseat Valens from power, but victory for the emperor was not easy. The brothers had perhaps underestimated the self-esteem of Constantinople and the dangers of leaving once powerful men to kick their heels in relative inactivity. For a year after the Betravi at Sirmium had given so violent a demonstration of the army's devotion to Julian's name, Procopius lived quietly at Caesarea in Cappadocia, closely watched by the imperial secret police, but as time passed and he did nothing to suggest that he planned treachery, police vigilance slackened, and a day came when he could slip undetected out of his enemies' sight. The next news that anyone had of him he was actually in Constantinople, wearing imperial purple and calling for revolt. The rising was well-planned and backed with ample finance arranged through a rich eunuch discharged from palace service during recent attempts at economy. Possibly through the same source, Procopius was enabled to seize Constantius' posthumous child Constantia, then aged two, and used her to demonstrate to the soldiers his devotion to the family of Constantine: "he carried in his arms the small daughter of Constantius, whose memory was still revered," Ammianus says, "emphasising also his own relationship with Julian. In addition, he made use of yet another favourable fact: that he had been clothed with the purple in Faustina's presence"—though whether the

Empress Faustina, Constantius' widow, was a willing or unwilling
supporter of his rebellion is not on record.[8]

His propaganda was not unsuccessful at first. Within a very short time he
held not only the city of Constantinople but most of Thrace in addition, the
whole of the Black Sea coast of Asia Minor, and several important inland
cities. Although local commanders in these areas gave him support which
they could not in safety refuse, the armies of the east generally did not rally
to him. He was forced to rely to too great an extent on disgruntled civilians
and to hire cavalry from among the hated Goths living beyond the Danube
frontier. By engaging these mercenaries, he sealed his own fate, for his was
essentially a "national" and regional rebellion of the kind which if it is to
succeed at all must succeed at once by the brush-fire spread of public
enthusiasm for the cause. By early in 366, however, Procopius' eventual
defeat was not yet obvious; his forces were judged to be as powerful as
either Valentinian's or Valens' separately, although mere head-counting
was not decisive in itself. What mattered in the long run was the loyalty of
the army to its oaths. Valens seemed not to know how to meet the threat,
but his Praetorian Prefect understood the psychology of the soldier and by
skilful propaganda persuaded a significant minority of Procopius' regular
forces to change sides before the first battle of the rebellion at Thyatira in
Lydia. The outcome remained in doubt only until Procopius' leading
general changed sides while fighting was actually in progress. Then
nothing remained for Procopius but flight. Valens himself crossed the
border from Syria and "met Procopius . . . in Phrygia, capturing him alive
through the treachery of . . . two of his generals and putting him cruelly to
death, together with his betrayers. They say that he had sworn to reward the
two generals, but nonetheless he had them sawn to pieces. And as for
Procopius, he ordered him to be tied by the legs to two trees bent to the
ground and afterwards allowed to spring back up again." So Sozomen tells
the story. "When the trees were allowed to return to their normal
positions, the victim was torn in two."[9] Procopius' head was recovered and
Valens sent it to his brother as proof of his victory. Constantia Posthuma
was safely rescued and survived to play a significant part in the later
history of the century as the wife of the Emperor Gratian.

While Valens was fumbling through his troubles with the Persians and
Procopians, Valentinian was learning something of the true magnitude of
the problems facing the empire in the West, problems of finance, staffing
and morale, as well as the more immediately obvious difficulties created by
invasion. Gold especially was in short supply and war was expensive. Later
in the reign, the export of gold by the purchase of barbarian slaves had to
be forbidden, but such marginal savings could not underpin the inherently
unstable economy. Over a five year period, Count Theodosius restored the
stability of the Britains, and Valentinian himself cleared the Saxons
temporarily from the Channel coast and pushed the Alamanni back from
the Rhine. But most of his victories were hollow triumphs. The nature of

frontier warfare had changed radically during the previous half-century. Pressures from the east on the Germanic tribes increased year by year. The Huns were moving westwards, bringing with them the Alani of the Caucasus, squeezing the Sarmatians, Goths and Quadi, Alamanni and Franks ever tighter against the Danube and the Rhine. Gone for ever were the days when a sound thrashing given to one people and permission for limited numbers of settlers from another to farm within the empire would give the whole frontier several years of peace. The Alamanni were already desperate for land; soon the Goths would be driven to equal despair. They were fighting for existence and would continue to fight for it, year after year, ignoring their losses. To such peoples as the Alamanni, the bitter irony of the situation was that the people they were fighting were in the main not Romans, but men of their own blood whose grandfathers or even fathers had been allowed to cross the rivers which were barred to them. To the true Roman, Valentinian was a barbarian. In all his reign, he appointed only two true Romans as consul; acting like a German king, he handed out such titles as decorations to his war-leaders. At the battle of Maintz in the spring of 368 one of the most important Alamannic chieftains captured and crucified was a man whose father had long been a trusted commander of Roman auxiliary cavalry. Inevitably in times so confused men's loyalties were divided. Although Valentinian could soon proclaim himself *Triumphator gentium barbarorum, Saxonicus maximus* and *Alemannicus maximus*, under the terrible emotional strain which such division entails, as much as through physical and economic weakening, the western empire had begun to crumble away.

Valentinian would have denied that collapse was inevitable, but he realised that the war with the barbarians deserved all his attention. When in the winter of 365–6 he was very ill, and Christian and pagan factions at court began openly to argue about the succession, he closed the argument as abruptly as earlier he had closed the Thracian frontier, by appointing his six-year-old son Gratian as his heir. The boy had no policies yet, and could not interfere. But not all internal problems could be ignored. Embassies from the provinces continually sought out Valentinian; he regularly lost his memorable temper with them before sending them away with laws generally offering reasonable compromises but threatening terrible punishments to all who would not accept them. What Valentinian wanted above all was to be left in peace to get on with the war.

His single-minded outlook explains his attitude to the religious problems of the day. He was a Christian and a consubstantialist, but was unwilling to make an issue of religion. On his coins, he celebrated Serapis and Isis as well as Christ. At the beginning of his reign, he issued an edict of religious toleration, and refused to allow himself to be budged from that position subsequently. He restored to Christians the right to teach in the schools, but promulgated two valuable laws requiring would-be teachers to obtain a state diploma and a licence from imperial education commissioners before opening classes.[10] Bishop Ambrose of Milan records that he once said, "It is not for me to judge between bishops"[11] and his refusal in practice to do so was notorious. The only sects he banned were the Manichees, because they were involved with practitioners of magic, and the Donatists of Africa, because their teachings about sin and repentance led to violence and intolerable breaches of the peace. He restored to the bishops as judges the privileges Julian had taken from them, but forbade them to judge any but Christians; he ruled that Christian soldiers were not to be ordered to act as sentries at pagan temples but refused all Christian pleas that he should close the temples themselves. He began the practice of giving an amnesty to criminals at Easter and ordered that executions should not be carried out on Sundays. But otherwise, he remained indifferent to religious questions as long as the peace was kept.

At Rome, the peace was not kept. Nor was it in Africa.

The troubles in Africa had begun fifty years earlier, with the "Donatist" schism among the Christians over discipline following the great per-secution—a schism which Constantine I hoped that he had ended at the Council of Arles by condemning the rigorist Donatus and recognising his more lax opponents as the "Catholic" sect. By Valentinian's reign, the origins of the conflict were lost in the past but the Donatists of Africa seemed as strong as ever, partly at least because theirs was a "national" and not an imperial church. Whatever went wrong in Africa and Numidia, the Donatists seemed to gain strength from it; even when, during Constantius' reign, the Moors of the Atlas broke their treaties with Rome and mounted an invasion which culminated with the sack of Leptis Magna, the Donatists succeeded in feeding on the peril. Soon after Valentinian's accession, he appointed a certain Count Romanus as his *vicarius* in Africa, with orders to restore the situation there. A blunt soldier like his master, Romanus set about the problem head-on, imposing swingeing taxes to pay for the military solution he intended to impose. Whether he was also corruptly enriching himself and his friends from these funds, as the Africans and Numidians soon complained, must be a matter for conjecture. The same accusation had been made against several of his predecessors in office. However, while Valentinian was still at Milan in 365 a deputation from North Africa wrung from him the appointment of a special legal commissioner, the Notarius Palladius, to look into Romanus' activities. Palladius took with him to Africa the donation which Valentinian had promised the legions on his accession, but when he reached Africa he claimed that he was unable to distribute the money because the Moors had again broken out of their mountain fastness and were ravaging Tripolitania. As before, Leptis bore the brunt of their attack. When the situation had been partly restored, and it was impossible any longer to delay distribution of the emperor's gifts, the news was broken that the money had vanished. In the winter of 367 another deputation from Africa sought out the peripatetic Valentinian and renewed the provincials' complaints. The plot thickened. Valentinian sent to Africa his favourite general, Jovinus, who had fought brilliantly successful campaigns against the Alamanni and had been rewarded with the consulate that year. But hardly had he begun his enquiries in Africa before he too was sucked into the swamp of corruption. Months and years passed without any improvement in the situation. Ultimately, Romanus, Palladius and Jovinus all had to be executed to prove the government's good faith, but by then it was too late. War came to Africa once more in 371 when the prince of the Moors died and the leadership was usurped by his younger son, whom the Romans called Firmus. Firmus united under himself not only the Moorish peoples but everyone in Africa dissatisfied with life under the empire and its corrupt officials. Legionaries and veterans defrauded by Palladius and Donatists oppressed by Catholics all joined the revolt. The fighting worsened after 373, when Valentinian outlawed the sects. The moment finally arrived when Mauretania and Numidia actually declared themselves independent. In the end, Valentinian was driven to the extreme measure of weakening the northern frontiers to restore the south. He detached Count Theodosius from the Rhine army and gave him troops trained in Pannonia and Moesia by his son, the future Emperor Theodosius, to reconquer North Africa. Their landing at the tiny port of Sitifis, in the middle of rebel-held territory, brought consternation to Firmus' supporters, and Theodosius' swift action in fulfilment of his initial proclamation that he had come not to exact retribution but clean up corruption shook their confidence in their prejudices against Roman justice. Firmus' strength melted away; he himself withdrew to the Atlas Mountains, where he committed suicide. An unhappy story seemed to be reaching a happy conclusion, but then suddenly, when Theodosius had restored loyal obedience in Africa, he was recalled and executed. No one knows why. But dictators (and Valentinian was a dictator in all but name) are notoriously suspicious of too much success.

The picture of widespread corruption emerging from these events in Africa forms a sombre backcloth to the fundamentally even more important troubles at Rome during the same period. Corruption and local feeling entered into Rome's story, too, though in a rather different way.

The real problem at Rome was that after the chaos of the third century, and especially after the battle of Mulvian Bridge had destroyed the Prince of the Romans, Maxentius, she had become superfluous to the empire, and her citizens sensed this even if they would not have admitted it. The Pannonian emperors from Constantine to Valentinian fought not so much for Rome as for themselves and *Romanitas*, the concept of Romanness. Although individual members of the Roman aristocracy were immensely wealthy, the real riches of the empire lay outside Italy. The Roman senate was mocked by the existence of a second senate at Constantinople, and the actual rulers of the empire, the members of the imperial Sacred Consistory, were drawn from the circle of the emperor's non-Roman friends. It took a rare man, like Praetextatus, to carve for himself a career in the civil administration which overcame his real disability in being born a Roman of Rome—and even then, like Praetextatus', his career was likely to be interrupted by anti-Roman sentiment. Rich young Romans had nothing but their wealth; poor young Romans nothing but their meagre privileges. Neither wealth (in land) nor privileges were readily exportable. Offered no real trust, and so no real opportunities, Rome naturally became introverted, falling prey to the vices of introversion: luxury, vanity and above all snobbery, a life-style in which boredom could be relieved only by petty intrigue and quarrelling.

The city of Rome had always been corrupt, but corruption had never essentially weakened her until now, when there were no real challenges for her citizens, her institutions were being undermined by semi-barbarian rulers hundreds of miles away, and her very gods were being—as it seemed—stolen from her. There is a brilliant account of this, her fourth-century degradation, in the *Roman History* of Marcellinus Ammianus, a man who loved Rome so much that he could only magnify her shortcomings, the better to bewail them. It would certainly not be boring, but unfortunately would be impractical, to quote all that he has to say in tracing the stages of Roman degradation and corruption from the time of Constantine's sons. But three brief paragraphs must suffice to spotlight areas he rightly felt to be of deep concern:

The failure of the religious sensibilities of the rich: "Many of them deny the superior power in heaven, but yet will not appear in public, or dine, or believe even that it would be at all prudent to bathe, before carefully consulting an almanac and learning where, perhaps, the Planet Mercury is, or in what degree of Cancer the Moon lies."[12]

The corruption of the nominally poor, pampered by the corn-laws, but fettered by edicts governing what they might do, and especially what they might not do, to earn a living:

"Some spend the whole night in the wine shops; some lie hidden in shady corners of the theatres. . . . Some play dice so zealously that they quarrel . . . from sunrise to sunset, through sunshine and rain. They stand gaping at the charioteers and horses, giving their best and worst qualities thorough examination . . . it is a wonderful thing to see such countless crowds of people so intent . . . on chariot racing. These and similar occupations prevent anything noteworthy . . . from getting done there."[13]

And worst of all, perhaps, the injustice and corruption of officialdom, reflected here in an incident during the reign of Constantius, but rife throughout the period of Rome's decline: "Once, not long ago, when famine threatened, foreigners were hurriedly expelled from the City, and those who practised the liberal arts were driven out so quickly that they had not time to draw breath. But the associates of actresses, and such as pretended to be so, were allowed to stay, while three thousand dancing-girls did not have as much as a single question put to them."[14]

Only administrators belonging to such a world could hope to make sense of it. When Valentinian became emperor, the City Prefect, recently appointed by Julian, was just such a man, an aristocrat well known in the city and respected by the senate, whose father had been consul in 330. Valentinian replaced him by Lampadius, Constantius' former Praetorian Prefect, who had been deeply involved in the conspiracy against Gallus, described contemptuously by Ammianus as "a man of such infinite arrogance that he grew very indignant if he were not praised for as much as spitting, as though he did even that more gracefully than anyone else". With a conqueror's arrogance towards private property, he did not purchase but commandeered the materials he needed for public works and finally roused small proprietors to such a pitch of frustrated fury that in 367 they forced him to flee from the city in fear of his life. His successor in office was Viventius, a legal officer, "formerly quaestor of the palace", and director of the enquiry into magic ending in the arrest of Maximus and Priscus in 364. Though "a man of integrity and prudence" he was not a Roman. The situation into which he was plunged was a particularly Roman one and because he failed to understand Rome, his period of office was very brief.

As long before as the year 355, when Pope Liberius had been banished, the clergy of Rome—or a certain section of them, perfectly orthodox in doctrine—had chosen a deacon named Felix to be their bishop, although Liberius still lived. Eleven years later, it happened that both Liberius and Felix died within a short time of one another, and instead of holding a single election to find a successor to them both, the clergy held two elections, and produced twin popes, Damasus and Ursinus. One of the first problems brought before the alien Viventius when he arrived in Rome was that of deciding who should be the pope, and have the jurisdiction—granted by the laws of Valentinian—over the bishops and clergy of the City Prefecture. Ammianus' (the pagan) account of what happened is the most unbiased—and his comment on events very revealing:

"Damasus and Ursinus, being both immoderately eager to win the bishopric, founded parties and carried on a conflict of the utmost asperity, the partisans of each of them carrying their violence to the point of actual battle, in which men were wounded and killed. Viventius was quite unable to put an end to or even mitigate these disorders, and in the end he was forced to withdraw to the suburbs because of their violence. Ultimately, Damasus—by the mighty efforts of his adherents—got the best of the fighting. But it is indisputable that one particular day one hundred and thirty-seven corpses were found in the Basilica of Sicininus [*now S Caecilia-in-Trastevere*] which is a Christian church. It was only with difficulty that the people, having been roused to such ferocity, could be brought back to order. (I do not deny that, bearing in mind the ostentation reigning at Rome, I can understand the justification for those desiring such rank and power labouring as hard and vehemently as they can to gain what they want, for after they have succeeded, they will be secure for the future, being made rich by the offerings of matrons, riding in carriages, dressing splendidly, feasting luxuriously, to the point where their entertainments outclass even imperial banquets.)"[15]

If Roman bishops behaved more like humble country priests, Ammianus goes on to say, they would be more convincing. But the point (which he recognised as well we can) was that Damasus and Ursinus were not country priests. They lived in the city, and theirs was essentially a Roman quarrel following years of typically Roman intrigue. Viventius was not equipped to deal with them. Because Ursinus' seemed the smaller of the factions, he ordered him into exile, and himself withdrew to the country, out of reach of rioters, while Rome tore itself apart.

Two Prefects had now lost control in less than a year. Valentinian's choice of a man to replace Viventius was a very bold one. He called on the ultra-pagan Praetextatus to go to Rome and restore the situation.

Praetextatus was appointed to uphold the law, and immediately showed that he intended to do so. Viventius had ordered Ursinus out of the city; Praetextatus confirmed that ruling, and when he learned that Ursinus' followers were still holding churches around the city, and from them were plotting a violent return to power inside it, banished their leader to Gaul. Leaderless, the Ursinians could only plot to recover what they believed had been stolen from them, but there were no further disorders among the Christians while Praetextatus ruled Rome.

His firm, swift action in this affair gave pagan extremists hope that he would support them against the Christians, but his innate justice led him to be equally firm with them. The law forbade private divination, as it had generally for many years. The public altars were available for use; private temples, a threat to the state, were banned. But magic-making had largely replaced true Roman religion, and the law had long been widely ignored. Praetextatus enforced it rigorously, despite all complaints. It is a fitting memorial to him that during his years of office there was dedicated the last pagan public building known to have been erected in Rome, the restored colonnade of the *dii consentes*, the twelve gods of Rome who assented to senatorial decrees from the terrace above the *tabularium*, where copies of the laws were anciently preserved.

The peace at Rome under Praetextatus could not long survive his retirement from office. He retired because Valentinian, the senate felt, despised Rome, and was letting his scorn for her institutions overcome any respect he might originally have felt for her antiquity. When he began to press for full implementation of his draconian law against theurgy, the senate staged a quiet rebellion, Praetextatus resigning, and a legation of senators, including Aurelius Symmachus Eusebius, the brilliant son of a former City Prefect, travelling to Trier, ostensibly to convey to the emperor congratulations and gifts from the senate and people on the occasion of his *vicennalia* and Gratian's promotion to Augustus but in fact to represent to him the senate's misgivings about his policy. The senators remained in Gaul for about a year. Symmachus won Valentinian's friendship and respect, but the city gained nothing from the embassy.

Meanwhile the situation at Rome itself worsened. The man who succeeded Praetextatus as Prefect was Hermogenianus Olybrius, an ambivalent figure with unusual family connections. His father was a man of great riches but little distinction, but both his mother and his wife were prominent Christians: his mother, Proba, had won respect as a poet, one of the first Roman Christianity had produced, and his wife, Anicia Juliana, was a daughter of the first of the great Roman families to abandon paganism for service under Constantine. On marrying her, Olybrius had been formally adopted into her family and so was protected by one of the proudest names in Rome.

His mandate was to keep Rome quiet and submissive. In himself, he might have been acceptable to the senate, but Valentinian foisted upon him as subordinates a group of Pannonian adventurers who were quickly to make themselves infamous. Chief of them was the Prefect *annonae*, responsible for collecting taxes in kind, a man named Maximinus, an ambitious member of a self-seeking family. His grandfather had been one of the Carpi tribesmen who had been allowed to settle in Dacia at the beginning of the century. His father had kept the records for the civil governor of his province, and had Maximinus educated to the law. Maximinus' own son was with the army in the new northern British province of Valeria, while his wife's brother was in the same diocese of the Britains as an exile, plotting rebellion there. This thrusting, bustling man seized his opportunity at Rome when Olybrius fell sick (diplomatically, one wonders, when he realised the full implications of his instructions?) and all but appointed himself to the post of vice-Prefect, winning confirmation of the appointment by the vigour with which he set about the work.

Bluntly expressed, that work was murder, but murder under cover of the law. The senate was to be broken and with it, its unlikely ally, the Roman church under Damasus.

Two complaints gave Maximinus his opening. In the list of cases awaiting Olybrius' attention when he fell sick had been an appeal for swift justice on behalf of a musician, a wrestling-master and a soothsayer charged by a couple named Chilo and Maxima with attempting to poison them, and left in very unsavoury imprisonment until their defence could be heard. The importance of the case lay, of course, not in the identity of the prisoners themselves, but of their patrons, who were bound to be wealthy if they could afford to procure poisoners, and who could be shown by any competent lawyer to have aristocratic connections. Maximinus notified the importance of the case to Valentinian and was granted permission to hear it with his servant Leo, another Pannonian, as his assessor. The three prisoners were heard, found guilty and executed. But, more importantly, before they died enough names had been wrung from them by torture to open the way to a succession of other cases. As Ammianus put it, "Bellona", the bloody goddess of battle and revenge, "raging through the Eternal City, destroyed everything".[16] Many cases were swiftly disposed of. A significant one among them was that of Lollianus, the son of the arrogant failed Prefect Lampadius. Convicted before Maximinus "of having copied out a book on the subject of the unlawful arts . . . he was, it seemed, on the point of being sentenced to banishment when, at his father's suggestion, he appealed to the emperor, and on being brought before the [imperial] court . . . was handed over to . . . the Consular governing Boetica, and put to death."[17] The terror was not, then, of Maximinus' own devising, but deliberate imperial policy.

When it became obvious that this was the case, those most horrible of human creatures, the political informers, naturally started their deadly work. The acquittal of Terentius Bassus, his brother, and two other prominent men on charges of "having protected the charioteer Anchenius and having been his accomplices in the act of poisoning" proved, however, that even this infamous court had some respect for justice—a weakness in the eyes of Leo the Assessor, who soon succeeded Maximinus as its president, and after discarding his own first chosen assessor as too slow and careful, replaced him with "a murderer of the worst kind", Simplicius of Emona. Under the court as now constituted, judicial liquidation of the opposition went on apace.

The opportunity for the court to break Pope Damasus came fairly early in the terror, when a certain Isaac laid an information against him, as the real instigator of the rioting after the double election of himself and Ursinus. The supposition must be that Isaac was paid to lay the information by Ursinus who, when he heard that Praetextatus had retired, had crossed from Gaul into Italy and was waiting in the wings, as it were, at Milan for a call to power. But Damasus was too powerful, too well protected, to be murdered as lesser men—some of them senators—had been, and he appealed to Valentinian. The case dragged on for years, Damasus being alternately charged, acquitted and charged again with new crimes until he was finally cleared by a church council given judicial powers in 378.

Some of the evidence in this and related cases concerning the Christian clergy brought from the thoroughly irritated Valentinian a very strongly worded re-enactment of one of Julian's most anti-Christian edicts—a development suggesting that Julian's original law had not been so much against true Christian interests as it has sometimes been represented:

"The Emperors Valentinian, Valens and Gratian, to Damasus, Bishop of the City of Rome:
Ecclesiastics or former ecclesiastics and those claiming to be vowed to chastity

shall not enter the houses of widows and female orphans, but shall be banished by the magistrates if after this relations or kinsfolk shall suspect them of having done so; we believe that they should retain nothing of what they might acquire privately under the guise of religion from such women by whatsoever form of gift or testament they may gain possession of it, and any [bequest] shall be null which might be left to them by any such person."[18]

It would appear that some at least of Damasus' clergy were not beyond bringing themselves down to the level of the bequest-hunters, a form of social pest common in Rome at the time, as Ammianus regretted having to record. Damasus himself was once called "the ladies' ear-tickler" and Jerome's attacks on the wealth and luxury of the Roman clergy of the era are notorious.[19] But Valentinian refused to condemn Damasus and left it to Damasus, as judge, to condemn individual ecclesiastics.

It is easy to sympathise with the hard-pressed Valentinian in his struggle with the senate and the church of Rome. The issues on the frontiers were clear-cut and could be resolved only by determined action. The senators, however, were right to be anxious about his attitudes, not only because of the activities of his special commissioners, Maximinus and Leo, but also because they led directly to the question of what the emperor and the Roman army were fighting for, if it was not for Rome. "These and similar affairs led everyone to fear," Ammianus wrote, "that the treatment now being experienced by a few lay in store for all, and that these evils should not by being glossed over be allowed to grow ever bigger until they reached intolerable proportions. So the senators sent a deputation consisting of Praetextatus [the former City Prefect] and Venustus [once vice-Prefect] and Minervinus [a former consul] to beg the emperor not to allow justice to be excessively severe, and not to permit senators to be indiscriminately and illegally tortured." When the deputation arrived, Valentinian, feigning ignorance, disowned his servants, "denying that he had ever ordered such things". But the Praetor Eupraxius, a braver man than most, realised that the emperor was going too far. "Very restrainedly" he called the emperor a liar to his face and "in consequence of his freedom, the cruel laws were amended." Maximinus was kicked upstairs, as Prefect of the Gauls, but the question still remained: what—or whom—was the emperor fighting for?

The answer to this fundamental question was not a simple one, although in very general terms the army saw itself as Rome, and fourth-century emperors believed themselves to be the embodiment of *Romanitas*, however alien the Eternal City itself might seem to them. Every emperor fought naturally for his own survival. Procopius' use of Constantius' daughter as a kind of living battle-standard, and Valentinian's promotion of the infant Gratian as not Caesar but Augustus suggest that in their time the tendency towards dynasty-building discernible long before in imperial history was becoming an ever more important factor in imperial thinking. And as its importance rose, Rome's fell.

The story of Valentinian's marriages seems to underscore the significance of this element in his own attitude to the world. When he himself had been elected unexpectedly to supreme power by the army, he was married to an insignificant lady. She had given him his son Gratian, whom he promoted Augustus in 366. In 370, he divorced her to marry Justina, second cousin and widow of Magnentius, the long-dead enemy of the emperor Constantius. The reasons for this marriage are ambiguous. Justina was reputedly one of the most beautiful women in the empire and Valentinian was so infatuated with her, it is said, that he proposed a law permitting bigamy to allow him to marry her. He had known her for some years, ever since his father, in retirement after a chequered career, had sheltered her and her rebel husband after he had been expelled from Italy. At that time she had been a child-wife, too young to bear children; now she was fully nubile and Valentinian was ready to surrender much to win her—although it may be that his plan to marry her had political as well as amorous facets. Non-Roman by origin though Magnentius had been, he had represented Latin hopes to many, and by marrying his widow Valentinian could hope to bind these people to his dynasty. If it was his plan to unite the empire in this way, it failed in the long term because although in the five years 370–5 Justina helped the family by becoming the mother of four children—Valentinian *Junior*, Justa, Grata and Galla—in later years she became a virulent Arian and was the trigger of violent disruption in Italy. In 370, however, all that lay in the future; by marrying Justina, Valentinian was not only pleasing himself but also healing old wounds. Three years later, after Justina had given him his second legitimate son, he took a further step to bring stability by arranging the marriage of Gratian to the last surviving descendant of Constantine the Great, Constantius' daughter, Constantia Posthuma.

The vice-Prefect Maximinus began his campaign against the theurges and senators of Rome shortly before Valentinian's second marriage. Only a year or so later, a similar terror was instituted against the sophists and magicians of the east by the Emperor Valens. It is impossible not to see a connection between the two campaigns. Once again, Valens was following his brother's lead.

By 370–1, Valens had become a much more active Christian than Valentinian would ever be. His wife, the Empress Domnica, appears to have exerted a great influence over him: she was an Arian Christian, a devotee of the bishop Eudoxius of Constantinople, a member of the most extreme sect of the Arians who denied that Christ shared the divine nature in any way. Between them, the empress and the bishop persuaded Valens that he must actively promote the Arian Christian cause. Under their influence, he banned the bishops Constantius had banned (although Athanasius of Alexandria was allowed to return to his city only four months after being exiled, so great was the furore created by his banishment: he was still reigning triumphant at Alexandria when he died in 373). When sees fell vacant, Valens secured the election of Arians to fill them, and he sent Arian bishops to preach to his enemies the Goths. But he never went back on the toleration for paganism proclaimed as his policy at the beginning of his reign: the temples remained open and sacrifices were publicly offered; processions in honour of Demeter and Dionysos were reintroduced at Antioch itself and elsewhere, after an interval of thirty years; and the governor of Isauria, a devout pagan, rebuilt the shrine to Proserpine at Corasion partly at least with official funds.

So Valens shared his brother's ambivalent attitude—and his ambiguity would seem inexplicable except by fear; his main impulse was not religion but superstitious terror. It was certainly superstition that ruled his actions when he instituted the persecution of the theurges in 371.

The years after the suppression of Procopius' rising were not easy for Valens. When he disbanded the military units which had fought against him, he enslaved the Gothic mercenaries of the cavalry, selling them in various eastern cities, far from their homes, then carried the war against them across the Danube, deep into the mountains of central Europe, from headquarters at Marcianopolis, the chief military depot in Thrace. Although once Procopius was dead the Goths were the main threat to his empire, Marcianopolis was not a suitable centre from which to direct affairs. It was too remote from the Euphrates and the Nile. Valens certainly recognised the dangers; he several times visited Constantinople between 366 and 370 and occasionally ventured into Asia. But in the circumstances of his frequent absence, sedition against him was inevitable. When it was detected, the theurges were inevitably said to be involved and punishment followed, for it did not stop with those proved guilty. Realising the difficulty of his situation, Ammianus was nonetheless driven to condemn him for his violent injustice, and we must concur in that condemnation: "he can be excused for taking every precaution to protect his life, which traitors were trying to take from him. But it was an unforgivable crime in him that with a tyrant's pride he hastily . . . visited the same severe punishment on the innocent as upon the guilty, not discriminating between their deserts, so that while the magistrates were still deliberating about their guilt, the emperor had made up his own mind about their punishment, and people were informed that they had been condemned before even they realised they were suspected."

Valens felt persecuted. Not even the Christian clergy in his realm offered him peace of mind. They quarrelled continually about the nature of Christ, and expected him to take sides in their disputes. His empress Domnica brought him joy when in 366 she presented him with an heir, Flavius Valentinianus Galates. But when in 369 the prince sickened and died at Caesarea in Cappodocia, while some talked darkly of magic and poison, others claimed that the true divinity in heaven was punishing Valens for trying to persuade the great orthodox champion Basil of Caesarea that he should turn Arian. That year should have been a happy one, for peace was made with the Goths at last, a peace that left them north of the Danube frontier, free to cross it only in two places, to visit imperially appointed trading stations. But the young prince's death cast a cloud over everything.

In the winter of 371–2 Valens felt that it was safe at last to leave Thrace and visit the southern half of his empire, setting up his headquarters in the palace at Antioch. But hardly had he arrived there before his secret police uncovered a very tangled tale of a plot to depose him—a tale so tangled, indeed, that as it has come down through the centuries to us its details seem quite incredible because so many of them are distorted or missing. Putting all the versions together, it is obvious that the whole affair was concocted by *agents provocateurs* to give grounds for the persecution of the sophistical friends of Julian, and specifically to trap Maximus.

Valens did not admire Maximus, but he was afraid of him. Immediately after Valens' promotion to Augustus, Maximus had been arrested, but released into a kind of house-arrest through the intervention of powerful friends. According to Eunapius, who only reluctantly affords him a place of honour in his *Lives of the Philosophers* (because he allowed his love of magic to override his reason) he barely survived his experiences at that time: having failed to find grounds for executing him, "they inflicted the greatest possible punishment on him, fining him so huge a sum that no philosopher was likely ever to have heard of so much money (for they believed that he was in possession of what had belonged to all [Julian's friends]). Then they had second thoughts, on the grounds that it was not enough. And he was sent to Asia to find money for the fine." Sallustius, now the Prefect in Asia, was specially charged with keeping close guard over him. Probably at the instigation of a local commander exceeding his orders, tortures were inflicted on him which brought him to the point of suicide; he could not reveal where Julian's friends' treasure was because no treasure existed. In the end, Eunapius says, unable to endure any more, he made a suicide pact with his wife. She purchased poison. Maximus watched her die, and then could not bring himself to end his own life. Admirers, among whom was the civil governor of Asia, nursed him back to some semblance of mental health and, about the year of Valentinianus Galates' death, he was recalled to Constantinople to give advice on magical subjects. When the court moved to Antioch, he went with it. It was now that the trap was laid for him.

"There was among the imperial secretaries [at Antioch] [Zosimus' version of the story runs] a certain Theodorus. He was well-born and well-educated, but nevertheless little more than a boy. . . . Some men approached him, persuading him that they were rich in knowledge, experts in seeing into the future by a special kind of divination."

They persuaded Theodorus to join them in this piece of illegal magic-making, asking their spirits the one question forbidden above all: "who should reign after Valens?"

Their method was to set up a tripod, lighting a fire in a bowl placed upon it, say their prayers, invoke the divine and mystical names of god, and read the future in the ashes.

"In the tripod, they saw letters written: θ, E, O and last of all Δ, letters clearly indicating that Theodorus would succeed Valens."

Theodorus—if he ever existed, which we may doubt not only because the secret police were capable of inventing a detail like him when required but also because (as everyone knew by the time the story came to be recorded) Valens' actual successor was named Theodosius—the boy-like Theodorus could not keep his excitement to himself, but talked about the glorious future in store for him. He was arrested and tortured. When part of the story emerged, Maximus, the real victim, was called in to act as an assessor of the magical element in the evidence. He saw the trap, knew he could not avoid it, and was inspired—or driven to the frenzy—of himself making a prophecy about Valens' end:

"After a general and universal slaughter
In which murderous work we ourselves shall be annihilated,
The emperor shall die in an alien place,
Without honourable burial or a worthy tomb."

It was illegal to make any prophecy about an emperor's doom, let alone ill-wish him in so baleful a manner. But even with such clear evidence against the sophist Valens dared not order his execution at Antioch. He was put to death at Ephesus in the presence of the *Magister memoriae*, "a murderous man with a butcher's soul".

After Maximus died, and all those involved in the Theodorus conspiracy, "the Emperor became suspicious of all individuals known to be philosophers or have any kind of culture. . . . On all sides, a universal howl of lamentation went up," Zosimus relates, "as the prisons were filled with people unjustly detained."[20] The terror—which so closely paralleled that instituted in Rome three years earlier—nauseated and frightened those it did not directly threaten and though Valens never persecuted "orthodox" paganism, confidence between him and the non-Christians of his empire was never restored.

Magic—or rumours of magic—played a part also in Valens' complex and not very creditable dealings with his neighbours in Armenia and Persia during these years. What Valens wanted above all was peace in this area, and knowing his unwillingness to fight, King Sapor never ceased to make trouble but took care not to carry provocation to extremes. By the winter of 373–4, when Valens celebrated his *decennalia* at Antioch, Armenia had been lost to its pro-Persian, pagan aristocracy; its king was a fugitive; war rumbled on the Mesopotamian frontier so relatively recently established by Jovian's shaming peace. It was said that the king could only have escaped his enemies so long by his skill in the black arts, and such was Valens' fear of magic that he allowed the king to be murdered by an imperial officer, and recognised a usurper in his place. Manifestly, Valens did not understand the east.

In 364 the brothers had believed that there were sound reasons for dividing the empire and during their first ten years nothing had happened conclusively to demonstrate that their division was ill-conceived. When in about 371 the horde of the Huns broke the Alani and absorbed them, the moment for that demonstration was at hand. In 373, the east Gothic kingdom in the steppes crumbled, and the Ostrogoths flooded westwards. One tribe pleaded with Valens to allow them to settle in the empire, but he stood by the terms he had made with the Goths of the west, and the refugees had to try to settle where they were, north of the Danube. The domino shunt of people on people along the river valley did not stop opposite the frontier of Valens' territory. "At that time an atrocity for which there could have been no expiation was very nearly committed, one which would have had to be accounted among the most shameful catastrophes ever to fall upon the Roman world. The daughter of Constantius had a narrow escape. She was almost taken prisoner while dining at a posting-house while she was on her way to her wedding with Gratian. She was saved only by the prompt action of Messala, the governor of the province, who, with the help of a beneficent god, was able to put her in a carriage and . . . convey her to Sirmium."[21] The raiders who so nearly brought off this coup were not Huns or Goths, but Quadi, operating with the remnants of the Sarmatian peoples, disturbed by events further east. Valentinian, obviously expecting trouble, but not quite sure where it would occur, had moved his court north from Milan to Trier, and had given orders that fortifications throughout the Alpine area should be strengthened, while he came to terms with the Alamanni which he hoped would keep the peace on the Rhine. The Quadi were driven back over the Danube by the reduced garrison commanded there by Theodosius *Junior*, whose father at this time was still tidying up the ends of Firmus' revolt in Africa. All the forces of the empire were now needed on the Danube, but Valens was too preoccupied with his involvement with the Persians to realise it. Valentinian wintered at Trier, but judging aright the direction from which danger would come, left there as early in spring as travel became possible, about the second week in April, to set up headquarters at Carnuntum, ordering the rebuilding of the fortress for what was to prove the last time.

While he was there, the western Goths first felt the inexorable pressure of the Huns. They lacked the unity to make a determined stand. Valens' Arian missionaries had made unhealable breaches within their federation. Their only proven war-leader was the *Iudex* Athanarich, a pagan who had persecuted converts to Christianity, hating them as much as he did foreign enemies. Athanarich tried to organise a defence against the threat from the east, but his Christian subjects would not stand and fight for him, even if he had been willing to use them. They left their homes and spread the length of the Danube searching for food and shelter, begging to be allowed to settle within the empire. An unimaginable number died before the local commander in Valens' Dacia allowed two hundred thousand to cross the river on their promising to live according to Roman and Christian law.

Meanwhile further west, Valentinian at Carnuntum was trying to read the developing situation from his own point of view. The Sarmatians who eighteen months previously had broken all their oaths to join the Quadi in attacking the empire were now suffering pressures they could not endure. Soon, they sent an embassy to Valentinian, suing for peace. He temporised, waiting to see how the situation developed further. The pressure from the east increased as the summer wore on. About 12 August, leaving the Empress Justina and her children at Carnuntum, the Emperor moved to Aquincum on the Danube, and crossed by a bridge of boats into Quadi territory, to see for himself the position there. Hunting through the mountains, he found nothing living. Early in October, he withdrew to proposed winter quarters at Brigetio in Illyricum. Here, a deputation from the Quadi found him. They were in a desperate state. Harassed by the Romans from the south, and by marauding bands from the east, they were broken and starving. Now winter had fallen upon them, exceptionally early. Would the empire give them refuge? Their pleading annoyed the quick-tempered Valentinian; when they accused the Romans of being the aggressors in the recent troubles, his temper exploded, in an outburst of vituperation. He went on cursing till he broke a blood vessel in the brain and collapsed speechless. He lived until 17 November. His body was taken to Constantinople and buried there before the year ended.

Valentinian's death left his widow and her four children in a very difficult and exposed position. Gratian her step-son was only sixteen and could not be relied upon to protect her. Besides, he was far away in Gaul. Fortunately the winter proved a severe one and while it lay heavy over central Europe, there was little threat of further fighting. Justina and her brother Cerealis, an officer on the dead emperor's staff, acted promptly, throwing down a challenge to the army of the Danube by carrying Valentinian's children off to Aquincum, and proclaiming Valentinian *Junior* Augustus there only five days after his father's death. Boldness was rewarded. First Gratian and then Valens accepted Valentinian II's right to wear the purple. He was given the Italian and African dioceses, with residence at Milan. Aged only four in 375, for several years afterwards he naturally played no part in the struggles of the empire. They were years during which Justina, robbed of the intense life to which marriage with the explosive Valentinian had accustomed her, turned to religion and found an outlet in ecclesiastical intrigue in support of the Arian party at Milan. Till December 374, the Arians had been dominant there, but then, on the death of their leader, Bishop Auxentius, popular opinion had forced the consecration to the see of the Catholic Ambrosius, a former governor of Liguria, born the son of a Prefect of Gaul and educated at Rome, a man in whom the frustrated empress found an opponent worthy of her metal.

Meanwhile on the Danube front the local commanders had to deal as best they could with a rapidly worsening situation. The Christian Goths permitted to cross the frontier into Moesia and Thrace to save themselves from the triple threat of starvation, Judge Athanaric and the Huns quickly discovered that all was not paradise on the south bank of the river. They complained that Roman officials first disarmed them and afterwards stole their rations. In the summer of 376, they turned upon their new persecutors at Marcianopolis. Urgent messages were sent to Valens, warning him that his presence alone could restore confidence, but he was deeply engaged in conversations with the Persians and was not free till the spring of 377. Perhaps realising that he had lost control of events, he fumbled a path through 377 and the first half of 378, while Goth marauders—soon followed by parties of even wilder Huns and Alans —fought through northern Thrace and finally broke through to the Black Sea. When Valens appeared at the circus in Constantinople in May 378 he was jeered at as the *anandros* and *phugopole*, "the not-man" "who fights running away". Leaving for the front shortly afterwards, he swore that he would flatten the city on his way back from the war.

Almost a year earlier, he had sent legates to Gratian asking for additional troops to fight in the Danube provinces. But Gratian had troubles of his own and although he did not refuse reinforcements there were many to accuse him of sending too few men too late. (Widespread famine that year, and a murderous epidemic of plague subsequent to it, were probably enough in themselves fatally to delay the movement of western forces.) As it was, as soon as the Alamanni on the Rhine learned that the garrisons facing them had been reduced, they crossed the river in a determined attempt to conquer Gaul, and part of the army had to be recalled to repulse them. So when Valens at last began a drive against the Goths, it was with only minuscule western help, a restless people at his back and a determined—and probably desperate and frightened—enemy before him. At Hadrianopolis on 1 August, he found a letter awaiting him from Gratian, warning him against precipitate action. But his hand was being forced. The commander under whom the invaders had found temporary unity, drove him on to the defensive, with ambushes, threats of pitched battle, and pleas for talks. It seems, however, that control of the unruly tribesmen was imperfect, for on 9 August, while negotiations were actually in progress, Ostrogoth and Alan horsemen stormed down from the heights above Hadrianopolis, smashed through the Roman lines, and killed Valens himself, together with thousands of his soldiers. So Maximus the Sophist's prophecy was fulfilled: the emperor died "in an alien place, without honourable burial or a worthy tomb". The dead were stripped where they lay, and Valens' body was never identified. The advance the tribesmen began that day carried them on to the very walls of Constantinople, where they were finally halted only with the payment of a huge tribute in gold offered by the Empress Domnica.

At the age of nineteen, Gratian thus suddenly found himself in sole control of the tottering empire, sharing the name of emperor only with a boy of seven. Even allowing for the fact that he had been educated to rule, the burden on him was intolerable. He was naturally surrounded by admirers, but they all pulled in different directions and he was probably following his own inclination when he sent messengers to Spain to bring back from premature retirement as his Master of Soldiers the former Duke Theodosius, a general of thirty-two who knew the Danube region well and whose only crime was that his father had been too successful.

Theodosius arrived in the east probably before the year ended and immediately plunged into the task of unravelling the tangle which Valens had left. He set up his headquarters at Thessalonika and was quickly successful—if not in the field, certainly with the morale of the army. If Gratian had not proclaimed him Augustus in the East with Macedonia on 19 January 379 it is certain that some soldier, pinning his hopes to the rising star, would very soon have done so. By promoting him, Gratian forestalled a revolution, but precipitated a catastrophe.

Notes

1 Zosimus, III, 34; see Ammianus, who relates the whole story in vivid detail.
2 Sozomen, *Ecclesiastical History*, VI, 4.
3 Zosimus, III, 34.
4 Zosimus, IV, 2.
5 Cod. Theod. IX, 16, 7.
6 Zosimus, IV, 3.
7 Ammianus, XXVI, 5, 13.
8 Ammianus, XXVI, 7, 10.
9 Sozomen, *Ecclesiastical History*, VI, 8.
10 Cod. Theod. XIII, 3, 6 and 7.
11 Ambrose of Milan, *Letters*, 21, 2.
12 Ammianus, XXVIII, 4, 24.
13 Ammianus, XVI, 6, 25f.
14 Ammianus, XV, 6, 9.
15 Ammianus, XXVII, 3, 11f.
16 Ammianus, XXVIII, 1, 1.
17 Ammianus, XXVIII, 1, 26.
18 Cod. Theod, XVI, 2, 20.
19 Damasus: *matronarum auriscalpius*, in C.S.E.L. vol. 35 (Vienna, 1895) pp. 4, 5.
20 Zosimus, IV, 13ff. Maximus was *the* enemy both as the most famous theurge then living and because he had accused Valentinian of "impiety towards the sacred rites" during Julian's reign: Zosimus, IV, 2, 1.
21 Ammianus, XXIX, 6, 7.

The Battle for the Altar of Victory

There have been those throughout history—and there are, perhaps, more of them today than ever before—to whom what a man believes is a private matter, between himself and his gods. Valentinian I was one of them, but not many Roman emperors shared his indifference. Because most of them felt that the beliefs of their people were of the deepest, most immediate significance to the life of the state, the story of the death of Zeus and his family is largely one of political and even military ineptitude and disaster: in the empire, religion and politics were one and indivisible.

With Valens dead, the empire was left in the hands of Theodosius, Gratian and Valentinian *Junior*, a man, a youth and a child, a catholic in an Arian world, a semi-pagan in a catholic world, and a child whose world was as inchoate as his own thinking.

Theodosius set himself two public tasks (and the private one of making himself supreme and indispensable): he worked to rid the world of Gothic invaders and to establish catholic Christianity as the sole religion within his borders. Gratian had one primary aim: to stay alive. Valentinian Junior had no aims as yet.

To achieve his public aims, Theodosius fought with the greatest determination. Even before his military programme had achieved its first limited goal of containing the Goths, he took extreme measures in the religious field, actually going so far as to become formally a Christian by baptism during a severe illness and, upon his recovery, working tirelessly to make everyone else a true Christian also.

His working definition of "a true Christian" was one who held the faith of Theodosius, which was the "catholic" faith of Damasus of Rome and the ruling bishop, Peter, of Alexandria. Declaring Arian bishop Demophilus of Constantinople deposed and precipitating into retirement his chief supporter, the dowager Empress Domnica, he nominated the bigoted Gregory of Nazianzus to rule the eastern church and set to work with new laws to ensure that his ecclesiastical deputy should have the necessary powers to operate effectively. But not even Theodosian loyalists could accept the idea of a church governed by Gregory. The bishops refused to ratify his appointment and Theodosius was compelled to name another bishop, Nectarius, to preside in his place.

On 10 January 381 the emperor decreed that all dissension in the

Christian world should cease, commanding that every Christian place of worship not already controlled by catholics—that is, Theodosian loyalists—should immediately be surrendered to them. Shortly afterwards, he ordered that a council should be held at Constantinople to fix the faith once and for all time and to write canons giving total control of the church to the emperor through his bishop of Constantinople. It was this council which imposed on Christianity the rigid "Nicene" creed and declared the Patriarch of Constantinople equal in power with the pope of Rome "because Constantinople is the New Rome", a declaration with political as well as religious significance.[1] Finally, also during that same year, 381, an edict was promulgated in the names of all the emperors designed permanently to upset in the Christians' favour the delicate balance established under Valentinian and Valens:

"If anyone betakes himself to the old sacrifices whether diurnal or nocturnal as an insane and blasphemous enquirer into the unknown, or if a shrine is believed criminally to have been used for this purpose, or may be suspected of having been so used, the punishment therefore shall be proscription. As we gave notice at our legal appointment [there shall be an] honouring of God with chaste prayers, not blaspheming with songs to the godlings."[2]

The orgy of destruction and despoliation to which this law ultimately led was delayed a little, until the Theodosian new world was firmly on its feet. But the delay was only temporary.

The empire no longer had the resources—or perhaps, the reserves of courage—to deal effectively with such invaders as the Goths. Theodosius' long-drawn illness made his appointment as supreme commander for the first three years of his reign largely negative. In October 382, he was forced to accede to a treaty made with them by Gratian in his absence. Under its terms, the empire granted to the West Gothic tribes what they had first asked from Valens, the right peacefully to settle on the Danube frontier south of the river, paying a tribute in corn and keeping watch on the movements of the Huns from behind the river barrier. Theodosius' Christians immediately set to work among the settlers, trying to convert them from Arianism. It proved to be a very long, slow task.

This much at least can be said for Theodosius, that he knew what he wanted to achieve. In contrast, Gratian generally found himself torn in several different directions at once. Successfully to control the West—and counterbalance the massive figure of Theodosius in the East—he needed to be a great military figure. But he did not have it in him. Part of the blame for his early failure must rest with his father, who had dominated him throughout his boyhood and had found as a tutor for him the perfect instructor not for a warrior prince but for a boy destined to rule a world of peace and plenty. He was the poet Ausonius, who for thirty years had been a teacher at peaceful Bordeaux.[3]

Ausonius was nominally a Christian, but he was too bland and urbane a man to disagree seriously with anyone about anything. The author of delicate pornography as well as down-to-earth letters, the friend of bishops, monks and pagans, ambitious in a gentle, persistent way for his family as well as for himself, he exerted an influence upon Gratian which, although not demonstrably pernicious, was nonetheless undeniably anachronistic, out of keeping with the demands of the times. That his influence was deep is undeniable. Gratian himself admitted it, not only in words but also in deeds by promoting Ausonius' aged father titular (but financially well-rewarded) Praetorian Prefect in Illyricum and his brother Proconsul in Africa, as well as naming Ausonius himself first as Prefect in Gaul, as successor to the enemy of the senate Maximinus, and then Consul in 379.

What responsibility Ausonius had for the most far-reaching policy decision of Gratian's reign, the determination legally to end state support for the pagan cults, it is difficult to estimate, but it is morally certain that, with Bishop Ambrose, he cannot escape some degree of culpability for it.

From the outset, Gratian's religious policy differed from his father's. In 375, he allowed complete toleration to all religious sects except the hated Manichees, but the following year he permitted the first tentative step towards intolerance at Rome during the brief rule as City Prefect of Furius Maecius Gracchus, who can be shown to have exercised authority there only during the two months December 376 and January 377. During those two months—and probably immediately before the great feast of 25 December—Gracchus suppressed the worship of Mithras at the cave on the Vatican hill, leaving the feast-day free for his rival Christ; he then himself became a Christian. The details of the story are lost. It would be especially interesting to know if the Prefect had given his emperor prior warning of what he intended to do and what reaction, if any apart from a great deal of excited talk, his vandalism provoked. But the only surviving record of the events of those weeks is in a letter which St. Jerome wrote to Laeta, a relation of Gracchus', worried, some years later, because her husband and father were still not Christians although they left her free to bring up her daughter Paula in her own religion:

"You yourself were born of a mixed marriage," Jerome reminded her, "but from you and Toxiotianus has come my Paula. . . . Do not despair of your father's salvation. . . . Was it not only a few years ago, when he was ruling the City Prefecture, that your kinsman Gracchus (and what patrician nobility echoes in that name!) destroyed the cave of Mithras and all the monstrous idols—the Raven, the Nymph, the Soldier, the Lion, the Persian, the Sun-runner, the Father of the Initiates—broke it up, laid it bare, and offered these perilous things as his first-fruits, as it were, when he sued for the baptism of Christ?"[4]

It would appear (although there is room for controversy about this) that after Gracchus' personal assault on Roman Mithraism no further action was taken against paganism in the West until 381 or 382, after the promulgation of the edict making suspicion of divination an offence and after the Council of Constantinople inspired by Theodosius had given definitive formulation to Christian orthodoxy while declaring all other religions unacceptable (already in 379 the law had withdrawn toleration from Christian "heretics"). When precisely the first legal steps were taken to disestablish paganism in the West is not clear, but from the fact that measures aimed at strengthening Christianity were more or less parallel in both halves of the empire and followed so immediately upon the appointment of Theodosius, it would seem that a joint policy was formulated at Sirmium in 378. None of the edicts ordering the withdrawal of subsidies from western temples has survived, but the story can be pieced together from the record of the protest which began in 382.

After the conclusion of the talks with the West Goths which allowed them to settle in Pannonia, Gratian withdrew from the frontier provinces to Milan where he quickly succumbed to the influence of Bishop Ambrose, whose battle with the heresy of the dowager Empress Justina—a fight ultimately for control of the infant Augustus Valentinian *Junior*—had taken a very bitter turn since heresy had been made illegal. Christians like Ambrose whose backgrounds were strictly Roman-orthodox did not always find their new lives as Christians easy to justify to themselves. To those educated with Ambrose in the old values at Rome, his Christianity looked like unpatriotic treachery, and if he was not to find himself secretly agreeing with their assessment of his defection, he had to formulate a new philosophy of history to excuse himself to himself. The theory he accepted was that the purpose of the Roman empire had been to prepare the world for Christianity: Rome was not anti-Christ, but ante-Christ. Now Christianity had spread so widely, Rome could disappear. His disciple, the Spanish Christian poet Prudentius, likened Rome to a tree whose sole purpose had been to bring to flower in its old age a single branch, Christianity. Because without the tree, the branch could not have lived, the story of Rome was interesting to Christians as that of their own origins.[5]

The appeal of this kind of thinking to men like Gratian was obvious; for if the Ambroses of the Empire were traitors to Rome, her Gratians were aliens to her. They did not understand Rome. It was satisfying to them to be told that they were the future and that the mystifying past could safely be destroyed.

These conclusions were naturally not so welcome to such men as Symmachus and his friends at Rome (and elsewhere in the empire) whose whole lives grew out of, and found their meaning in, the past history of their city. The number of priesthoods and official offices within paganism collected in his lifetime by Praetextatus has already been noticed (p. 81). Such interests were not merely antiquarian, but reflected genuine concern for both the past and the future, for the past as the birthright and inheritance of the future. Men like Praetextatus believed in the gods, and

believed also that it would be a great evil for them to allow the Roman past
to die. In Symmachus' surviving correspondence this devotion to the gods
and to the past is made clear over and over again. A true Neoplatonist,
Symmachus was very much aware of the Oneness, the Fulness, of all things
in all things, past, present and future, human and divine. To him and his
friends the One and the Many were not opposite and often antithetical, as
they were to the Christians, but complementary and mutually fulfilling.
Their attitude to the past is perhaps most clearly illustrated in the
reverential approach to it shown in their friend Macrobius' *Saturnalia*, a
Platonist dialogue itself constructed on the oldest models and set in
Praetextatus' house at Rome. Macrobius actually speaks of us "always"
showing the highest degree of reverence towards antiquity "if we are
sensible beings". There is a delicately old-fashioned flavour about much
that these Roman Platonists did, as well as what they wrote and said; it
is to be felt, for instance, in the gracious gesture of Caelia Concordia, the
chief of the Vestals, in setting up a statue honouring Praetextatus, and
Praetextatus' return of the compliment, commissioning a statue of Caelia
Concordia. Again, there was an old-world feeling about Praetextatus'
devotion to his wife Paulina "the confidante of truth and chastity, guide to
the temples and friend of the gods" as the epitaph composed for this
couple after Praetextatus' death in 385 calls her, "Paulina, our hearts'
adviser".[6]

Some time around 381-2 a deputation went from Rome to offer Gratian
the high-priestly robe of the Pontifex Maximus, the robe marking him as
head of the College of Pontiffs, leader of the priests and flamens of Rome,
director of the Vestals, and *Rex sacrorum*. His reception of the delegates is
described by Zosimus:

> "The sacerdotal robe used to be offered to every emperor at the time when he
> took possession of his sovereign power, and at that time he was inscribed
> among the sovereign pontiffs with the title *pontifex maximus*. Up till [Gratian's]
> time all the emperors evinced the greatest zeal to receive this honour and bear
> the title: this remained true even when the *imperium* passed to Constantine . . .
> and his successors . . . down to Valentinian and Valens. But when the pontiffs
> brought the robe to Gratian, in accordance with custom, he spurned what
> they offered, considering that a Christian ought not to wear such a garment.
> When the pallium was returned to the priests the leader of the delegation
> cried out, or so they say: If the emperor does not want to be called *pontifex*,
> Maximus will become *pontifex* very soon."

"Or so they say . . .": the pontiff's prophecy could only have been
mysterious before Count Maximus of the Britains began his rebellion
against Gratian in 382, and Zosimus politely questions whether the
prophecy in the form he heard it was made before the event it foretells.[7] A
formal curse—a priestly ill-wishing—of some kind would, however,
clearly have been in order, for a bigger insult to the traditional life of the

state than Gratian's it would have been difficult for the College of Pontiffs to imagine. However, almost immediately afterwards, the emperor doubled the impiety he had offered to the gods by issuing commands designed to end Roman religion altogether, forbidding imperial officers to support pagan sacrifices and priesthoods from state funds and ordering that the statue and altar of Victory was to be removed from the Senate where (except briefly under Constantius) it had presided over the destiny of the empire since Augustus, the first emperor, had placed it in the debating chamber in the year he celebrated his triumph at Rome and the doors of the temple of Janus were closed (29 B.C.).[8] Under the new laws, the endowments of the temples were to be taken from them and given partly to the public fisc, partly to the prefect's treasury. And—worst of all in the opinion of some traditionalists—the fire on Vesta's hearth was to be permitted to go out: the Vestal Virgins were to lose their endowments and immunity from taxation, and all their privileges were to be taken away. The tiny order of six Vestals was particuarly hated by the Christians, to whom they seemed—although they were not—a diabolical anticipation of the peculiarly Christian communities of nuns. Their Christian enemies feared them as mysterious and magical: they did not understand them and did not want to do so; they wanted only to see them destroyed.

The law-abiding Romans swallowed Gratian's painful purgatives without rebelling, though not without revulsion. But no pagan was surprised, or even pretended to be distressed for the emperor's sake, when a series of disasters fell upon the empire within months of his vicious insults to the gods. First, death claimed both Gratian's son and his wife, Constantia Posthuma, the last of the Flavians: Gratian married again almost immediately, but his new empress Laeta was soon widowed. Harvests failed in provinces as far apart as Egypt, Africa and the Belgiums. Plague followed hunger, and war plague. The Alamanni crossed the frontier into Rhaetia and while Gratian was leading his troops against them through the northern foothills of the Alps, Maximus was proclaimed Augustus by troops in Britain and, crossing to mainland Europe, had already won control of all the north to Paris before Gratian's year of disaster ended with his murder by his own Master of Cavalry Andragathus at Lyons on 25 August 383.

Like Theodosius, Maximus was a Spaniard and an orthodox Christian. He had actually had himself baptised before assuming the purple, and throughout his years of power strove continually to demonstrate how orthodox he was in his approach to everything. He had served the elder Theodosius in Britain and possibly also in the Moorish wars, and there may have been some substance in his claim that he had an understanding with Theodosius the Emperor before beginning his revolt, though he told Bishop Martin of Tours that his troops had forced him to accept supreme command. He made so many conflicting claims that the truth about him is hard to come by. After Gratian was dead, he maintained that he had not wanted him murdered, and he certainly refused to allow his head to be circulated, an object of mockery, through the provinces—but, on the other hand, saw no incongruity in keeping his body as a kind of bargaining-counter at the palace at Trier, to be used as required in negotiations with his family.

The family reacted as honour dictated—but not too violently, lest the *status quo* be disturbed. Theodosius armed additional troops, but did nothing decisive with them. Valentinian *Junior*'s Master of Infantry closed the Alpine passes. But no one actually moved against the murderer, and when he sent an embassy to Theodosius, asking for recognition, after only a token delay it carried back to him the emperor's blessing in a grant of the title Caesar.

A similar attempt by envoys led by Maximus' son, Count Victor, to reach Valentinian *Junior* was foiled by an unexpected (and very temporary) alliance between his mother Justina and Bishop Ambrose. Both were determined to protect Valentinian from outside influences—for each was set upon playing the greater part in shaping his mind and opinions. They agreed that the bishop should go north to meet Count Victor before he could reach the court. Justina held one very powerful card: the usurper's brother had been arrested when the rebellion had begun and been kept in prison ever since. During talks at Maintz, Ambrose negotiated his release in exchange for promises from Maximus that he would remain north of the Alps. Rufinus says that Valentinian offered "simulated peace" to Maximus; events later proved that Maximus simulated acceptance of it. But at the time, probably no one believed that he was feigning anything. Peace was much more important than revenge for Gratian's murder. Soon Maximus was recognised as Caesar at Milan as well as at Constantinople.

While Maximus' legates were trying to reach the court of the boy-emperor, another embassy was also endeavouring to see him. This was a party from the Roman senate, a very powerful delegation led by Symmachus. It seems to have been allowed to meet the emperor, and individual members of it made a good impression, for although none of Gratian's legislation was withdrawn, Symmachus himself emerged from the meetings with the cherished appointment of City Prefect for the year 384 while Praetextatus was asked to serve as Praetorian Prefect in Italy, winning one concession from the administration immediately in the form of an edict ordering those who had taken material from public buildings for private construction projects to make good what they had stolen. Christian thefts from pagan buildings were not specifically mentioned, but it was notorious that some people had made fortunes out of temple marbles and treasures, and everyone knew that it was these profiteers who were in Praetextatus' mind. The whole pagan world took heart at his success. But it reckoned without the influence of the Christian Pro-Prefect Petronius Probus appointed to represent Italy at the court while Praetextatus travelled. As soon as the senators left Milan Ambrose and

Probus began to work against them. The propaganda was so successful that Symmachus' prefecture appears to have lasted only seven months, from June 384 to January 385.

Probably right at the beginning of that term, Symmachus led his senators back to Milan to plead the pagan's case again. The winter following the closure of Rome's temples had been one of the worst in history, with widespread famine and sickness following Gratian's murder. People had already felt the anger of the gods before they knew of any reason why the gods should have been angry. To superstitious minds, accustomed to seeking causal relationships between coincidences, that they were suffering because of Gratian's ordinances seemed obvious, once they had all the clues. The gods were angry because the Victory of Rome had been denied: everyone except the Christians knew it; Christ's people did their best to deny the facts—but they understood nothing about the gods.

Attempts were made to ensure that Symmachus' delegation should not win a hearing, and for a time they were successful. But in the end Symmachus did succeed in delivering a protest—his famous *Relatio III*—which was instantly recognised as a model in manner and style even by those who thought its arguments pernicious distortions of the truth. Its message was simple (and the underlying warning clear): "To be held in friendship, honour and love is better than to dominate." If he is to be loved, and respected, an emperor must follow the traditions of Rome: "We beg you again, therefore, to restore the religious situation which was for so long beneficial to the state."

"There have, of course, been emperors belonging to other sects, other persuasions: the earlier of them honoured the ancestral cults; the more recent have sometimes tried to do away with them. If you cannot take as your guide the religion of those long before you, at least share the tolerance of the most recent in time. How alien the family [of the empire] has become not to want an altar to Victory! . . . Your Eternity owes much to Victory and shall yet owe her much more. . . . Devotion to tradition is a precious thing. What Constantius of Blessed Memory did [when he removed the altar] did not deserve to endure. You should follow the example of those even closer to you in time. We are concerned for the eternity of your fame and name, lest a future time should find something to be deprecated in you. Let your Eternity take other actions of his as your guide, actions more worthy of him. He deprived the Sacred Virgins of none of their privileges; he filled the priesthood with noble men; he did not refuse to meet the expenses of the Roman cult. Indeed, he followed the rejoicing senate through all the streets of the Eternal City; he observed with pleasure all the golden treasures, read the names of the gods written on temple gables, asked about the foundation of shrines, wondered at their builders [*during his vicennial visit in 356*]: although he himself followed another religion, he behaved towards them imperially!

Everyone has his own way of doing things: everyone his own religion: the Divine Mind has given every city its own protecting deity. . . . Even if time seems to have taken authority and power from our gods, we still want to follow them because they are old, because our fathers honoured them. . . . [The City of Rome begs] 'Because I am free, let me live in my own way'.

So we are pleading for peace for the gods of our fathers, the gods of our founders. What all worship, one [you] should have some regard for. We all look up to one common sky—and it encloses us within a common world.

Do not rob the priests: good emperors can live without that. . . .

Let no one think that I am merely defending the cause of religion. As a result of what has been happening trouble has come upon the whole Roman race. Ancestral law honoured the Vestal Virgins and the ministers of the gods with sufficient maintenance and legal privileges. The rights of these people are now in the hands of ignoble bankers who may appropriate the substance of sacred chastity to trade in the commonest commodities. And what has followed from that? General starvation. It is not due to the corruption of the soil: we cannot attribute it to the stars . . . for it is only inevitable that those who deny religion should perish.

So let us now all pray for the empire [in whatever style]. That elder divinity [your predecessor], looking down from heaven's arch, perceives the tears of the priests and holds himself scorned to see customs violated which he himself truly held in honour. . . ."[9]

This powerful petition was addressed to the emperors of both east and west. They ignored it, but no one else had the strength of mind to do so. It is, of course, special pleading and in its appeal to history it ignores all those aspects of it which do not suit its case. In the long perspective—as Ambrose was quick to point out—its plea to freedom must appear especially specious. Pagans had persecuted Christians when they could. Yet many must have felt the force of the city's plea, *Vivam meo more, quia libera sum*, "if I am free—not a slave-city nor a puppet-city: not the home of slaves, or prisoners, or orphan-wards—let me live according to my custom, in my own way". Read together with the appeal to antiquity (and that to superstition) this call for freedom could not fail to make an impact.

How many senators supported Symmachus is not known. Probably the majority were still pagan. A Christian delegation was organised by Pope Damasus to go to Milan at the same time as Symmachus' party and present its own petition through Ambrose. What it said has not survived, but among Ambrose's letters there are two setting out his replies to the arguments of the *Relatio* in terms which the eleven-year-old Valentinian might be expected to understand, but naturally looking beyond him to a wider Christian audience. The first of them (Letter 17) seems to have been composed hurriedly, before Ambrose had been able to study the details of the senatorial petition, and sets out in general terms what a Christian's attitude to such a plea ought to be, while warning that if Valentinian does not make this attitude his own he will be excommunicated from the life of the church:

"All men who live under Roman sovereignty serve you, the emperors and princes of the world, but you yourselves serve almighty God and the holy faith. For your present happy estate [*salus*] would not long endure if the one true god—that is, the God of the Christians—was not properly honoured. [He can be so honoured only by rejecting the worship of other gods.] So I wonder how anyone can have convinced himself that it could possibly be your duty to authorise the reconstruction of the altars of the gods of the nations. . . . People are asking you for mercy who took our blood, destroyed our churches: they are pleading for privileges who a short while ago forbade us, under Julian's laws, as much as to teach. . . .

Let no one abuse your youth. When a pagan asks these things of you, do not let your mind be trapped in the chains of his superstition, but let what you have learned teach and admonish you. . . .

If a man is worried by a military problem, he goes to a soldier for advice; when the question is one of religion, he should turn to God. . . . What will you reply to the priest who says to you: the church wants no favours from you who have bedizened the temples of the pagans with gifts? The Altar of Christ rejects your gifts, because you have set up an altar to an idol! . . . God's sacred virgins will have no privileges from you—the virgins of Vesta have already laid claim to you? . . . What will you say? That it was a youthful lapse? But every age is mature in Christ, every age is full of God."

This first letter is throughout an appeal to Christian emotionalism: it even ends with a "What would your father say?"—implying "now that he knows better, being dead, than when he tolerated pagans on earth." The second letter (Letter 18) attempts to answer the *Relatio* point by point, although, like Symmachus' work, it begs important questions, the most fundamental of them (never answered at any stage in this controversy) being the atheist's: why, if one is deserting the gods, does one not go all the way and abandon religious belief entirely?

The letter is too long to translate here in full. It concentrates on answering what Ambrose considered Symmachus' main arguments: that "Old Rome needs her [old] religions", that it is unjust to withdraw subsidies from the priests, and that famine has resulted from the insults offered to the gods.

"Forgive me," Ambrose writes, "if I do not put things very elegantly. Elegant expression—the rhetoric of the pagans—is dangerous." He then goes on at great length—and with some elegance—to deny that the old gods ever did anything to help or protect Rome, sneering at examples Symmachus and his friends had offered of divine interventions in the past: "When a goose sounded the alarm, was Zeus speaking through the goose? . . . Why do you offer me examples from olden times? I hate the religion of a Nero! And what am I expected to say about two-month emperors?—the end of whose reigns was as contemptible as their beginnings? . . . And why look for the nature of god in dead cattle? . . . God himself, who created them, teaches us the divine mysteries, not some man who was once ignorant of them himself. . . ."

"Have pagan emperors," he asks, "put up altars to Christ?" The answer to this question being "no", there was, in Ambrose's opinion, no need for a Christian emperor to do anything for any pagan foundation, be it temple, priesthood or order of Vestals. The Vestals, and the fact that there were only a handful of them, he was particularly scornful about, contrasting them with Christian nuns, all volunteers, of whom there were probably thousands.

It rankled with Ambrose that Valentinian I's (and Julian's) law forbidding the clergy to receive bequests still continued in force: "A gift from a Christian widow to the priests of a pagan temple would be valid: one to the ministers of God, invalid." Pagans do not need property: "Let them be like us, whose only property is faith."

The famine, he claimed, could not have been a punishment, else either it would have been universal, or it would have fallen only on Christian fields. He also rejected the idea that old institutions had value because they were old. Things have to change. "The world itself reached its present beautiful form by change", by the evolution made familiar by *Genesis* and some classical creation stories "of the skies, seas and land" from "the orb containing the seeds of things".

As for Victory, she is no goddess but "a gift given, rather than a power, ruling—one given by the grace of the legions, not one in the power of religion. What a fine goddess it is who owes her very being to the multitude of the legions, her very existence to fighting!" There are still altars at the temples, Ambrose said: let the pagans go to them, and not seek to force their Victory on the Christians in the senate; "Is it not enough for them that bathing establishments, arcades and public squares are cluttered up with gods?"

Ambrose did not anywhere take up Symmachus' argument for the liberty of a free man to live according to his own code, except negatively, with his claim that an emperor was bound to serve "the one God, the God of the Christians".[10] In this debate, whichever side was winning forgot all about freedom and began to talk about compulsion. It is a sad reflexion on the age that, as in this, as soon as any group had power it began to seek means of exerting it over some less fortunate group. At precisely the time that the pagan senators were appealing for freedom to follow their own way of life, the now-dominant "catholic" Christians were trying to force uniformity not only on their open enemies, the pagans, but also upon dissident members of their own religion. This generation, which saw the victory of Christianity, also saw the beginning of heresy-trials and state-sanctioned executions for deviation from the orthodox Christian line.

Priscillian of Avila was the first victim of this new militancy, hounded to death for what he was said to have believed. Priscillian—like Theodosius and Maximus—was a Spaniard. He was charged with magic and Manichaeism, although as torture was freely used to substantiate these charges they should be regarded with caution. His main fault seems to have been that without becoming a monk he preached extreme asceticism; laying great stress on blessed poverty, and using such books as the uncanonical *Acts of Thomas*, he seemed to his enemies to be teaching a dualism that made this world an evil place, and the devil as powerful in it as the deity. In the year 380 the Bishop of Merida asked Pope Damasus for a ruling on Priscillian's doctrine, and when the pope declared that he saw nothing heretical in it, appealed from him to a synod of bishops meeting at Saragossa. Like the pope, the Spanish bishops also cleared Priscillian and shortly afterwards he was elected bishop of Avila. The Bishop of Merida was still not satisfied. In the light of the edicts against Manichees and other heretics of 373 and 378, he applied for a rescript against "pseudo-bishops and Manichees", and was authorised to oversee the expulsion of all heretics from Spain. He set about his task with a will, not only forcing Priscillian and his associates to leave their homes, but also ensuring them a bad reception in Italy and elsewhere by writing to Ambrose of Milan, warning him and others to expect their coming, and blackening their names as far as he could before they arrived to speak for themselves.

With two fellow bishops and their wives Priscillian went to Rome, once again to argue his case before Pope Damasus. The fact that any of the party were married should have been enough in itself to prove that they were not "perfect men" in the Manichee tradition, and when Pope Damasus had heard the story he did indeed clear them all once more of suspicion. The three "pseudo-bishops" returned to Spain.

At this point in their story, a tragedy occurred for them. Maximus' soldiers clothed him with the purple, and Gratian was murdered. Learning that Maximus was concerned above all things to prove what an orthodox emperor he was in every respect, the Bishop of Merida left Spain and went to Trier, complaining that he had been driven out by "heretics" who had made it impossible for him to live and work there. In his anxiety to do the right thing, Maximus ordered that a synod should be convened at Bordeaux and Priscillian arraigned before it, together with his friend Bishop Instantius, one of the others whom Damasus had already cleared. The charges were immorality, magic and heresy. Priscillian refused to plead, and appealed to "the emperor". The appeal could not be legally refused, so both bishops were conveyed to Trier, where they were, quite illegally, tortured to make them give evidence against themselves. Ambrose of Milan, who was then at Trier, expressed himself shocked and horrified at their treatment and refusing to be associated in any way with their tormentors left the city in protest. On the basis of the confessions obtained under torture, the Prefect of Gaul applied to Maximus for warrants authorising the execution of the criminals, and finally Priscillian, two other men, and a widow named Euchrocia were put to death.

Ambrose's protests availed nothing. Martin of Tours' denunciation of the executions as "murder" could not change the spirit of the age. When a fanatic could so hound fellow-bishops to death, the appeal of a Symmachus to be allowed to live as he liked had no chance of being heard. The altar of Victory was not returned to the senate, and the House of the Vestals remained officially closed, although it is said that for some time yet the sacred flame continued to be tended on their hearth.

Ambrose's record in the case of fellow-bishop Priscillian was not unworthy of the public image of himself he was trying to create, as the arbiter of imperial affairs. But he could not restrain himself in the witch-hunt which followed Symmachus' attempt to win the sympathy of Valentinian *Junior* for the pagans. Everyone was talking of Symmachus as a great and coming man, therefore for the church's good he had to be forced out of public life, at least until the danger he seemed to embody had been destroyed. Against Symmachus himself, nothing detrimental could be unearthed, so the attack on him was made through his wife, Rusticiana, the daughter of a former City Prefect.[11] A whispering campaign was initiated, alleging that when Symmachus' father-in-law, the present City Prefect, had himself held that office during the reign of Constantius, he had enriched himself from public funds and persecuted Christians in a variety of ways. When the rumours were at their loudest, Ambrose and his friends demanded that the present City Prefect should be brought before the courts to answer the charges against his predecessor. As the days passed, the stories grew ever more circumstantial and ever wilder. More and more great names were dragged into the affair. It was remembered that Symmachus' own father had once made himself so unpopular with the mob that his house was burned down. In December 384 a law was promulgated making it all but impossible for Symmachus to fulfil his office by forbidding him to punish state officials by fines. As though to underline the gravity of the situation, Praetextatus, then serving as Prefect in Illyricum, was named as one of the consuls for 385, as he had been named for offices at Rome when trouble had threatened with the senate in the past. But he died[12] before he could take office, a few days after Pope Damasus, the validity of whose election he had once been called upon to vindicate. When there were violent disturbances at the election for a new pope, and the pagans were blamed, Symmachus, as chief magistrate, was accused of dereliction of his duty in not keeping order. He endured continual calumny until the early autumn of 385, when final preparations were being made at Rome to celebrate Valentinian II's decennalia there. Then he resigned, and went to live on one of his properties overlooking the bay of Naples.

So the first stage in the final confrontation between the pagans and the Christians, the conflict over the removal of the altar of Victory from the senate, ended with the complete eclipse of the pagan party and the celebration of a Christian emperor's jubilee at Rome. In later years, the Victory was to be heard of again, but the main centre of strife now shifted to the East. However, Symmachus' *Relatio* continued to be regarded as perhaps the most powerful defence of traditional paganism ever published, and nearly twenty years after it had first appeared was considered still to be dangerous enough to require further undermining.

The task was undertaken by the Spanish Christian poet Aurelius Prudentius Clemens, who was twice governor of Tarraconensis before retiring, at the age of about forty, around the year 390, to devote himself to the self-imposed task of "hymning the Lord day and night" and combating heresy wherever he found it. Fifteen years later he attacked Symmachus and his religion in well over a thousand lines of powerful if predictable verse. Prudentius believed that it was the gods themselves who had brought Rome close to destruction, by introducing confusion into people's minds and promising a vision of true divinity which they could not supply. His theology is Ambrose's throughout, and like Ambrose he is particularly scathing about the Goddess Victory (although like Ambrose also he draws back from carrying his argument to the logical conclusion of thorough-going atheism):

> "Tireless labour, crude force, surpassing strength of mind, zeal, power . . . and strength in handling arms: if those who fight lack these, although the gilded marble Victory in the temple unfold her wings . . . she will not be with them. Why, soldier, if you lack faith in your own powers, arm yourself with the feeble solace of a woman's shape? Never yet has an armoured legion seen a winged girl guiding the weapons of the fighting men. . . .
>
> Do you seek the lord of victory? It is a man's right hand and almighty God, not a coiffeured virago hanging barefoot, bound round with a bust-improver, while her flowing gown wraps itself around her bulging breasts. . . ."

Such a description of Victory as the soldiers' pin-up was perhaps legitimate, if tasteless, invective. But when Prudentius came to discuss the (now vanished) institution of the Vestals, his generation's fear of the continuing strength of Symmachus' arguments and party overcame his good taste, and he sank to mere insult of the cult, its motives and methods:

> "So to the legate's last, tearful, sorrowing complaint:
> Sacrificial flour is refused to the hearths of Palas
> Money grants to the chaste Virgins and maintenance to the dancers;
> The Vestals' Fire is cheated of its wonted upkeep—
> And hence, he says, our fields are barren. . . .
> But if arising from a world we cannot trust
> This pestilence for the Vestal maidens is revenge
> Why does it not waste our Christian fields alone
> Ours, through whom the ancestral gifts are stopped . . . ?
> But, I ask now, is the virginity of the Vestals honest—
> That Virginity they call the standard for all devotion?
> Notice, first, that they are taken in childhood's early years;
> Before they can decide by their own will, freely,
> Burning with zeal for chastity and love for the gods,

From righteousness to reject the bonds of sex in marriage
Their chastity is made captive, dedicated on a thankless altar.
Poor things. Their sexuality perishes not from their scorning it, but by theft.
They keep a body intact—but not an intact mind.
On the bed where lies a wretched woman, betrayed, wounded, by such a
    marriage, there is no rest. . . ."

And so on to nausea if not—fortunately—to infinity.

Notes

1 See "Constantinople", art. in *The New Catholic Encyclopaedia* (McGraw-Hill, 1966) and the bibliography there.

2 Cod. Theod., XVI, 10, 7.

3 *Decimus Magnus Ausonius*, ed. H. G. Evelyn White (Loeb, 1919–21). See also S. Dill, *Roman Society in the last century of the Western Empire* (2nd ed., Macmillan 1899).

4 Jerome, *Ep. ad Laetam de institione filiae.* The Raven, Nymph, and so on were degrees within Mithraeism rather than "idols" in the usual sense, although they were sometimes depicted symbolically and may thus have appeared as "idols" in the grotto on the Vatican Hill.

5 *Aurelius Clemens Prudentius*, ed. H. J. Thompson (Loeb, 1949–53).

6 *C.I.L.* 6, i, 1799.

7 Zosimus, IV, 36. On the problem of the actual date, see Jean-Rémy Palanque, *L'empereur Gratien*, art. in *Byzantion* (Viii) pp. 41ff.

It is significant that Ausonius, a careful man, called Gratian *pontifex* in his *Gratiarum actio* (35, 42) in 379.

8 On this controversy, see J. Wytzes, *Der Streit um den Altar der Viktoria* (Amsterdam, 1936).

9 Latin text in O. Seeck, *Symmachus*, (Mommsen, *Mon. Germ. Hist. Auct. Ant.*, 1883) VI, 1, see also, A. Momigliano, ed., *The Conflict between Paganism and Christianity in the Fourth Century* (Clarendon Press, 1963).

10 On St. Ambrose and his beliefs, see F. Homes Dudden, *Life and Times of St. Ambrose* (Clarendon Press, 1935); also *Ambrose*, art. in *The New Catholic Encyclopaedia*, 1966, and art. *Ambrosius* in T. Klauser *Reallexikon fuer Antike und Christentum*, Vol. 1, Miersemann, Stuttgart, 1950.

11 Memmius Vitrasius Orfitus Honorius (*Paully-Wissowa, 17*: at *Symmachus n. 16*) was another of this century's dedicated pagans whose career suffered because of his devotion.

He began brilliantly enough, becoming Consular of Sicily almost out of the schoolroom (before the year 350), under Constans. He was then appointed Count of the Second Class *expeditionis bellicas gubernans*, "directing the military mission"—a rare appointment, possibly made to give him status in the legation from Magnentius to Constantius in the winter of 351–2.

Constantius appointed him Count of the First Class and after a short time gave him an appointment in the Sacred Consistory, before making him Prefect of Africa in winter 252.

On 8 December 353 he became City Prefect of Rome for the first time. Then wine shortages led to riots against the administration and forced his resignation in June 356. But within little more than six months, he had been returned to the City as Prefect for the second time, and held office throughout the period of preparation for Constantius' vicennial visit and beyond, from April 357 to March 359.

During this second period of office, he made the mistake of endowing a temple to Apollo in the City—one of the last new temples to be endowed there. In 364, long after he had retired into private life, he was denounced as an embezzler of public funds and sentenced to exile. He worked unceasingly to have his good name and property restored, and seems to have succeeded in regaining at least part of his inheritance, because it was his Villa Bauli at Baia which Rusticiana took to Symmachus as her dowry in 375, five years after Orfitus himself had died.

12 Praetextatus earned the special hatred—and perhaps the secret envy—of St Jerome. Jerome was at Rome—actually intriguing (unsuccessfully) to have himself elected pope in succession to Damasus—when Praetextatus died. Twice in his letters he contrasts Praetextatus' and Paulina's lives and deaths with those of true Christians: in Letter 23, to Marcella, offering her consolation on the death of the young and devout Leah, he writes of the dead girl's "brief labour bearing fruits of eternal bliss" while, on the other hand, in Paulina's world, "O! How things are changed! This man [Praetextatus], whom only a few days ago they were treating with the highest honour, and who ascended among the arches of the Capitol as though enjoying a triumph for having subjugated enemies, received by the people of Rome with applause and caperings, the man whose death troubled the whole city, is now abandoned and naked, not in a milky celestial palace, as his wretched wife lyingly says, but held in filthy darkness. . . ."

In Letter 39, writing to Paula on the death of Blasilla, he again used Praetextatus as the archetype of the doomed pagan, insulting his memory by a pun on the word *infidelis* which many have found inexcusable. Using quotations from earlier Christian sources to support his argument, Jerome maintains that it is wrong to mourn the dead:

"The rule I draw from the Apostle is that we should not mourn for those who have fallen asleep in the same way as the gentiles [pagans] do. Blush, if you behave no better than the pagan woman [Anconia Paulina], the handmaiden of the devil. She conceives of her faithless [?*unbelieving-or adulterous*] husband transported to heaven . . . (yet she weeps)."

Jerome makes a third reference to Praetextatus as the typical pagan in his *Book against John of Jerusalem* (in Migne, P.L., 23, II, 415): "The wretched Praetextatus who was designated consul and died: a sacrilegious man and worshipper of the idols, who jokingly said to Pope Damasus: Make me bishop of the City of Rome and I'll become a Christian right away."

Praetextatus' religious appointments as recorded on his epitaph have already been listed (p. 81). The record continued: "and in public life, imperial legate to the senate, Prefect of the City, Corrector of Tuscany and Umbria, Consular of Lusitania, legate from the senate, Praetorian Prefect in Italy and Illyricum, nominated consul."

The epitaph commemorates also: "the Most Illustrious Anconia Fabia Paulina, devotee of Ceres and Eleusis, devotee dedicated by the taurobolium of Hecate of Epina, temple guardian."

Its final note is: "Having been married, they lived as one for forty years."

The Defeat of the Gods

The Augustus Theodosius was a man of boundless ambition. From the moment of his appointment in January 379 until the day of his death in 395 he worked ceaselessly to make the whole world Theodosian.

At the time of his accession, he was married to a lady with claims to nobility named Aelia Flacilla and had one son, Arcadius, whom, on 16 January 383, when he was aged five, his father caused to be proclaimed Augustus at Hebdomon, the military headquarters at Constantinople, so claiming for him equality with Valentinian *Junior* and the right to succeed to absolute power. The claim was accepted, and so it was that Symmachus addressed his *Relatio* on the restoration of the old religion to a man and two boys "the Lords Valentinian, Theodosius and Arcadius", though it was intended primarily for the court of the West.

The following year, a second son was born to the imperial couple and named Honorius, in honour of his great-grandfather and his late uncle, the emperor's brother. So the foundations were laid for a new dynasty to supersede that of Valentinian.

Others before Theodosius had set out to remake the Roman world, but none, apart perhaps from Augustus and Constantine, had set about it with the same determination. The illness which struck him immediately after he reached the headquarters he had chosen at Thessalonika probably convinced him that his life was precarious, and that he must work fast if he was to achieve his ends. As we have already seen, he opened his attack on the old world with a vicious decree against divination in any form and by a determined endeavour to impose his own brand of Christianity on the churches of the Roman world through the Council of Constantinople, an imperial council whose decrees had the effect of laws.

The first edict against surviving theurges and sophists was followed by another in 382, while Gratian still lived, issued perhaps simultaneously with the Western decrees against paganism at Rome. It was addressed to the *dux* of the frontier province of Osroene in Mesopotamia:

> "Any building sacred in former times where people used to congregate and which is, as it were, now in public ownership, and where images may be set up as it might be suspected in readiness for the art of divination is, we decree, to be kept continually open by the civil authorities, so that no surreptitious oracle may be permitted to operate there."[1]

The wording of this edict is difficult, partly because an attempt was made to keep it precise. The aim of the law was not to bring about the destruction of the temples or the statues. Theodosius was not yet strong enough to take actions which might provoke civil war. Even later in the reign, when all sacrifices were forbidden, no general order was made for the destruction of pagan shrines; they became museums, containing fine examples of sculpture and painting, and as such were open for visits by the public. But, like Valens before him, Theodosius was afraid of the diviners, partly on superstitious ground, partly lest they should provoke his assassination by predicting it. It is clear that some of the shrines which Julian had despaired of seeing frequented again were being used from time to time at least for the oracular purposes for which they had been founded. So Theodosius forbade divination, and—in the law of 382—ordered the opening of all secret rooms and chambers so that secret divination became theoretically impossible.

No more than Valentinian's advisers in the West could Theodosius afford to provoke an outburst against himself from those who remained pagan, although in the great centres of the east, at least, this was a smaller proportion of the total population than in most of the West. But in the course of the following decade a stream of laws poured out from the sacred notary's office against divination in all its forms, laws which, although not formally condemning pagan belief, made all pagan practice extremely difficult, especially when they were over-zealously or even criminally misapplied to the pagans' disadvantage. Theodosius' laws from these years surviving in the *Codex theodosianus* compiled under his grandson's authority in 438 include (from 385):

"Let no living creature be bold enough so to make sacrifices that by inspection of the liver and inward parts he may have some vain hope regarding promised things by prophecy—and again, what is even worse, that he may know the future by such abominable consultation. For more bitter punishment than used to hang over him tortured by crucifixion awaits those who contrary to justice try to explore the truth of present and future things."[2]

and, from 391:

"Let no one defile himself with sacrificial victims, no one fell an innocent victim, no one go to the sanctuaries, frequent the temples and hold in honour images shaped by the world of mortal beings, lest he be held responsible under sanctions human and divine."[3]

and from the following year:

"No power is to be attributed to anything concerning sacrifices; no one is to go the round of the temples, or have respect for the sanctuaries. Let it be recognised also that our law excludes even profane persons from approaching them, to the end that if anyone . . . attempts anything contrary to the prohibition and against piety, he may know that he has no grounds for claiming exemptions for himself. . . ."[4]

All these laws were accompanied by schedules of penalties usually envisaging equal punishments for magistrates failing to accept denunciations or inflict sanctions. They were paralleled by another series of ordinances, beginning in the first year of Theodosius' effective government—381—forbidding any baptised Christian to desert his religion for paganism. Never before had apostacy from Christianity been a punishable offence:

"To Eutropius, Praetorian Prefect: Rights in respect of the law and of making wills are [hereby] stripped away from those who, having become Christians, become pagans, and the will of any such person, being dead, is to be rescinded".[5]

Three years later, the sanctions were even more clearly spelled out: "Let Christians . . . who go over to pagan rite and cult . . . be outside Roman law."[6]

Except in one special instance, Theodosius never authorised the destruction of temples with a law banning their existence. But neither did he take any action to prevent their being razed. In fact, it would seem that he let it be known that he would welcome the news that outbursts of what modern propaganda might call the just or uncontrollable anger of the masses had destroyed pagan shrines. As France long ago had its revolutionary mobs and China more recently its Red Guards, both groups bent on wiping out all traces of the reactionary world, so too the empire in the closing years of the fourth Christian century had its propaganda-directed gangs of rioters who went from place to place smashing, burning, looting and destroying in defiance of the laws and defence of their own cultural revolution.

Moreover, like other administrations since, Theodosius' government was not unwilling to advocate and promote secretly what its own declared policy forced it officially to deprecate. Nor was it unready to stiffen the ranks of popular protesters with government agents when public fury failed.

The monks and hermits formed the spearhead of the Christian revolutionary army. Often, they were invited into new areas by local bishops especially to undertake the "depaganisation" of the place. But when the monks were few, or insufficiently aggressive, government officials and even soldiers were used to provoke incidents which were bound to end in the destruction of state property.

Theodosius' chief agent in this work was a fanatical Christian named Cynegius. It was to Cynegius, as Prefect of the East, that there was addressed in 385 the law forbidding any mortal creature to offer sacrifice in an attempt to unlock the secrets of the future. No balanced account survives of the life and character of this much hated man. The only quasi-official record of his career is to be found in a later chronicle, under the date 388, the year of his death:

"In the consulate of Theodosius, for the second time, and Cynegius: in this consulate Cynegius, the Prefect of the East, died while he was consul. He had brought back to their original condition all those provinces which had for so long been going to ruin, penetrating as far as Egypt and throwing down the images of the pagans—for which with great mourning the whole population of the City accompanied his body to the Apostles (Church) on 14 April. . . ."[7]

Cynegius was appointed Prefect in 384, so that his rule over the East lasted about four years. What secret orders the Sacred Consistory gave him regarding "bringing back the provinces to their original condition" can only be surmised. It is probable that the law regarding the temples used for divination represents only a small part of his work. But it was a part which he carried out with extreme thoroughness, a dedication so complete that neither pagans nor Christians ever found it possible to describe it objectively. So far, this chapter has related historical events: much of the rest of it will consist of folk-tales, atrocity-stories, propaganda and downright lies. The blame for this confusion rests with the ruthless Cynegius.

With his large staff and bodyguard Cynegius travelled south-east from Constantinople through Asia Minor, then due east to the Mesopotamian provinces (carefully avoiding Antioch, which at this time was still the chief city of the East and had certain privileges with regard to sacrifice). Finally, he turned west into Egypt and possibly Libya, from where he was recalled to become consul on 1 January 388.

From the popular Christian account of the events of these years presented to his sensation-loving readers by the Syrian historian Theodoret, the first bishop aroused to go beyond the law and destroy the temple in his area by the approach of Cynegius and his troops was a certain Marcellus of Apamea in Phrygia:

"First of all the bishops to start the destruction of the pagan temples in the city he ruled on the basis of this law was the most excellent Marcellus . . . a man who, like the Apostles before him, was on fire with the spirit. The Prefect of the East came to Apamea with two tribunes and the men under their command [*perhaps as many as a thousand fully armed troops*] and the mob held its peace for fear of the soldiers. They had come to destroy the temple of Jupiter. It was very big, very richly decorated, and very richly endowed. But they found the construction excessively strong and stable—so much so that it was believed that human beings could not loosen the bonding between the stones. . . . And when the holy Marcellus saw that the Prefect had lost heart and did nothing, he sent him away into other towns, and begged God to grant him some way of destroying the temple. . . ."[8]

Jupiter at Apamea was a very famous shrine. Theodoret is anxious to show how the Christians' god, his bishop, and a clever workman co-operated to destroy it without outside help. But it is clear that there were fears of riots if soldiers were not within easy reach of the town. The very morning after the troops had left, Theodoret relates, Marcellus had a visitor "a man, coming of his own volition, who was not an architect or a stonemason, nor a follower of a related trade, but whose job it was merely to carry wood or stone on his back". He offered to bring the temple down and finally did so by undermining three of its pillars "propping up the part of the building standing above it with logs of olive wood. . . . When he had undermined three of the pillars in this way, he set fire to the wooden props. Immediately a black devil appeared, and refused to allow the wooden timbers to be destroyed by fire as their nature required them to be."

But Bishop Marcellus had the answer to black devils. He blessed some water and sprinkled the spirit with it: the devil vanished, the flames bit into the olive timbers and "their support being taken away not only the three pillars fell, but twelve others with them".

So Jupiter the Black Devil was driven in visible form out of his temple at Apamea, and thereafter, Theodoret, the master story-teller, would have us believe, Bishop Marcellus had nothing to fear from the pagans. The treasury of the Prefect was enriched by the endowments of the temple and the pagan mob was forced to stand by in sullen silence while their heritage was destroyed.

The story is fanciful enough as it stands, but unfortunately for its credibility, there is another entirely different story of how a certain Bishop Marcellus tried to destroy a temple at Apamea, and what became of him that same year. Marcellus was a fairly common name, and there were three towns named Apamea, but the coincidence is to say the least remarkable:

> "Hearing that there was a very large temple at Aulone, a district of Apamea, he [Marcellus] went there with a force of soldiers and gladiators. He made his own headquarters at some distance from the scene of the conflict, beyond the reach of arrows, because he was suffering from an attack of gout, and was unable either to fight or to run away if defeated. While the soldiers and the gladiators were employed in the attack upon the temple, a party of pagans, discovering that he was alone, hurried to the place where he was waiting the outcome of the struggle, seized him and burned him alive."[9]

His sons wanted to avenge him, Sozomen (who relates the story) records, but the council of the province forbade it.

There is no pagan account of events at Apamea (or at either Apamea, if two different bishops Marcellus are involved in these stories). But even these favourable Christian accounts suggest that there were some very ugly scenes in Asia and the East in that year 385.

What the rioters, backed by Cynegius' open-ended authority as Prefect, accomplished in Mesopotamia after they had finished with Asia Minor and Northern Syria, stung Libanius into one of the most reasoned defences of the temple produced during these troubled years, his speech *In Defence of the Temples*. It is probable that he never delivered it before Theodosius in person. By this time the emperor was far too deeply committed to his policies to be persuaded to withdraw from them. But it represents what Libanius would have liked to have said to his emperor, if he had dared.

It is not easy to read. Libanius was an old-fashioned, somewhat pedantic Greek stylist and followed the unfortunate convention of seldom referring to persons or places by name. The following extracts are not a strict translation but do, I hope, convey some of the powerful—all but unanswerable—points he made in a style not too far removed from his own to deserve quotation marks.

The year, it should be remembered, was 386, expected to be the year of doom for the great temple of Serapis, and all the shrines of Egypt:

"Many will think that I am broaching a delicate subject choosing to talk to you about the temples and the wrongs they have been forced to suffer in these times. But I think that those who fear for me in this are not familiar with your character. . . . So keep your eyes fixed on mine and do not, I beg, look across to those who would like, by some means or another, to erect a barrier between us. I beg those people down there to let me develop what I have to say without interrupting. . . .

After I have done, they can have their turn and try to refute what I have said.

The first men who inhabited this world, my emperor, lived on the heights. Finding shelter in caves or huts, they had their own consequent concept of the gods . . . built temples to them—as best the skills of early man allowed—and set up statues to them. When their skill allowed them to build cities and the arts of construction were sufficiently well advanced, towns appeared in great number; some were at the foot of hills, others in the plains, but in them all the first buildings put up after the ramparts were shrines and temples. The thinking behind this was, of course, that with such protectors they would be most secure. And if you go now through the lands occupied by the Romans, you will find the same everywhere: the first town after Rome still has temples even now—although stripped, to be sure, of all honour. Where before there were many, there are now few, I admit, but at least temples have not entirely disappeared there.

It was with the help of their gods that the Romans carried on operations against their enemies, gave battle to them, won victory over them—and after their defeat gave to the conquered, from compassion for them, a better life than they had had before, freeing them from all fear and letting them participate in their own political system [*1–5; 6–7 summarise religio-political events from Constantine's defeat of Maxentius onwards; 7 ends:*]. Of what Julian did or wanted to do I shall not speak at this time. The sacrifices continued for a little, but unforeseen events intervened and the two brothers [Valentinian and Valens] forbade them, incense apart: and this last exception is confirmed by your law. You have not caused the temples to be closed nor forbidden visits to them: you have not banned temples, nor altars, nor fires, nor incense, nor other perfume offerings. Yet men in black who eat more than elephants and exhaust themselves with the number of cups they drain, who have drink served to them in the middle of their psalm-singing and hide their misdeeds under an artifically-induced pallor—these people, my Emperor, have brought scorn upon the law that is still in force. They rush upon the temples, carrying baulks of timber, stones and fire—some of them with nothing more than their bare hands and feet—and then: O Moesian spoil! Roofs are knocked off, walls undermined, shrines thrown down, altars totally destroyed. And as for the priests: they can choose between silence and death. When one temple has crashed to the ground, they run to a second, and after that, a third, adding trophy to trophy. And all contrary to the law.

Their exploits are perpetrated even in the cities. But in the countryside, matters are worse. They go about in gangs, attacking each village in turn. Then, when as individuals they have created a thousand evils, they all join up together again to take stock of what they have done, and each think themselves dishonoured if they have not committed the worst crimes. So they rush through country places like flood waters—ravaging them by the very fact that it is the temples that they destroy. For every country place where they destroy a temple is a place made blind: a place knocked down, assassinated. For the temples, my Emperor, are the souls of the countryside. They are the first buildings put up in the fields, and they have come down to us through the generations.

It is in the temples that labourers put their hope for men, their wives, children, beasts, cultivated and sown land. A country district put through so much is a country district lost: the labourers' heart has vanished with their hope. . . .

. . . [The monks] say they are making war on the temples but their warfare is a way of pillaging what little poor unfortunates do have, the produce of the fields and the cattle they feed. Then the attackers withdraw, carrying off the goods whose surrender they have compelled. But even that is not enough for them. They grab people's land, claiming the place is sacred. Many have been robbed of their patrimony on such a pretext. They who (as they say) give honour to their god by fasting are getting fat on the wretchedness of others.

And as for those others, the victims of such a sack, if they go to the town, to a 'shepherd'—he will be called that, though he may not be a good shepherd precisely—and tell him, weeping, of their injustices suffered, the shepherd will approve of the pillagers, and chase their victims away, saying that they should count it a gain that they have not suffered worse. (8–11)

If they hear of a place with something worth raping away, they immediately claim that someone is making sacrifices there and committing abominations, and pay the place a visit—you can see them scurrying there, these guardians of good order (for that is what they call themselves), these brigands, if brigands is not too mild a word; for brigands at least try to conceal what they have done: if you call them brigands, they are outraged, but these people, on the

contrary, show pride in their exploits . . . : they believe they deserve rewards!
(*12*)

In the city of Beroea there used to be a bronze statue of Asclepios . . . in
which art surpassed nature [*Phidias had sculpted it, centuries earlier, using
Alcibiades the Beautiful as his model*]. . . . No one has ever been impertinent
enough to suggest that sacrifices were ever offered to it. But this statue, which
must have cost such labour to produce and was the work of an outstanding
genius, has been smashed. It now no longer exists. . . . So they behaved at
Beroea . . . and you can be sure they have behaved in precisely the same way
in the temples of the countryside . . . without any sacrifice having been
offered there. (*21–3*)

But even if there had been criminous activities, it would be for them to
show that they deserved punishment, and for a judge to order that
punishment. . . . I believe I am right in saying that the law gives the duty of
ascribing punishment to the judge. . . . (*25–26*)

They have not dared to suppress the sacrifices at Rome. If sacrifices are
vanities in every respect, why has this particular vanity been allowed to
continue? . . . (*33*) And in fact it is not only at Rome that sacrifices are still
continuing. They are still going on also at the great and populous city of
Serapis. . . . (*35*) So what is the real position, then?

The temples are imperial property, like other monuments. Would it be the
act of a wise man to drown his possessions under the waves? . . . Why destroy
a monument when you might make another use of it? . . . (*43*)

There used to be on the frontier of Persia a temple beyond all compare . . .
I have even heard discussion about which was the greater marvel, this temple,
which as of now no longer exists, or that of Serapis, which may the gods
preserve from a similar evil fate! . . . That temple is now destroyed, lost. (*44–5*)

It was not you yourself who brought this about, but that man who deceived
you [Cygenius], an enemy of the gods, craven, avaricious, ill-intentioned
towards the world which gave him life, a man who has profited by Fortune's
disruption and served Destiny ill. A slave to his wife, he has done everything to
please her, taking her as his guide in everything. But she, for her own part,
had made it her own rule to obey in everything the instigators of these
exploits, these people who demonstrate their virtue by living in mourning
clothes—or rather, garments woven by sack-weavers. . . . (*46*)

So all has come from treacherous deception. . . . (*48*) But why have they
destroyed this famous temple? Was it because it seemed good to the
emperor? . . . If that is so, tell me why the temples of Fortune, Zeus, Athena
and Dionysos [*all temples at Antioch*] have been left unmolested? Is it because
they—and you—want to leave them standing? No. It is because no one at all
has ever given authority for their destruction. But in that case—did they ever
receive it for those they have destroyed? Again, no. They, why have they not
been punished? (*51*)

What you must do, my emperor, is hand down the following edict:

'Let none of my subjects revere the gods, or honour them. Let none invoke
them to receive benedictions from them, either for himself, or for his
children, even in silence and in secret. Let everyone believe in the god I
worship, participating in the cult offered to him, making prayer in the form
prescribed for his worship, and bowing his head under his hand as guide to

the people. Let it be mandatory that anyone disobeying shall be put to death.'

It would be easy for you to promulgate such an edict. But you have not chosen to do so, because you are unwilling to put such a yoke on human consciences. (52–53)

If, my emperor, such acts [as the destruction of the temples] were to receive your approval and sanction, we should support them, although not without unhappiness: we should demonstrate that we knew how to obey. But if without your support these people go on to attack temples which have hitherto escaped their fury, or those which have been so speedily rebuilt after attack, you must realise that the true people of this land will defend both their property and the law." (55)[10]

Libanius knew that at the moment when Cynegius turned his attention from the County of the East to Egypt, the empire risked being torn apart by religious conflict. Daily reports were being received of temples closed, treasures smashed or stolen, priests robbed and beaten. He also knew that the empire existed because of the average citizen's acceptance of the law, a fact of life in the empire which fanatical Christians were using to their own advantage, both using the laws against divination (and abusing them) to gain their own ends, and breaking the laws against damage to property and persons in the belief that law-abiding citizens would hesitate to defend themselves by action outside the law. But the temper of the people was wearing thin. Bishop Marcellus—and probably others also—had died already. Phidias' Asclepios had been wantonly smashed. The temple-hospital at Aegaea lay in ruins: so did the temple at Carrhae, the second most beautiful in the world. Now, the rumour was, the most beautiful of all temples, the Serapeum, was in danger. And Libanius believed—rightly as events proved—that unless Theodosius himself ordered its destruction, together with all other temples, the people would fight to defend it.

The fighting, however, was mainly in Egypt. Libanius misjudged the temper of his fellow-citizens, although only by a hair's breadth. The law still held the allegiance of most citizens most of the time. The Serapeum was defended for about three years, until in fact Theodosius did give a direct order for its destruction, but there was no general revolt, not because there were no pagans left to rebel, but because most people remained loyal to the state, and to the laws of the state forbidding violence to persons and property.

There are five accounts of the fall of the great temple of Serapis, accounts which, when they are put together, reveal a very ugly picture of the bitterness of the times and the violence smouldering just below the surface of life during Cynegius' mission and after. The person most brilliantly spotlighted by all the accounts is not Cynegius, who was long dead before the temple fell, but Archbishop Theophilus of Alexandria, an unsubtle advocate of Christianisation at any price, who survived until 412. On appointment to the archbishopric in 385, Theophilus was given a building sequestered from the Arians to be consecrated as an orthodox church. He decided that it was not big enough for his congregation's needs, and planned to extend it. During the work of digging out new foundations, his workmen discovered the remains of an underground shrine, possibly dedicated to Mithras but more probably to Dionysos, a shrine suppressed, perhaps, during the reign of Constantius and never reopened. Within the remains of the sanctuary were discovered certain cultic objects, hidden there for safety. During Cynegius' visitation of Egypt, while the army was at hand in strength to protect the Christians, Theophilus used these objects as visual aids in a propaganda war against paganism conducted with the ultimate aim of whipping up his supporters to the point of destroying all pagan shrines in the area. His main pagan opponents throughout the vicious conflict which ensued were Helladius and Ammonius, both well-known grammarians, and a sophist named Olympius.

The version of events at Alexandria which found favour among unsophisticated Christian audiences, who preferred to see their enemies destroyed by miracle and ridicule rather than by violence, was composed by Theodoret and included in his history immediately after his story of the black devil of Apamea. It is a cheerful account of the speedy cleaning up of the whole Delta and ignores the controversial background story of Christian provocation, together with the army's role in the affair, while setting out to make the much-revered gods of Egypt look ridiculous and their end long overdue:

> "[Theophilus] not only destroyed the temples of the gods from the ground up, but also disclosed to the ignorant and misguided the tricks of their deceitful priests. They used to leave the inside of their bronze and wooden statues hollow, fastening their backs close to the wall, but leaving undetectable passages in the walls themselves, so leading the people to believe that they were of incredible holiness: they got into the interior hollow spaces and thus made them do whatever they chose. Being deceived in this way, the Hearers would do whatever they were commanded. The bishop, a man of real insight, revealed all this to the deceived people and brought it to an end for ever.
>
> When he reached the temple of Serapis (which some claimed as the biggest and most beautiful temple in the whole world) he saw there a huge likeness of the god, so big that by its very dimensions it struck terror into those who saw it. Connected with this huge object there was an oracle which said that if anyone came near this image of the god the earth would shake and general disaster overtake everyone. But Theophilus held this oracle to be the sort of nonsense talked by drunken old women, and did not let the huge size of the statue disconcert him either. It was, when all was said and done, only a lifeless thing. So he commanded a man with an axe to let fly boldly at this Serapis. While he was hitting at it, everyone around cried out for fear of the notorious oracle. But as he was made of wood the Serapis felt no pain at all when he took the stroke and, being lifeless, neither did he cry out because of it. However, when his head was knocked off, a whole swarm of mice ran out from inside: the Egyptians' god had become an apartment-block for mice! So they broke him into pieces and fed them to the flames. But the head they dragged

through the whole city, so that his worshippers could see it, and with it the impotence of the gods they had prayed to."[11]

This is a very cunningly constructed story, on several levels. Suffice it here to point out that although the great Serapis was powerless to help himself in any way—was in fact a mouse's nest—the fate he suffered was that of a deposed tyrant. Bishop Theophilus is several fairy-tale figures all at once, but primarily Jack-the-Giant-Killer. Serapis' fate is that of a Maxentius or Maximin Daia, whose name and portraits were destroyed and all his acts annulled.

The atmosphere is wholly different—and so are most of the details—in all four other versions of the story. The greatest contrast to Theodoret's is, as might be expected, offered by Eunapius' brief but sorrowing account, which he included in his *Life of Antoninus of Canopus*, a sophist who shortly before his death had foretold the complete destruction of the temples and their worship:

"No sooner had [Antoninus] left the world of men than the therapy [*saving and healing cult and culture*] of the Alexandrian temples—and above of the Serapeum—was scattered to the winds. And not only the therapy alone, but also even the very buildings themselves. Everything happened as in the myths of the poets, where they tell of the Giants winning control [*and chaos returning*]. The same thing happened to the temples of Canopus. It was while Theodosius had the imperium and Theophilus was presiding over the filthy, a man comparable to Eurymedon 'ruler over the proud giants'. Evagrius was the prefect of the city and Romanus commanded the legions of Egypt. Without any kind of justification—not even as much as a rumour of war . . . these people . . . raided the temples, razing the temple of Serapis and giving battle to the temple offerings, so winning a victory with no adversaries and no fighting. They fought so manfully against the building and the offerings that they not only beat them but thievishly carried them off as well. . . . Of the Serapeum, all that they did not take was the floor, because of the weight of the stones.

So they boasted that they had defeated the gods! Then they brought into the holy places those they call monks, men according to their appearance but swine in their way of life. . . . For among them, every man is given the power of a tyrant who has a black robe and is prepared to behave badly in public. . . . They settled these monks at Canopus also, and so they fettered the human race to slaves' worship—and not that of honest slaves either. They collected the bones and skulls of criminals put to death for a variety of crimes—men whom the courts of the city had condemned to punishment—and made them out to be gods, honouring their tombs, claiming that they made themselves better by defiling themselves at sepulchres . . ."[12]

The third version of this same story is to be found in the *Ecclesiastical History* of Socrates Scholasticus, a fifth-century writer who had special knowledge of affairs at Alexandria. He recorded an attempt by the pagans in the delta area to concert their opposition to the plans laid by the prefect, the bishop and the monks for the destruction of the temples under military protection. His story begins with the bishop's fiery propaganda against the pagan therapy:

> "The mystery of Serapis especially, when phalluses were carried aloft around all the public squares amid rejoicing, and the mysteries of the other gods also were shown up in all their absurdity."

It was at this stage in the campaign, no doubt, that propaganda use was made of the objects found in extending the church. When Theophilus' preaching became ever more perfervid, and the Christian mob grew agitated, longing for action, the pagans resolved to take steps to defend themselves—a fact mentioned by neither Theodoret nor Eunapius, each for his own reasons:

> "The pagans then still living at Alexandria—and particularly those who claimed to be philosophers—decided that they could no longer endure their suffering in silence, but must give powerful expression to it in horrible outrages."

Socrates seems to be admitting here that the suffering was real and the provocation very great. The patience of the pagans generally through the fourth century and their loyalty to the law were remarkable. But now at Alexandria a counter-campaign to the bishop's was mounted and a plot laid:

> "At the giving of a signal, they all with one accord fell upon the Christians, cutting them down wherever they found them."

Contrary to the best Christian tradition based upon the New Testament, the Christians fought back: they

> "began to defend themselves, fighting evil with evil. The conflict went on in this way until satiation with massacre [and perhaps military intervention, or the threat of it] supervened. And in this set-to, few pagans were killed, but many Christians."[13]

When teaching years later at Constantinople, Helladius the Grammarian, one of the instigators of the pagan counter-plot, used to boast that he personally had killed nine people during the siege. It was possibly from him that Socrates learned the details of the story, for as a boy he attended his school at the eastern capital.

The most circumstantial of the five accounts are those given by Sozomen in his *Ecclesiastical History*—which we have been using to provide the editorial background for the other accounts—and that of Rufinus of Aquileia, a church historian who had travelled in Egypt, where he collected material he incorporated into the two books by which he extended Eusebius' *History* down to his own times. Both he and Sozomen give remarkably similar details of Archbishop Theophilus' campaign and propaganda war against the pagans of Alexandria. Sozomen emphasises pagan violence, and makes it clear that the temple itself was ultimately destroyed, and monks settled on the site on the strength of an imperial rescript specially obtained to prevent any recurrence of fighting.

Here is Rufinus' story, as he heard it in Egypt, probably less than twenty years after the events he describes:

"Meanwhile, new disturbances against the current of the times and the faith of the church arose at Alexandria. It all began in this way: there was a certain basilica in public ownership which had been to some degree neglected even after Constantius the Emperor had given it to the bishops preaching his heresy. After being left so long without maintenance, nothing remained of what had once stood there but the walls. It seemed to the bishop who was then ruling the church [Theophilus] that he should petition the emperor that as the nation of the faith was growing, its house ought also to be made to grow with it. And when it had been agreed that it should be improved, they discovered in certain concealed places and caves dug out in the ground villainous objects and evil things relating to magic and fitted for ceremonial use. Whereupon, seeing their crimes revealed in these hiding places and even more incriminating caves, the pagans, whose custom it is to do their evil deeds not overtly and publicly but to reserve them for secret darkness, all began to rave and openly go mad, as did the Dragon when he had drunk from the cup. They reacted not merely with their voices and seditious utterances as they usually did but this time with their fists and steel. [*Street battles followed until*] the streets ran slippery with the blood of the citizens. Their leader in wickedness and audacity was one Olympius by name who wore the dress of a philosopher. Under him as commander they stormed the citadel and held the palace district. [*The citizens wrote to the emperor, who offered an amnesty to everyone, but ruled that the true cause of the trouble, the statues, should be destroyed. Unwilling to accept this ruling, the pagans then took refuge in the Serapeum at Alexandria*] a temple almost everybody must have heard of, famous everywhere. The site is not a natural one, but man-made, built on a hundred wide steps, so that it is raised up high; it spreads over wide squares and remarkable open spaces, lying off in every direction. . . . The temple in the middle of this complex was built generously and magnificently with precious pillars and marble blocks imported from abroad. The likeness of Serapis within was so huge that the right hand touched one wall and the left the other. This huge object had been made out of metals and woods of many kinds. The inmost hidden layer was robed first in a sheet of gold, with over that one of silver, and finally one of bronze decorated with other precious metals [*Windows in the temple were so arranged that the Serapis and the rising sun appeared to greet one another when the first light fell on the god's crown, and similar devices, including magnets, were used to produce other effects].* The rescript ordering its destruction was read, but no one dared to make any move against it, for fear of divine punishment as threatened by an oracle, until at last a soldier threw a javelin at it . . . [*whereupon, as he survived, the statue was destroyed*]."[14]

According to Rufinus, the temple itself survived for some time, until its destruction was ultimately decreed. Monks were settled on the site to prevent the continuation of pagan worship there. Marcellinus' annals date the final destruction to 389 "by the edict of Theodosius" but this date may be a year or so early.

We now have a working picture of the mechanics of the campaign: at Alexandria and Canopus, as at Apamea (and credibly elsewhere) the bishop led the Christian mob, with soldiers in reserve and behind them again the full weight of the civil authority, ready to declare dissidents proscript throughout the empire. When, as at Apamea, the pagans stood sullenly by, and watched their treasures carried off and temples ruined, the local Christian leadership did the evil work, but when resistance was organised, as at Alexandria, troops were used. In Egypt—and elsewhere also it would seem, from the number of pagan sites "desecrated" with Christian shrines—monks and hermits were settled among temple ruins to prevent any re-use of them by continuing pagans, although in the west at least it was many years before temples were actually converted into churches.

Atrocity-stories have been common in all wars, and because Christian congregations had been conditioned into a state of morbidity about sexual matters (a morbidity they had learned partly from contemporary Jewish teachers, but largely through converts from the more esoteric and ascetic gnostic religions) their "favourite" pagan atrocities, guaranteed to shock and anger them, were those alleging sexual enormities at temples. Writing around the year 400—when the propaganda war was still raging—about the period of the enforced Christianisation of Alexandria, Rufinus tells an atrocity story which—even if its main facts have some connection with truth (which is doubtful)—is clearly designed not to inform but to enrage its readers, and is worthy of a place in any history of propaganda:

". . . and omitting other evils that were done elsewhere, such as the slaying of weak and despised infants so that their virgin entrails might be inspected for omens,[15] I would recall just one other thing that went on at the temple of Saturn—as everyone now knows—from which many related evils took their origin: among the priests of Saturn was one named Tyrannus. Claiming to be speaking for the divine spirit, he would say to noble and prominent men worshipping at the temple that they should give him their wives for sexual purposes: Saturn himself commanded that a man's wife should pass the night at the temple. A man who heard this, rejoicing that his wife should be judged worthy of the divine being, would load her with jewels and cash, so that he might not be thought penniless and send her to the temple. In the sight of all, the woman would be securely locked away: Tyrannus would close the door, give the key to someone, and leave. Then in silence he would creep by a secret subterranean passage into the wide hollow inside of the statue of Saturn—for that particular statue was hollowed out inside and the back was fixed right up close against the wall. Then torches and lights would appear in the temple, and the praying woman would suddenly receive a Voice from the hollow bronze statue such as to make the wretched little thing shake with awe and joy, to think that she had been chosen as worthy of such intercourse with a divine being. And after he had so delighted her, stirring her mind to either great consternation or lust, the filthy spirit vanished by degrees, spirited away by a trick with linen cloths, and suddenly all the lights went out. So, passing on down, the bemused and confused female was led by a trick to commit adultery in the midst of her meditations. But after many unfortunate women had been so served over a long period of time, it chanced that a certain woman of chaste mind, being urged to this crime and picked for such solicitation, recognised Tyrannus' voice and going back home told her husband about this wicked deception. Upon learning of the injury which had threatened his wife, he burned with rage and had an indictment drawn up, committing Tyrannus to questioning on the rack. And he being convicted on his own confession, and the filthy and evil deceit thus exposed, there spread everywhere universal shame and repugnance against the pagans with their fornication by mothers, incest by fathers, and embarrassment by illegitimate children. And all this having been revealed and proved, he [Tyrannus] was taken, together with his statue and temple, and demolished. . . ."[16]

If this sort of story was deemed worthy of publication, we are left wondering what others adapted from Eastern fairy tales and Greek novelettes circulated behind closed doors.

The greatest Christian hero in all the orgy of destruction at the close of the fourth century in the east was not, however, Theophilus of Alexandria, but John Chrysostom, himself a hermit before he became a priest at Antioch in 386 and later forced against his will to accept promotion to the archbishopric of Constantinople. In most matters, John was Theophilus' enemy: in his attitude to paganism, he was his closest ally. The temples of Antioch—still chief imperial city in 386, though soon to be demoted after riots over new taxation there—were not yet closed when John became a priest. Theodoret relates how he set about closing them:

"When he realised that the Phoenicians [Syrians] still felt warm towards the mysteries of the devils, he collected a band of mystics glowing with zeal for God, armed them with imperial edicts, and sent them out to confront the temples of the gods. He did not take from the imperial treasury the money with which to pay the labourers and their helpers to whom the work was entrusted, but persuaded women blessed with riches and believing minds to give it voluntarily, promising them that if they did so they should have greater blessings from God. So he was enabled to bring total devastation to the temples of the devils which had survived thus far."[17]

It was not an easy task. The temple of Artemis at Ephesus stood at least until 405–6 when a mad Christian, inflamed by this same John, burned it down. The gods were loved in Syria. John's attacks on temples under the edicts of 385 and later years provoked riots along the Mediterranean shore of Syria and Phoenicia, especially at Antioch. In 386 he preached a series of twenty-one sermons "On the statues", proving that the earthquakes and political troubles which beset Syria that year were not marks of the anger of the gods. His preaching earned him a great reputation among Christian ladies and brought large donations to his vandalistic cause. Forty years later, the patriarch of Constantinople preached a sermon in praise of him, claiming that he "had freed places everywhere from error: in Ephesus he stripped the treasury of Artemis; in Phrygia, he left without sons her whom they called the Mother of the Gods; in Caesarea, he robbed the valueless public prostitutes of the honours paid to them; in Syria, he emptied the god-defying synagogues; in Persia, he sowed the word of devotion . . ."[18] For all of which, naturally, he and his monks were hated.

In the west also the ascetics pursued their fanatical work wherever social and political upheaval made their illegal activities possible. The most famous scourge of the "devils" in the west was Martin, a hermit who, like John Chrysostom, became a bishop against his will. Martin was a theurge as dramatic as any pagan sophist-magician, and his story lost nothing in the telling when at the end of the century Severius Desiderius came to relate it for the delight of unsophisticated Christian audiences and as propaganda to be used in preaching:

"Martin originated in the town of Sabaria in Pannonia, but was brought up at Ticino in Italy. By the standards of this world his parents were not unworthy people, but they were pagans. His father was first an ordinary soldier, and afterwards became a tribune of infantry. He himself followed the profession of arms in his youth, serving in the cavalry of the guard under Constantius, and then under the Caesar Julian. . . . [But already] at the age of ten he sought refuge in the church without his parents' knowledge and asked to be made a catechumen. . . . [He wanted to be a hermit but] the princes having decreed that the sons of veterans were to be enlisted in the army his father—being inimical to his good way of life—made him a prisoner, putting him in chains, when he was fifteen years old, and bound him with the oaths of military service . . . He was in the army for three years before his baptism . . . Then, when he was eighteen, he became most anxious to be baptised; but he did not immediately desert his military status, for he was overborne by the prayers of his tribune . . . who promised when his period of office as tribune ended to renounce the world. . . ." (2. *1–6*)

So, for two years, Martin soldiered on, finally to win his discharge by refusing the donation Julian offered to the troops at Paris. Hilary of Poitiers became his teacher in the arts of driving out devils and resisting the temptations of the eremetical life, and soon he felt well enough equipped to travel to Illyricum and Italy, working as an exorcist, and living for a time in a hermitage at Milan. A few years later he wandered back into troubled Gaul, founded the community of ascetics which later grew into the abbey of Marmoutiers, and was elected bishop of Tours. The Emperor Maximus put up with a good deal from him—including a sound ill-wishing in a prophecy of his downfall—and he was influential in many of the developments in Gaul while Ambrose was at work in Milan. He used his ascetic brothers to destroy the temples of the Loire Valley and—according to his biographer—his powers as a theurge to drive out devils, raise the dead, and confuse the ungodly. The devil fought back:

> "Often the devil, in his attempts to deceive the holy man by his two thousand wicked arts, revealed himself to him in the most varied of forms; sometimes he showed himself with the facial features of Jove, very frequently of Mercury, often also of Venus and Minerva. On being so attacked, ever unperturbed, he defended himself with the sign of the cross and the help of prayer. . . ."

It is an Arabian Nights story with a Christian hero—but the shape-changing genii is the old Supreme God in all his manifestations: Whatever-rules-in-heaven transformed into Whatever-threatens-from-hell. But behind it lies the truth: Martin was a mystic—many would say, a sick mystic—projecting his visions on to the temples, so when he went out to destroy them, he was doing battle with the "devils" in his own mind, and seeking to destroy all trace of the way of life he had betrayed:

> "Once at a village, when he had destroyed a very ancient temple, he undertook also the cutting down of a pine tree standing close to the shrine, when a priest of the place and a crowd of pagans began to resist him. And these people who by the Lord's command had been quite unable to move while the temple was being destroyed would not allow him to cut down the tree. And he was careful to point out that there is nothing sacred in a tree-trunk. They should rather serve the god whom he himself served: the tree must be cut down, because it was dedicated to a devil. . . ."

So after some argument, one of the pagans, bolder than the rest, told the bishop that if he would catch the tree, the pagans themselves would cut it down. Naturally, the bishop agreed, arrested the tree in its fall with the sign of the cross, and set it flying back to crash down so close to the pagans as to frighten them into conversion.

> "At about the same time and in the same district, he showed the same power at work again. For when in a certain village he had set fire to a most ancient and celebrated shrine, the next moment balls of fire were carried by the wind to a house standing up alongside it. When Martin realised this, he ran up to the roof very fast so as to be able to intercept the flames as they came . . . and so the fire retreated against the wind . . . the most ancient and celebrated shrine was destroyed, and the people converted.

In another village called Leprosum, Martin again wanted to demolish a temple which the religion of superstition had made exceedingly rich. But a mob of pagans withstood him, so that he was driven back—and not without injuries, either. [So he retired for three days to pray and then] two angels armed with spears and shields, as a heavenly guard, appeared to him, saying that they had been sent by the Lord to disperse the local mob and guarantee Martin's safety, so that there would be no resistance during the destruction of the temple. . . . So he returned to the village and while the pagan crowds stood around motionless watching him he destroyed that godless edifice to the foundations, reducing all its altars and statues to dust. . . ."[19]

So in both east and west fanaticism was illegally destroying the most ancient and celebrated treasures of the civilised world, and the heroes of the time were violent men with warped outlooks on many aspects of life. In the West, Symmachus and his pagan friends defended the cause of the Empire in such appeals as the *Relatio* on the Altar of Victory. In the east, Libanius voiced his protest against the illegality and waste of the destroyers' activities. Here and there—as at Alexandria—swords were drawn and atrocities committed: crucifixion seemed to the Alexandrians a fitting end for as many as they could catch of the soldiers of the cross. But generally, initial distress among the continuing pagans of the population gave way to a listless apathy as they realised that what was left of the empire as a result of Theodosius' policies towards Christians and barbarians was not worth their fighting for, so that when the war of religion predicted by Libanius did break out the pagan cause was defended only half-heartedly by those in the west who might have been expected to champion it, and found no active support in the east.

Notes

1 Cod. Theod. XVI, 10, 8.
2 Cod. Theod. XVI, 10, 9.
3 Cod. Theod. XVI, 10, 10.
4 Cod. Theod. XVI, 10, 11.
5 Cod. Theod. XVI, 7, 1.
6 Cod. Theod. XVI, 7,2; the laws were further strengthened in 391 (Cod. Theod. XVI, 7, 4), 396 (Cod. Theod. XVI, 7, 6) and 426 (Cod. Theod. XVI, 7, 7).
7 *Consularia Constantinopolitana*, under the year *Theodosio Aug. II, et Cynegio, Coss.*, in Mommsen, *Mon. Germ. Hist. Auct. Ant.* IX, 244; cf. also Zosimus 4, 37 and 45.
8 Theodoret, *Ecclesiastical History*, V, 22.
9 Sozomen, *Ecclesiastical History*, V, 15.
10 Text in *Libanii opera*, ed. R. Foerster, 1909–27. Misson, J., *Sur le paganisme de Libanios*, (*Université de Louvain: recueil de travaux, fasc. 43*, 1914.). The date of *In Defence of the Temples* has been much disputed: it was obviously written while the

temple of Serapis still stood: how much earlier is the difficult question to answer. The reasons for my choice of date I think emerge from my general argument.

11 Theodoret, *Ecclesiastical History*, V, 23.

12 Eunapius' quotation is from the *Odyssey*, vi, 59. These years of the destruction of the temples were great ones—perhaps the most lavish after the reign of the Empress Helena—for the invention of impossible relics. The head of John the Baptist was rediscovered in Cilicia (it had previously been reverenced in Jerusalem, but mislaid). The Prophet Habakuk and the Prophet Micah were disinterred in Syria and the Forty Martyrs at Sebaste (Samaria). Lesser finds were almost daily occurrences, it would seem.

13 Socrates, *Ecclesiastical History*, V, 16.

14 Rufinus, *History*, II, 22ff.

15 The same calumny precisely was spread by propaganda and rumour against Maxentius, as we have seen. Fourth-century Christians liked their enemies to be really diabolical. There is, as far as I know, no evidence for this nastiness at any pagan shrine under imperial jurisdiction.

16 Rufinus, *History*, II, 25.

17 Theodoret, *Ecclesiastical History*, V, 30.

18 Proclus, Patriarch of Constantinople, *Oratio, 3*, dated after 434.

19 Severius Desiderius, *Vita S. Martini*; text with French translation and notes in Fontaine, "*Vie de Saint Martin*", in *Sources chrétiennes* (1967, No. 133).

The Years of Barbarian Domination

Libanius' warning went unheeded. The demolition of the old world continued at an increasing pace. The time was fast approaching when, in the image the pagans themselves used, the battle of the gods and giants would be fought again, the great battle of the beginning of time, and now the giants would win. With their victory, the civilised order over which the Best and Greatest had presided would be swept away. Chaos would return. And out of the chaos would grow . . . only the Christians like Ambrose claimed that they knew what.

Some pagans continued, as they and their fathers before them had done for eighty and more years, to ignore Christianity in the hope that it would go away. There was an optimistic prophecy which said that "a year of years"—three hundred and sixty-five years—after it had first appeared, it would vanish again as mysteriously as it had come. But the more honest of the pagan leaders realised that their world was almost beyond saving. There is in Eunapius' *Life of Julian* the record of a prophecy of the end of the old world in Greece made by the last of the Athenian Eumolpidae to hold the office of high priest at Eleusis, a position which had been filled by members of his family since records began. Its baleful shadow overhangs the events of the last years of Theodosius' reign, the years leading up to the "catastrophe of the temples and the ruin of all Greece".

Julian, Eunapius says, while he was at Athens learned the "higher wisdom" from this hierophant, who also initiated Eunapius himself and,

"in [my] presence he foretold the catastrophe of the temples and the ruin of all Greece: he clearly prophesied that after him there would be a hierophant who would have no right to touch the hierophant's seat, because he would be sworn to other gods and would have taken a most solemn oath not to preside over temples other than theirs. Nevertheless, he said, this man would preside, although not even an Athenian. And he also said that during his own times the temples would be ruined and sacked, and that while the other man still lived he would see their total destruction. . . . The worship of the goddesses would come to an end, and stripped of all honour, he would not enjoy a long life. And so it all fell out. Hardly had the man from Thespiae become [hierophant], he who was already a Father of Mithras, than many great evils came inexplicably gushing in. . . . Alaric the Goth with his barbarians poured in through the gates of Thermopylae as easily as though they had

been running the length of a stadium or a cavalry ground. For this gateway to
Greece was thrown open by the impiety of those who wear black robes, who
came into Greece unhindered with him, and by the fact that the laws and
ordinances of the hierophant had been broken. . . ."[1]

The Caesar Maximus had firmly established himself by 387 as ruler of
the north-western quarter of the empire. In that year, Valentinian *Junior*
and his mother decided that the time had come for the young emperor to
exert himself in his own dominions. The way he chose initially to make his
mark was the typical one for his Theodosian and Ambrosian times of
unifying the Christians by wiping out his former allies, the Arian heretics,
so that, blessed by the orthodox bishops, his reign might go from strength
to strength.

For this task, he needed Maximus' help and co-operation in Gaul, and
as it happened at just this time Maximus also needed his, in operations on
the frontier. Complicated negotiations led to the establishment of what
was said to be a token force, expressive of mutual trust and friendship
between the emperors, of Maximus' troops at the southern ends of the
Alpine passes in summer 387: in late July or early August, Maximus
himself led his main army through those passes in a drive on Milan.

His aim appears to have been to seize Valentinian as a hostage, but by the
time he reached the palace, that formidable lady Justina had won help
from her old enemy Ambrose in spiriting her children away, first to
Aquileia on the Venetian Gulf, then to Thessalonika. With Valentinian
fled, there was no opposition to Maximus in Italy. After all, Theodosius
himself had sent him the purple. Moreover, he was careful to offend no
one's susceptibilities. As he had done in Gaul from the beginning of the
reign, so now in Italy, he set out to prove himself the most law-abiding of
emperors. The only scuffle during his occupation of the peninsula
occurred at Emona, the frontier-post with Illyricum. At Capua, on 22
November, Valentinian II's accession-day was celebrated by his fellow-
emperor with due solemnity, and preparations were begun in Spain, which
had also surrendered to him, for the proper ceremonies to mark
Theodosius' *decennalia*. But it was significant that this most orthodox of
emperors set up his headquarters at Aquileia, the last big town on the route
to the east: he was a legitimate emperor, but he was willing to fight his
fellow-emperors to prove it.

The pagans of Rome, and the frustrated, neglected senators, welcomed
Maximus as their saviour from futility. In January 389, when he named
himself consul for the third time, Symmachus addressed to him a most
flattering panegyric. But the pagan party's hopes were misplaced.
Maximus was a Christian. The time for the pagan rising was not yet.

Meanwhile in the east Justina was working indefatigably to win support
for her son's cause. She not only pleaded with Theodosius and his
ministers, she also subverted the throne, using as her fifth column her

daughter Galla, now aged fifteen and universally admired (as Justina herself had been twenty years earlier) as one of the beauties of the empire. Theodosius was a recent widower. In Galla, he saw not only a desirable child but also the blood-line of Valentinian I. He married her with alacrity—and so committed himself to restoring her family's fortunes in Italy. His obligations to Maximus, his legitimate Caesar, were entirely forgotten.

He planned a campaign to destroy Maximus which demonstrated that he had lost none of his old flair as a strategist. Calculating that with the Gothic and other mercenaries available to him, his forces far outnumbered those Maximus would dare to withdraw from the north Rhine frontier, he boldly decided to divide his own legions, landing troops in southern Italy simultaneously with an attack through Pannonia into Noricum, from where roads ran west into Gaul and south into Italy.

The sea-borne invasion was brilliantly executed. Sailing from Thessalonika and heading south around Sicily to avoid an ambush laid at the normal landing at Brindisi, the east Roman forces suddenly appeared at the port of Ostia and took Rome against the lightest of resistance.

Meanwhile Maximus advanced an army to Sirmium, to meet the land army Theodosius and Valentinian were bringing through from Thrace. It was beaten soundly there and again at Poetovio only a few days later. Maximus himself hung on at Aquileia, no doubt longing for a miracle. Although Gaul under his son's rule was still loyal to him and retreat thus still practical, he despaired when he heard that Theodosius' forces had entered Italy and, asking for a safe conduct, surrendered to the first east Roman officers his bodyguard encountered. They accepted his parole, stripped him of the purple, fettered him, and led him to Theodosius, who ordered his execution on 28 August 388 in fulfilment, propaganda afterwards maintained, of the just demands of the soldiers.

So Theodosius entered Italy as a victor, and to a general welcome from all except those like Symmachus who had in any way encouraged the usurper. Symmachus took refuge from the wrath of Theodosius in a church when the conqueror entered Rome, but was quickly pardoned. The speech of apology he made to the emperor still survives.

Theodosius remained in Italy throughout 389, and during that year showed singular favours to several members of the pagan party at Rome, especially during a summer visit to the city. But on 1 January 390, when he entered upon his "victory" consulship, he did so at Milan, and Symmachus, although asked to speak, wrote from Rome that he was unable to do so. Relations between the emperor and his pagan subjects seemed to be cooling, until during Lent news reached the court of a rising at Thessalonika. Enraged that his most favoured city should so scorn him, Theodosius ordered that extreme measures should be taken to bring the rebellion to an end. Thousands—some reports says tens of thousands—were killed. Ambrose excommunicated the emperor, and

Theodosius replied by cultivating the pagans of the senate. The affair dragged on for months. Before reconciliation between the emperor and the bishop was announced on Christmas Day, it had been well publicised that the new western consul for 391 would be Symmachus, with another pagan as his partner in the east. Reconciliation between the emperor and the bishop before those consulships began made them embarrassing to Theodosius and he eagerly seized on the opportunity to exile Symmachus from the court when in his thanksgiving speech the senator repeated all the old pagan demands.

Not all Theodosius' force marched with him into Italy in 388. An army nominally led by Valentinian II struck west into Gaul from Noricum. Its actual commander was Arbogast the Frank, one of the many ruthless barbarians to whom Theodosius entrusted so much so unwisely.

Arbogast's early life was wrapped in mystery, although it was known that before he entered the Roman service he had been exiled by his own people for crimes the nature of which he afterwards sought successfully to conceal. He had come to prominence in 381, when Gratian had appointed him to command reinforcements sent from the West to support Theodosius in Thrace. In 385 he had been appointed Master of the Infantry on the death of General Bauto, the previous barbarian holder of that key appointment. Now, as Praetorian Prefect to Valentinian in Gaul, he had his chance to prove himself in his first fully independent command. He took it with relish. In a succession of battles, and at subsequent peace conferences, he not only brought the rebellion to an end but also established personal ascendency over both the army and the young emperor. Maximus' son was quickly captured and killed. Gradually, order was restored among the tribes settled within the empire. All seemed to go well until about 391, after Theodosius had returned to the east, when it soon emerged that a very unpleasant situation had come into being in Gaul.

The Frankish Prefect had certainly led his armies to overwhelming victories, including several of special brilliance against rebellious members of his own race settled in the north Rhine area. But at the same time, he had established barbarian-born officers loyal to himself in all the highest ranks in the army. His career, and his methods of advancing it, was a vivid adumbration of those of the later Merovingian Mayors of the Palace: like Pepin of the Franks, he kept the lord in whose name he ruled a virtual prisoner while conducting the country's affairs as seemed best to himself.

Valentinian endured this arrangement until he reached the age of twenty-two, in the year 392. That year, the barbarians were troublesome in Pannonia. The commanders of Italy closed their frontiers and asked Bishop Ambrose to go as their legate to the court, then at Vienne, with an urgent request for troops to reinforce the southern army. Ambrose reported that Valentinian seemed anxious to lead these forces himself, but Arbogast had forbidden it: although reinforcements would be sent, the emperor would not lead them. Hardly had the bishop reached Milan with this news, however, when there arrived there not the promised soldiers but an anguished letter from Valentinian himself begging him to return to Vienne, baptise him, and help him to win his freedom from the Prefect. The emperor and the general had actually come to blows. Arbogast had murdered a young Roman in the emperor's presence, although Valentinian had tried to shield him with his own cloak. . . . Ambrose hurried north once more, but while he was still on his journey, a messenger brought him the news that Valentinian had been found hanged. Whether he had despaired and committed suicide, or had been murdered at Arbogast's orders, no enquiry was ever able to determine.

On the surface, all this story has little to do with the religious battle still being fought out in the empire, but developments in the next few months showed that the confrontation between Arbogast and Valentinian reflected issues of the deepest significance through the whole range of imperial affairs. For three months Arbogast pleaded his innocence of the murder—if such it was—and made gestures towards the recognition of Theodosius' dynasty as sole rulers of the empire. Then, on 22 August—apparently as soon as news reached him that Flavius Rufinus, a ruthless advocate of "Theodosianisation" in all its aspects—had been appointed Prefect of the East, he threw all pretence aside and proclaimed a new emperor in Gaul, a fellow Frank named Eugenius.

The new emperor had been Master of the Offices to Valentinian II, the head of his civil service. He was a friend and protégé of the Frankish chief Richomer, a man related to Arbogast, powerful among his own people and respected at Rome. Obviously, Eugenius was intended to be a figurehead, but he was not without value of his own to the soldiers Arbogast and Richomer, for he was well known to the Romans of the City, where he had studied rhetoric and possibly even taught it himself.

Immediately upon his appointment, Eugenius wrote to Ambrose, asking for support at Milan. Ambrose prudently did not reply. He also sent an embassy to Theodosius, asking for recognition. Theodosius also did not reply, except negatively, by refusing to allow Eugenius' name to be published in the East as that of consul for 293, an honour usually afforded emperors in their first year of office. But a pagan embassy from Rome was only too anxious to extend its welcome to the new emperor. It begged him to restore the old religion—which was his religion, and the religion of Arbogast. Still not certain at this stage whether or not Theodosius would recognise him, Eugenius temporised. But in November 392 and January 393, Theodosius struck first against the pagans, then against Eugenius himself.

On 8 November 392, he signed an edict forbidding all reverence for the old gods—the very edict, in all but its wording, that Libanius had said in his *Defence of the Temples* would test the loyalty of pagans to its breaking-point—and at a disputed date in January 393 he named his second son Honorius as Augustus in the West.

The new edict and the orders circulated with it show that Theodosius had come to believe that any survival of paganism was a threat to him and his family. Under its provisions, the most intimate worship of the family gods, the *lares*, *genii* and *penates*, was forbidden under the most ferocious penalties:

> "No one at all shall offer veneration by way of propitiating even in private the guardians of the hearth with fire, the guardians of the family with wine, or the guardians of the house with perfumes, by lighting lamps, sprinkling incense, or hanging up garlands. . . ."

The courts were empowered to overturn pagan wills in favour of Christian relatives of the deceased. Governors of provinces and other officials were forbidden to attend pagan festivals; within two years, all celebratory games excluding those commemorating some anniversary or exploit of the emperor himself were suspended, it became a crime to consult any oracle for any purpose whatsoever, and no one was permitted to take a holiday on former pagan festivals.[2]

Eugenius' response to this legislation was immediate. Hitherto, Theodosius had been careful not to alienate the pagans of the West, where his rule was not direct but through intermediaries, and to some extent dependent upon the co-operation of the great families, many of which were still pagan, or partly so. Thus he had used Symmachus both in contending with and propitiating Ambrose, playing off one against the other. But now the battle-lines were clearly drawn. Even if Eugenius had not wanted the role of the pagans' last straw, they would have clutched at him nonetheless. He was, however, very willing to be of that service to them. In the spring of 393, while marching on Italy, he sent a message ahead of his army to the Senate, ordering the re-establishment of the Altar of Victory. Ambrose—retreating first to Bologna, then to Florence, as the now overtly pagan army marched into Italy—was stung into writing to him, reminding him of all the trouble that altar had provoked in bygone years and arguing casuistically that as it had not been Eugenius who had ordered the altar removed, he could not now order it restored: "My letters [to Valentinian] were read in the Consistory [and found favour]. Valentinian heeded my advice then, to do nothing which was not in accordance with our religion . . . but now that Your Clemency has himself taken over the steering-oar, we find that benefactions are being given to these men—men most noble indeed, but dedicated to pagan ideals. People can with truth say that you, the emperor, have not rebuilt the temples. But you have made gifts to those who have seemed to deserve well of you. . . ."

So, indeed, Eugenius had. Realising that if he restored to the pagan priesthoods the endowments of which they had been stripped there was no hope at all of his ever being formally recognised as a legitimate emperor (except in the remote chance of a total pagan victory everywhere), he had tried to compromise by making grants to pagan aristocrats of priestly families on the understanding that the money would be used to restore the sacrifices.

As he advanced into Italy, he published the names of those to whom he intended to entrust the administration there. The most significant of his appointments was that of Nicomachus Flavianus, Symmachus' cousin and brother-in-law, as his prefect in Italy with his son—also called Nico-machus Flavianus, as City Prefect at Rome.

Flavianus was already Theodosius' Prefect of Italy, Illyricum and Africa. By accepting re-appointment in his own office from the usurper, he was repudiating the person and the policies of Theodosius in an unforgivable way;[3] the battle, as far as he was concerned, was already joined.

(It is not known what part Symmachus played in this last struggle for the old world. If he played any significant role, all reference to it was edited out of his letters by his son, who prepared them for publication. It is possible that he was not actively engaged, but was already partially incapacitated by the illness which kept him out of public life certainly from the autumn of 394 until his death in 402.)

Eugenius' officers took control in Italy without difficulty. Spain also submitted to him, but Africa remained shakily loyal to Theodosius, with the inevitable result that Italy soon began to suffer crippling food shortages. The Christians fought a vigorous propaganda war against the new government, a war growing ever fiercer as Flavianus proved himself a pagan reactionary with a flair for giving offence, selecting for immediate revival all the oldest and oddest cults he knew, from original Etruscan haruscopy to the special invocation of Bellona, Goddess of Battles, and the public performance of the most obscure eastern rites.

The last known inscription recording a pagan foundation with official backing (if not, strictly speaking, imperial authorisation) within the area of the City Prefecture dates from this year and bears the name of Eugenius' Collector of Taxes in Kind. Ironically, it also carries the ultra-Christian names of Theodosius and Arcadius, because Eugenius was still claiming to be the legitimate ruler of the West. Found at Ostia, it commemorates the restoration of a shrine of Hercules:

"In honour of our devout and blessed Lords Theodosius, Arcadius and Eugenius, the eternal emperors, victors throughout the world, the Illustrious Numerius Proiectus, Prefect of Supply, has restored Hercules' shrine-room."[4]

Flavianus' activities were not merely of antiquarian interest. He knew that Eugenius would have to fight to survive. He toured Italy drumming up an army to defend *Dea Roma*, divine Rome.

Meanwhile, Theodosius seems at first to have hesitated as to what he should do. But in the winter of 393–4 he took the advice, Sozomen tells us, of the Empress Galla and sent his eunuch-minister Eutropius to Egypt to consult the Christian equivalent of the oracles of former days, a venerable monk known as John of the Thebaid, and ask him to prophesy the outcome of the war. No doubt Theodosius would have fought even if John had not foretold that the conflict would be satisfactorily ended without bloodshed, but in those interim years a favourable prophecy was a potent weapon; Theodosius knew that his men would listen respectfully to chaplains with a cheerful message to convey. For the same reason, Eugenius consulted the augurs before deciding when and where to commit his forces to battle and let it be known that he had discovered an ancient prophecy—the prophecy of "the year-of-years"—foretelling that Christianity was on the point of foundering.

By midsummer, Theodosius had advanced an army into Sirmium. There was an easy propaganda-point for his enemies to make in the fact that it consisted so largely of barbarians under barbarian command.

Although Eugenius owed his appointment to Arbogast, a Frank who had openly rebelled, much was made of the fact at Rome that the supreme commander of the eastern forces was a Vandal, and that his cavalrymen and shock troops were mostly Goths.

The supreme commander was Stilicho, a name long to be remembered in the West. Aged about thirty at this time, he had already been well known for a dozen years, ever since in 383 Theodosius had approved him as one of the delegates to represent the empire at a peace conference with the Persians. He was the son of a Vandal commander of auxiliary cavalry and an obscure Roman mother, but on returning from Persia had been given permission to marry Theodosius' niece Serena, who had lived at court since infancy. On his marriage, Stilicho had been named Colonel of the Mews (*tribunus stabuli*); very shortly afterwards he had been given the title Count and appointed Master of the Household. In 393, he had attained the ultimate military rank of *Magister utriusque militiae*, Master of both arms of the forces.

The Goths who had so important a rôle to play in Stilicho's plans were under the dual command of Gainas and Alaric. To Alaric—an unproven commander still in his twenties—this campaign was of great significance. Although his family was prominent among the Goths, he was not an hereditary king (despite the fact that contemporary historians often describe him as such). When he was a child, his clan had still lived outside the confines of the empire, in lands north of the Danube. His only education had come from Arian Christian missionaries at work among the tribes, and he had become a fanatical Arian. His family had been among the invaders of Thrace during the reigns of Valens and he had won notice as a very young man during his people's wars with Theodosius. After the peace of 383, he had played a prominent part in the negotiations which converted the men of his tribe from enemies to mercenaries of the empire, transforming them instantly into "Roman" soldiers by giving them Roman arms and armour. But despite the brilliance of his career, his position was not secure. He had enemies as well as rivals among the tribes, and success in a major campaign was very precious to him.

While the main body of Stilicho's forces were at Sirmium, Alaric's Goths were already probing much further west, into Noricum and Rhaetia. Theodosius—in mourning for Galla, who had died of a miscarriage in May—joined the main forces during the summer. Eugenius, Arbogast and Flavianus marched from Milan at the end of July (Ambrose returned there on 1 August). Soon it was obvious that the decisive battle must be fought in the passes of the Alps. To proclaim the allegiance of Italy's rulers, Flavianus had a gigantic statue of Jupiter erected on a high mountain overlooking the route his armies took.[5]

Battle was not joined until 5 September, at Flavia Frigida. The day was a disaster for the Goths. So many died that Theodosius is said to have groaned, "Where is Theodosius' god?" By next morning, however, his generals had recovered the initiative, marching through the night over a high, unguarded pass in order to be able to strike next morning at Arbogast's main camp on the plain beyond. The issue of the battle which ensued hung in doubt until suddenly a strong north wind, the dreaded *bora*, began to blow, raising the dust and throwing it into the eyes of the southern troops . . . or so the story runs. Both armies were so occupied with omens and prodigies that when the very wind appeared to open fire for Theodosius, his victory was assured. Eugenius fled, but was caught and killed before the day ended. Arbogast and Flavianus successfully concealed themselves in the mountains for a few days. Then both killed themselves.

So the war which Libanius had predicted was finished in two great battles, on 5 and 6 September 394. In a sense, Roman paganism died then, for never again did the Best and Greatest preside as patron and protector over a Roman army. Although the true Romans were, it is said, happy that it was a Roman army, and not the barbarian Gothic cavalry, which destroyed their hopes, there was very little else for the pagans among them to delight in. As Theodosius advanced unopposed into Italy, the old life of the country was destroyed. The laws of the east were rigorously enforced in the peninsula and men like Symmachus had to retire into private life in order to survive. Once again, the Altar of Victory disappeared from the senate.

Four months after the great victory of Flavia Frigida, on 17 January 395, Theodosius died at the palace at Milan. Shortly before his death, his two youngest children, the eleven-years-old Honorius and the five-years-old Galla Placidia had joined him there. In his will, he left them in the West under the care of his niece's husband, Stilicho the Vandal, while the Augustus Arcadius inherited the empire ruled from Constantinople. This meant that Stilicho in the west and his rival Rufinus, Prefect of the East, were in effective control of the empire, though in the centre-north the

Goths were still a power to be reckoned with, and Africa, under its Prefect Gildo, was all but independent.

Alaric was shamed by the Goths' failure in Roman warfare at Flavia Frigida and it rankled with him that the Roman world he had chosen as his own was relieved and delighted at his failure. His young fighting men needed a victory—and so did the Arian clergy whose cause was very close to his heart. That winter, he was elected leader of all the Western (Visi-)Goths with the obvious first duty of restoring the morale of his people. He found an excuse and a first enemy in Arcadius. His Goths were technically Roman soldiers, but on succeeding to his father Arcadius had not sent them a donation. By early Spring 396 thousands of Gothic tribesmen were camped within sight of Constantinople, having come, as their leader announced, to collect what was due to them. The Prefect Rufinus himself went out from the city to their camp to argue with Alaric. His arguments and his gold were accepted. The Goths turned back from the Bosphorus and, unimpeded by the legions, sacked Greece.

Eunapius and his pagan contemporaries were certain that this attack on Greece was a deliberate crusade, supported by the Christian clergy, against Hellenism and its temples. It is difficult indeed to believe that Rufinus did not at least sanction it, if only because the Greek peninsula was the most expendable of the territories of the eastern empire, and it was obvious to him that Gothic energy and anger would have to boil over somewhere. Our suspicion must be that Alaric himself saw the raid confusedly as revenge on the Romans (in the widest sense) for the slights offered to his people, an opportunity of proving the flair he would bring to the leadership, and some kind of extension of the religious war against the ideas inspiring Eugenius' supporters, for many in Greece clung to the old gods, the mysteries still survived there, and to Alaric and his clerical friends that country must have symbolised the whole past of the Helleno-Roman and pagan world.

"The ruin of all Greece" foretold by Eunapius' master in the Eleusinian Mysteries of Demeter and the Maiden, the ruin brought about by Alaric's destruction of the sanctuaries and opening of the country to "the men in black", needed a great pagan poet to lament it. But there was none. There was no one—or no one whose work had survived—but an ambiguous friend and sycophant of the enigmatic Stilicho, the Alexandrian Claudius Claudianus. A successful secret policeman by trade, Claudian crept out of the shadows to become Stilicho's court poet. Like his master, he was one who never let his right hand know what his left was doing, so that in one line of his verse he is a Christian and in the next he is fervently praying to the old gods. St. Augustine called him "a foreigner to Christ's name" and Orosius "a most obstinate pagan", but he would no doubt have resented being so clearly labelled. Most of his verse is indifferent, but when he was touched by an event, he could write vividly. His description of Alaric's invasion of Greece, from Thrace, through the mountains and over the rivers of the east to Athens and on to Eleusis and so into Arcadia recalls not only the landscape of the country but also many of the greatest incidents in her history and legend:

> "Wheresoever the waves of fate drove [the host]
> Hailed down ritual sickness along lonely secret ways.
> Pouring through closed places, they rushed on:
> Neither rivers nor crags helped [the Greeks] to defend their land:
> Neither Rhodope, nor massive Athos, nor Thracian Hebrus avails—
> Strymona is leapt over with scornful ease—
> And with deceptive speed they spurn the Bessian [River] Haliacmona.
> From Macedon they see Olympus, unmasked by clouds,
> Sticking up foolishly from the fields.
> Thessaly's [beautiful Vale of] Tempe sighs in vain
> And—laughable now—Mount Oeta is painlessly subdued.
> In Sperchius, and Eripeus beloved by virgins,
> The barbarians wash their hair. Pindus saves not
> The Dryopians, nor the Leutrians the cloud-making Attic shore.
> The great gates of Thermopylae, which once so powerfully
> Defied the Persians, are smashed at the first assault;
> The ramparts of the Scironian Gulf are broken
> And the unpierced parallel wall of the Isthmus.
> They force the narrow confines of Lechaea
> And you, Parrhesius, are not allowed to save
> The ever-leafy columns of Arcady.
> And so, on, still riding, till from the highest peaks of Taygetus
> Behold! Anxious Amyclae. . . ."[6]

Claudian expected his readers to know that cloud always hid some part of Olympus because it was the home of the gods, discreetly veiled from mortal eyes. That Alaric's men should have seen it "sticking up foolishly from the fields" meant that the gods had gone from Greece, never to return.

In another poem, *On The Rape of Proserpine*, Claudian describes the horrible assault on civilisation which was Alaric's sack of "Cecrops' city" of Athens and the holy sanctuary of Eleusis, the home of the goddesses and their mystery, where destruction was so complete that hardly a stone was left on another and Eleusis, one of the most evocative names in religion, has ever since been for the visitor one of the most barren of sites. Fittingly—for Demeter and the Maiden were corn-goddesses—the destruction of Eleusis was marked by widespread shortages of food grains in the years 396 and 397, so that Claudian's epic, which is largely devoted to a retelling of ancient myth and legend, can be read either as a lament for the shrines of Greece or a hymn of hate against famine.

> "A full heart moves me to versify. Impious—back a pace!
> A tumult drives human feelings from our breasts

So that they breathe now only the Phoebus of Inspiration.
I see the sanctuaries move on trembling foundations. . . .
A great shaking is heard from the depths of the earth—
The Cecropian temple quivers, and the sacred forms Eleusis holds holy.
The soothsayers of Triptolemus cry out. . . .
O Gods . . . lay open now the inner secrets of your sacred treasures to me
And your hidden Antipodes: as love prevailed upon the God
So that, led by him, bold Chaos seized plundered Prosperpina
As his bride. . . ."[7]

Zosimus, for once letting his heart openly rule his head, has a vivid but quite untrue story of the stalwart defence of the acropolis at Athens by divine figures, who drove the barbarians away. Eunapius' story is the true one: all sacred Greece was deliberately ruined, and never recovered. He relates that many despaired at the destruction they saw. One of those who died at this time was the Emperor Julian's friend, the sophist Priscus:

"Priscus died at last, having reached a great age—for he was over ninety—at the time of the destruction of the temples of Greece. And there were many who at that same time threw their lives away for grief while others were butchered by the barbarians, among them being Proterius, a native of Cephalonia, of whose worth and probity there is plentiful proof. Hilarius was another—a man known to the present writer, a Bithynian by birth. He had grown old at Athens and had mastered the art of painting, as well as the whole gamut of learning. . . . He was taken outside Athens and was beheaded by the barbarians together with all his servants. . . ."

Hilarius was murdered while returning home from a visit to Eleusis, the last pilgrim known to have worshipped at the shrine of the goddesses while it still existed.

So the ruin of all Greece was accomplished. The battle of the gods and giants, fought out at the beginning of the world, was restaged, and the giants won. The men in black took over the holy places of Greece. The Erechtheum, where once had run the salt spring struck from the rock by Poseidon's trident, was converted into a Christian sanctuary, the first sacred place in Greece so to be alienated from its ancient usage.

Chaos ruled again.

Notes

1 There is a translation of Eunapius' *Lives of the Philosophers* by W. C. Wright (Loeb Classical Library, 1922).

2 All sacrifice, even in private houses, was forbidden by Cod. Theod. XVI, 10, 12; XVI, 8, 8 forbids *Clarissimi* and *Illustres* to attend the games; II, 18, 9 forbids holidays on former pagan festivals.

3 Like all pagan aristocrats of his generation, Nicomachus Flavianus enjoyed—or endured—a very mixed career.

Born about 334, he followed the traditional path through offices in the city, becoming first Quaestor, then Praetor and a member of the College of Pontiffs before being appointed Consular of Sicily in the year that Symmachus the Elder was City Prefect (364–5). After resigning from Sicily, he was offered no further appointment, presumably because of his paganism, until he became Vicar of Africa in 376. He soon fell into trouble there, pursuing the only anti-Christian policy pagan administrators felt to be open to them, by favouring local schismatics—in this case, Donatists—against the Catholics; this policy brought him censure in October 377, when Gratian ordered him to intensify persecution of the Donatists (Cod. Theod. XVI, 6, 2). Clearly, he took no notice of this direct order, because a new law dated 27 February 378 complained bitterly of the "wickedness" (*improbitas*) of "secular judges" in not putting down schismatics. So Flavian was retired and spent several years making himself one of the most learned men of his age, becoming especially famous for his knowledge of augury and methods of divination. He also wrote *Annals*, running down to the time of the death of Procopius; these drew to him the attention of Theodosius, who appointed him Quaestor of the Sacred Palace at Constantinople, then sent him in February 383 to be Prefect in Illyricum, Italy and Africa.

Within six months of his appointment, however, he had retired to his villa in Campania to think and to write, either because (as he claimed) public life bored him, or because he was dragged down into disgrace with his son, who had risen with him to become Proconsul of Asia in 383, but almost immediately earned exile and sequestration of his property by ordering a town magistrate to be scourged.

Nicomachus' retirement proved to be only temporary. When Theodosius rested in Italy after the defeat of Maximus, he called his ex-Prefect to court and rewarded him—probably in 389—with reappointment to his old Prefecture. He held the post until 392.

Then he joined Eugenius' revolt, was Prefect in 393, and Consul in 394.

Theodosius could scarcely have let him live, even had he not committed suicide; but he mourned him in a speech to the senate.

His son—Eugenius' Prefect in Rome—survived the war, and saved his property by becoming a Christian, losing only what Eugenius had given to his father.

4 Published by H. Bloch, *Harvard Theological Review* (38, 1945) pp. 199ff.

5 The bitterness of the Arian controversy during these and subsequent years is well brought out, with dry and somewhat malicious humour, in a famous passage in Gibbon's *Decline and Fall of the Roman Empire*, Vol. II, pp. 345ff. (Bury's Edition, 1900).

6 Claudius Claudianus, *De Bello Gothico*, 173ff. (some of the references to places have been simplified).

Augustine's reference to Claudian is at *De Civ. Deo*, 5, 26 (P.L. 41); Orosius in his *Historiae adv. Paganos*, 7, 35 (P.L. 31).

7 Claudius Claudianus, *De Raptu Proserpina*, 1, 1ff.

Chapter Eleven
"The Roman race then struggled to survive . . ."—Rutilius Namantianus

Alaric and Rome

Arcadius was eighteen when his father died, and could have been a force for survival in the empire if there had been any spark of leadership in his character. But there was none. As a child, he had been weakly, undersized, and purblind, given to outbursts of excitement and intense rage. As he grew older, he seemed to withdraw into himself, becoming mentally torpid unless his deepest emotions were directly aroused. When Theodosius died, and barbarians from beyond all the frontiers invaded the east, Arcadius seemed not to care. Caught up in Byzantine dreams, he left all the problems of empire to Rufinus. One of the few things that did move him was religion. Hardly had the news of his father's death reached him before he addressed a new law against the pagans to his overworked Prefect:

> "Arcadius and Honorius to Rufinus:
> Let no one at all have permission on any grounds to put fire to or to celebrate accursed sacrifices at any shrine or temple whatsoever at any place or time. . . ."[1]

These sacrifices were continuing unlawfully in Egypt and Syria, although at fewer places every year and in ever greater conditions of secrecy and even furtiveness as confiscations of buildings and land continued under the laws of Theodosius. Libanius had threatened in his *Defence of the Temples* that pagans would fight for their shrines: "if these people go on to attack temples which have hitherto escaped their fury, or those which have been so speedily rebuilt after attack, you must realise that the people of the land will defend both their property and the law".[2] Since he had written those words, the pagans had tried to defend their heritage, both in Egypt and in Italy. Now the law had been changed. It was still not legal for bands of Christian fanatics to roar through the countryside destroying public buildings and monuments, but every form of devotion to the gods was forbidden, and any defender of the old ways could expect neither advancement in his career nor even the protection of the law for his property and family. He might still be promoted: he might be protected. But he could not expect it.

Arcadius' other preoccupation beside religion in the year his father died was a young girl named Aelia Eudoxia who had won some notoriety for

herself even among the women of that idle and fast-living court. She was
the orphan daughter of the General Bauto who had taken reinforcements
from Gratian's army to the east during Theodosius' Gothic campaigns in
the early eighties. Nothing would satisfy Arcadius but that he should marry
her. Rufinus saw this marriage as further barbarisation, a disaster, but he
was unable to prevent it. Three months after Theodosius' death, before his
corpse had been brought to Constantinople for burial, and while Rufinus
was in Antioch on urgent state affairs, Arcadius married his Eudoxia with
the connivance of Eutropius, the eunuch Master of the Bedchamber—
after which (for the emperor was absurdly happy) Eutropius could do no
wrong, and Rufinus very little right.

Nor were Arcadius and the barbarians Rufinus' only problem. He had
a mortal enemy in the virtual ruler of the west, Stilicho. No two historians
have ever agreed about Stilicho—not even about what he did, let alone
what sort of man he was. Decisive and wavering by turns, he surrounded
himself with a peculiarly odd assortment of personages. When he
hated—as he certainly hated the Prefect Rufinus—he permitted nothing
to deter him from the destruction of his enemy. But when he feared and
admired—as he feared and admired Alaric—he could not bring himself to
act with determination however great the needs of the empire it depended
upon him to save.

The dead Theodosius had put Stilicho in command of the combined
armies of the empire to bring about the defeat of Eugenius, so that in 395
and 396, he found himself militarily the strongest man in the empire. He
decided then to bid for supreme power, eliminating Rufinus, and bringing
both Theodosius' sons under his influence. But events outran him. Alaric,
as we have seen, collected his army in Thrace and camped them under the
very walls of Constantinople for the winter, till Rufinus bought him off,
and sent him to sack Greece, while in the depths of the coldest months a
vast horde of Huns swept over the Caucasus and through eastern Asia
Minor into Syria. Stilicho moved troops into Thessaly, but indecisively, as
thought not certain whether the aim was to fight Alaric or take
Constantinople and threaten the Huns. When Alaric's men swept through
Greece, the Westerners seemed unable to do more than contain them
within the peninsula, but, at the end of the year, when under pressure from
Rufinus Arcadius demanded troops from Stilicho's combined command
for the defence of the east, he took firm action at last, sending men to the
military headquarters at Hebdomon outside Constantinople with orders
to murder his rival. Rufinus was cut down in Arcadius' presence on 27
November. Whether the emperor had been privy to the plot beforehand is
not known. He certainly condoned the assassination afterwards by
declaring all Rufinus' property forfeit to the state, giving leadership of the
court and country to his minister Eutropius, a man who apparently offered
no threat to Stilicho's military supremacy. Eutropius held office for almost
four years.

While Alaric's men were actually ravaging Greece, Stilicho absented himself from the troubled area, making a tour of the defences of the north Rhine area and perhaps even leading in person the naval expedition which landed troops in North Britain to relieve the hard-pressed defenders of the Wall. It was not until after Rufinus was dead that he returned south, to confront Alaric at Corinth and compel his withdrawal into the Danube provinces. Even then, it is doubtful whether western forces were very effectively deployed against the Goths. Alaric did not actually quit Greece, despite western pressure, until Eutropius named him Master of the Infantry serving Arcadius in Illyricum and paid him to go there and defend eastern interests against the west. However, Alaric did finally leave Greece and this ambiguous victory left Stilicho free to turn his attention to the winning back of Africa. He spent a large part of the following summer equipping an army for service against Count Gildo there. Once again, hesitancy cost him dearly, for the news of his intending invasion soon reached Africa, whereupon Gildo offered his provinces to Arcadius, and Eutropius declared them part of the east. The once-united empire stood on the brink of civil war but not even the gambler Stilicho dared to push it over that edge in the desperate hope of regaining all that he had already lost.

Although Eutropius would have been justified to feel that he was serving his master well in the political confrontation with the West, he was given no time to preen himself upon his success. He found a new rival in Caesarius, the newly-appointed Prefect of the East who, although he was unable to offer practical support to Gildo in Africa or even to mount a major drive against the Huns in the east, nevertheless found a good deal of time for intrigue among the various sects of Christians at the court. In 396, while Alaric's men were still in Greece, a further edict against leading pagans forbade anyone to accord them any of the privileges granted "under the old law",[3] and when Eutropius came to supreme power he seemed as opposed to the old religion as anyone in the east. But gradually, perhaps because of his bickering with Caesarius, his attitude changed, until the year 398 found him simultaneously oppressing both the pagans and the Christians, advocating an edict ordering the physical destruction of pagan buildings, bringing pressure on Bishop Theophilus of Alexandria to secure the election of John Chrysostom (a man with many enemies) to the Patriarchate of Constantinople, stripping churches of the right of asylum they had enjoyed as the successors to the temples, and forbidding the bishops to ordain those he defined as "criminals" in order to save them from what he defined to be the law.

By this time he had lost Africa, through Caesarius' inability to give Gildo military backing. The food shortages of the west had become so acute that Stilicho had been goaded into action. Typically, he did not at first attack the problem head-on, but tried to undermine Eutropius' position in the east—and in consequence was declared proscript by the senate of

Constantinople. Only then did he appeal to the senate at Rome for men and money to fight in Africa.

How confused the whole situation was at this moment in Rome's history when clear thinking and national unity were so desperately needed is illustrated by the muddle instantly created by Arcadius' promulgation at this point in time of the edict requiring the destruction of pagan temples, the edict for which eastern Christians at least had been agitating for so long:

"If there are temples in our domains, let them be razed without alarms and tumults. When they have been thrown down and annihilated, the fundamental support of all superstition will have been eliminated."[4]

This law was signed at Damascus in July 398. Copies of it reached Africa and the West at just about the time when Stilicho felt strong enough to reconquer the granary of Rome—when, in fact, he had reached the height of his powers by marrying his daughter Maria to the Emperor Honorius, and won approval from the senate for everything he planned. To start the war, all Arcadius' laws were declared null in Africa so that when Africa was regained, this edict against the temples was also rescinded. Nevertheless, in Gaul, Spain and Africa, the work of destruction went ahead. Saint Augustine later recalled with satisfaction the day when the temples were destroyed in Carthage, several months after the law ordering such destructions had already been annulled. Augustine had also heard the oracle which had heartened Eugenius' pagans, foretelling the disappearance of Christianity "a year of years" after it had first troubled the world during the consulate of the two Gemini, in A.D. 29. The oracle foresaw the end in 398, the consulate of Honorius and Eutychianus, "three hundred and sixty-five years after that Ides of May when the Holy Spirit was sent forth. Then, the following year, in the consulate of Mallius Theodorus—when according to that devilish and man-imagined oracle nothing ought to have remained of the Christian religion—it was not necessary to enquire into what might perhaps be happening in other parts of the world; for as we know in this most noteworthy and prominent city of Carthage in Africa the Emperor Honorius' Counts Gaudentius and Iovius threw down the temples of the false gods and broke their images on the sixteenth day of March. And there is no one who has not seen how the worship of Christ's name has not grown through the thirty years more or less from that time till now."[5]

In fact, the destruction of the temples caused resentment and dissensions which the regime could not afford. About three months after the sanctuaries of Carthage were destroyed Honorius—or rather, Stilicho, acting in Honorius' name—sent two new orders within a few days to the new Proconsul in Africa:

"Although with beneficial legislation we have done away with profane rites, we will not sanction the abolition of those festivals which bring people together and are a source of common enjoyment to all. What is desired is that these should be publicly promoted while abominable and criminous activities should be ended with fitting and most severe fines. . . ."[6]

With Christians screaming that every manifestation of paganism was abominable and criminous, and the pagans on the verge of rebellion in defence of their way of life, the burden of decision which this law laid on the Proconsul was not an enviable one. The second law was more direct in its provisions:

"Let no one attempt to destroy the temples already stripped of unlawful objects. . . . We require that the integrity of such buildings shall be preserved. . . ."[7]

Whatever the law might say on this subject, however, there were some western Christians ready to go to extreme lengths to obtain their ends. Not only were they willing to risk skirmishes with the pagans in order to fulfil their dreams of a "purified" world, they were ready also to sacrifice their personal integrity: in September, Macrobius, the Prefect of Spain, received the following instruction:

"Although we have forbidden sacrifices, nonetheless it is our desire that the fabric of public buildings should be preserved. So let no one be seduced by any order purporting to require them destroyed. If by any chance any persons should present such a rescript or edict, seize the document from them for our information. . . ."[8]

Some Christians were prepared even to forge documents, it seems, to gain their ends. Those ends were, however, no longer the aims of the western administration. What Stilicho needed was unity and peace—any compromise, so long as it was willingly accepted by everyone in a moment of great danger.

It was partly in pursuit of this elusive unity that he decided to cut all communication with the east in 399. On 1 January Eutropius, the man he regarded as the west's chief enemy since he had settled Alaric permanently on the frontier of Italy and tried to win Africa for the east, had become consul at Constantinople, the first eunuch ever to hold the office. Stilicho had refused to recognise him and to underline his opposition had declared all the laws of Arcadius of no effect in the west. How far this was a declaration of war against the east, and how far it was a gesture towards western pagans it is impossible now to decide. What seems indisputable is that the pagans of the senate took it as licence to them to continue to exist (in the old legal phrase) and there was an upsurge of pagan sentiment, at least in central Italy, sufficient to win for Stilicho's regime the enmity of Christian fanatics.

Was the altar of Victory once again restored to the senate at this time? In spirit, certainly, although perhaps not in physical reality; however, in describing Stilicho's third consulate this year, Claudian seems to imply that it was:

"What real joy when thought is given
To bringing back to her sacred sanctuary
Victory, who drives out all hardships with her full wings:
O green palms of rejoicing and delightful trophies [of Victory]!
Guardians around this Virgin of Dominion
Who alone heals wounds and teaches [men] to feel no burden.
[Victory!] The stars of Ariadne's Crown delight you!
In summer heat, you are the Lion's companion!
You share the sceptre of sublime Jove and Pallas' aegis!
With a breath you soothe the hurts of Mars!
Be an abiding presence here in Latium!
Assent, O Goddess, to the deliberations of the senate!
Stilicho, who has oft adorned your dwelling,
Having made you commander in this war
Now carries you back to camp. So take upon you now
The robe of Counsellor. . . ."9

The meaning of these lines is, on one level, plain enough, but as many commentators on them have denied as have affirmed that they refer to an actual restoration of Victory to her ancient place. One thing is certain, however: this was not the language for a good Christian to use when the outcome of the conflict between religions and ways of thinking was still in doubt. At the very least—even if they are translated (as they can be) with an emphasis different from that given to them here—they show no disrespect towards the mythographers and astrologers to whom Ariadne's Crown and Leo were important constellations, and they seem to imply that Jupiter, Pallas Athene and Mars are no less "real" (whatever that is taken to mean) than the *diva* Victory. Equivocation and ambiguity were the marks of Stilicho's rule, and in these lines his poet-panegyrist reflected precisely the mood of the times.

At that moment in time, Victory was indeed living in Stilicho's camp. Apart from small trouble spots, there was peace everywhere, the corn supply was assured, and there was no usurper anywhere to challenge the authority of his son-in-law. The western barbarians were asking permission to settle in the empire rather than forcing their way over the frontiers. At a superficial glance, the world must have seemed much as it had been throughout living memory. True, there were differences between the western and eastern halves of the Roman world, but one could hope that they would prove temporary. When it was announced that Stilicho would be consul for the year 400, many must have felt that this clever barbarian deserved the honour. For a few months, the sun shone on the western world.

Meanwhile in the east there was a growing—but in 399 still underground, still largely unexpressed—realisation that the recent settlers threatened destruction of the old world. After the failure of Caesarius to support Gildo in Africa, Eutropius—till now still only Master of the Bedchamber—had secured his dismissal from the post of Prefect and secured it for himself, together with the honourific title Patricius, "the Patrician". In this new rôle, he took on direction of the army in the war against the Huns and their Ostrogoth allies, slowly driving them out of Asia Minor and Armenia, back to the Caucasus. Although he could not bring them to a decisive battle, and relieve them of their accumulated booty, he was granted a triumph at Constantinople, and—as has already been mentioned—was named consul for 399.

His days of glory were very short. The year 398 had seen widespread earthquakes and flooding in Constantinople itself and throughout Thrace. The people were nervous—the patriarch had them all out in the streets waiting for the end of the world when he foretold in a sermon the destruction of the whole city—and the superstitious were looking for an explanation of their troubles in imperial religious policies. When John Chrysostom became patriarch, he quickly proved a divisive force, alienating many of the clergy with his constant demands for stronger powers, and using his preaching skill and his seemingly inexhaustible supply of wonder-working relics to influence policy through popular agitation and in particular to encourage fulfilment of the ordinances against the temples. Then, as though earthquake and John Chrysostom did not represent troubles enough, in the spring of 399 a Gothic Tribune named Tribigild gave expression to the strong underlying discontent which Eutropius' way of running affairs had aroused; he complained against delays in his receiving his pay. Within days, it seemed the whole of Asia Minor was threatened by rebellion, as both dissatisfied auxiliary troops and hitherto trusted slaves rose against the authorities in the names of Tribigild and the romanised chief Gainas. While this mob still threatened the peace, news reached Constantinople of a change in Persia's government and preparations for war on that frontier. Showing rare initiative, Arcadius appealed over Eutropius' head for western help. Stilicho replied that his price would be Eutropius' dismissal, a demand which left Arcadius helplessly wondering what he should do. Throughout his life, he was childlike in his devotion to the friend of the moment, and at that moment he could not imagine Constantinople without Eutropius. Others knew—Stilicho's secret service had made sure that they did know—how corrupt Eutropius' administration was proving, and how overbearing he himself had become in his hours of glory. But Arcadius preferred not to know such things. It was only when Eudoxia approached him as a suppliant, declaring that the consul had threatened her and the imperial children, the two-year-old Flacilla and the newborn Pulcheria, that Arcadius was forced to a decision. Eutropius fled, taking refuge in a church. His property was confiscated. A mob raged through Constantinople, screaming for his death. John Chrysostom preached a sermon calling the people back to sanity, telling his congregation to go to the palace and ask forgiveness for themselves and the fallen minister. Such was his power, that a penitential procession was formed, but before it reached the palace it had become a riotous, murderous mob. Eutropius barely saved himself, and was smuggled away to a brief exile in Cyprus. But even in disgrace the character-assassins would not leave him in peace, and with Arcadius it was ever a case of out of sight, out of mind. Soon the former minister was recalled and executed.

During his days of glory, his predecessor in office, Caesarius, had found a new role to play, as interpreter of the barbarians to the court. He had made himself the friend of the Goths and spokesman of the Vandals. But if he had played any part in Eutropius' fall, he gained nothing from it, but lost rather, when his own brother Aurelian was appointed Prefect in August 399. The brothers were bitter enemies. Their differences polarised around their different attitudes towards barbarians. Caesarius wished to see them prosperous and peaceful citizens, fully integrated into the empire. Aurelian believed that this policy had already caused untold damage to the state. He was determined to see the empire "re-Romanised". For better or worse, Aurelian had the ear of the Empress Eudoxia, and Eudoxia had learned that with the help of her children and her clergy, her superstitious fears, her smiles and tears, she could do as she chose with Arcadius. So at the beginning of January in the year 400, when Stilicho the Vandal became consul in the West, Aurelian, the declared enemy of barbarians, became Consul in the East, while Eudoxia was formally endowed with the title Augusta.

Re-Romanisation under the Consul Aurelian began with the dismissal of the barbarian-born from the higher ranks of the army and the civil service. The policy might have made more sense if it had been evolved fifty years earlier. Now, although it was ultimately successful in the East, it came too late to save the united empire. Even at Constantinople the struggle was a hard one. There were not enough Roman-born officials with the experience necessary to fill essential posts. Both Gainas and Tribigild had to be reinstated after their rebellion had failed, and when Gainas, as commander at Chalcedon, again made trouble, the only commander whom Aurelian could find to use against him was Frevitta, his rival for leadership of the Goths.

Stilicho naturally found Aurelian's policy a wonderful opportunity for trouble-making. He refused to recognise Aurelian's consulship and persuaded Honorius of the need to write to Arcadius disapproving of Eudoxia's promotion. There has been much speculation as to how far he pushed his interference into eastern affairs; many feel that the hand of

Stilicho could be seen at work in Caesarius' decision a few weeks later publicly to show his adherence to the barbarians by leaving Constantinople and joining Gainas in his camp. For a moment, it looked as though the east would be plunged into civil war until, in one of those sudden changes of policy for which Arcadius was notorious, Aurelian was dismissed and Caesarius replaced in the Prefect's office. He opened the gates of Constantinople to Gainas and the Goths, carrying his views to the extreme limit of their expression by actually expelling the Roman garrison from the city and manning all its defences with barbarians. For two months, till the Goths' behaviour drove the citizens to violence, Gainas ruled the east. His Goths' expulsion was achieved by a wonderfully apt combination of coincidences: while Gainas himself was at a country church outside the city, seeking a miracle-cure for a chronic ailment, his Arian chaplains offended the catholics by celebrating their masses in a catholic church in the city, and in precisely the same week a great comet appeared in the sky overhead . . . By the time the killing stopped, thousands of Goths were dead; Thrace, in the hands of the survivors under Gainas, had become an enemy country, and the stage was set for the final onslaughts against Rome. For of course Alaric, the faithful ally still in command in Illyricum, watched these events and drew his own conclusions from them.

When Gainas had marched the remnants of his men into the mountains of Thrace, Arcadius' government suddenly realised that the city of Constantinople was defenceless. John Chrysostom was sent to beg Gainas to return. He refused, so Fravitta was commanded to drive him back to the Danube. By December, Gainas' people had decided that they had suffered enough in the empire and elected to cross the river northwards, seeking a secure home in the lands their tribes had left twenty years earlier. But their old home was now in the hands of Uldin of the Huns. His men hunted Gainas down; on 23 December 400, they killed him. Uldin sent his head to Constantinople as a peace-offering. The citizens dragged it through the streets. Fravitta was named consul for 401. The administration sent Uldin a great present in gold and declared him Friend of the Roman People.

Less than a year later, the army of Illyricum invaded Italy. There was no declaration of war—indeed, such were the circumstances of the invasion that Alaric's diplomatists were in a position to argue that there was no war, but that Alaric the Prefect had merely taken steps to protect the people of Italy from troubles to the north. Both sides maintained the fiction that Alaric was no more than protecting Italy and attempting to reform its institutions until long after the story became quite incredible. Alaric himself, in fact, continued to wrap his actions around in the ragged tatters of this cloak of respectability until the end.

As the Prefect for Arcadius in Illyricum, Alaric's official sphere of activities ended at the frontier-post of Emona. Only extreme peril to the empire could justify his sending troops into the domains of the Prefects of

Italy or Gaul. A very plausible excuse for him to do so arose late in 401 when after several years of relative peace along the whole Rhine frontier, a confederation of Vandals, barbarians of Stilicho's own race, smashed its way over the frontier into Rhaetia, where the Rhine and the Danube, both young streams, all but met. Stilicho took the army of Italy north to meet the threat. Alaric, acting in his guise as faithful ally, moved troops west and south, to form a rearguard closing the Alpine passes. In recent years, these had been standard tactics. But it was not established practice for him also to advance men actually into the plain of Lombardy and to take ransom from the towns of northern Italy while spreading his creed among the people with the sword.

The Vandals were held on this occasion in Rhaetia, but it took well over a year's fighting and argument for Stilicho to free the Italian peninsula from Alaric's Goths.[10] Under the peace agreement, Honorius' government recognised Alaric's rights in Illyricum, and paid him well to exercise them; a few months later, Stilicho claimed that Theodosius' testament had been misinterpreted: Illyricum belonged to the west, and Alaric was Honorius' Prefect there. While the war lasted, Italy was reduced to desperate straits: the court was forced to Ravenna for safety, a large part of the garrison was withdrawn from Britain to fight in Italy, and recruits were accepted into the legions from any tribe, however barbaric. Every form of petition to every sort of god was acceptable to all but fanatics. Although very slowly, the military position in the west was restored, all frontiers were crumbling, and barbarianisation continued apace.

In the east, the struggle to free the Roman world from barbarians continued. Fravitta, despite his successes (or perhaps because of them) was twice charged with having secretly aided Gainas. On the second occasion, in 402, Caesarius was charged with him, as a traitor to his race. Both men were found guilty and executed, and Aurelian, the enemy of all barbarians, was restored to power.

That same winter there was a tragedy in the imperial family which had wide repercussions upon later history. Its occasion was a struggle for power in the eastern church between John Chrysostom of Constantinople and Theophilus of Alexandria. Whatever the rights and wrongs of the theological aspects of their disagreement, the Empress Eudoxia reduced the argument to a very human level. She liked John; she admired—and feared—his collection of potent relics; she could usually rely on him to support whatever cause she had in hand, because he wanted her support in the fight against the temples. But then one day in her presence he preached a sermon against luxurious and loose-living women which enraged her because it so obviously referred to herself and her ladies. As Augusta in her own right, the mother of four children (the youngest of them, Theodosius Junior, already Augustus at the age of one year) and pregnant with a fifth, Eudoxia felt that she had all the authority she needed to deal summarily with cruel-tongued clerics. She denounced the archbishop and declared herself (and her purse) at the disposal of Theophilus. Her public stand brought rioting crowds into the streets and her appeals, supported by theirs, drove Arcadius to declare John Chrysostom exiled. Fighting continued as John's supporters took to the streets in their turn. A mob broke into the palace and the Princess Flacilla was murdered.

Arcadius' reaction to her death was terrible in its melancholy intensity. He withdrew into a black cloud of gloom from which he rarely again emerged before his own death on 1 May 408. Neither Eudoxia's repentance and the return of John Chrysostom, nor the birth of another princess, Marina, could stop him mourning for his dead child. Until, in mid-404, John Chrysostom was again exiled at the insistence of an ecclesiastical tribunal of his enemies, and the empress herself died (of a miscarriage, on 3 October of that same year), the empress, the archbishop and the prefect ruled the east. After the empress died, Aurelian—and from 405 onwards, his successor, Anthemius—directed affairs all but single-handed. Anthemius, like Aurelian, dedicated himself to re-establishing Roman control over the empire and its emperor. Until after he died in 415, not a single barbarian name appeared among the lists of those appointed to high office in the Eastern Empire.

From the eastern Roman's point of view, this may have been a valuable development. The Byzantine Empire survived at Constantinople for another thousand years. But it meant that while Stilicho lived, and Alaric held Illyricum, normal relations between east and west were impossible. The east did nothing until the very last moment to prevent the coming disaster in the west—nor would her earlier intervention have been welcomed. In fact, at the official level, everyone desperately maintained Alaric's fiction that the whole world was as it had always been, difficulties were merely temporary, and normal circumstances would soon be restored.

Anthemius' appointment marked a turning point, in as much as his declared policy of Romanisation in every sphere left Alaric exposed and insecure. The years 403 and 404 had passed quietly in the west; in 404, Honorius had reached his twentieth birthday and entered his sixth consulship at Rome. But now in 405, indubitably egged on by threats and promises from Illyricum, Stilicho refused to recognise Anthemius' promotion, pressed the west's claim to the middle Danube and Illyrian coast with the Greek peninsula, and prevailed upon Honorius to give Alaric security and his men guarantees of employment by naming him Master of the Soldiers in the West. Suborning auxiliaries and stealing provinces was cause for war, but before fighting could break out all contact, diplomatic and military, along land routes between east and west was severed by the appearance of a mixed band of desperate adventurers in Pannonia. They were led by an Ostrogoth named Radagais. Their invasion was apparently quite unheralded by the intelligence and security services—which suggests either that Alaric had allowed all normal Roman standards to decay beyond belief during his command of this vital area, or that some at least of his officers were open to bribes from beyond the frontier. For the horde was a huge one, and cannot have moved undetected before it crossed the Danube, unless no watch was kept. The invaders swept aside Alaric's Visigoths and Romans, destroyed Pannonia so utterly that as a Roman province it never recovered, and poured into Italy from the north-east. They were no half-civilised frontiersmen, with reverence towards Rome's glorious past. Their leader showed no desire to emulate Alaric and become a Roman general. There was no question as to whether or not these men were a threat. Neither the Arians nor anyone else could welcome them. They were not saviours, but savages bent on destruction. Orosius' account of the disaster they created,[11] though it may not be accurate in detail, and is certainly biased, echoes the true horror of these terrible days:

"In an unexpected onslaught Radagais, the most monstrous by far of all enemies, ancient or modern, flooded over all Italy, for there were among his people more than two hundred thousand Goths. The man over this incredible, unbeatable horde was a pagan and an Ostrogoth [*Scytha*], from those barbarian tribes whose habit it is to offer in sacrifice to their gods the blood of everyone of Roman race. And when they came to the Roman lines, all the pagans in the City got together to oppose them with whatsoever wealth of forces they could, including the maximum protective power of the gods, on the grounds that the City having lost its gods and sacred places was now left destitute and dying of old age. The result was that there were massive disturbances everywhere and, with their ceremonies and sacrifices continually going on, the whole city was full of blasphemies. The name of Christ was infamously oppressed by the mob, as some sort of plague peculiar to these modern times. . . . [Everyone] shook with terror that such a degree of vengeance should be permitted [to fall on Italy] and as the terror continued they began to wonder if obedience might not win favour from the gods of the sacrifices, so a still more immoderate carnage [of offerings] was sent up in smoke, and there developed a new error worse than the former in as much as not only was the pagan residue . . . convinced of the need to restore the worship of idols, but the Christians also became dangerously confused."

However, all seemed to come right in the end, because, Orosius claimed, "the Just Disposer of human affairs elected that the pagan enemy should perish and permitted the Christians to prevail, so that the pagans, and blaspheming Romans, and those confused by them, vanished. . . ." But the perishing and the vanishing were not easily accomplished. Radagais' horde was broken up and finally scattered, but only after many anxious months. He made the mistake of dividing his forces, himself laying siege to Florence while lesser chiefs led smaller armies foraging north and south. Alaric, acting in his capacity as Roman commander, defeated him with a motley army. Radagais' forces were badly mauled in the hills behind Fiesole, then gradually driven back to Pannonia, where they regained some measure of coherence, and stayed. After this victory, Alaric not unnaturally felt that he had earned his place at the head of Roman military affairs, and relations between him and Stilicho's party quickly became strained.

The next invasion of the west was staged before the threat of Radagais could be discounted. Its leader was the Vandal king. He led his people through the wastes of what had been the Danube provinces into Gaul, but was stopped near the frontier by a local defence force made up chiefly of Franks settled there after invasions long before. The Vandal king was killed, but when, shortly afterwards, his son led a second wave of invaders over the frontier in the north Rhine area, there were no forces left sufficiently cohesive to organise a defence. "He burned Germany first, and after that . . . the land of the Belgians . . . and later, the wealth of the luxuriant Aquitainians, and then the main mass of all the Gallic provinces."[12] Pretence became impossible for the court: this was catastrophe. Every last man was withdrawn from Britain's five provinces to reinforce the armies, and from Ravenna there issued two of the most frightening decrees ever promulgated by a Roman emperor—frightening because as far as the government knew there were no officials left to whom they could be addressed, so that they were superscribed simply: "To the people of the provinces" and sent out from Ravenna, dropped into flame-filled chaos:

> "In the face of the enemy's attack, let us not think of individual persons, but of forces; and believing it to be right to appeal to inborn love of the fatherland, we exhort slaves to come forward on the authority of this [proclamation], promising them as soon as they offer themselves for the fatigues of battle the reward of freedom (if they prove fit to bear arms) and two *solidi* as enlistment-money.
>
> By reason of the pressing need [of the present situation] we entreat all living in the provinces to select and set forward those fit to serve militarily as freed men. And the freeborn who make it their business to take up arms for love of peace and the fatherland should know that they too shall receive two *solidi* from the fund which we have collected. . . ."

To anyone familiar with the traditions of the fatherland, these were edicts of panic and despair, and the policy advocated by Stilicho in this crisis, and forced upon Alaric, seemed to many not to match the needs of the situation. Instead of directing regular forces to the relief of Gaul, he ordered the army to drive Radagais still further back towards the Danube and out of all Illyricum, including the Greek peninsula. So once again, Alaric found himself fighting in the provinces he had ravaged a decade earlier. Not surprisingly, the Romano-Greek population there did not wait to be liberated by him of all men; many of them left all that they owned to him and to Radagais, fleeing to Italy as refugees—where when they landed the policy was to treat them as defeated enemies, shackle them, and sell them as slaves. Incredibly, it looked as though Stilicho was ready to sacrifice the whole of the north in order to pursue his vendetta against Constantinople. Orders were issued that no sailor or trader from the east was to land in any western port, and no trade between east and west to be carried on. The situation was crazy by anyone's standards except Stilicho's and from what little evidence survives it would seem that plots were made against him from this time onwards, at Rome and elsewhere. In the British provinces that year, no less than three new emperors were proclaimed: although the first two of them, Marcus and Gratianus, may have been mere adventurers, the third, Constantinus, asked to be seen as more. Both by assuming that illustrious name, and by his subsequent action in crossing the Channel to fight his way south through Belgica and Germania towards Rome, he declared that the time had come for a new start, just a century after the last. Perhaps from fear of him—or perhaps because there was nothing left in Gaul to make the region worth fighting for—the Vandal leader retreated before him and led his displaced people in an attack on hitherto untroubled northern Spain. Meanwhile, Alaric waited in the Epirus for fresh orders and a promised relief force which did not come.

Throughout 407 the news received at Rome grew worse almost day by day. Slowly but inexorably, Constantine III liberated all Gaul from both barbarians and the remnants of Honorius' administration. Displaced and desperate bands of would-be settlers from the north roamed northern Italy. Stilicho was forced to break off operations he had commenced in Illyricum against the remnants of Radagais' horde and so abandon his dreams of a west-Roman Danube. The pleas from Alaric (still in Greece) took on a threatening note. By December the now adult Honorius, surveying with Stilicho from the relative safety of Rome the chaos they had helped to create, realised that he must do something positive to demonstrate his strength and effectiveness. The action he decided upon was apparently trifling and futile, but in fact provocatively dangerous, in as much as it could only make him still more enemies. To placate the Christians he ordered that the Sibylline Books should be burned on Christmas Day. On the face of it, such an action would seem a small thing beside all the insults already offered to the gods, but Rutilius Namantianus, a highly-educated and sensitive Roman traditionalist, saw it as a symbolic act of murder, a proclamation of the coming death of old Rome. Many probably shared his view. In a bitter attack on the memory of Stilicho, "the traitor who was secret emperor", he later compared burning the books with two similar symbolic murders from the mythological past, Althea's dooming to death of her son Meleager by burning the firebrand upon which his life depended, and Scylla's destruction of her father Nisus' kingdom by cutting his sacred hair (after which, the gods made both of them sea-birds). So to this contemporary pagan, the deliberate destruction of the Oracles was an evil act, an ill-wishing the meaning of which could scarcely be overlooked in a world where omens might be seen in events far less obviously fateful:

"The Roman Race then struggled to survive—Frenzy mingled with the worst
of cruelty!—Fearing that there now had come what men had ever feared: the
barbarian net weaving the death of Latium. . . .

Rome itself lying open to leather-clad auxiliaries, a slave before ever she
grew withered—

The traitor lying in wait with so many Gothic troops! But first he burned
the treasure, the Sibylline Oracles—It hurts to see Althea burn the sacred
firebrand: to hear those birds named Nisus and Scylla scream—Stilicho
choosing to destroy the fateful pledges of eternal rule. . . ."[13]

Many shared Namantianus' opinion that all Rome's troubles lay at
Stilicho's door. They would have been happier with the eastern Prefect
Anthemius' anti-barbarian policies than they were with those of the
western administration, although many of them would have scorned the
Greek's devotion to the cause of Christianity. To Namantianus, Stilicho
was "the traitor" who, with his leather-clad auxiliaries, lay concealed till
the moment should come when he could destroy Rome—a moment he
himself precipitated by burning the sacred books guaranteeing Rome's
sovereignty.

But was it in fact Stilicho who ordered the burning of the books? Roman
gossip told Namantianus that it was, but although he may actually have
given the order, it is probable that the inspiration came from Honorius
himself and his Christian advisers. Relations between the emperor and his
prefect were probably already strained. In the coming months, they were to
deteriorate rapidly. Stilicho's son, Eucherius, was a pagan, and was widely
suspected later of having been involved in plots against Honorius'
Christian government. It may well be that by Christmas 407 Honorius felt
that it was time to assert himself. Only shortly afterwards, he promulgated
new laws underscoring his determination to rule through orthodox
Christian administrators and to end the dangers of a pagan revival: the first
of them, issued simultaneously with the order to burn the oracles, barred
Christian heretics from public office, and made the bishops judges in these
matters; another, dated 408, forbade "those antipathetic to the catholic
sect" to serve as imperial guards; and a third, addressed to the Praetorian
Prefect appointed after Stilicho's death, ordered the bishops to see that no
pagan rites were celebrated anywhere, even in cemeteries, and suggests, by
what it proscribed, that during recent years paganism had largely been re-
established, public money having been allocated for its support:

"Means of subsistence [*annonae*] of the temples are to be withdrawn. What
statues there now are in temples and shrines are to be thrown out from their
places, as we are well aware has been frequently reiterated in former decrees.
The structures of temples, whether in cities or towns or outside towns are to
be converted to public use, and altars everywhere destroyed."[14]

On that Christmas Day 407—the day of the undying sun—when the

Sibylline books were burned, that last order lay a year in the future. But
Namantianus and his friends saw it coming, when they watched the oracles
destroyed and the priesthood of the Quindecimvirs thus emptied of
meaning. The books had been destroyed before—but only by enemies in
open warfare. The case now was different.

Early in 408 the Empress Maria died. A very young child when her father
had made her marry Honorius, there is nothing to suggest that her life had
been a happy one. Now, exerting his influence over emperor yet again,
Stilicho made his second daughter Thermantia empress. The marriage was
at Rome in the spring. Hardly had the celebrations ended before more
disturbing news sent the imperial couple hurrying from Rome to the
supposed safety of Ravenna. All Gaul had submitted to Constantine, and
Spain had freely offered him her allegiance. Tired of waiting in Greece for
money and men, Alaric had marched north through stricken Illyricum to
Noricum and from there, poised either to invade Italy himself or to make
an alliance with Constantine, was demanding a vast tribute in gold for
himself and his men, to compensate them for the hardships they had
endured for Rome. After an acrimonious debate in the senate, Stilicho won
approval for the money to be raised and sent to him, but there was a good
deal of speculation about whose side Stilicho was really on. The question
became even more acute when, while Honorius and his bride were still on
the road to Ravenna, the news reached Italy that Arcadius had died at
Constantinople, leaving as his heir the seven-year-old Theodosius III, and
barbarian admirers of Stilicho proposed that his son Eucherius should be
sent to the east to depose Anthemius and act as Theodosius' guardian. As
Eucherius was already betrothed to Honorius' half-sister Galla Placidia,
such an arrangement would have made it all but certain that at some stage
a member of Stilicho's family would make a bid for the throne. This
prospect the soldiers of Honorius' bodyguard could not accept. They
staged a rebellion against Honorius, which he turned into a mutiny against
the tyranny of Stilicho by setting himself at the head of the revolutionary
troops.

While Honorius had been going to Ravenna, Stilicho had marched his
mixed army of Romans, Goths and Huns to Bologna, from where he was
expected to march on Gaul. Alaric, acting correctly, advanced troops to
guard the passes. But the news of Arcadius' death, and the ambitions it
aroused for Eucherius, decided Stilicho to halt his troops where they were
while he went to confer with Honorius.

Honorius, it was rumoured, had his own plan: to go himself to
Constantinople and act as adviser to the infant prince—so making himself
in all but name Autocrator, sole ruler of the empire.

What happened next is very fragmentarily reported in surviving records.
It seems that as soon as Stilicho had left his camp, Sara led his Visigoth
auxiliaries on a raid on the Hunnish cavalry in a search for better weapons,
so that in an hour the army was reduced to a bickering, ill-tempered mob,

and Alaric was the only leader in Italy with effective and coherent forces under his control.

When Stilicho reached Ravenna, he was arrested and executed:

"In the consulate of Bassus and Philippus: Stilicho, being contemptuous of Honorius and his rule and hotly in favour of the Alans, Suevians and Vandals, incited [men] against Honorius' rule, to make his son Eucherius, a pagan and opponent of the Christians, Caesar by a plot. Being detected in his wickedness he was executed along with Eucherius."[15]

The new empress, Stilicho's daughter, was sent back to her mother. In an attempt thoroughly to re-Romanise the state, Honorius appointed true Roman Christians, Olympius and Curtius, as his Master of the Offices and Praetorian Prefect, setting them as their primary task the elimination of barbarians from positions of power. They busied themselves with treason trials at Ravenna, but bloodshed did not stop there. As though an ugly abscess had burst, virulent hatred poured out over Italy. For months, no barbarian was safe from it. Soldiers turned on their comrades in the ranks, and even on their comrades' wives and children. Probably at Olympius' persuasion, Honorius promulgated laws banning heretics and pagans, as well as barbarians, from holding any official position, and ordering bishops to oversee the destruction of all temples. That winter, Italy promised to be a miserable place.

One of the victims of the new policy was Alaric, the barbarian heretic. He now found himself in the invidious position of having been dismissed as a barbarian by both eastern and western emperors. He asked for an explanation, and received none. He demanded hostages for the safety of his Goths in Italy; his demand was ignored. So, demonstrating that he was no mere tribune of auxiliaries to be waved aside when governments pleased, "he advanced again upon Rome, planning to take it by storm until the citizens supported him by declaring against Honorius,"[16] when he diverted his forces to take the port of Ostia with its essential granaries.

It is sometimes suggested that Rome did not surrender until Alaric had induced famine there, but it is all but certain that there was collusion between him and enough members of the senate to make his a token siege and the city's a token defiance. When appearances had been satisfied, serious negotiations began. It was a world turned upside down, with the Arian barbarian talking treason with senators to whom both his Christianity and his foreign blood were abominable.

After very little delay—not even long enough for the touchy Alaric to lose his temper and forget his purpose—the gates of Rome were opened to the Goths and Alaric, the City Prefect Priscus Attalus, and a group of leading senators conferred about the future of the state. Although formalities were observed, Alaric was unquestionably the master of the situation and—as Zosimus relates—"following his instructions the Senate set Attalus the City Prefect upon an imperial throne, putting the purple and diadem upon him. And there in the hall he proclaimed Lampadius his Praetorian Prefect and Marcianus his City Prefect . . . and so he filled all the offices in turn."[17]

The Emperor Attalus' name does not usually appear in name-lists of legitimate Roman rulers, but there must have been many among the senators who could persuade themselves that this was an authentic election, although one made under foreign protection, for genuine emperors—they could believe—ought to be nominated by the senate. Besides, Attalus was one of themselves, a man to be trusted, above all, not a fanatical Christian, a ruler himself ruled by bishops. When they looked at the list of Attalus' appointees, they found much satisfaction in it, realising that "they now had magistrates who were tried and experienced administrators, and above all the Consul, Tertullus. Only the family named Anicii were troubled by the fact that everything was apparently going well for the state because, as they were now in possession of almost everyone else's property, what made everyone else happy made them unhappy."

Zosimus was a pagan, writing his history about the year 500 as the servant of a suspicious Christian administration. He had to be careful what he said. Superficially he is suggesting here that the new régime at Rome frightened the powerful Anicii (and their dependants) because they feared that it would attempt to restore to its former owners property sequestered by earlier emperors and either granted to or purchased by Rome's richest family, property which is known to have included vast estates in southern Italy as well as numerous holdings on the fashionable and extremely expensive Bay of Naples. What he is careful not to say openly is that in the course of the previous century the Anicii had become what they now were through the allegiance of many of them to the Christian cause, or perhaps more accurately to the cause of the Christian emperors since Constantine I, for, like those emperors themselves, many of the family were not actually baptised. So what Zosimus is really implying in this passage is that upon the enthronement of the Emperor Attalus and his appointment of good *pagan* administrators like Tertullus everyone except Rome's Christians took heart.

The same point was made less deviously by the Christian historian Sozomen, writing from an entirely different standpoint and with a different end in view:

"From this circumstance [the appointment of Attalus] a situation arose in which both the pagans and those among the Christians who were followers of the Arian sect became very troublesome. The pagans for their part, basing their plans on Attalus' appointment (and bearing in mind especially his own background) hoped that their pagan superstition would once again become dominant and that the temples, and ancestral sacrifices, and festal days would be restored. . . ."[18]

Whether any sacrifices were offered and feasts commemorated following Attalus' appointment is not known, though it is likely that offerings, at least of incense and wine, were made to Fortune and Victory, if not also to *Roma dea* and other gods. It would seem certain that divination was once again practised in some traditional forms if not in all, for in 409 Honorius addressed the following law particularly to the "mathematicians"—the numerologists and astrologers—of Rome: at that date, he not being in control of the city, it can only have been a warning to them to halt their reported activities:

"Unless astrologers, after burning with fire the books of their particular errors before the bishops' eyes, are prepared to convert to the faith and worship of the catholic religion, and not afterwards to return to their former error, we are resolved to drive them out not only from the city of Rome but from all cities. . . ."[19]

The other sacrifice which seems certainly to have been restored was that made in the Flavian amphitheatre by the gladiators in their dying. Fourth-century tradition saw their blood as poured out in propitiation to the gods of death and the underworld. As sacrifices, gladiatorial contests were certainly forbidden by the law against the temples of 408, even if at Rome no account had been taken of an earlier law, promulgated in 405, forbidding them.[20] But Zosimus is most explicit—in a most horrible context, which will be cited below—that gladiators still fought in Attalus' Rome.

Such restoration of paganism as did occur under Attalus, however, eixsted only with Alaric's licence and could continue only during his pleasure. It was to the pagan senators' advantage as well as to Alaric's that Attalus' authority should be recognised outside the City Prefecture as soon as possible. But it was one thing for him to make appointments outside that area; another to have them acknowledged. And everyone knew that the strength of Attalus' government stemmed ultimately from the hated Goths. Where there were no Goths, no one cheered for the Emperor Attalus.

Central Italy's great weakness, demonstrated time and again through the years, was its inability to feed itself. The granary of Africa was indispensable to Rome. Once more now, under Alaric and Attalus, the City's dependency on outside resources was about to prove fatal to her rulers' plans. While a deputation from the senate was at Ravenna, trying to persuade Honorius either to accept Attalus as his co-ruler or to abdicate, Heraclianus, Honorius' representative in Africa, closed all ports to shipping routed to Italy, so that from late spring 409 onwards "neither grain, nor oil, nor yet any other necessity, was carried to the port of Rome". With the whole of the north already closed to Roman traders, there was even less hope than in other times of making good the deficit. The outcome was inevitable. As the summer passed without the new year's corn supply arriving to fill the depleted granaries, locally grown produce soon disappeared from the markets, and famine enveloped Rome, a famine worsening day by day until, as Zosimus relates, "at the games of the Circus people yearning for a taste of the combatants' corpses shouted: 'Put a price on human meat!'"[21] The dowager empress Laeta, widow of the Emperor Gratian, who had subsisted at Rome for years on a pension from Honorius, actually starved to death, as also did uncounted numbers of less prominent people. No government as artificial as Attalus' could survive for long in such circumstances, and Alaric soon began to realise that his plans had gone awry: rebellion had won Rome for him, but a Rome impoverished and impotent, no longer the heart of a great empire. There were two ways by which he might restore to his Rome something of the old Rome's glory, war and diplomacy. He chose first to explore the way of diplomacy.

Legates from the senate made their way to Ravenna. The demands they carried were reasonable and Honorius received them with some sympathy. The racial tensions of the previous autumn had slackened during the winter, partly perhaps because the government had realised that it could not survive without barbarians, and partly also because, shocked by their own ferocity, the soldiers had returned to their senses. The legates required that Olympius, the rabid Christian Master of the Offices, should be retired. Honorius dismissed him, and offered the leading senators of the delegation appointments, which they accepted, as his Prefect of Italy and chief treasury officer (*comes sacrarum largitionum*). But Alaric's own personal request, that he should be re-established as Master of the Soldiers, and his demand that Attalus should be recognised as Caesar, went unanswered.

As the weeks went by, Honorius could believe that his position was improving. A delegation arrived from Constantine III, asking that he should be acknowledged as Honorius' fellow emperor—an indication that all was not going well for him in the war. Part at least of the garrison remaining in Dalmatia (no more than a long day's sailing from Ravenna) swore its allegiance to Honorius' rule. And finally, at long last, vague but encouraging promises of support arrived from the east. Abruptly, the negotiations with Rome were broken off, and Olympius reinstated. An army was hastily mustered to march on Rome. It was cut to pieces in the Apennines. The reigning pope, Innocent I, journeyed to Ravenna, to suggest to Honorius that now might be the moment for him to make his peace with the senate, because Alaric was daily expecting reinforcements, under his brother-in-law Athaulf, to reach him from Pannonia. Honorius would not treat with the rebel—and starving—Romans, but scratched together another army to send against them and their allies. It also was destroyed, after Olympius had betrayed its movement out of the lowlands around Ravenna by attacking Athaulf's Rome-bound forces with a party of only 300 Hunnish cavalry. Athaulf broke through to Rome, and the luckless Olympius, not daring to face his master, fled to Dalmatia, where he was murdered.

Despite these setbacks, the intensity of Honorius' feelings concerning barbarians had by now so weakened that he was persuaded to appoint a governor for Dalmatia with the un-Roman name Generic and to grant him—a pagan—an edict of toleration for pagans in his province. But this conciliatory attitude did not survive the events of the following year, and after the sack of Rome toleration was brought to an end.

The year 409 ended with yet another shift in the balance of power, once again ultimately in Honorius' favour. In Spain, a certain Gerontius, British-born Prefect of the rebel government, led a counter-revolution against the administrators appointed by his master Constantine III; the resulting confusion allowed the Vandals under Gunderic, hitherto confined to the Pyrenees, to break into the central and coastal areas of Spain, but this weakening of Constantine resulted in greater credibility for Honorius' claim to be the only true Western Emperor.

By early in 410 Alaric knew that Rome must win control of Africa soon or collapse. He therefore prevailed upon the Emperor Attalus to name a proconsul for the diocese and despatch him from Rome to take up his appointment. He seems to have been provided with no more bodyguard than would normally have accompanied a new administrator, as though it was expected that Heraclianus would merely hand over to him, as to his legal successor in office. Perhaps the senators were so blinded by their own sense of importance that they expected this result. In the event, Heraclianus arrested the man and executed him. Alaric's response was immediate, but miscalculated. Instead of throwing his whole force into a do-or-die attack upon the African ports, he mounted an ill-planned revenge attack upon Ravenna. It may be that he had heard that the promised reinforcements from Constantinople were actually on their way at last. Honorius prepared to flee, but the eastern ships reached the port of Ravenna before the Goths could lay siege to its walls, so Alaric was forced to retreat.

Frustrated and no doubt very angry, he now decided that his Roman policy was bankrupt. The world would never recognise Attalus and his overlord as the heirs to Augustus and Constantine. Abruptly, he broke with the senate and tossed his toy emperor aside, stripping him of the purple in the gesture of demotion sanctioned by tradition and forcing him afterwards to live as a hostage, promising that "when peace had been concluded with Honorius, he would secure safety of life and body for him and his son". One wonders what in these circumstances the family of Attalus found to say to the Princess Galla Placidia "who was also living at Alaric's house".[22]

This bloodless execution having been efficiently carried out, after only a brief delay Alaric once more took the road (cap in hand and tongue in cheek, as it were) to Ravenna, to point out to Honorius how valuable a servant of the state he had proved himself to be by putting down so threatening a revolution. His whole army and his hostages travelled with him to add weight to his arguments. For a time it looked as though Honorius would reach an agreement with him but, as Zosimus wrote in the closing sentences of his history, "Fortune was pointing down the road to the ruin of the state" and nothing could now avert the bitter end.

Among those angered by Alaric's arrogant behaviour and envious of his success was the chieftain Sara whose tribal connections made him in any case the hereditary enemy of Alaric's brother-in-law and second-in-command Athaulf. Sara was also ambitious in the service of the empire, and at Ravenna he argued so powerfully against anyone giving trust to Alaric that Honorius was persuaded once again to break off negotiations with him. In a fit of pique—or, more grandiloquently, a demonstration of strength—Alaric led his men back to Rome and sacked the city.

"He assailed Rome," Philostorgius wrote, "with an extraordinarily dangerous hostile force. So by fire, by the swords of the enemy, by men becoming the slaves of barbarians, simply as the dice fell, the greatness of so much glory and fame of power was brought to an end. The City of Rome lay in ruins."[23]

Modern commentators agree that in the course of the three days during which Alaric gave his men the freedom of Rome, the 24th, 25th and 26th of August of the year 1163, from the founding of the city, the buildings of the city suffered relatively little damage. But the psychological damage was immense.

It is said that the Falerian Gate was treacherously opened at midnight to the Visigoths, either by rebel slaves, or by Goths remaining in the city. The greatest structural damage occurred when leading troops fired the first buildings within the walls, perhaps accidentally, perhaps to light the way for the rest of the army. Some citizens, Christians as well as pagans, were killed, but the tally of the dead was not huge. The fact that Christian dead lay unburied in the streets after the sack concerned contemporaries, for Christian superstition at the time required extreme reverence towards the body which was one day to rise again. Augustine, in a passage written to calm superstitious fears, has left an indelible picture of corpses lying in the streets and markets in rotting, tangled heaps.[24] Some Christians found refuge in the Basilica of St Peter on the Vatican Hill, which Alaric ordered to be spared. Other citizens, as Rustilius mentions, found temporary refuge on the tiny island of Igilium in the Tyrrhenian Sea, "which received many shattered refugees from the City, arriving here exhausted".[25] Still others fled even further. Jerome's friend Proba, the widow of Petronius Probus, former head of the Anicii, took her daughter and grand-daughter to Africa. But most could afford to find no such relief in flight. Goths and rebel slaves killed some. Disease killed others. Many were made slaves and sold on the open market, although the price of redemption was set especially low to encourage a swift flow of cash into the mule-borne coffers acting as the Visigothic national treasury.

When after only three days the terror ended and Alaric ordered his men south to ravage Campania, where so many rich and successful Romans had their summer homes, "the City of Rome lay in ruins" psychologically and spiritually if not physically, because "the greatness of so much glory and fame of power" had been destroyed. Although most of the city buildings still stood, the senate could still meet, some of the essential bakehouses still operated, and some of the old men still dreamed, the legend had been shattered on 24 August and the two following days.

Zosimus' history breaks off suddenly a matter of days before that fateful midnight. No one knows why. The last few pages of the text obviously lack editing, and the speculation has always been that Zosimus died suddenly before he could finish his work. But how long before his death did he lay his unfinished manuscript aside? It may have rested for years at the back of a cupboard waiting for the day when its author could steel himself to describe "the ruin of the state". Many pagans did refuse squarely to face the new world. Rutilius survived the siege; poems he wrote afterwards, however, do not describe the horror of the time when the Roman race lost the struggle for survival. They refer to it obliquely in an account of a journey he took through Italy to Gaul in 417, when he could bear to live in dead Rome no longer. It is to Christians that, in the main, we have to listen for echoes of the traumatic effects of Rome's fall. So, for instance, there is in Augustine's *City of God* a most interesting note about the possibility of the existence of giants suggesting obliquely (and therefore the more convincingly) that one of the effects of Alaric's attack was an outbreak of mass hysteria, an outbreak quite credible in the circumstances although recorded by no one else. As we have seen, Zosimus tried to persuade himself that in 395 Athene and Achilles appeared on the walls of Athens to save the city from Alaric and Christianity; other sources make it quite clear that Athens was not then saved. In 410, according to Augustine, *Roma Dea*, the divine spirit of Rome, appeared in the streets of the city but made no attempt to defend them, although crowds gathered to see her and as it were to take leave of her:

> "Is it not true that when only a few years ago the City of Rome was all but annihilated by the actions of the Goths, warning of it was given to everyone by the female figure of Rome appearing with her father and mother, physically so tall as to appear gigantic? One and all gathered together to see this wonder. And the most remarkable thing was that neither of her parents was any taller than the tallest persons we are accustomed to see. So it is possible for giants to be born. . . ."[26]

Augustine had made it a rule of his theology that occult phenomena do not occur; to him the gigantic female figure of Rome could not be anything but a human being of phenomenal proportions. But he did not deny its manifestation: its appearance was so well attested by eyewitnesses that he felt safe in using it as an argument for the existence of giants. . . . Would that there existed an eyewitness account of the Spirit of Rome pacing through the City, and of the awe her visionary presence evoked while men, women and children waited for the dice of destiny to fall!

Notes

1 Cod. Theod. XVI, 10, 13.

2 *In Defence of the Temples*, 55.

3 Cod. Theod. XVI, 10, 14.

4 Cod. Theod. XVI, 10, 15.

5 Augustine, *De Civ. Dei*, 18, 54; see Idatius' Chronicle: *Mallio Theodoro et Eutropio Coss.* "In this consulate the temples of the pagans were demolished by Jovian and Gaudentius."

6 Cod. Theod. XVI, 10, 17.

7 Cod. Theod. XVI, 10, 18.

8 Cod. Theod. XVI, 10, 16.

9 Claudianus, *De cons. Stilichionis III*, 202ff. Text and an English translation in, M. Plautnauer (Loeb Classical Library, 1922).

10 According to Prosper's Chronicle, the great battle was fought at Pollentia "fiercely on both sides". Other sources say that it was fought on Easter Day 403.

11 Orosius, *Historia adversum paganos*, VII, 37, 4f.

12 Chronicle of Salvianus, *in loc. De gubernatione Dei*, ed. F. Pauly (Vienna Corpus, 1868); an English version, E. M. Sanford, *On the Government of God*, (Columbia University Press, 1930); see also P. Courcelle, *Histoire littéraire des grandes invasions germaniques* (Hachette, Paris, 1948).

13 Rutilius Claudius Namantianus, text ed. L. Mueller, Teutoner, Leipzig, 1870); see also E. S. Duckett, *Latin Writers of the Fifth Century* (Holt, New York, 1930).

14 Cod. Theod. XVI, 10, 19.

15 Marcellinus' Chronicle, *in loc.*

16 Zosimus, 6, 6.

17 Zosimus 6, 6; for this troubled period cf. also Olympiodorus fragments in Photius, *History*, 80.

18 Sozomen, *Ecclesiastical History*, 9, 9.

19 The date of this law is not certain, but it would be in keeping for Honorius to attempt to re-assert his rights at Rome in this way. It is interesting to notice how the authority over religious matters has passed completely from the old authorities to the bishops. The drive against astrologers was, of course, never completed, in this century or later.

20. Theodoret's account of the closing of the Colosseum is another of his popular Christian folk-tales, but it is the only record of the law closing the amphitheatres in Honorius' Italy:

"Honorius . . . put an end to the ancient gladiatorial contests customary at
Rome. The name of Telemachus, a man of ascetic life coming from the east, is
revered at Rome for this: going to the amphitheatre where this horrible
spectacle was to be produced, he went down into the arena to interpose his
own body between the weapons of the men fighting there. In a frenzy of
bloodlust and filled with the devils' anger the spectators—who found delight
in this bloodletting—showered stones on the Herald of Peace. When the
illustrious emperor was informed of what had happened, he proclaimed [the
monk] one of the victorious martyrs and forbade the evil spectacle for ever."

21 Zosimus 6, 11. The actual cry is said to have been *Pretium impone carni
humanae!*

22. Zosimus, 6, 12. Orosius tells the sad end of what he calls "this farce", "this
game of kingship", "this wretched parade": when after Alaric's death, the Goths
under Athaulf ultimately left Italy "This ludicrous likeness of an emperor, Attalus,
was taken as far as Spain by them where, as the ship was making landfall, uncertain
as to where it was, he was captured at sea and carried to Count Constantius, and
after he had been shown to the Emperor Honorius, his hands were cut off, and he
was allowed to live" *(Hist. adv. paganos.* VII, 42).

23 Cf. also Orosius, *op. cit.* I, 8, 39 and Procopius, *de Bell. Vandal.*, 1, 1, 2.

24 Augustine, *De Civ. Dei*, I, 1, 12.

25 Namantianus, *Itin.* I, 325ff.

26 Augustine, *De Civ. Dei*, 15, 23.

The Failure of Pagan Morale

Superficially, the sack of Rome was only one incident in a very tangled chapter. In the Western Empire generally at the time, life scarcely paused because of it. Looking back, it might easily appear more important that Alaric failed to win control of Africa. His invasion fleet was wrecked by a storm at Rhegium and he himself died at Consentia in Bruttium before the year ended. His successor as leader of the Goths, his brother-in-law Athaulf, divorced Alaric's sister to marry Galla Placidia, and so win a place by adoption in the imperial family, making the Goths respectable citizens at last. As a man with a certain position, he could make terms with Honorius without losing face, and in 412 felt justified in accepting an offer to settle his men outside Italy, in the area around Toulouse and the Pyrenees. With their help and assistance from the East, Honorius achieved a major victory, the destruction of the army of Constantine III. But his later years were made bitter by would-be usurpers. In 421, the court was actually forced to flee to Constantinople under the threat of one of them. But all this was normal chaos, by the standards of these new times and by 421 everyone, Christians and pagans alike had recognised that the really significant date had been 24 August 410, a date as pregnant with meaning as that of the Fall of Troy or the Founding of the City. In the sack of Rome "so much glory and fame of power" had been destroyed that the new Italy was essentially different, so far as quality of life went, from the old.

The Christian Sozomen's account of the sack suggests a reason, largely supported by modern research, why life changed so radically after it. He maintains that the new world was essentially Christian and pinpoints the moment of its conception as that of the issuing of an order by Alaric that the Basilica of the Apostle Peter established by Constantine the Great on the Vatican Hill should be spared:

"Alaric seized Rome by means of a treacherous siege. And he permitted his forces to carry away as much as each man could manage of Rome's riches, and all the houses were sacked. But from reverence he ordered that the Basilica of the Apostle Peter . . . should be left untouched. This prevented the whole city of Rome from being destroyed. For what was preserved there was used to rebuild the whole city."[1]

The treasures preserved at St Peter's, he goes on to say, were not only the portable riches of certain Christian citizens but also their female children. So, he implies, the new Rome was totally Christian, built on the foundation of Christian money and Christian blood-lines. Archaeological and other historical researches confirm that although not many of the old city's buildings were destroyed during the sack, Rome thereafter was almost wholly Christian. The pagans were not all killed, or suddenly converted. They despaired.

Honorius and his advisers seem almost immediately to have grasped the enormity of the shock the pagans had suffered. There is a new confidence in the law against paganism he sent to the City only two months afterwards:

> "We command that now all superstition has been set aside what was formerly ordained about the catholic faith or decreed concerning it by the devout authority of our father, or again has been confirmed by our serenity, is to be preserved whole and inviolate..."[2]

Even before this, in mid-September, he had addressed a law to Heraclianus in Africa equalling in ferocity any that had emanated from the east, and especially remarkable because it reflects a new Christian attitude towards paganism, the attitude of the middle ages, when paganism was seen not as a rival religion, but as a Christian heresy, punishable by ecclesiastical courts as such:

> "Let all who act contrary to the sacred laws know that their creeping in their heretical superstition to worship at the most remote oracle is punishable by exile and blood, should they again be tempted to assemble at such places for criminal activities. . . ."[3]

So the new world had come. Now the Christians had to learn to live in it and direct it. They had set out to destroy the old world of the gods with a creed which expected the sudden disappearance of the old creation and the appearance of a new kingdom ruled by the visible Christ. But the new, problemless kingdom did not immediately follow upon the fall of Rome. The life of this world went on, and the Christian leaders were forced to come to terms with it, evolving for themselves a new dialectic of history which would permit them to take responsibility in the imperfect world while still looking forward to the advent of the perfect.

Many, of course, played their part in the evolution of this Christian dialectic of history. But three men filled rôles of special significance in it. They were Augustine, who elaborated the theory of the City of God as an idea and ideal to be set up in place of the failed City of Rome; Paul Orosius, who accepted a challenge from Augustine to compose a Christian *History against the Pagans*[4] to replace earlier histories and correct earlier historical theories; and the friend of them both, Jerome, whose main memorial has been the Latin version of the Bible bearing his name, but whose chief task he himself saw as one of education, involving him, together with the production of the Latin Bible, in the development of a system of Christian instruction (such as the Emperor Julian had proposed) to replace the methods and materials used in earlier times. In his letters, he frequently warned Christian friends against the dangers of pagan literature: "what children are obliged to do", he once wrote of reading pagan books, "it is a crime for you to do of your own free will".

This sentence highlights the dilemma in which the Christians found themselves, as far as education was concerned. There were still no Christian schools within imperial frontiers, nor in fact would there be for some time to come. But as future Christian administrators had to be educated, Christian children still attended pagan schools, where they learned to read and write as imperial citizens had done for centuries: the alphabet first, then syllables, then wordlists made up principally of the names of the gods and heroes, and afterwards grammar and syntax from the myths themselves. Although the dangers to adults of any contact with paganism was fully realised (and exaggeratedly stressed), children were permitted to use texts which adults viewed as criminal propaganda. It was this situation which Jerome set himself to correct.

There can be no doubt that when Augustine, Jerome and Orosius put themselves to the task of reforming the Christian's way of seeing the world, they were fully conscious of what they were doing. All had received extensive pagan educations and were determined that theirs should be the last generation to be so burdened. The philosophy of history which they sought to impress upon their contemporaries was in essence that simplistic scheme already to be found in Eusebius and Lactantius, and which Ambrose and Prudentius had used in a form scarcely modified, but which they now expanded to cover the whole of human history. As the old testament led to the new, their argument ran, so the Roman Empire was intended by God to prepare the way for the universal kingdom of Christ. Anyone standing in the way of this inevitable development can only expect to suffer. (It is noteworthy that they were as strongly anti-Jewish as anti-pagan.) The theme of inevitable suffering for opponents recurs time and again in Christian literature. There is an especially explicit statement of it in Orosius' summing up of history from Constantine I to his own day:

"Thus Constantius [Chlorus] having died, as I have said, Constantine became the emperor, the first Christian emperor apart from Philip, in the few years since when, it seems to me, Christians have increased to their present huge numbers: then a thousandth of all Romans worshipped Christ rather than idols, but from Constantine on all emperors have been Christian down to today with the sole exception of Julian, whose unbelieving life earned for him, as they say, a deadly destiny. So the punishment of pagans is slow but sure: the healthy fall sick, the unwounded fall fighting one another, the laughing are made to weep, the full of life fail, some are secretly afflicted whom no man pursues. . . ."[5]

Living as they did after the sack of Rome and consequent dismay of the pagans, Augustine and Orosius believed that total victory was possible in their own generation. Augustine directly related the genesis of his own most powerful attack on the credibility of the pagan world with the blow his god had struck at Rome through Alaric:

> "Rome was ruined by the agency of an invasion of the Goths under King Alaric, suffering a great disaster—in reaction to which ruination those who cultivate the false gods and godlings, whom we generally call pagans, began at once to blaspheme even more pungently and bitterly against the true God than formerly, trying to put the blame on the Christian religion. Wherefore I began from zeal towards the house of God to write my books about 'the City of God' against their blaspehemies and errors . . ."[6]

What Augustine had to say in his twenty-two books about the City of God destined to replace divine Rome coloured all mediaeval thinking in the West and deeply influenced the protestant and puritan reformers. Although he would have denied that he was a fatalist, with no true concept of human freedom, his philosophy of history was in fact wholly mechanistic: he saw his god as inexorably redeeming the world in spite of itself, and acceptance of this fundamental Augustinian tenet was what fastened the fetters upon mediaeval Europe. Monks and bishops like John Chrysostom and Martin of Tours forced the destruction of the material treasures of the old world. Thinking men like Augustine squeezed men's minds into a new and constricting mould.

There was an instant reaction even among Christians against the narrowness of Augustinian concepts of sin and salvation. In Britain—a Britain perhaps mentally freed by the withdrawal of the legions and the consequent need to draw on her own resources— the dangers of imposing a rigid doctrine of time and salvation on the world were quickly appreciated by a monk named Pelagius who realised that such expressions of Christian feeling as Augustine's prayer "Give me what you will"[7] were altogether destructive of human freedom, and that the tendency of Christian teaching was towards rigid conformism and worse, a fatalism influenced by gnosticism and Manichee dualism. The Augustinian Christian might speak of a god "whose service is perfect freedom" but he was in danger of thinking of himself as free only to perform ritualistic acts of choice in servile obedience: the concept was no longer what it had been when the devotees of Venus had used the same phrase of the service they offered to their goddess.

In Rome before 410, then afterwards in Africa and in Palestine, Pelagius fought untiringly to preserve the concept of human free will in the face of virulent attacks by Augustine and Jerome. A church council was called in the east not so much to try as to condemn him. Significantly, the man chosen to prosecute him before it was Paul Orosius, whose dialectic of history excluded true freedom. The details of "The Pelagian Controversy" belong to Christian history:[8] what must interest us here is that Pelagius' attack on Augustine was in essence a restatement of Plotinus' argument against Christian thinking as stated over a century earlier: "Providence cannot be of such a kind that we ourselves are nothing." Plotinus was Augustine's chosen mentor, but he had failed to understand Plotinus here, as in so many other contexts. To Porphyry, Plotinus' disciple and companion, interpreter of his ideas, contemporary Christians were atheists because they knew nothing about the divine nature: in the years since Plotinus, they had still learned nothing about it.

The fascinating thing is that Augustine and Pelagius reached their diametrically opposite views of the relation between man and his world from very similar philosophical beginnings: both found the roots of their teachings not so much in the Christian Bible as in the ideas of Plotinus and Porphyry. The first book which Augustine wrote after becoming a Christian contains only one direct quotation from the Christian scriptures—and that the most Hellenist of all Jesus' reported sayings, one worthy of the sophists of Julian's reign, "Seek and ye shall find". It is much to be regretted that his intellectual grasp was so limited in some directions that once he had fixed on a fanatically narrow interpretation of the destiny of man and the universe, he resolutely closed his mind around it, shutting out any other view whatsoever.

Augustine[9] was so much a Christian of his times that, familiar as his story is, we must be forgiven for once more outlining it here. Born about the year 354, when Constantius ruled the world, he was of Roman birth on both sides and a native of Numidia, a province of that most Roman of dioceses, Africa. His mother Monica was a Christian; his father, Patricius, was not. Under his father's direction, he studied the normal school courses in grammar and literature, later advancing to rhetoric, which he taught for a while, first at Carthage and afterwards at Milan. At the age of nineteen, reading Cicero converted him to philosophy (of which he often later wrote as though it were a religion in its own right). A little later, he became a Manichee, dedicated to beliefs he never afterwards wholly lost about the absolute power of evil and total corruption of the physical universe.

From Carthage he moved first to Rome where, flattered by the patronage of the elder Symmachus and the friendliness of the younger, he dropped his Manichee friends, dismissed his mistress, and planned to make an advantageous marriage. It pained him afterwards to remember that he never quite succeeded in making himself acceptable as a Roman philosopher and sophisticate. He applied unsuccessfully for the professorship of rhetoric and was never fully admitted to that circle of friends which later writers distinguished as the Aristocracy of Letters. One may wonder what part envy played in his subsequent development.

In 383–4 he followed the senatorial delegation led by Symmachus to Valentinian II's court at Milan, there met Ausonius, and finally won the teaching post he coveted. In 386, he was converted yet again, this time to the dominant Christianised neoplatonism of Ambrose, from whom he learned not only the particular version of Christian teaching then passing as orthodoxy but also the rudiments of the philosophy of history which he and his own follower Orosius were later to perfect, together with the theory of the monastic life as pursued by the followers of Anthony of Egypt. Ambrose baptised him at Milan at Easter 387, after a dramatic conversion which must inevitably appear to have been at least in part a flight from failure, and he returned to Africa to attempt to combine the ascetic and academic in a life of semi-retirement, living privately with a handful of friends. In 391 he was forced out of retirement by a Christian mob at Hippo Regius which compelled the bishop of the city to ordain him priest, and in 395 he succeeded to the see, which he held until his death in 430, during the siege of the Vandals under Gaiseric the son of Gunderic. His influence on the development of Christian doctrine, and especially in the theory of freewill and predestination, has been immense. No doubt, like Alaric's rampaging Goths, he did "carry away from Rome as much as he could manage" of her treasures. It is a pity that he could not have managed more.

Jerome[10] was his slightly older contemporary, born about 348 at Stridon in Dalmatia, but educated at Rome, where he was privileged to study under the great pagan Aelius Donatus, whose textbooks on grammar survived long into the middle ages. It was at Rome that he was baptised, although he studied his Christian theology at Trier, the Greek language and its literature at Antioch, and Hebrew at a monastery in the desert near Calchis.

Later, he returned to Rome, where he began his new Latin version of the Bible, but in 386, after the death of Pope Damasus, he was driven from the city by the enmity of Christians who believed that he had overstepped the bounds of acceptable underhandedness in his intrigues to have himself elected pope. Scornfully summing up his enemies' reasonably accurate estimate of his character in a letter to a friend, he wrote, "I am notorious: I am deceitful, a slippery customer. I am a liar. I deceive with the arts of the devil."[11] He withdrew to Bethlehem and founded a monastery, from where he issued the completed "vulgate" Bible, a chronicle continuing Eusebius' history of the church down to the year 381, a study of one hundred and thirty-five Christian writers entitled *de viris illustribus*, numerous biblical studies, and a volume of correspondence unsurpassed in its antifeminism, antisemitism, and general vituperation against every aspect of life and manners offensive to his own excessively narrow view of the world. Yet this unpleasant man also carried treasures from Rome into the new era. The purity of expression he had learned from his earliest teachers influenced generations of mediaeval scholars. He was a bundle of contradictions. Although very learned and proud of it, he claimed that his love of literature was a pain to him. In one letter, he wrote that he had had a dream in which he was accused at the bar of heaven of having lived as a *Ciceronianus* rather than a *Christianus*, and had since sworn never again to read "secular books".[12] Yet later, when Rufinus accused him of having done precisely that, he defended the practice[13]—although in another place he rejoiced that the old authors were being forgotten: "How few now read Aristotle. How many as much as know Plato's name?—to say nothing of his works! Even old men sitting in corners with nothing to occupy them can scarcely remember them."[14] This was to some extent wishful thinking, but it was a cause for boasting among Jerome's younger monastic contemporaries that they were ignorant of everything except Christian literature. Soon they were to force the world into ignorance also.

Theodosius' harsh laws, the violence of Alaric and the distortions of Christian teachers marked only the beginning of the West's long death agony. The continuing pagans watched in powerless anguish. Augustine's City of God could be built without Rome. Until now, there had always been pagans and philosophers close to the heart of imperial affairs—which is why their family lives and political fortunes have been as important to us as the stories of the temples. But from now on for centuries to come those who kept alive classical concepts of learning, faith and freedom were men on the fringes of European and Byzantine life. Soon, if a man did not believe in Christ's redemption of the world, he had to make himself a hypocrite and dissemble his opinions or suffer for them. Before we look at the generally unhappy careers of those who in the early days would not dissimulate, it will be enough, therefore, merely to summarise political developments in the now Christian empire from the fall of Rome to the total triumph of the Christian barbarians.

In the west, the ineffectual Honorius ruled alone until 421 when he was prevailed upon to take his half-sister Galla Placidia's present husband, the nobly-born Roman Constantius, as fellow emperor.

During the intervening years since Alaric's death, Galla Placidia had achieved a colourful if uncomfortable life as the plaything of politically-minded soldiers, a queen with no more real freedom than a slave. Till Athaulf's death in 415 she was his wife first at Toulouse, the capital of the new Visigothic kingdom, then at his Basque headquarters for the conquest of Spain, Barcelona, where she bore him a son, who did not survive infancy. When Athaulf was murdered, she became for a week the concubine of his murderer until he in his turn was assassinated. Next, the new Visigothic King Wallia included her in the price he agreed to pay Rome for a supply of corn and his recognition as ruler of all Gaul south of the River Loire. In 417, she married the "Illustrious Count", Constantius, whose task it had been to settle the Visigoths with the minimum of friction among the Roman provincials; the solution he had found to that problem laid the foundations of the later feudal system, for under it Visigoth overlords "protected" the citizens of Gaul and received in exchange proprietary rights in the old estates, together with one third of their incomes as rents.

A year after her marriage, Galla Placidia bore a son, the future Emperor Valentinian III. Her husband Constantius was made co-emperor with Honorius in February 421, only to fall victim to the plague in September of the same year. When Honorius died childless in 423 she became, and remained for a quarter of a century, until her own death in 450, the effective (but often inefficient) ruler of the remains of the western empire, devoting much of her time to the beautification of Ravenna and the advancement of the careers of her favourite clergy. It was during the early years of her rule that a second disaster almost as great as the sack of Rome fell on the economy and organisation of the Roman world, the conquest of Africa by Vandals from Spain.

Gunderic, who had led the Vandals into Spain in 409, maintained a kingdom there, despite threats from first the Roman armies of Constantine III and later the allied forces of the Visigoths, until his death in 428. By then, his men had reached the sea on the southern and western coasts of the peninsula, and had quickly learned to be as good sailors as their forefathers had been horsemen. Despite their often proclaimed devotion to Roman civilisation, they were still nomads and robbers at heart. Having learned to build and sail ships, the Vandals looked for somewhere to go in them—and Gunderic's son, Gaiseric, led them to the conquest of the diocese of Africa, whether or not at first by invitation of the Proconsul there, who was in difficulties with Moorish rebels, has never been established. By 430, at any rate, the Proconsul had realised that the Vandals had not come to Africa merely as raiders or adventuring auxiliaries, but were intent upon conquest, and he fortified Carthage, Hippo and Cirte against them. But they did as they liked in the countryside, and by 435, when Galla Placidia advised her son to appoint them his confederate allies in Africa, they had done enough for "vandalism" to have become a way of life and death never afterwards forgotten in the West. Although they represented themselves as settlers, preserving ancient monuments and customs, like clumsy children they crushed whatever they touched at the second or third if not at the first approach. Gaiseric's chiefs became the lords of the best Roman estates (the rest paid crushing taxes) and his men the patrons of Roman provincial clients who were never actually called slaves. The Vandals were Christians of a sort but that never stopped them doing anything they felt like doing. However, they did not lean to the worship of the old gods, so their Christianity meant the end of culture and civilisation in Africa for they made it their business to see that those pagan institutions which had survived Roman laws and the Roman clergy were battered into non-existence under their own rule.

From the early thirties onwards, Galla Placidia had the support in her attempts to preserve the West of the able general Aetius but more and more as the years went by real power passed into the hands of the Visigoths whose kingdom, after the Vandals had migrated to Africa, stretched from Southern Spain to Northern Italy and included all Gaul north to the Loire. Even though Aetius is given credit for the destruction shortly after his appointment as Patrician in 433 of the independent Burgundian kingdom centred on Worms, the Visigoths were the real gainers by his victory.

Just as in the West the leading figure was Galla Placidia while she lived, so also in the East for many years power was in the hands of the imperial princesses and their advisers. After Anthemius' fall from power at Constantinople in 415, the Emperor Theodosius II's elder sister Pulcheria was the greatest single influence in his life until the early forties, even after his marriage in 421. The ladies of the eastern court were rivals only in piety and a stream of laws issued from the palace putting ever greater disabilities upon those who would not accept Christianity. The way things would inevitably develop under Pulcheria's gentle rule was made obvious as early as 416 when a law was sent to the Praetorian Prefect ordering that,

"Gentiles, those who deviate into the profane rites of the pagans or otherwise pollute themselves with criminality, shall not be admitted to the armed forces or be promoted to any administrative or judicial honour."[15]

In just one hundred and twenty years the wheel had turned full circle and the Christian revolution, which had begun with Galerius' purge of Christians from the armies at the behest of his pagan mother, was completed with this law made through the influence of a Christian princess.

Only the richest, who could buy privacy and loyalty, and the lowest, who had nothing to lose, could now afford to be pagans. A century later, in the reign of Justinian, it was the prostitutes and employees of the circus who were regularly accused of un-Christian practices, women like Theodora, the bear-keeper's daughter who became empress, and Antonina, the wife of Belisarius, of whom Procopius wrote in his *Secret History* "her grandfather and father had been charioteers who raced in Byzantium and Thessalonika, her mother a prostitute employed at the theatre, while she herself at first lived a life of vice and depravity and associated with sorcerers like her parents".[16]

In 421, after a victory had been won by the purged eastern armies over the perennial enemy, the Persians, and while east Roman troops were fighting in Italy to help restore Honorius by putting down his would-be usurper there, a further law was issued which looks like a distorted mirror image of the edict with which Diocletian had initiated the great persecution in 303:

"If at any time any of those pagans still surviving should be apprehended in
the act of making the abominable sacrifices of the devils, although they ought
to be subjected to capital punishment, let rather their gods be proscribed and
they themselves be forced into exile."[17]

The final destruction of everything pagan surviving above the surface of
the ground—many treasures had been buried for safety, both in east and
west—was surprisingly delayed until 435, when it was decreed that

"*fana, templa, delubra, signa*—everything remaining intact until now is to be
destroyed by order of the magistrates."[18]

Even before that date, an attempt had been made to establish a new
Christian law code, based on decrees issued since the reign of Constantine
I. Undertaken by the Praetorian Prefect in 429, this first attempt foundered
because of the complexity of the task. But in 438 the same minister
produced the great collection known as the *Codex theodosianus*, which was
promulgated in both east and west to replace the old law of the empire. Ten
years later, in 448, the works of Porphyry were solemnly burned. In a sense,
the Dark Ages had begun.

The great weakness was that neither half of the empire produced an
inspiring leader of any race, so that both were at the mercy of the mediocre.
Unhampered by any action from within the empire, and fed by the gold
paid in annual tribute to Uldin and his successors as "allies" by
Constantinople, the Huns gradually built up a vast if amorphous empire
from the Rhine to the Caspian. In 422, the year after Theodosius II's
generals had used vast resources in men and money to defeat the Persians,
the Hun leader found an excuse to demand that the annual tribute should
be increased to 350 pounds of gold. His demand was met, but even this did
not end Hunnish raids for slaves and booty; the average Roman prisoner
was worth one gold *solidus* (weighing seventy-two to the pound) in ransom
money. When Attila and his brother jointly inherited leadership of the
Huns in 434 they summarily demanded that the tribute should be doubled.
Eight years later Attila led the horde on a devastating attack into
Macedonia and Thrace before allowing himself to be bought off by
promises of an annual subsidy of 2,100 pounds of gold and the raising of
the redemption-price of a Roman to twelve *solidi*. Just two years earlier, in
441, the Eastern armies had suffered a major defeat at the hands of Vandal
pirates. No government could long survive such incompetence. After
months of bickering and intrigue at Constantinople, the princesses and
their friends lost power, but Theodosius II himself survived, to die in 450,
in the same year as his aunt Galla Placidia.

Attila meanwhile had murdered his brother in 445 to make himself sole
Khan of the Huns and in a demonstration of his right to leadership had
collected his Roman allies' tribute in 446 and 447, then given his men a free

hand in the East, letting them sack such cities as they felt inclined. Four years later, it was the turn of Gaul to meet the challenge of the Huns, and for the last time a truly Roman army fought north of the Alps, with Aetius commanding a force made up partly of the old legions and partly of Visigoths. It won a great victory, in the battle of the Catalaunian Plains on the banks of the Marne in Belgica, but exhausted itself in the fight. When Attila brought a horde into Italy in 452 there was no Western army capable of meeting his horsemen and all that stopped him from sacking Rome, legend maintains, was Pope Leo I, armed with the authority of Saints Peter and Paul, and encouraged by the power given him over all the churches of the Western world by Valentinian's Novella 17 of 447, an early western appendix to the *Codex theodosianus*. Fortunately for what remained of Western civilisation, Attila died during a wedding orgy the following year, and the Western khanate found no comparable leader among the survivors of the feast.

Aetius, who had for so long managed western military affairs, could not live down his humiliation at Rome, and differences between him and Valentinian embittered relations between them until in 454 the emperor murdered the patrician with his own hands, in the first and last truly independent action he had ever performed. After a decent interval, two barbarian admirers of Aetius assassinated his murderer and one of them briefly became emperor in his place.

In June that same year, the Vandal pirates succeeded in doing what superstition had prevented Attila from achieving two years earlier. Led by Gaiseric, the conqueror of Africa and victor over the eastern fleets, they landed at Ostia and sacked Rome, refraining from massacring all its citizens only because Pope Leo talked them out of it. Alaric had remained only three days in Rome; Gaiseric allowed his men two weeks there, partly because it took them so long to hack the solid bronze roof off the Capitol. Even then part of it had to be left behind, but among the treasures the Vandals did load into their ships were Valentinian's widow and two daughters. The dowager empress became queen of the Vandals by marriage to Gaiseric's son Huneric.

For twenty-one more years the western empire continued a shadow existence. For seventeen of them, its real ruler was "Flavius" Ricimer, who bore the courtesy title of Patrician. He was a Burgundian from one of those families allowed to settle in central Gaul—the modern Burgundy—after Aetius had destroyed the independent Burgundian kingdom. In 456, he forced the cardboard emperor Avitus to abdicate; in 457, he secured the election of Majorian, who at least tried to act imperially until Ricimer tired of him in 461 and killed him for failing to defeat the Vandals. His next four-year emperor was Liberius Severus, who died in 465, and the next Anthemius, whom he executed in 472, the year he himself died after appointing his last emperor, Olybrius.

With Ricimer dead, Burgundian control over Roman affairs was maintained for a further three years by his nephew Gundabad, while the Romans quarrelled among themselves over who should claim the ghost of imperial power. The last pathetic creature to do so was Romulus "Augustulus", forced unwillingly by his father Orestes to assume the purple at Ravenna in 475 and persuaded easily to take it off again the following year by Odoacer, the powerful leader of the Ostrogoths. In the funereal phrases of Marcellinus' Chronicle:

> "The Second Consulate of Basiliscus Augustus, and Armatus: Odoacer the King of the Goths took power at Rome. Orestes, Odoacer cut down; Augustulus, Orestes' son, Odoacer condemned to punishment in exile at Lucullanus, a fortress in Campania. The sunset of the rule of the Roman people, which governance Octavius Augustus, the first of the emperors, had begun to hold in the 709th year from the founding of the City, was completed with this Augustulus when the reign of the emperors had lasted 522 years, the kings of the Goths thereafter holding Rome."

Odoacer had been quietly building up a strong holding in northern Italy for some years before he murdered Orestes and thrust his son, the puppet-augustus, aside, to proclaim himself Odoacer *Rex* and send Romulus' discarded robe to Constantinople in token that Italy now had a king to rule her, and stood in no more need of Roman emperors.

By the standards of the hereditary system which had been creeping into eastern law and practice over the previous century, the man who received it there, the Emperor Zeno, had little more right to accept it than had Odoacer to send it. For he, although not strictly a usurper himself, was the second husband of the wife of a usurper now dead, a general named Leo who had seized power in the east in 457 and ruled for fifteen years by the swords of his bodyguard. The dynasty of Theodosius the destroyer was no more.

Against all this background confusion of barbarian and Christian activity contrary to the ancient institutions of the Roman world a handful of men can be seen attempting to preserve the standards of learning and religion handed down to them from their forefathers. We have already mentioned Rutilius Namantianus, the poet and public servant who described in verse Stilicho's "treachery" to the state and symbolic murder of Rome in the burning of the Sibylline Books. He survived Alaric's sack, and watched the shameful negotiations which permitted the Visigoths to leave Italy in 412, carrying the treasures of Rome with them to line the treasuries of their newly-founded kingdom at Toulouse. In that year he was, in fact, Master of the Offices to Honorius, responsible, as head of the Civil Service, for keeping what to him must have seemed the terrible records. Two years later, he savoured the bitter-sweet honour of ruling as Prefect of the City, retiring—possibly before his period of office was legally bound to end—to withdraw from public life and preserve what he could of his family estates in the area then being resettled with Visigoths under the treaty negotiated through Constantius. From Gaul, he regretted the dead years in accomplished verse, presumably addressed to survivors of the old world who thought as he did (although, unfortunately, the dedications of his two long narrative poems, as well as many of the lines of the second, are lost).

In Africa, too, old traditions were maintained, and not only among the lower classes, whose devotion to the old gods Augustine so often deprecated in the years between 410 and his death during the siege of Hippo. Realising the emotional hold exerted by familiar objects and places over the human mind, Augustine himself advocated the "baptism", as it were, of the sacred treasures of paganism, once his first flush of enthusiasm for the razing of the temples had died down. "When temples, idols, lamps are converted to the worship of the true god, it is the same with them as it is with people when they are changed from sacrileges and impieties to the true religion," he wrote to Publicola.[19] But how dangerous this applied psychology could be was soon demonstrated at Carthage itself, where an early attempt was made to convert the temple of the Mother of Heaven into a church. Writing about the year 440, Salvian of Marseilles records that Bishop Aurelian of Carthage was tempted to use the site of this temple for a church long after its original dedication had apparently been forgotten and the place itself had become overgrown with brambles; but once services were started there, it was discovered that so many of the "Christians" attending them were in fact making their devotions to the old goddess that the bishop felt compelled to have the whole area razed.[20]

In the 420s Augustine wrote of paganism's continual and rapid decline from the reign of Theodosius onwards, but that neither classical paganism nor Manichaeism was dead, while astrology flourished, at least until the invasion of the Arian Vandals, is clear from several sources, including his own works. There was even a competent, although not inspired, encyclopaedist at work in Africa during Augustine's own lifetime, one who managed to carry away a great deal of Rome's treasures, preserving them for the new world to use. While Augustine was propagating his theory that the classical gods were fallen angels—devils—who had adopted the names and nasty habits of long-dead but historical Greeks and Romans, this scholar, named Martianus Capella, was devoting his life to making a compendium of all the arts under the title *The Marriage of Philology and Mercury*.[21] Although Martianus taught at Hippo and practised law there while Augustine was bishop, he remained quite untouched by Christianity. He was not a great scholar, although when later Christian teachers found that they could not base education solely on the scriptures and church fathers, his book proved invaluable to them as a handy introduction to the first principles of the seven liberal arts. (It is in part at least because Martianus, following Varro, did not account law and medicine as arts that they were not among the basic studies at mediaeval schools and early universities, but became special subjects.)

The form that Martianus gave his book is usually ridiculed, but if it is a failure, it is one of execution, not of imagination or intention. Martianus was a man of great vision and courage. Writing for his son (as the convention was) partly in prose and partly in verse, he described the apotheosis of *philologia* and her marriage in heaven to Mercury, the God of Eloquence; thus in defiance of the chaos of barbarian rule and depreciation of human knowledge by the Christians, he proclaimed that through knowledge the human mind can reach the sphere of the divine.

In this allegory, Martianus gives Philology seven attendants at her wedding. The seven maidens are the seven arts: Grammar, Dialectic, Rhetoric, Geometry, Arithmetic, Astronomy and Music. The main body of the book consists of the detailed description by each of the seven in turn of the scope of her interests, mainly in the form of long quotations from earlier specialists (whose works Martianus rightly judged in grave danger of being lost). The study ends with Harmony conducting Philology to her marriage bed.

Attempts were made also to continue the tradition of compiling histories and chronicles, now with the added difficulty of keeping them unaffected by the Christian dialectic of sin and salvation. Olympiodorus of Thebes,[22] a contemporary of Namantianus and Martianus, continued the story of philosophy left unfinished by Eunapius shortly after the fall of Eleusis. Unfortunately, his book survives only in fragments quoted by Zosimus and the later Byzantine historian Photius. From these it appears that he probably lived in Rome for part of his life, around the time of Alaric's sack, and must have known the life of the court at Ravenna, for he was sent from there on a mission to the Huns in 412. But he lost either favour with or faith in the west: in 415 he was at Athens, and by 423 in Egypt, where he visited Thebes and Talmis, Syene and the Oasis of Siwwa, all centres where even then something of the old traditions were preserved. When precisely he died is not known, but it must have been after 431, for he was in Alexandria that year. Although remembered as a historian, Olympiodorus described himself as a poet, possibly because he dared not call himself a sophist, the times being as out of joint as they then were.

As far as is known, he never visited the school at Constantinople, where the arch-enemies of the régime, Helladius and Ammianus of Alexandria, survivors of the terror directed by Bishop Theophilus, had succeeded in establishing themselves as teachers of rhetoric at the very heart of their enemies' country. But at Athens he met and conversed with the men struggling to refound the Academy in the face of constant harassment, Leontios the philosopher and Philtatios the grammarian. Their brave efforts were rewarded by scant success, and during Olympiodorus' lifetime the centre of learning moved from Athens to Alexandria, where the library still in part survived. It was Alexandria which first nurtured Proclus, the most dedicated of the philosophers of the fifth century and the last great teacher of the ancient world.

The life of Proclus, as related by his friend and disciple Marinus offers on the one hand interesting parallels with the lives of the sophists of earlier and more peaceful generations, and on the other stark contrasts with the careers of the triumphant and fêted Christian teachers of his own day. He was born at Constantinople in the year 412, but while still a child returned with his parents to the family home at Xanthus in Lycia. He learned his grammar there. His father wanted to make a lawyer of him, but so safe a career was not to be his. He was a mystic by temperament and several times during his childhood the protective goddess of old Byzantium, the goddess Hecate, appeared to him, directing him to the more dangerous study of philosophy. During an illness, he was also honoured by a vision of Apollo, which brought him back to health. (It may be that he suffered from epilepsy, the "divine falling sickness", as the Emperor Julian is sometimes said to have done. But if this is so, like the emperor before him, he drew strength from, rather than despairing on account of, the peculiar aural and visual disturbances produced by his disease.)

Higher education being impossible in his home town, his father sent him to Alexandria, "the metropolis of ideas", when he was still well under twenty. There he studied under the rhetor Leonas who, discovering in him a great gift for words, made him the pupil also of the grammarian Orion and saw to it that he learned enough Latin to be fluent in that language, although in later life he naturally wrote and taught in Greek. The bond between Leonas and Proclus was clearly a close one, for when the master went to Constantinople on business, Proclus travelled with him. While he was there, his goddess appeared to him once more and told him that when the time was right, he must go to Athens. But first he returned with his master to Alexandria, having found nothing to tempt him to stay in Christian Constantinople. Back among his old companions, he studied under Hieron the mathematician, who introduced him to the elements of Aristotelianism, and then under Olympiodorus, the poet-historian-sophist, who conceived such admiration for him that he offered him his daughter's hand. But Proclus felt no desire to marry.

It was in 432 or 433, when he was aged twenty, that Proclus at last went to Athens. In deliberate rejection of the new Christian city, he lived as close as possible to the Acropolis, on the site of the old temple-hospital of Asclepios. Visits to the Parthenon were still permitted and it had not yet become a Christian church, although the nearby Erechtheum was already used for Christian worship. The law ordering the destruction of all surviving monuments of paganism had not yet been promulgated, and the edict then in force allowed those temples to remain open "where statues of rare artistic merit are displayed". It may fairly be assumed that it was before the great statue of the Maiden that Proclus meditated much of his life's work.

Syrianus, the successor to Leontios as head of the shrunken school of Athens, drove Proclus to take up the serious study of philosophy, bringing him into his own household and setting him as his first task the duty of re-reading all Aristotle's works. Further studies were arranged for him with Plutarch, a neoplatonist, and as a result Proclus became a platonist with an interest in theurgy. His views on theurgy we have already quoted (p. 18 n. 10). The material for his prayers and meditations came not only from Plotinus but also from the Chaldean Oracles, a series of metrical incantations based on platonic ideas, in aim and effect not unlike the incantatory prayers of modern Buddhism. The Oracles—which had been used by Porphyry in his attempts to achieve union with the One—were introduced to Proclus by Plutarch's daughter Asclepigenia, who also taught him the Orphic Hymns. Although still young, he himself took a disciple named Archidias and living in platonic friendship they pursued the contemplative life together. Despite the cold, hostile environment, a warm community of learning briefly existed at Athens, where every new idea was welcome. The contrast with contemporary monastic communities is self-evident.

In about the year 450, Syrianus died and Proclus became the head of the school. By now, the government was burning books of philosophy apparently inimical to Christian thinking, the remaining temples had been destroyed, and no known pagan was permitted to occupy any office under the state. For thirty years Proclus lived in seclusion, never actively persecuted but never completely free. At one stage, his life did seem to be in danger and he moved from Athens to Asia, but as he himself relates at the beginning of his *Outline of Astronomical Theories*, his goddess recalled him to his duties at Athens.

Every day of his working life, he taught five courses and wrote seven hundred lines of commentary. His surviving works, none of them deeply original, but all valuable, include studies of Platonist theology, textbooks of physics and astronomy, and commentaries on Plato, as well as hymns and poems. He died about the year 485 and was buried beside his old master Syrianus near to Mount Lycabettos. His grave bore the epitaph: "I am Proclus, a Lycian, whom Syrianus raised up to teach his doctrine after his day. This grave unites our two bodies. May a single dwelling-place be set aside for our two souls."

Around himself during his thirty years as head of the Athenian school he had collected a group of disciples which, if the times had been more normal, might have established itself as comparable with the great literary and philosophical circles of the past. His closest disciple, and successor as *diadochos*, head of the school, was Marinus. Next in stature to him, and dear to Proclus' heart for Syrianus' sake, was Ammonius of Alexandria, the son of the lately-dead head of the Alexandrian school and Syrianus' niece. With him, Proclus accepted also his less-talented brother Heliodorus.

During the rule of Marinus two of the pupils of the school, Severianus and Panegraphius, emigrated to Constantinople and there earned the school unwanted notoriety by an inept plot to overthrow the ultra-Christian emperor Zeno and restore the old religion. It was far too late for any such attempt to be taken seriously. Although Severianus was executed, Panegraphius, who had won the emperor's friendship and respect before revealing himself as an enemy, was merely exiled in disgrace.

Meanwhile, at Athens the school declined under Isidore, Marinus' successor, partly at least because of the suspicion the plot cast upon it. But it was still capable of nurturing independent minds. In its last quarter-century it produced three totally different thinkers in the last master, Damascius, his disciple Simplicius, and Simplicius' own follower, Asclepiodotus. In the midst of the final upheaval, when in 529 the Emperor Justinian declared the school dissolved (in a rescript which has not been preserved), Damascius found the mental energy and application to evolve an entirely new interpretation of Platonism while Asclepiodotus earned himself notoriety for his self-doubt, as a man torn between the atheism native to himself and his devotion to his master and his master's wholly orthodox platonist ideals.

Rather than cease to teach and to contemplate at the command of a Christian emperor, Damascius and the six disciples remaining loyal to him fled to Persia in 529, where they were made welcome by the reigning King Chosroes not only because non-Christian philosophers always were welcome in Persia but also because they had great propaganda value. When three years later a peace was signed between Persia and the empire, one of its provisions was that the philosophers should be permitted to return to Athens and live there unmolested. The clause was fulfilled, but the break in continuity, short though it had been, proved to have been long enough to destroy everything. Pagan neoplatonism was dead.

As a threat to the unity of the Byzantine empire at the imperial and official level, the old gods were gone, but in the secret places of the East they lingered still, as they did also in those of the West. Where before there had been splendour, there was now furtiveness and fear. But in the high hills, and in desert places, offerings were still made and oracles consulted down to the time of the Arab invasions and beyond. In the cities, too, the old ways were not forgotten entirely. Zosimus, whose *New History* has been so often quoted in this book was a pagan financial officer, who attained the title of Count under Anastasius I: it is impossible to believe that he was a pagan in a vacuum, as it were. But in his History, he is careful not to parade his beliefs and within a few years of his death continuing pagans were forced to be even more circumspect than he. "Pagan", "hellene", and "gentile" had become terms of abuse. As the gossip about Belisarius' wife Antonina already quoted shows, depravity and sorcery were reckoned to go hand in hand. It was not unnatural that paganism should so often have been associated in later times with the circus because, like the superstitious gladiators of earlier generations, charioteers knew how much their lives depended upon good luck, a spiritual blessing under the old religion which the new offered no official ritual for winning. Prostitutes and players, tavern-keepers, gamblers and most medical practitioners (because of the knowledge they had and the company they were forced to keep in following their profession among all classes) were also banned from the Christian kingdom and found little incentive to serve the bishops' god. So theurgy survived, both as medicine and as popular magic, together with astrology, despite the attacks made upon it by the more rigorist clergy.

But was it only degraded survivals of the old religion which lived on? Probably not, although it is only rarely that we catch a glimpse of the persistent paganism of the Byzantine world, as in this (designedly unfriendly) account of John of Cappadocia, who, as the author was at pains to point out, rose from humble origins to become Justinian's Praetorian Prefect, the great enemy of the Empress Theodora. "A man drunk every day but never before lunch" he:

> "gave no thought to God and whenever he did visit a church as though to pray there, he did not behave in the least like a Christian, but would put on a rough cloak, the proper dress for a priest of the old faith which people nowadays generally call Hellene, and all through the night he would repeat certain unholy words which he had previously got by heart, to the end that the emperor might be brought still deeper under his influence and he himself might be kept safe from harm by anyone."[24]

Obviously, John of Cappadocia was a student of theurgy—and equally obviously, he was not an isolated phenomenon in Justinian's Constantinople. Someone had taught him his prayers (the Orphic Hymns, perhaps), and had instructed him how to dress while repeating them "all through the night"; moreover, Procopius himself knew enough about both prayers and dress to recognise them as "Hellene". So the old religion undoubtedly still survived in Justinian's capital, where porphyry pillars from the temple of Artemis at Ephesus were being built into the grandiose church of Holy Wisdom, *Hagia Sophia*, and where draconian laws were rigorously enforced against hellenes, apostates and Jews. Indeed, the same author hints at the strength of this underground opposition to the received religion when he relates that, on the Empress's plotting to murder the Prefect, he was able to organise a powerful bodyguard for his own protection and "call upon sorcerers and oracle-mongers who" (fully in the tradition of Maximus of Ephesus) "declared that he would one day attain the imperium."[25]

From this time onwards, however, although the study of ancient literature continued at Constantinople and elsewhere, and new editions of the classical writings with commentaries were sometimes produced, it is difficult to trace the continuing story of paganism in the East, not only because believers in the old gods dissembled their faith but also because words such as sophist, magician and hellene, which once had precise meanings, had degenerated into insults, to be hurled at any enemy whatever his true persuasion. It was not until the execution by burning of

Basil the Bulgarian, the ascetic "bearer of the script" as a Cathar, a pagan Manichee, in the year 1118 that the continuing opposition to victorious Christianity again emerged defiantly onto the public stage.[26]

Notes

1 Sozomen, *Ecclesiastical History*, ix, 9.

2 Cod. Theod. XVI, 10, 20.

3 Cod. Theod. XVI, 10, 21.

4 Paulus Orosius, *Historiae adversum paganos*, ed. K. Zangemeister, Teubner, 1889.

5 *Hist. adv. pag.*, 7, 28; see Jerome's sneer against Julian: "The Augustus Julian vomited up seven books against Christ while on a trip to Persia, and then chopped himself up with his own sword" (*Letters*, 70, 3).

6 *De civitate Dei, lib. II in retractionem, cap.* 43.

7 *da quod iubes*, in *Confessions*, 10, 40.

8 His life and struggles are discussed in many books and articles. See, e.g., J. Ferguson, *Pelagius*, (Heffer, 1956). R. F. Evans, *Pelagius* (A. and C. Black, 1968).

9 Aurelius Augustinus, *Works* in *P.L.* vols. 32–47. See also art. *Augustinus* in *Reallexikon fuer Antike und Christentum*, vol. 1 (Hiersemann, Stuttgart, 1950), and the bibliography there. P. Brown, *Augustine of Hippo*, (Faber and Faber, 1967).

10 Eusebius Hieronymus, *Works* in *P.L.* vols. 22–30 and G. Morin, *Anecdota Maredsolana*, vol. 3, Maredsous, 1895–1903 Art. *Hieronymus* in *Reallexikon fuer Antike und Christentum*, and the bibliography there.

11 Jerome, *Letters*, 45, 2.

12 Jerome, *Letters*, 22, 30.

13 Jerome, *Letters*, 30.

14 *Comm. in Gal.*, at *P.L.* 26, 428c.

15 Cod. Theod. XVI, 10, 22.

16 Procopius, *Secret History*, I, 11 in his *Works*, ed. J. Haury, 3 vols. (Loeb Classical Library, 1914–40).

17 Cod. Theod. XVI, 10, 23.

18 Cod. Theod. XVI, 10, 25.

19 Augustine, *Letters*, 47.

20 Salvian, *De gubernatione Dei*, 8 (*Works*, ed. F. Pauly, in *C.S.E.L.*, vol. 8 (Vienna, 1898).

21 *Works*, ed. A. Dick, Teubner, 1925; cf. art. W. H. Stahl in *Speculum*, 1965, pp. 102ff.

22 *Fragmenta* in Dindorf, *Hist. Graec. Minor.*, I (Leipzig, 1870).

23 Marinus *Vita Procli*, ed. J. Boissonade (Paris, 1814). L. J. Rosan, *The Philosophy of Proclus* in "Cosmos", New York, 1949. P. Bastid, *Proclue et la crépuscule de la pensée Grecque* (Paris, 1946).

24 Procopius, *Wars of Justinian*, XXV, 10, in his *Works*, ed. J. Hanry, 3 vols. (Loeb Classical Library, 1914–40).

25 *Ibid.*, XXV, 580.

26 The Empress Anna Comnena, *The Alexiad*, 15.

The Survival of the Pagan Ideal

When Rutilius Namantianus left sad Rome in the summer of the year 417 on his journey into retirement, he had reached a certain place "near to Faleria" one noontime when a great lassitude swept over him, and he decided to rest through the heat of the afternoon. By chance, the day was the feast of Isis and Osiris, and "the country people with country jollifications delighted our weary hearts with sacred jests: for it was the very day when reborn Osiris awakens copious new seeds in the produce of the fields. . . ."[1] So Namantianus found new heart in a country harvest festival banned by the emperors, banned by the bishops, but celebrated heartily by the people nonetheless.

It was a chance happening at a golden noontide. How many other travellers through mediaeval and barbarian Europe found themselves unexpectedly spectators of pagan ceremonies during the centuries to come we can never know. Perhaps it happened much more often than is usually suspected—although naturally as the old world grew more remote and the penalties for nonconformity with the new more certain, the nonconformists were driven ever deeper into the woods, and tended to transfer the time of their celebrations from noon to night, while the celebrations themselves must gradually have degenerated into the crudenesses of later satanism. The cities were generally easy to police. It was the country people who most often escaped the vigilance of their overseers and worshipped in the old ways as far as they remembered them. So it is that the canons of church councils bristle with prohibitions against country "witchcraft" and the worship of the devil. It would be easy to dismiss these as little more than ritualised warnings, especially as the evidence for the survival of the old religion in any recognisable form is so scanty, but such few records as there are suggest that in some parts of the West at least the clergy were right to be on their guard.

What partly obscures the record is that at the end of the fifth century the kingdom of Theodoric, the successor to Odoacer in Italy, won the services, if not the enthusiastic support, of the most prominent of the Anicii of his generation, Anicius Manlius Severius Boethius,[2] whose gifts as a scholar and reputation as a Christian with no fear of the gods opened the way to the development of a more healthy Christian attitude to the past running parallel with the unhealthy attitude of outright rejection typical of less cultured and more fanatical monks and bishops. Theodoric, a hostage in Zeno's Constantinople, sent by the emperor to assassinate and replace the less-Romanised Odoacer (a usurpation he achieved in 493), was anxious to retain the appearance of normality in Italy; although the army was now largely Goth, and many also of the civil officials had little Roman blood, the old names were preserved for the new things, and the novelties themselves made to reproduce old institutions as far as possible. It was therefore of the greatest encouragement to Theodoric that such men as Boethius, although dreaming, as the king must have been aware, of the day when true Roman freedom would be restored, were meanwhile willing to work for him. In his turn, he encouraged them with rewards and honours. Boethius became his Master of the Offices and was named consul for 510. His primary gift to mediaeval scholarship was a primer of arithmetic preserving what had been taught in the old schools. But he also translated some of the works of Aristotle into Latin—a translation showing dependence on the latest master of the school of Athens, Syrianus—and in doing so showed no hesitation in using the old names for the things of the past, including the gods. He ultimately earned the distrust of Theodoric, who imprisoned him on charges of not only favouring a restoration of direct imperial rule but also having tried to further that end by astrological and magical means. While in prison he produced a study in five books *On the Consolations of Philosophy* in a style which earned him in some circles a reputation as a pagan, although it is pagan only in so far that in it Boethius used everything he knew from whatever source it originated. His five books are full of quotations from earlier authors and set a precedent for their use among the best Christian scholars—a precedent which the West was on the whole slow to adopt, but which could not but be a partial antidote to the ravings of the anticlassical fanatics.

What was begun by Boethius was continued by his near-contemporary Cassiodorus "Senator",[3] whose career in the Ostrogothic kingdom was assured when his father, a former friend of General Aetius and notary to Valentinian III, gave the allegiance of the whole of southern Italy to the new kingdom of Theodoric without the need for a battle. Already prominent soon after 500, and untouched by the suspicion which ruined Boethius' political career, the younger Cassiodorus became first the Quaestor of the Palace at Ravenna, then a Patrician, next Consul (in 514), and afterwards, till the death of Theodoric, Master of the Offices. His public career continued under succeeding Ostrogoth kings until the empire was temporarily restored under Justinian, when he withdrew to family estates in the extreme south of Italy where—rather in the style of Augustine before his ordination—he founded a house of scholar-contemplatives, wrote a history of the Goths (now lost) and tried to continue the work begun over a century earlier by Martianus Capella in producing an encyclopaedia of all the arts. His house of studies—the Vivarium—outlived him by a full century (and he himself survived until

570), preserving, in the course of its most valuable life, many ancient texts which must otherwise have been lost for ever. As a preservation society, however, its great weakness was that it was generally under Christian direction and there were therefore classes of literature that it was happy to see die.

In the early centuries of Christian domination, Christians as liberal as Boethius and Cassiodorus were, however, extremely rare. Most Christian leaders of wide influence stood in the tradition of Augustine and Jerome. After Capella's death, nothing seems to have survived in lowland Africa but Vandal Christianity, until Byzantine Christianity was restored there, only to be swept away in its turn by Islam. In the Visigothic Kingdom of Gaul and Spain, the great problem was always reckoned to be Arianism. Gradually, Christian fears of a resurgence of paganism died away. Yet there is evidence that even two hundred years after Theodosius had destroyed the old priesthoods and their temples, the names of the old gods and the form of honours to be offered to them had not been forgotten, at least in the north-west of Spain and the Pyrenees, the former province of Galicia.

During the great resettlement of the fifth century, this area had become temporarily (until it was absorbed by the Visigoths in 585) the independent kingdom of the Suebi, a tribe from central Germany, which had crossed the Rhine with the Vandals in 409. The Suebi were Arians, but they ruled an Hispano-Roman population which was nominally catholic. Around the year 560 a monk named Martin, a native of Pannonia but trained in Palestine, was made bishop of Bracara (Braga) and abbot of Dumio, and charged with the task of converting the ruling Suebians to the Christianity of the pope. In 560 he succeeded in converting the Arian King, and three years later had the satisfaction of receiving the submission of the great majority of the Suebian lords. But during his explorations into the faith of the nominally catholic native population, he discovered not only Arians to be converted, but also followers of the long-dead ascetic Pricillianus and devotees of the old gods of Rome and the countryside. Winning their lasting allegiance proved much more difficult than persuading the nobility to become catholics. From the wording of the first canon of the Second Council of Braga, held there in 572, it would appear that it was not so difficult to win converts as to keep them. The canon orders bishops to instruct new Christians intensively over a period of twenty days before baptising them "that they may turn their backs on the insanities of idols and other offences such as murders, adulteries, false swearing, giving false evidence, and other death-dealing sins". Apparently, converts less carefully prepared had been found simply to add the name of Christ to the list of their gods—and perhaps also often to drop it again when it did not immediately bring rewards. Now, the bishops under Martin thought, the time had come really to convert the countryside.

Shortly after the council ended, Martin received a somewhat agonised letter from one of the bishops who had attended it. He was not finding it easy to follow the instructions he had been given. What could he say to the simple people of the countryside, the *rustici*, which would put them off paganism for life?

Martin replied in a very long letter setting out a specimen course of instruction in the precise form of words he expected to be successful.[4] The formula he proposed was essentially that laid down nearly two hundred years earlier by Augustine of Hippo in his *Rudiments of Catechesis*. New Christians are to be taught about the creation of the world, the fall of man, redemption and salvation; they are to be given detailed instruction about what will actually happen at their baptism, and thoroughly frightened with threats of what punishment will fall on them if they do not live up to the promises they then make. I want to quote from this letter at some length, not only for the sake of the evidence it provides of how strong the old ways still were in Galicia at this late date, but also as an example of Christian preaching against the gods; it finds parallels right back to the second century. It is interesting to notice that it offers not one whit of proof that its teaching is true: the power of "the Spirit", the force of the preacher's personality and the dignity of his position were expected to do that.

Not surprisingly, the letter shows that the customs which had survived most strongly were for the most part the more primitive—and they were customs which, despite the efforts of Martin and his successors, were to survive for centuries yet, to be mentioned at the witch-trials of the fifteenth and later centuries: the making of offerings at trees, rocks and springs, the blessing of fields, and special rituals in courtship and childbearing. But Martin found an evil equally to be fought in the "biggest lie of all", the reckoning of the Kalends of January as the beginning of the year, the day the consuls had taken office under the *Dea Roma* (who is not mentioned at all).

Martin regarded the gods as fallen angels, or perhaps as "evil and wicked beings of the race of the Hellenes" whose names the fallen angels had adopted to deceive mankind. The blackest of all these devils, the most dangerous of them, is "Juppiter", the Best and Greatest.

> "I have received from Your Charity a letter [Martin began], in which you write asking me to send you something . . . about the origin of the idols and the evils relating to them for the correction of simple people who, trapped in their former pagan superstition until very recently, are still paying respect in worship rather to the demons than to God . . . (paragraph 1)
> [*Rustic sermons must be simple, so what I suggest you say is this.*]
> Most beloved brethren, we want to tell you in the Lord's name something that you need to hear at least a little about. . . . (2)
> When God first made heaven and earth, in the spiritual domain he made spiritual creatures, that is angels, who were in his presence and praised him. But one of them, the first made of all the archangels, seeing himself glowing with so much glory, did not give honour to God his Creator, claiming that he himself was as good as he. And for his pride he was thrown down with many

other angels who thought as he did from that heavenly domain into this lower air below heaven; and he who had been the first archangel lost the light of his glory and was made a dark and horrible devil. Similarly, the other angels who agreed with him were thrown out of heaven with him and losing their glory were made demons . . . And those expelled with Satan because of their pride are called fallen angels and demons." (3)

The following two paragraphs (4 and 5) Martin devoted to the story of the creation and fall of man, and the story of Noah's flood; in the next (6), still following the book of Genesis, he explained how polytheism began among Noah's sons:

"Men, forgetting the divine creator of the world . . . began to worship created things. Some adored the sun, some the moon or stars, some fire, some deep waters or springs of water, believing not that these things were made by God for man's use but that they were themselves gods in their own right (*ipse ex se orta deos esse*).

So then the devil and his servants, the demons, who had been expelled from heaven, seeing ignorant man forgetful of God his Creator and going astray with regard to created things, began to display themselves in a variety of forms and to speak with them and to desire of them that they would offer sacrifices to them on mountain tops and in leafy woods, and worship them as divine. One of them, assuming the ways of evil people who live out their lives in all sorts of crimes and wickedness, called himself Juppiter: he was a magician and involved himself in such immense incestuous adulteries that he had his sister, who is called Juno, for a wife, and corrupted his daughters Minerva and Venus, and filthily fornicated incestuously with his granddaughters and all his relatives. And another demon called himself Mars: he was the instigator of contention and discord. And yet another devil chose to call himself Mercury: he was the inventor of all theft and fraud. . . . And yet another demon took upon himself the name Saturn: it was he who, living in the utmost barbarity, used to eat his own newborn children. And another demon pretended to be Venus, a whore, who played the prostitute not merely in innumerable adulteries but also with her father Juppiter and her brother Mars (7). So that is how men in those times were lost. They worshipped . . . devils . . . as gods . . . building temples . . . making statues and altars. . . .

And there was yet more. For many were the devils expelled from heaven. So some ruled in the seas, or rivers, or wells, or woods. . . .

And those in the seas were called Neptunes, and in the rivers Lamias, and in the wells Nymphs, and in the woods Dianas: and they were all malign devils and nefarious spirits, who hurt and troubled unbelieving people who did not know how to protect themselves with the sign [of the cross].

Moreover, quite without permission, they corrupted the days . . . each day was given the name of a devil, and they came to be called the day of Mars and of Mercury and of Juppiter, and of Venus and of Saturn—none of whom had made the days, being actually most evil and wicked beings of the race of the Hellenes. (8)

It was God who made the days. . . . (9)

Similarly, let the ignorant and simple be relieved of this error, the belief that they have that the Kalends of January are the beginning of the year. This is the biggest lie of all. For Holy Scripture says that the very first day of all was the eighth day before the Kalends of April—March 22—the equinox. For it says there, 'and God divided the light from the darkness' and as any proper division is an equitable one, and on 22 March the day and the night each contains an equal spread of hours, it is not right that 1 January is the beginning of the year. (10)

Next, mention must be made of that most foolish of errors, the Day of Moths and Mice (*the feast of Tellus and Ceres, protectors of household stores, also in January*), when Christian people—if I may bring myself to say so—worship mice and moths instead of God. For if bread and cloth are not, as a protective measure, taken out of barrels and cupboards, and offered to them on their feastday, they will not spare what they find within. . . . [It must be explained that the whole year cannot be affected by such practices as these: the whole year belongs to God alone]. (11) Do you not realise that the demons lie to you in the customs you try so futilely to observe, and in the omens you expect to see fulfilled? [God does not allow us to see the future]."(12)

Paragraph thirteen is devoted to the story of Jesus and salvation: in fourteen the first threats appear:

"Those who are unbelieving and are not baptised, and especially those who have been baptised and fall back after their baptism to idols, or homicides, or adultery, or falseswearing or other evils, and die without penance, all such people will be damned with the devil and all the demons they worship and whose works they have done, and they shall be put physically into eternal fire in hell, where the inextinguishable flames burn for ever . . . and such a man shall long to die again, and not feel the punishment, but he will not be allowed to. . . ."

In paragraph fifteen, Martin described the rite of baptism and what it implied, listing in the following paragraph all the common practices which were forbidden after baptism:

"Take note what sort of obligations your confession before God binds you to! How could any of you who have renounced the devil and his angels and worship and evil works revert to the cult of the devil? But what is the lighting of wax lights at rocks or trees or wells or crossroads if it is not worship of the devil? Divination, and omens, and observing the days of the idols, what are these if they are not worship of the devil? Observing the Vulcanalia (*23 August*) and the Kalends, decorating tables, wearing laurels, taking omens from footsteps, putting fruit and wine on the log in the hearth, and bread in the well, what are these but worship of the devil? For women to call upon Minerva when they spin, and to observe the day of Venus at weddings and to call upon her whenever they go out upon the public highway, what is that but worship of the devil? To make evil incantations with herbs and to invoke the names of the demons in those incantations, what is that but worship of the devil? And so many other things too long to relate. . . ."

Christians, Martin said, would do none of these things: they would, rather, use the sign of the cross, say their prayers, refuse to work on Sundays. Then they would go to heaven (17). Sunday observance he saw as one of the most important of all Christian practices: "It behoves the Christian man to venerate the day of the Lord. It is very unseemly and wrong that those who are pagans . . . honour the day of Juppiter and suchlike demons, and refrain from work, when in fact no demon ever created a day, or owned one, while you, who adore the true god . . . do next to nothing to reverence . . . the day of his resurrection. . . ."

Martin of Braga eventually died and was canonised for his work in converting the pagans of Galicia, but throughout the Latin world the second day of the week still belongs to the moon, the third to Mars, the fourth to Mercury, the fifth to Jupiter, the sixth to Venus and the seventh to Saturn. But no one is worried by it now: the Christian fear of the gods died not long after St. Martin himself.

Visigothic Spain swallowed up the kingdom of the Suebi in 585, and four years later King Recared of the Visigoths decided to become a catholic, instead of continuing as the Arian he had been all his life until then. It did not, of course, satisfy him that he alone should submit to the pope, and the main concern of the (Third) Council of Toledo[5] held that year was to ensure the swift conversion of the whole nation. The canons adopted by the council are concerned chiefly with the bleak future of continuing Arians. But in its twenty-first canon, a law binding upon the whole kingdom, the council wrote:

"Although almost all Spain and Gaul have now been freed from the sacrilege of idolatry (*an assertion which in itself suggests that the opposite was true*), with the concurrence of our most glorious Prince, the Holy Synod ordains the following:
   That every priest shall make most careful inquisition in his own area, together with one of the magistrates of the district, for survivals of the sacrileges, and shall not hesitate to destroy whatever may be found. And those people who have fallen into such errors shall be coerced from this danger to their souls by whatsoever warnings may be required: which, if any neglect to do, let them understand both parties are in danger of excommunication. And if any lords omit to extirpate this evil from their holdings, or refuse to prohibit it among their people, they too shall be driven from communion with the bishop."

So in Spain the witch-hunting season began, a season which was to last, with a few intermissions, for well over a thousand years. But in other parts of the old western empire the fear of the gods had begun to recede and superstitious terror of witchcraft had not yet taken its place. Pope Gregory

I, who reigned from 590 to 604, felt it safe to adopt a rather more indulgent attitude not, indeed, to the gods themselves, but to the weaknesses of those who had worshipped them. It was he who began the practice, which had far-reaching consequences, of converting former pagan shrines into Christian churches. As we have seen, it had long been the practice in the east for monks to bivouac on expropriated pagan sites to prevent their re-use by their former owners: so monks had been settled at Canopus in Egypt, for instance, on the site of the Serapeum, and in the Erechtheum on the Athenian acropolis. But an early attempt to convert the temple of the Mother of Heaven at Carthage into a church had failed, and in general bishops had followed the advice of Theodoret,[6] that materials should be taken from pagan temples, blessed to purify them, and used in Christian buildings, rather than pagan buildings themselves made Christian: so the ruin of the temple of Artemis at Ephesus had been cannibalised for the building of both the double church of St Mary and St John at Ephesus and Hagia Sophia at Constantinople. There was, in fact, a canon of an obscure council, widely adopted and quoted, which read: "We disdain to apply to sacred purposes the basilicas of heretics, which we have vilified with so much execration. And we believe their pollution to be beyond purging."[7] Although originally referring to the churches of dissident Christian sects, its sentiments were generally felt to be applicable to the fabric of former temples. So the temple sites were left deserted in the east, rendered harmless perhaps by the construction of a monk's cell and a small chapel containing relics in one corner, and visitors to the sites of ancient temples in Asia Minor today will often find the ruins of a small Byzantine brick church nestling close to the mighty pillars of an even more thoroughly ruined pagan temple.

In the West, the problem remained unsolved until Pope Gregory (like Augustine before him) had the insight to realise that people may be attached to places as well as to ideas, and was bold enough to act on his insight. Writing to Abbot Mellitus at the close of the sixth century concerning the instructions to be followed by Augustine in the mission to Britain, he suggested,

"the temples of the idols in that nation should be subjected to as little destruction as possible, though the idols within them should be destroyed. Let holy water be prepared, to be sprinkled in such temples, let altars be built and relics placed in them—for although such temples may be well constructed, they do none the less need to be converted from the worship of the devils to the service of the true god, so that seeing the temples left undestroyed the people may turn aside from the dry desert of error and, acknowledging and worshipping the true god, may meet in places which are familiar to them. . . ."[8]

Similarly, he goes on to say, there is no reason why the English should not kill and eat cattle to mark the festivals, decorating their homes with branches cut from the trees . . . as long as they do these things in honour of the Christian god.

The first such conversion of a temple into a church at Rome itself was not, however, made until some five years after Gregory's death when the Pantheon was dedicated by Pope Boniface IV as *Sancta Maria ad Martyres* and protected from the demons formerly inhabiting it by a large collection of bones brought from the catacombs.

After these initial steps had been taken on the edge of outer darkness in Britain, and at Rome itself, a continual flow of such conversions was reported, so that many famous churches from Châtres to Syracuse incorporate pagan buildings in their structure. Moreover the Christianisation of many seemingly innocuous pagan ceremonies also became common: the pagan origins of Christmas decorations and the Easter egg are now generally recognised. A specially evocative survival of this kind is that of Argive Hera as "our Lady with the Pomegranate" at Capaccio Vecchio on Mount Soprano near Paestum, in Western Italy.

Paestum was originally Poseidonia, a colony of Sybaris, itself a colony of the Achaean League. Its protecting goddess was Hera of Argos, to whom votive offerings of small boats filled with flowers and candles were made at her great festivals, laid at her feet as she sat with a child on one arm and a pomegranate in her hand.

The shrine of "our Lady with the Pomegranate" was established by the people of Paestum in the twelfth century, when they migrated from their low-lying town to Mount Soprano to escape an outbreak of malaria. And even today pilgrimages are still made from Paestum to our Lady with the Pomegranate, and small boats offered to her, as she sits with her child on one arm and her pomegranate in her hand.[9]

But even with the christianisation of harmless pagan ceremonies[10] and useful pagan buildings, the gods themselves were not forgotten, although apart from Liber and Venus, whose names constantly recur in mediaeval literature, and especially in popular songs, the memory of them did rapidly fade, as simple people everywhere were "coerced" into catholicism, and the ignorance of the dark ages settled upon Europe, with the final decay of all but the monastic schools and the gradual destruction of books by time and neglect.

The little knowledge of the classical world which did live on was disseminated chiefly by the encyclopaedists, one of the most famous and influential of whom, Isidore of Seville, was a near contemporary of Pope Gregory I.

Isidore was educated in Carthage (once again during his youth under Roman—that is, Byzantine—rule). His two brothers also became bishops and his sister an abbess. His upbringing was totally Christian and in his works the gods have no reality at all, but have become mere figures in books, items in the corpus of universal knowledge, although he still makes ritual references to their diabolical wickedness.

Isidore suffered very badly from the encyclopaedist's complaint, overeagerness to believe that the name is the thing, and that if therefore the etymology of a word can be determined, the essence of the thing named will somehow have been captured. He was also a Christian neoplatonist, in the tradition of Augustine. Everything was to him in some sense an emanation from the divine—everything, it would seem, except the pagan gods, for there is no trace of neoplatonist generosity in his treatment of them in the section of his vast *Etymologies* entitled "On the Gods of the Pagans".[11] To Isidore at least, the gods were truly dead:

"Those the pagans defend as gods were once human beings who for some aspect of their life or some merit came to be worshipped by men after their death, as Isis in Egypt, Jovius in Crete, Juba among the Moors, Faunus among the Latins. . . . Sometimes they were accredited with the discovery of arts or aspects of civilisation, as medicine by Aesculapius, smith's work by Vulcan. . . .

Saturn is called by the pagans Cause of the gods and all that comes after: he is so called from the Latin *satu* (filled) as one in himself filled with all things. . . . The Greeks call him *Chronos*, that is, time who consumes his sons, time which revolving produces the years. . . . They say this father of heaven cut off his genitals because nothing in heaven is born of seed. He carries a scythe, to signify agriculture. . . . Jovius is so named from *juvandu* (*supporting*) and called Juppiter as 'father of help': he is pre-eminent before all. They also call him Juppiter Optimus, the Best—yet he was incestuous with his family and shameless with strangers. They make him in the form of a bull for the rape of Europa because there was the sign of the bull on her ship; in Danae's case, he aroused her to copulation with him with a shower of gold, for it is understood that the chastity of women may be corrupted with gold; they make him in the likeness of an eagle because of a boy he snatched away to defilement, a serpent because he crept about, and a swan because he sang serenades. And these things are not mere figures, but truly are real evils—whence it is also evil to believe in such gods, who are the very sort that human beings ought not to be.

Liber they call that from *liberamento* (*freely*), because of the sea, as it were, of his blessings liberated in the emission of seed in copulation, and they show this same Liber with a womanly delicate body, for they say that women are his, and wine which excites to lust. . . .

They call Venus by that name because she has no desire to be a virgin without womanly vigour. The Greeks call her Aphrodite, because of the bloody spume from which she was begotten: spume is called *aphros* in Greek. . . . They say this woman Venus is the wife of Vulcan, because the venereal function is not performed without heat: hence 'the old man is cold in love'.

They have given Cupid his name on account of [the cupidity of] love, for he is the daimon of fornication. He is shown with wings because nothing lighter and more volatile than loving is to be found anywhere. They show him as a boy, because love is stupid and unreasoning. And he is made to hold an arrow and a torch, because love wounds the heart and because it sets on fire. . . ."

So the gods sank down into oblivion, although never into total darkness. By the time the kingdom of the Franks replaced that of the Visigoths in old Gaul, warnings against pagan superstition in the law-books of the kings had become vague and mechanical. The names of the gods had been forgotten—or had become dark mysteries whispered only in secret, out of hearing of the kings' and bishops' men.

> "We decree in accordance with the canons [reads the fifth of the Capitularies of Carloman, dated 742], that every bishop should give attention in his district—bearing it actively in mind that he is the defender of the church—that the people of God does not become pagan, but that every pagan defilement should be rejected and spurned, whether it be sacrifices of the dead, or soothsaying and divining, or amulets and omens, or incantations, or the offering of sacrifices—by [all of] which ignorant people perform pagan rites alongside those of the church, under cover of the names of the sacred martyrs and confessors. Sacrilegious fires, such as are called 'needfire' or any other such things whatsoever they may be belonging to pagan observances provocative to God and his saints are to be strictly prohibited."[12]

More than forty years later these essentially primitive, pre-classical observances had still not died out, and were once more condemned in the sixty-fourth chapter of the General Capitularies of Charlemagne of 789:

> "Again, in the law of the Lord there is the command: thou shalt not observe omens, and in Deuteronomy: Let no one consult soothsayers, or observe dreams, or favour omens. And again: Let no one consult an enchanter, or a wizard, or a possessed sorcerer (*pithon*). On these grounds we command that astrologers, or enchanters, or weather-makers, or spell-binders are not to exist, and wherever they do, they are to change their ways or be condemned.
> With regard to trees, and rocks, and springs, wherever ignorant people put lights or make other observances, we give notice to everyone that this is a most evil practice, execrable to God, and wherever they are found, they are to be taken away and destroyed."

So the tone of the Middle Ages was set by the omniscient ignorance of the successors of Isidore, and the blanket condemnation of the laws. But not everyone everywhere was content to let the insights of the past simply die. There were new editions of the poets at Constantinople—although, being written in Greek, they were meaningless in the West. And from the West itself, a handful of meticulously-copied manuscripts survive from the empty centuries to prove that the love of learning and literature was not wholly dead. The fact that most of these copies are of relatively late date is evidence in itself that the texts were still used, for only valued manuscripts found copyists. Among the most noteworthy survivors are the "Vatican" and "Basilican" manuscripts of Terence, both copied at Courbie, the earlier between 826 and 856 and the other between 893 and 898.[13] The Basilican was obviously made from the Vatican manuscript, but interestingly enough whereas the frontispiece facing the title page of the earlier depicts a group of men of very grave Carolingian aspect upon a screen held by actors wearing comedy masks, the frontispiece of the later copy shows a cupboard full of actors' masks, some male, some female, looking like decapitated heads, all drawn so badly as to suggest that the illuminator did not know the real appearance of what he was trying to draw. But the inference must be that someone knew and suggested the subject to him, probably offering him a drawing now lost as his model; someone in Carolingian France still had regard for the classical world, centuries after the last actor's mask cupboard had been turned into a book-chest or broken up for firewood.

An even more surprising survival from much the same date is the prayerbook of Walafrid Strabo, composed in Alsatia.[14] Its main text consists entirely of prayers to the gods of Olympus and the Capitol. Interlaced between the main paragraphs are other pagan prayers and commentaries upon them. Later mediaeval secular writings are of course full of conventional references to the gods, but there is nothing conventional about Strabo's prayer book, which provokes a multitude of questions to which at present there can be no satisfactory answer.

The Carolingian revival of learning reintroduced the seven liberal arts into northern Europe from the few small Byzantine schools surviving in Southern Italy, and through the works of Martianus Capella and Isidore of Seville stimulated a revival of interest in the books in which that learning had originally been presented, although on a very limited scale. Joannes Scotus Erigena made his own version of Capella's study of the seven arts under the title *The Marriage of Mercury and Philology* and such new editions of old works as this no doubt played their part in inspiring the copying of such texts as the Vatican and Basilican *Terences*, or the careful preservation of Donatus' Commentary[15] on books 6–12 of the Aeneid made at Tours perhaps as early as the eighth century and brought to Florence in 1446, at the height of the Italian renascence. But the names of great scholars in the old style are pitiably few, and the booklists of even the most important monastic libraries are so thin in fields apart from Christian theology as to be all but non-existent. William of St-Thierry's school at Chartres, which produced its own handbook of the seven arts, owned treatises on grammar by Donatus and Priscian, rhetoric by Cicero, dialectics by Aristotle and Porphyry, and arithmetic, music and geometry by Boethius; that appears to have been all, apart from fragments of Plato, Macrobius and Apuleius. The true revival of interest in the classical world began not with the reintroduction of Aristotle through the translations of the justly-famous Arab scholars of Spain, but with the revival of Latin itself stimulated by Petrarch and his pupils, a revival almost contemporaneous with the rejuvenation of interest in forms displayed by the early architects and painters of the Siennese and Florentine schools, and the mania for manuscript-collecting which led humanist popes to the extravagance of authorising mercenary captains in the pay of the papal armies to sack monastery libraries in search of lost treasures.

It was the interest in all things ancient stimulated by Petrarch, and turned in the direction of all things proudly Italian by the publication in 1454 of Poggio's *Urbis Romae Descriptio* and a few years later of Florio Biondo's *Roma instaurata, Roma triumphans, Italia illustrata* which at last brought action to preserve what remained of the buildings of pre-Christian antiquity. In 1462, Pius II, the great humanist scholar Aeneas Silvius Piccolomini whose novel *Lucretius and Euryalus* shows him to have been at least as much at home among the gods as he was in church, pro-mulgated a bull forbidding the quarrying of the buildings of old Rome for marble to be burned to quicklime. After that, public opinion changed so rapidly with regard to the antique that it was only relatively few years later that all Rome—and Michelangelo—gaped at the Laocoön newly excavated from the Baths of Titus and stared open-mouthed at the Apollo in the Belvedere.

Here at least was something: the skill and the art of those who had produced such treasures of literature and sculpture no longer lacked appreciation. Through recognition of their artistry, the gods were no longer mocked. But could they themselves ever return, to reign beside Christ, perhaps, if never to replace him? There were those who dreamed that they could, although no movement to revive them ever found favour except among small circles of (often unbalanced) intellectuals, cut off by their aspirations, their vocabulary, and usually by their affluence from the mass of the people around them.

As the classical gods, worshipped with classical blood-sacrifices, the family of the Best and Greatest are dead. The dead do not return. And yet—

It is five centuries since Aeneas Silvius Piccolomini saved for the tourist, and the more thoughtful visitor, the city of Rome. It is fifteen since the second battle of the gods and giants, which the giants lost by winning—for at last, many are beginning to realise that after the battle, the gods did not die. They are the immortals.

They went on talking, as they had talked in the hills above Troy, long after the sun had set. They are talking still. They let themselves be heard in beauty, in nature, in dreams, in imaginings, in the researches of psychologists and the explorations of mystics. And as time passes, more and more are listening to them—and being surprised by what they hear.

The altars will not be restored: altars are not of our times (though to pour a libation for whatever gods there be can be no evil thing). The temples cannot be restored; they are memorials of how things once were managed. But the gods remain. And what they say is: your god is too small; there is divinity in things that his followers have ignored and decried; above all, there is divinity in generosity and acceptance of difference, though none in narrowness and exclusivity.

The story we have been tracing of the destruction of what in Italy are still called "the old things" is a poignant and unhappy one, full of fanaticism and madness, lies and distortion, terror and blood. The darkness lying over so many of the Christian centuries since has been a scandal to all Europe. Yet the story could have been so different.

The next chapter in man's eternal quest for the divine may yet be.

If the gods will. And we also.

For "providence cannot be of such a kind that we ourselves are nothing".

Notes

1 Namantianus, *De reditu suo I*, 371 ff.

2 Works in Migne, *P.L.*, 43 and 44; *Theological tractates and the Consolations of Philosophy*, text and an English translation, Stewart and Rand (Loeb Classical Library, 1871).

3 Works in Migne *P.L.*, 69–70.

4 *De correctione rusticorum* in C. W. Barlow (ed.), *Martini Episcopi Bracarensis Opera Omnia* (Yale University Press, 1950), 183ff.

5 The acts of this and other councils referred to in this chapter are collected in Hefele, *Histoire des conciles* (Paris, 1911), *in loc.*

6 Theodoret, *Sermon*, 8; works in Migne, *P.G.*, 80–4; see also *Graecarum affectionum curatio*, ed. J. Raeder (Teubner, 1904).

7 Council of Epaona, A.D. 517, canon 33.

8 Gregory the Great, *Letters*, XI, 76, "to Mellitus, an Abbot in France".

9 See *Paestum* by P. C. Sestieri, published by the Italian Ministry of Public Instruction, p. 38.

10 A certain softening of attitude was discernible even before the time of Pope Gregory, although only in very narrow directions. In the middle of the fifth century, Leo I wrote to Januarius, Bishop of Aquileia: "if what [offenders] have done is merely go to a pagan gathering and eaten food offered in sacrifice, they can be cleansed by fasting and by laying on of hands, so that, staying away from sacrifices thereafter, they may be participants in the sacraments of Christ; but if they have either worshipped idols, or have committed murder or fornication, it is not fitting to admit them to communion in them except by public penance."

11 *Etymologiarum libri 8, xi: de diis gentium*, the extracts are from 1ff., 30ff., 43, 76ff., 80; see Fontaine, *Isidore de Sévile*, Paris, 1952.

12 The following law, number 6, seems to link sexuality with paganism as they appear to be linked in Pope Leo's letter quoted in note 10:

"Similarly, we lay it down that after this synod—the date of which is 29 April—if any of the servants of god or handmaidens of Christ fall into the crime of fornication, they shall do penance in prison, with bread and water. . . ."

Four of the Canons in the collection Dionisio-Hadriani, of slightly earlier date, appear to make the same connection by juxtaposition:

Canon XII: If anyone has paid attention to soothsayers, or haruscopes, or has made use of amulets, let him be anathema.

XIII: If anyone has violated in any way the command of the Apostolic Church regarding olive groves and other places, let him be anathema.

XIV: Let Hadrian, son of Exhileratus, who after taking part in the sacrament of apostolic confession illegally used Epiphania the Deaconess as his wife, be anathema.

XV: Let Epiphania the Deaconess, who after taking part in the sacrament fell back into connubial living with Hadrian, son of Exhileratus, the son of aversion, be anathema.

13 Terenzio Vaticano is registered as Vat. Lat. 3868; Basilicano as Arch. S. Pietro H. 19.

14 Walafrid Strabo's prayer book is registered as Reg. Lat. 1703.

15 Donatus' commentary is registered as Vat. Lat. 1512.

Chronological Chart: Principal persons and events

(Numbers in brackets refer to chapters)

1. Date A.D.	2. Emperor(s) († murdered)	3. Pagan leaders, writings and events	4. Edicts on religion	5. General Events	6. Christian leaders, writings and events
235	Alexander Severus † Maximinus†	Ammonius Saccas (1)	Persecuting Christians (2)	Beginning of the years of chaos (2)	Origen of Alexandria (d. 254?)
238	Gordian I† Gordian II Balbius† Pupienus† Gordian III† (6)	Origen (1) Plotinus (d. 270) (1) Longinus of Athens (d. 273) Porphyry (b. ?232	(2)	Piecemeal loss of Mesopotamian Provinces to Persia	
244	Philip 'the Arab' (6)†	d. ?305) (1) Mani active from ca. 240 (1)	Tolerating Christians	241— Accession of Sapor I in Persia	
249	Decius		Persecuting Christians (2)		Origen's *Contra Celsum* (1)
251	Trebonius Gallus			Fall of Armenia to Persia	Cyprian active at Carthage
253	Valerian (*vanished in 260*) and Gallienus†		Persecuting Christians (2)		Pontius' *Life of Cyprian*
268	Claudius II 'Gothicus' (2)			Revolt of Palmyra. Beginning of first recorded pandemic of plague. Movement of peoples in Asia brings first probing attacks on Rhine and	various dates: Acts of the Martyrs

1.	2.	3.	4.	5.	6.
				Danube frontiers by the Alamanni and others (2)	
270	Aurelian†		*Sol invictus Deus* named supreme god (2)	273—Fall of Palmyra	
275	Tacitus†				
276	Florian†				
	Probus†			277—Execution of Mani (1)	
282	Carus† Carinus Numerian†				
284	Diocletian (Augustus 286 with) Maximian		Restoration of Jupiter the Best and Greatest (2)	287—Revolt in Britain	
293	'The Tetrarchy' Constantius Caesar and Galerius Caesar	?296— Porphyry's *'Against the Christians'* (1)		296—Restoration of Britain; revolt in Egypt and Africa	
			297—Edict "*Against Malefactors and Manichees*" (*Cod. Greg. XIV. 4*)		Purge of Christians from the Danube Armies
		303— Porphyry's edition of Plotinus "the Enneads" published (1)	303—Edicts of "the Great Persecution" (2)	Diocletian's *vicennalia* at Rome (3)	
		305— Hierocles' *Friend of Man* published (2)		Abdication of Diocletian and Maximian (3)	Origin of Donatist and Meletian Schisms
305	Severus Caesar† Maximin Daia Caesar				305? Lactantius' *Divine*

1.	2.	3.	4.	5.	6.
					Institutes published
306	Constantine (self-appointed Augustus; recognised Caesar) (3)		306—Maxentius self-appointed Prince of the Romans (3)		
308	Licinius† named Augustus			307—Death of Severus 308—Conference of Carnuntum 309—Murder of Romulus 310—Death of Maximian	309—Exile of Popes Eusebius and Marcellus 310—Election of Pope Melitiades
		Iamblichus prominent (4 and 6)			
311		Foundation of Daia's Pagan "Church" (3)	Edict of Toleration for all sects, especially favouring Christians (3)	Death of Galerius (3)	Cessation of persecution except in Egypt and the East (3)
312	Constantine Augustus Maximus	*The Acts of Pilate* Published	State support ordered for those recognised as "catholic" in Africa (3) 313—*The Edict of Milan* (3)	Battle of Mulvian Bridge Death of Maxentius 314—Death of Maximin Daia (3) 315—Constantine's *decennalia* at Rome: Arch of Constantine dedicated (4)	Anthony of the Desert active in Egypt; Arius active (4) 313–Synod of Rome on the Donatist Controversy 314—Council of Arles on Donatism (3 and 4) 315–?Eusebius' *History* (bks. 1–9) published

1.	2.	3.	4.	5.	6.
317	Crispus Caesar† Constantine II Caesar Licinianus† Caesar		318— Christian bishops granted privileges of the priesthoods (*Cod. Theod.* I. xxvii. 1) Converts from Judaism protected (*Cod. Theod.* VI. i, 1) (4)		318? Lactantius' *Deaths of the Persecutors* published
			321— Sunday observance laws (*Cod. Just.* III. xii, 3). (*Cod. Theod.* II. viii 1) (4)		321—First Persecution of African Donatists
323	Constantine Autocrator			323— Rausimond the Sarmatian driven across the Danube by pressure from Goths	
		326— Constantine at Rome insults the gods by refusing to attend sacrifices (4)	324— Licinius' acts annulled	324— Licinius murdered	325—The Council of Nicaea: Arius banned (4)
				326—Fausta, Crispus, *et al.* murdered	?Eusebius *History* (bk. X) published
		328—First stripping of temples to beautify Constantinople (4)		328—Constantinople consecrated	328—Athanasius of Alexandria appointed. Helena's discovery of the True Cross.
330—	Constantius II Caesar	From *ca.* 330— closure of		330—Constantinople dedicated	The Cult of Relics intensified.

1.	2.	3.	4.	5.	6.
		certain temples (4)		332—First invasion of Moesia by Goths	
333—	Constans Caesar†				
				335—Constantine's *tricennalia* (4)	335—The Synod of Tyre; dedication of Holy Sepulchre in Jerusalem. Athanasius exiled. (5, n. 10).
337	Constantine II, Constantius II, Constans, joint emperors (5)			337—Baptism and death of Constantine (4)	Return of all exiled bishops: emergence of semi-Arians (5) Election of Pope Julius I.
		340—Birth of Symmachus the Younger. Praetextatus' marriage. (5) Proaeserius (christian) head of Athens' School of Rhetoric (5)	340—Paganism banned by Constans (*Cod. Theod.* XVI.x, 2) (5)	339—Persian wars renewed: continued intermittently until 363 340. Death of Constantine II (5)	338—Return of Athanasius to Alexandria: Synods of Antioch and Alexandria (5, n. 10) Athanasius again exiled. Arian Gregory of Cappadocia appointed to Alexandria. 343—Council of Serdica (5)
		340—Libanius teaching at Nicomedia first then Antioch (6)	346—Public Sacrifice banned (*Cod. Theod.* XVI.x, 3; XVI.x, 4) (5)		349—Murder of Gregory of Cappadocia at Alexandria. Return of Athanasius (6)
350	Constantius II Autocrator (5)			Revolt of Magnentius; Constans murdered; Vetranio self-appointed	

1.	2.	3.	4.	5.	6.
				Caesar; Eutropia's rising at Rome (5)	
351	Gallus† Caesar in the East (5)	Retirement of leading pagans including Praetextatus (5)		Persian-Massagete Wars; Gallus' Persian Campaign (5)	352—Death of Pope Julius Election of Pope Liberius
		354—Julian's "conversion" to paganism (6)	353—Sacrifices permitted by Magnentius banned (*Cod. Theod. XVI.x, 5*)	353—Death of Magnentius; massing of Germanic tribes reported 354—Gallus murdered (5)	
355	Julian† Caesar in west (5 and 6)	Priscus, Maximus and other sophist/theurges prominent (6)		355—First Frankish invasion 356—Julian victorious in Gaul (5 and 6)	355—Pope Liberius banished; Felix antipope (7)
		356–7—Sack of temple of Serapis at Alexandria. Aelius Donatus teaching at Rome 360—Julian's *Letters to the Athenians,* et al. (6)	356—All sacrifices again forbidden (*Cod. Theod. XVI. x, 6*) (5)	356—Constantius' *vicennalia* at Rome (5)	356—Council of Sirmium. Death of Hosius of Cordoba (5)
361	Julian Autocrator	Recall of prominent pagans (Praetextatus et al.)	Edicts against Christian teachers in pagan	361—Baptism and death of Constantius II. Birth of	Violence at at Alexandria and elsewhere as exiled bishops again

1.	2.	3.	4.	5.	6.
		362— Julian's *Misopogon* (6)	schools Edicts reforming the united pagan "church" (6)	Constantia Posthuma (5)	allowed to return. (6) Last exile of Athanasius. Appointment of George "the pork butcher" to Alexandria.
363	Jovian Autocrator (6 and 7)	Religious toleration (7)		363— Julian's Persian	Jovian's declaration in favour of catholicism. Athanasius' final return to Alexandria (7)
364	Valentinian I and Valens (7)	Religious toleration apart from persecution of theurges. Execution of Maximus (7) Praetextatus saves the mysteries. (7) Symmachus the Elder City Prefect followed by Lampadius and then Viventius. (7) "The Aristocracy of Letters" distinguished for next 30 years at Rome (8)	Nocturnal sacrifices prohibited (*Cod. Theod. IX.xvi, 7)* (7)	Expedition and death. (6) 363—The Persian Peace (7) "Germanisation" of the empire becoming obvious. (7) Invasion of Alamanni on Rhine; Quadi, Carpi and Sarmatians on the Danube; Picts and Scots in Britain; Moors in Africa. (7) Persian intrigue in Armenia. (7) Procopius self-proclaimed Augustus (7)	Writings of poetess Proba; (7); Ausonius
365		Praetextatus City Prefect; Restoration *Dii consentes* (7)		Count Theodosius named commander in Britain (7)	Pope Damasus elected with Ursinus antipope (7)

1.	2.	3.	4.	5.	6.
366	Gratian Caesar† (7)			Defeat and death of Procopius (7) 366—First appearance in Europe of Huns and Alans (7)	
		367—Olybrius City Prefect			
		367 onwards-persecution of the theurges (7) 369—Symmachus the Younger *Oratio I* (7) 371—the Theodorus Conspiracy; execution of Maximus the Sophist (7)	Against clerical luxury, etc. (7) (*Cod. Theod.* XVI. ii, 20) Donatists and Manichees outlawed (7)	371—War in Africa (7) 373—Count Theodosius, victor in Africa, executed; retirement of Theodosius the Younger to Spain. Ostrogoths settled in old Dacia; Visigoths settled south of Danube (7)	371—trial of Damasus (7) 373—Death of Athanasius (7) 374—Ambrose elected at Milan (7)
375	Gratian Augustus and Valentinian II, Augustus (7)	Toleration of all but Manichees (8)		Death of Valentinian I (7)	
376		Mithras cult suppressed at at Rome (8)		376—Continued disturbances on the Danube. 377—Alamannic invasions in Gaul. Death of Valens; Theodosius the Younger made associate of the emperors (7)	Hilary of Poitiers and Martin of Tours active (9)
378					

1.	2.	3.	4.	5.	6.
379	Theodosius Augustus (7 and 8)		Heretics outlawed in the East (8)		Ausonius Consul in West (8)
380				War with Goths in Danube area (8)	380— Priscillian of Avila charged with heresy and Manichaeism in Spain (8)
					Baptism of Theodosius in the "catholic" faith of Damasus of Rome and Peter of Alexandria. Arian Demophilus of Constantinople deposed.
		381— Gratian's refusal of the title Pontifex Maximus (8)	381— Sacrifices at any shrine prohibited (*Cod. Theod.* XVI. x, 7) (8) Conversion to paganism forbidden (*Cod. Theod.* XVI. vii, 1) (8)		381—All churches ordered to be handed over to Catholics. The Council of Constantinople (8)
				382— Maximus' rising (8)	
383	Maximus Caesar in in North-West (8) Arcadius Augustus in the East (9)	382— Controversy over the Altar of Victory, etc. (8)	382— Divination at any shrine forbidden (*Cod. Theod.* XVI. x, 8)(8) Edicts withdrawing state support from western pagans.	383—Peace with the Goths. Visigoths settled in Moesia and Thrace. Gratian murdered (8)	383— Augustine at Rome (12)

1.	2.	3.	4.	5.	6.
384		384 Symmachus City Prefect Praetextatus Italian Prefect (8) Symmachus' *Relatio III* published (8) Death of Praetextatus (8)	384—*Cod. Theod.* XVI. vii, 2 (strengthening XVI. vii, 1) (9) All divination forbidden again. (*Cod. Theod.* XVI.x, (8) (9)	384— Stilicho married to niece of Theodosius	384— Priscillian executed for heresy (8) Augustine at at Milan (to 386). Death of pope Damasus: election of Siricius (8)
385		Symmachus' retirement under Christian pressure (8) 386— Libanius' *In Defence of the Temples* (9)		Cynegius' campaign against temples of the east (9)	Theophilus elected archbishop of Alexandria (9) 386— Jerome driven from Rome. John Chrysostom ordained priest at Antioch and leads hermits in attacks on Syrian temples (9)
		387—Pagan rising at at Alexandria in defence of the Serapeum (9) 388— Symmachus' panegyric of Maximus (10)		387— Maximus' invasion of Italy (10) 388— Theodosius' recovery of the West (10) Arbogast Prefect in Gaul.	Prudentius' first works published (8)
		?389—The Serapeum destroyed (9)	389—*Cod. Theod.* XVI. vii, 4, strengthening XVI. vii, 2 (9)	390—The Massacre of Thessalonika (10)	390— Ambrose's excommunication of Theodosius.

1.	2.	3.	4.	5.	6.
					?Desiderius *Life of St Martin* published (9)
		391— Symmachus Consul; exiled from court for repeating all pagan demands (10)	391—All sacrifices and prayers at temples banned. (*Cod. Theod.* XVI. x, 10) (9)		
			392— *Cod. Theod.* XVI. x, 11, reinforcing XVI. x, 10. Private Sacrifices forbidden (*Cod. Theod.* XVI. x, 12) (10)	392— Murder of Valentinian II (May) Rufinus Prefect of the East (August) Eugenius proclaimed Augustus in the west (10)	
		393—Altar of Victory restored to the senate. Last known pagan dedication in Rome prefecture (10)		394— Theodosius' campaign against Eugenius: commands held by Stilicho and Alaric (10 and 11)	
395	Honorius Augustus in the West (11)		395— Sacrifices again prohibited. (*Cod. Theod.* XVI. x, 13) (11)	395—Death of Theodosius (10) rise of Eutropius (11) Hunnish invasion of the East (11)	395— Augustine consecrated bishop (12)

1.	2.	3.	4.	5.	6.
				Alaric elected Visigoth leader. Alaric before Constantinople (10)	
		396—Death of Priscus the Sophist. End of the Mysteries in Greece (10)	396—*Cod. Theod.* XVI. vii, 6 strengthening XVI. vii.4 (11)	396— Alaric's rape of Greece and her temples (10) Widespread famine.	396/7— Conversion of the Erechtheum into a church (10)
		396–7— Eunapius' *Lives of the Sophists* published		Murder of Rufinus (11) Gildo's revolt in Africa (11)	
			397—All privileges stripped from continuing pagans (*Cod. Theod.* XVI. x, 14) (11)	397—Alaric named Master of the Infantry in Illyricum	397—John Chrysostom made Patriarch of Constantinople (11)
			398—All temples ordered destroyed (*Cod. Theod.* XVI. x, 15) (11) Popular festivals to continue (*Cod. Theod.* XVI. x, 17) (11) Despoliation of temples already closed forbidden (*Cod. Theod.* XVI. x, 18) (11)	398—Africa restored to western control. Arcadius' laws annulled in West. Huns massing in Black Sea area. Revolt of Gainas and Tribigild in the East	

1.	2.	3.	4.	5.	6.
		399— Destruction of the temples of Africa (11)		399— Eutropius Prefect of the East, replaced in August by Aurelian: attempted re- Romanisation.	399— Anastasius I, Pope.
		400—Poems of Claudius Claudianus ?Altar of Victory again restored to the Senate (11)		400— Stilicho Consul in the West. Caesarius Prefect of the East: Goths in control at Constan- tinople, then withdraw to Old Dacia. Eastern accords with Uldin of the Huns (11)	
				401—Alaric's first invasion of Italy; battle of Pollentia (11) Vandal invasion of Rhaetia (11) Aurelian restored as Prefect of the East (11)	
402	Theodosius II proclaimed Augustus (11)				402— Innocent I pope. *ca.* 404— Publication of Augustine's *Confessions*, Prudentius'
		405 ?Gladiatorial contests ended at Rome (11)		405— Anthemius Prefect of	*Contra*

1.	2.	3.	4.	5.	6.
				the East; re-Roman-isation continued. East-West tension. Alaric named Master of the Soldiers for the West. Radagais' horde in Pannonia, Illyricum and Italy (11)	*Symmachum* and Rufinus of Aquileia's *Ecclesiastical History*.
				406—Vandal invasion of Gaul under Godisel, then Gunderic; Constantine III proclaimed in Britain (11)	
		407— Burning of the Sibylline Oracles (25 December) (11)		407— Gunderic in N. Spain. Constantine III in Gaul. Alaric in Greece again (11)	
408	Attalus Augustus at Rome (11)	Pagans appointed to leading offices in city prefecture. Gladiatorial contests restored (11)	408—Edicts banning heretics from public office in the East. Destruction of W. temples ordered (*Cod. Theod.* XVI. x, 19) (11)	408—Death of Arcadius; execution of Stilicho and his son in the West (11) Alaric, dismissed as a barbarian, marches on Rome (11)	408— Pelagius in Rome (12) Pope Inno-cent I involved in negotia-tions between Rome and Ravenna (11)
			409?— Astrologers	408—Famine at Rome.	

1.	2.	3.	4.	5.	6.
			banned by Honorius (11)	Gerontius' rising in Spain restores Honorius' authority there (11)	
			410— Paganism totally outlawed (*Cod. Theod.* XVI. x, 20; XVI. x, 21) (12)	410— Attalus deposed by Alaric (spring) Alaric's sack of Rome (August) (11 and 12) Death of Alaric; Athaulf leader of the Goths, married to Galla Placidia. Goths withdrawn to Pyrenean region, settled there by Count Constantius. Constantine III defeated (12)	
		412—Birth of Proclus Rutilius Master of the Offices to Honorius (12)			
					413—*City of God* begun (12)
		414— Rutilius Prefect of Rome (12)			
				415—Death of Athaulf.	415—Pelagius tried for heresy at Jerusalem (12)
			416—All pagan practices forbidden (*Cod. Theod.* XVI. x, 22)		

1.	2.	3.	4.	5.	6.
		417—Rutilius' withdrawal from Christianised Rome (12 and 13)		417—Count Constantius married to Galla Placidia (12)	417—Orosius' *Historia contra paganos* (12)
				418—Birth of Valentinian III. 421—Honorius' flight to Constantinople. Death of Constantius III (12)	
421	Constantius III Augustus in West (in association with Honorius) (12)	421 (*circa*)—*The Marriage of Mercury and Philology* completed by Capella (12)			
423	Valentinian III Augustus of the West (12)		423—Proscription of continuing pagans in the East. (*Cod. Theod.* XVI. x, 22) (12)	423—Death of Honorius (12)	
		425—Olympiodorus of Thebes *History* published (12)			
					426—*City of God* completed (12)

428—Death of Gunderic the Vandal: accession of Gaiseric (12).

429—Vandal conquest of Africa begun (12). First attempt to edit the *Codex Theodosianus* at Constantinople to give Christian law-code to the empire (12).

430—Death of Augustine. Vandal siege of Carthage. Rise of General Aetius to prominence in the West (12). The School of Alexandria still teaching pagan philosophy under Leontios and Orion.

433—Aetius named Patrician (12). Proclus in Athens under Syrianus as head of school (12).

435—Vandals recognised as "confederate allies" in Africa. *Cod. Theod.*

XVI. x, 25 orders destruction of all visible remains of paganism in the east (12).

438—*Codex Theodosianus* of Christian laws published (12).

440—Salvianus' *de gubernatione Dei* composed (12): Leo I, pope (died 461) (12).

447—Attila's horde sacks eastern cities. Valentinian III's *Novella 17* gives authority over all western churches to Pope Leo I (12).

448—Porphyry's works burned (12).

450—Deaths of Theodosius II and Galla Placidia (12). Proclus head of the School of Athens.

451—The Huns defeated in Gaul by Aetius (12).

452—Attila turned from Rome by Pope Leo I (12).

453—Death of Attila (12).

454—Aetius murdered by Valentinian III, afterwards himself assassinated. Vandal pirates sack Rome (12).

456–475—Burgundian domination of Roman affairs (12).

475—Accession of Romulus "Augustulus" (12).

476—Resignation of Romulus: Odoacer "King" of the Romans (12).

485—Death of Proclus (12).

493—Accession of Theodoric in Italy (12).

500(?)—Composition of Zosimus' *Historia nova* (12).

517—Council of Epaona (canon 33) forbids conversion of temples and heretical churches into orthodox places of worship (13).

520–5—Boethius' *On the Consolations of Philosophy* (13).

529—Justinian's closure of the School of Athens (12).

555 (*ca.*)—Cassiodorus' foundation of the *Vivarium* (13).

560—Martin made Bishop of Braga (13).

572—II Council of Braga (canon I) orders more thorough catechesis of converts from paganism (13).

573(?)—Martin's composition of *de correctione rusticorum* (13).

589—III Council of Toledo (canon 21) orders an inquisition by every bishop into the question of continuing paganism (13).

597—Pope Gregory I encourages the "baptism" of British temples and customs (13).

609—The Pantheon dedicated as *Sancta Maria ad Martyres* (13).

620 (*ca.*)—Composition of Isidore of Seville's *Etymologiarum libri 8* (13).

742—Capitularies of Carloman forbid pagan practices (13).

789—Capitularies of Charlemagne forbid pagan practices (13).

800+—The Carolingian Renaissance: Erigena' *Marriage of Mercury and Philology*: the School of Chartres (13).

850–98—Vatican and Basilican *Terences* copied (13).

900 (*ca.*)—Walafrid Strabo's prayerbook composed (13).

1454—publication of Poggio's *Urbis Roma Descriptio* (13).

A Short Bibliography

Principal Sources

Ambrose of Milan, works in Migne, *Patrologiae Cursus, series Latina (P.L.)*, xiii–xvii; see also F. Homes Dudden, *The Life and Times of St Ambrose* (Clarendon Press, 1935).

Ammianus Marcellinus, text and English translation, *The Roman History of Ammianus Marcellinus* (Bohn Classical Library, 1848); see also, E. A. Thompson, *The Historical Works of Ammianus Marcellinus* (C.U.P., 1947).

Apuleius, *Metamorphoses*, text ed. R. Helm, 1913; English translation in R. Graves, *The Golden Ass* (Penguin 1950).

Athanasius, works in Migne, *Patrologiae Cursus, series Graeca (P.G.)*, xxv–xxvii; see also *Modern Authorities* on Arianism.

Augustine of Hippo, works in Migne, *P.L.*, xxiii–xlvii; see also H.-I. Marrou, *Bibliographia Augustiniana*, 1962, for an extended list of the more important of the many works inspired by aspects of Augustine's life and writings; on the life of St Augustine, see F. van der Meer, trs. B. Battershaw and G. R. Lamb, *St Augustine the Bishop* (Sheed and Ward, 1961); for an English version of *De civitate Dei*: see J. Healey's "Everyman" edition, 1945.

Aurelius Victor, *De Caesaribus*, ed Pichlmayr and Gruendal (Leipzig 1961).
—*Epitome de Caesaribus*, ed. Pichlmayr and Gruendal (Leipzig, 1961).

Boethius, works in Migne, *P.L.*, lxiii and lxiv; English translation, H. F. Stewart and E. K. Read, *Boethius: Theological Tractates and The Consolation of Philosophy* (Loeb Classical Library, Heinemann, London; Putnam, New York, 1871).

Cassiodorus, works in Mommsen, *Monumenta Germanicae Historica*, vol. 12, 1894; see also L. W. Jones, *Introduction to Divine and Human Learning by Cassiodorus Senator* (Columbia University Press, 1946).

Claudius Claudianus, text and an English version in M. Plautnauer, *Claudian* (Loeb Classical Library, Heinemann, London; Putnam, New York, 1922).

Consularia Constantinopolitana, in Mommsen, *Monumenta Germaniae Historica: Auctores Antiquissimi*, vol. 9. (Gesellschaft für altere deutsche Geschichtskunde, 1877.)

Cyprian of Carthage, works ed. W. von Hartel, in the *Corpus Scriptorum Ecclesiasticorum Latinorum*, vol. 3, Vienna, 1868; Pontius' *Passio Cypriani*, ed. R. Reitzenstein, Heidelberg, 1913; *Letters*, ed. L. Bayard (Paris, 1925).

Eunapius, text and an English version in W. Cave Wright, *Lives of the Philosophers* (Loeb Classical Library, Heinemann, London; Putnam, New York, 1922); *History*, fragments, in L. Dindorf, *Historici Graeci Minores*, vol. I (Leipzig, 1870).

Eusebius of Caesarea, *History of the Church*, text ed. G. Dindorf, four volumes, Leipzig, 1867–71, vol. 9; with French translation in *Sources chrétiennes*, n. 55 (Paris, 1958); with English translations in K. Lake and J. E. L. Oulton (Loeb Classical Library, Heinemann, London; Putnam, New York, 1932); in an English version, G. A. Williamson, *Eusebius' History of the Church* (Penguin 1966), with *The Life of the Blessed Emperor Constantine, etc.*, in the *Library of the Nicene Fathers*, vol. 1 (Parker, Oxford, 1890); the text and an English version of *Contra Hieroclem* in F. C. Conybeare, *Apollonius of Tyana* (Loeb Classical Library, Heinemann, London; Putnam, New York, 1912).

Eutropius, *Breviarum ab urbe condita*, text ed. F. Ruehl (Leipzig, 1887); English versions, J. S. Watson, *Justin, Cornelius Nepos and Eutropius* (Bohn's Classical Library, 1848).

Gregory of Nazianzus, works in Migne, *P.G.*, xxxv–xxxviii; an English version of the *Invectives against Julian* is included in C. W. King, *Julian the Emperor* (Bell, London, 1888).

Gregory of Rome, Pope, works in Migne, *P.L.*, lxxv–lxxviii; life in F. Homes Dudden, *Gregory the Great* (Longmans, London, 1905).

Historia Augusta, otherwise *Scriptores Historiae Augustae*, text and an English translation in D. Magie, *Historia Augusta*, Loeb Classical Library, 1922–23.

Idatius, *Fasti Hydatiani*, ed. in Mommsen, *Monumenta Germaniae Historica*: *Auctores Antiquissimi*, vol. 9. (Gesellschaft für altere deutsche Geschichtskunde, 1887.)

Isidore of Seville, works in Migne, *P.L.*, lxxxi–lxxxiv: see also, J. Fontaine, *Isidore de Séville* (Bibliothèque de l'École des Hautes Études Hispanniques, 1960).

Jerome, works in *P.L.* xxii–xxx and ed. G. Morin in *Anecdota Maredsolana* vol. 3 (in three parts, 1895–1903); see also D. S. Wiesen, *St. Jerome and the Satiric Tradition*, Cornell University, 1964; R. and M. Pernoud, *St Jérome*, trs. R. Shead (Cassell, London, 1963); J. Steinmann, trs. R. Matthews, *St Jerome* (Geoffrey Chapman, 1959). John Chrysostom: works in *P. G.*, xlvii–xlix; English translation, *Library of the Nicene Fathers*, vol. 9–14. Life, J. C. Baur, trs. M. Conzaga, *John Chrysostom and his Time*, Sandy & Co., 1959.

Julian, works with an English translation in W. Cave Wright, *Julian* (3 vols.), Loeb Classical Library, 1913–23; see also J. Bidez, *La Vie de l'empereur Julien*, (Paris, 1930).

Lactantius, works ed. S. Brandt and G. Laubmann, *Corpus Scriptorum*

Ecclesiasticorum Latinorum, xix and xxvii (Vienna, 1890); *De mortibus persecutorum*, with a French translation in *Sources chrétiennes*, n. 39, Paris, 1954; an English version (with *The Divine Institutes*) by A. Roberts and J. Donaldson, in the *Library of the Ante-Nicene Fathers*, vols. 21 and 22, (T. Clark, Edinburgh, 1867).

Libanius, works ed. R. Foerster, 12 vols., 1909–27; selections with English translation, A. F. Norman (Loeb Classical Library, 1969); see also, J. Misson, *Sur le Paganisme de Libanios*, (Louvain, 1914).

Macrobius, *Saturnalia*, ed. F. Eyssenhardt, Leipzig, 1893.

Martianus Capella, *De nuptiis Mercurii et Philologiae*, ed. A. Dick, Teubner, (Leipzig, 1925).

Martin of Braga, works ed. Barlow, *Martini Episcopi Bracarensis opera omnia*, Rome, 1959.

Olympiodorus of Thebes, works in K. and T. Mueller, *Fragmenta Historicorum Graecorum*, vol. 4, pp. 58f. (Paris, 1841).

Optatus of Milevium, *De Schismata Donatistorum*, Corpus scriptorum Ecclesiasticorum Latinorum, vol. 26 (Vienna, 1893).

Orosius, *Historiae adversus paganos*, Corpus scriptorum Ecclesiasticorum Latinorum, vol. 5 (Vienna, 1882).

Philostorgius, *Ecclesiastical History*, Societas Regia Scientiarum, vol. 21 (Berlin, 1913) and J. Bidez, *Art in Byzantion*, vol. 10, pp. 403ff. (1935). See also Walford, *The Ecclesiastical History of Philostorgius* (Bohn's Ecclesiastical Library, 1851).

Plotinus, works, ed. P. Henry and R. Schwyzer, Oxford Classical Texts (ed. major, 1951; ed. minor, 1964).

    E. Bréhier, *La Philosophie de Plotin*, 3rd edition (Vrin, Paris, 1968) and *Enneades*, text and translation, (Paris, 1924).

    For English versions of selected texts, see S. MacKenna and B. S. Page, *Plotinus: The Enneads* 4th edition (Faber, 1969). A. H. Armstrong, *Plotinus* (George Allen & Unwin, 1953), and G. R. S. Mead, *Select Works of Plotinus* (Bohn's Philological Series, 1895).

Porphyry. *Against the Christians*, fragments in A. von Harnack, *Porphyrius: Gegen der Christen: 15 Büche* in Proceedings of the Prussian Academy (Berlin, 1916) and the *Sitzberichte* of the Berlin Academy (1921). See also J. Bidez, *Vie de Porphyre* (Université de Gand: Faculté des Lettres, 1913) and the bibliography there, and Paully-Wissowa, *Reallexikon*, art. Porphyrius.

Procopius, works, with an English translation in J. Haury, *Procopius*, 3 vols, 1914–40, reprinted 1963–4 (Loeb Classical Library, Heinemann, London; Putnam, New York).

Proclus, *Life* by Marinus, ed. J. Boissonade (Paris, 1814), reprinted in Cousin, *Procli opera inedita* (Paris, 1864). See also L. J. Rosan, *The Philosophy of Proclus* ("Cosmos", New York, 1949).

Prudentius, *Works*, text and an English translation in H. J. Thomson, *Prudentius* (Loeb Classical Library, 1949–53).

Rufinus of Aquileia, *Ecclesiastical History*, ed. M. Simonetti in *Tyranni Rufini Opera*, Corpus Christianorum (Series Latina) vol. 20 (Turnholt, 1961).

Rutilius Namantianus, *De reditu*, text edited by L. Mueller, (Teubner, Leipzig, 1870): an English version in H. Isbell, *Last Poets of Imperial Rome* (Penguin, 1971) with the title *Concerning His Return*.

Socrates Scholasticus, *Ecclesiastical History* in Migne, *P.G.*, lxvii; an English version by A. L. Zenos in the *Library of the Nicene Fathers*, series 2, vol. 2 (Christian Literature Company, New York, 1891).

Sozomen, *Ecclesiastical History*, in Migne, *P.G.*, lxvii; an English version in the *Library of the Nicene Fathers*, series 2, vol. 2 (Christian Literature Company, New York, 1891).

Symmachus, works ed. O. Seeck, 1883; see also S.D. 11, *Roman Society in the Last Century of the Western Empire* (Macmillan, 1898).

Theodoret, works in Migne, *P.G.*, lxxx–lxxxiv; *Ecclesiastical History*, ed. Parmentier in the Berlin Corpus, vol. 19, 1911; English version in Bohn's Ecclesiastical Library, 1854.

Valesius, ed. J. Moreau, *Excerpta Valesiana* (Leipzig, 1961).

Zosimus, *Historia Nova*, fragments, ed. Mendelssohn, Leipzig, 1887; an English translation in Buchanan and Davis, *The Decline of Rome* (San Antonio's Trinity University Press, 1967).

Laws in the *Codex Gregorianus*

    Codex Justinianus in the *Corpus Iuris Civilis*, vol. 2, ed. P. Krueger (Berlin, 1954).

    Codex Theodosianus, ed. Mommsen and Mayer (Societas Regia Scientiarum, Berlin, 1905); with an English version and notes, ed. C. Pharr, Princeton University Press, 1952).

    Novellae in the *Corpus Iuris Civilis*, vol. 3 (ed. R. Schoell and W. Kroll, (Berlin, 1954).

    see also O. Seeck, *Regesten der Kaiser und Paepste* (Stuttgart, 1918–19).

Canons of the church councils are collected in chronological order in C. J. Hefele, *Histoire des conciles*, (Letouzey, Paris, 1907–52) which also contains the texts of the *Capitularies* of Carloman and Charlemagne.

Modern Authorities

(The literature is vast: in addition to those titles mentioned in the *Notes* appended to the individual chapters and under the heading Principal Sources, I propose the following, as having been of especial value to me in preparing this book):

A. Alfoeldi, *The Conversion of Constantine and Pagan Rome*, Oxford, 1948.

C. Bailley, *Phases in the Religion of Ancient Rome*, Oxford, 1932.

P. Bastid, *Proclus et le crépuscule de la pensée grecque*, Vrin, Paris, 1946.

P. Battifol, *La paix constantinienne et le catholicisme*, Paris, 1914.

N. H. Baynes, *Constantine the Great and the Christian Church*, Proceedings of the British Academy, 1929.

W. W. Buckland, *A Textbook of Roman Law from Augustus to Justinian*, Cambridge, 1963.

J. Burckhardt, *The Age of Constantine the Great* (Routledge and Kegan Paul, 1969).

J. B. Bury, *A History of the Later Roman Empire* (Macmillan, 1923).

C. E. Coleman, *Constantine the Great and Christianity* (Columbia University Publications in History, Economics and Public Law (60, 2), 1914).

P. Courcelle, *Histoire littéraire des grandes invasions germaniques* (third edition, Paris, 1964).

H. Crook, *Roman Law and Life*, 1967.

M. Deanesley, *A History of Early Medieval Europe* (Methuen, London, 1956).

A. Fliche and V. Martin (eds.), *Histoire de l'église* (Paris, 1934).

W. H. Frend, *The Donatist Church* (Oxford, 1952).

E. Gibbon, *The Decline and Fall of the Roman Empire*, Smith's edition, (J. Murray, 1862) and Bury's Edition (Methuen, 1909–14).

H. A. Gwatkin, *Studies in Arianism* (Deighton Bell, Cambridge, 1882).

A. H. M. Jones, *Constantine and the Conversion of Europe* (Hodder and Stoughton, 1948).

—*The Later Roman Empire*, three volumes and maps (Blackwell, 1964).

B. J. Kidd, *A History of the Church until A.D. 461* (Oxford, 1922).

P. de Labriolle, *La réaction païenne* (Paris, 1934).

Lebreton and Zeiller, *Histoire de l'église*.

F. G. L. Van der Meer, trs. M. F. Medland, Atlas of the Early Christian World (Thomas Nelson, 1958).

A. Momigliano, ed., *The Conflict between Paganism and Christianity in the Fourth Century* (Clarendon Press, Oxford, 1963).

F. X. Murphy, *Rufinus of Aquileia* (Catholic University of American Studies in Mediaeval History, new series, volume 6, 1945).

J. H. Newman, *Arians of the Fourth Century* (J. G. and F. Rivington, London, 1833).

J. H. W. G. Liebescuetz, *Antioch* (Oxford, 1972).

L. Petit, *Libanius et la vie municipale à Antioche au IVème siècle* (Paris, 1956).

Paully, Wissowa and Kroll, *Real-Encyclopaedie der Altertums Wissenschaft* (Mettzlerscher, Stuttgart, 1893)—in progress.

Reallexikon fuer Antike und Christentum (Hiersemann, Stuttgart, 1941)—in progress.

L. J. Rosan, *The Philosophy of Proclus* ("Cosmos", New York, 1949).

M. Rostovtzeff, revised by P. M. Fraser, *The Social and Economic History of the Roman Empire* (Clarendon Press, Oxford, 1957).

E. Stein, *Histoire de la Bas-Empire* (Paris, 1959).

O. Seeck, *Geschichte der Untergangs der Antiken Welt*, 6 volumes (Berlin, 1895–1921).

—*Regesten der Kaiser und Paepste* (Stuttgart, 1918–19).

J. Straub, *Heidnische Geschichtsapologetik in der christlichen Spaetantike*, Antiquitas, series 4, vol. 1 (Bonn, 1963).

J. M. Wallace-Hadrill, *The Barbarian West* (Hutchinson's University Library, London, 1952).

The Cambridge Ancient History, vol. 12.

The Cambridge Mediaeval History, vol. 1.

The New Catholic Encyclopaedia (McGraw-Hill, 1966).

J. Wytzes, *Der Streit um den Altar der Victoria* (Amsterdam, 1936).

G. Wissowa, *Religion und Kultus der Roemer*, 2nd Edition (Munich, 1912).

Index